More Machiavelli in B   s

More Machiavelli in Brussels

The Art of Lobbying the EU

Third, fully updated and revised edition

Rinus van Schendelen

AMSTERDAM UNIVERSITY PRESS

2002   First edition, titled 'Machiavelli in Brussels'
2004   Czech translation
2005   Polish translation
2005   Second, fully updated edition, same title
2010   Third, fully updated and revised edition, new title 'More Machiavelli in Brussels'

Cover design: Maedium, Utrecht
Lay-out: Het Steen Typografie, Maarssen

ISBN   978 90 8964 147 2
e-ISBN   978 90 4851 079 5
NUGI   654

© Rinus van Schendelen / Amsterdam University Press, Amsterdam 2010

CONTENTS SUMMARY

DETAILED CONTENTS

PREFACE TO THIRD EDITION

This book has two objectives. The general one is to clarify how interest groups can influence public authorities like civil servants and politicians on what they plan to do (or not do). As such, the book is about the *art of lobbying* both public officeholders and stakeholders on any playing field. Our notion of lobbying has nothing to do with the negative connotation it has acquired in mass media. Among most interest groups, including those representing governments, it is used today as the easy word for 'making a difference as desired' or gaining influence. It is embedded in a body of knowledge called 'public affairs management'. Its three main ingredients are: ambition to win, studying the arena and prudent lobbying. Embodying these three qualities is Niccolò Machiavelli, the advisor to the Ruler of Firenze in early 16th century. English moralists denounced him unjustly in the 18th century, demonising him as the devilish 'old Nick'.

The book's second objective is specific, as general knowledge can only prove its value when applied to a particular setting. Here we apply it to decision-making by the *European Union* (EU). Its main seat, in Brussels, has become the common capital for all groups and citizens of the member-states. This is the place where major legislation is produced binding all member-states and affecting their groups and citizens. Here, domestic governments being unable to rely on only their few formal powers, have to fight for their interests too and to behave like interest groups. They can learn much from the 'premier league' of mainly private groups who outpace them in influencing the EU.

The two objectives match in our underlying ambition to show that the EU can be influenced more successfully by applying the insights from public affairs management. This ambition has, of course, nothing to do with being in favour of or against europeanization. Knowledge takes no sides and can serve both camps. Lobbying successfully is largely a matter of *expertise* that, by nature and training, belongs to the few with talents and skills. Nature distributing talents we cannot change but, by publishing the collected insights of practitioners and researchers in this field of public affairs management in the EU, we might improve the skills of many more people, and hope to do so here. We feel inspired by two intellectual disciplines. One is political science, the mother of all studies of influence and focused on how an influencing process works. The other is management science, with its focus on how this process can be managed more successfully.

The first two editions of this book have earned a wide readership, as indicated by their many reprints and several translations. This third edition has been more than updated and revised and, in fact, is *largely rewritten*, so justifying a slightly modified title. One reason is that both political and management science and surveys among practitioners have produced more useful insights on how the EU can be influenced more successfully if the expertise of public affairs management and lobbying is applied. The second reason is that the EU machinery is ever-changing, and any textbook on it needs revision after a few years. In this fully new edition, we have included such new changes as occurring in the playing field, coming from recent enlargements, and caused by new trends in influencing the EU; we also have included much new research on the expertise needed for successful lobbying and many new lobby cases demonstrating that the art of lobbying the EU needs even 'more' Machiavelli.

In this third edition, we only refer to literature and documents in English, as it is the most common language in both the practice and the study of the EU. The authors, however, come increasingly from nearly every country, thus indicating a wider *awareness* that the EU can really be influenced and that its performances come from 'what all of us make of it'. The best practitioners on public affairs management at the EU level have long held this awareness. They always inspire me by their openness to inform me and their eagerness to enhance their knowledge in return. To them I also owe this third edition.

Rotterdam, August 2009

LIST OF FIGURES

LIST OF BEST WEBSITES

On European Union

www.europa.eu   The most important EU site
www.ecprd.org and www.ipex.eu   Sites of parliaments on EU
www.caselex.com   Site on national and EU Courts' cases
www.euractiv.com and www.euobserver.com   Search machines
www.agenceeurope.com   Daily news bulletin
www.publications.eu   Site on EU publications
www.europeanvoice.com   A weekly newspaper on the EU
www.euroreporter.co.uk   Weekly newspaper on European countries
www.europesworld.org   Magazine on the EU's foreign affairs
www.eufeeds.eu   All daily newspapers of the EU countries
www.presseurop.eu   EU clippings from European newspapers
www.europeanagenda.eu   Daily EU news on people and events
www.thebrusselsconnection.be   Site on Brussels' EU quarter

On Public Affairs Management

www.seap.be and www.epaca.org   Brussels-based PA networks
www.publicaffairs.ac and www.pubaffairs.org   UK sites on PA
www.dipa-berlin.org and www.degepol.de   Two German PA sites
www.afcl.net   The site of French PA practitioners
www.alpac.at and www.bvpa.nl   Austrian and Dutch PA site
www.pac.org and www.alldc.org   Two US sites on PA
www.publicaffairsworld.com   PA services site

LIST OF ABBREVIATIONS

ACEA	European Automobile Manufacturers Association
ACP	African, Caribbean, Pacific
AEA	Association of European Airlines
AEJ	Association of European Journalists
AEM	Association of Mountain Areas
AMCHAM	American Chamber of Commerce
BEUC	European Consumers Organisation
BINGO	Business Interested NGO
BONGO	Business Organised NGO
CASTER	Conference and Association of Steel Territories
CATS	Committee Article Thirty-Six
CCMC	Committee of Common Market Automobile Constructors
CEA	European Committee of Insurers
CEEC	Central and Eastern European Countries
CEFIC	European Chemical Industry Council
CEMR	European Confederation of Municipalities and Regions
CIAA	Confederation of EU Food and Drink Industries
CoA	Court of Auditors
COM	European Commission
CONECCS	Commission' Consultation of Civil Society (EU site)
COR	Committee of the Regions
COREPER	Committee of Permanent Representatives (-tions)
DG	Directorate-General
EACEM	European Association of Consumer Electronics Manufacturers
EACF	European Airlines Consumer Forum
EBF	European Banking Federation
ECB	European Central Bank
ECF	European Construction Forum
ECJ	EU Court of Justice
ECOBP	European Campaign on Biotechnology Patents
ECOFIN	Economic and Financial Council

ECSC	European Coal and Steel Community
EDA	European Defence Agency
EEB	European Environmental Bureau
EFC	Economic and Financial Committee
EFPIA	European Associations of Pharmaceutical Industry
EFSA	European Food Safety Authority
EIB	European Investment Bank
EIRA	European Industrial Regions Associations
ELTAC	European Largest Textile and Apparel Companies (now EuraTex)
EMF/FEM	European Metal Workers
EMU	European Monetary Union
END	Seconded national expert
EP	European Parliament
EPEE	European Partnership for Energy and Environment
EPHA	European Public Health Alliance
ERT	European Round Table of Industrialists
ESC	Economic and Social Committee
ETI	European Transparency Initiative
ETUC	European Trade Union Confederation
EU	European Union
EuroFed	European Federation (abbreviation)
FELPA	European Federation of Lobbying and Public Affairs
FIM	International Motorcyclist Federation
GAER	General Affairs and External Relations Council
GINGO	Government Interested NGO
GONGO	Government Organised NGO
GMO	Genetically Modified Organism
GS	General Secretariat (Council)
HDTV	High-Definition Television
IGC	Intergovernmental Conference
MNC	Multinational Company
MNGO	Multinational NGO
MEP	Member of the European Parliament
NATO	North Atlantic Treaty Organisation
NGO	Non-governmental Organisation
OCM	Open Coordination Method
OECD	Organisation of European Co-operation and Development
PA(M)	Public Affairs (Management)
PAP	Public Affairs Practitioners

PGEU	Pharmaceutical Group of the EU
PR	Permanent Representative (Representation)
PSC	Political and Security Committee
PURPLE	Peri-Urban Regions Platform Europe
QMV	Qualified Majority Voting
SCoFCAH	Standing Committee on Food Chain and Animal Health
SEA	Single European Act
SEAP	Society of European Affairs Professionals
SEM	Single European Market
SG	Secretariat-General (Commission)
SGAE	French EU co-ordination centre (formerly SGCI)
SME	Small and Medium-sized Enterprise
UEAPME	European Association of SMEs
UNICE	Union of Employers' Organisations (now BusinessEurope)
VLEVA	Flemish public-private PA desk in Brussels
WEAG	Western European Armament Group (NATO)
WHO	World Health Organisation
WTO	World Trade Organisation

Commission DGs/ Services (except few internal offices, year 2009)

ADMIN	Personnel and Administration
AGRI	Agriculture
AIDCO	Aid and Co-operation Office
BEPA	Bureau of Policy Advisors
BUDG	Budget
COMM	Communication
COMP	Competition
DEV	Development
DGT	Translation Service
DIGIT	Informatics
ECFIN	Economic and Financial Affairs
EAC	Education and Culture
ECHO	Humanitarian Aid
ELARG	Enlargement
EMPL	Employment and Social Affairs
ENTR	Enterprise and Industry
ENVI	Environment
EPSO	Personnel Selection Office

ESTAT	Statistical Office
IAS	Internal Audit Service
INFSO	Information Society and Media
JLS	Justice, Liberty (Freedom) and Security
JRC	Joint Research Centre
MARE	Fisheries and Maritime Affairs
MARKT	Internal Market and Services
OLAF	Anti-Fraud Office
OPOCE	Publications Office
REGIO	Regional Policy
RELEX	External Relations
RTD	Research
SANCO	Health and Consumer Affairs
SCIC	Interpretation Service
SG	Secretariat General
SJ	Legal Service
TAXUD	Taxation and Customs Union
TRADE	External Trade
TREN	Energy and Transport

CHAPTER 1

THE EUROPEANIZATION OF PUBLIC AFFAIRS

Living Together in Europe

'Europe' is almost a synonym for *variety*. In the year 2010, almost 500 million people live in the European Union (EU), which is more than the 420 million people of the US and Japan combined. The outcome of negotiations with more countries, such as Turkey and some new states of the former Yugoslavia, may bring in another 100 million people. All these countries are politically organised by way of a national state, frequently subdivided into more or less autonomous domestic (regional, provincial, local) governments, reflecting territorial idiosyncrasies and different power ambitions. Their histories usually have a long record of wars with neighbours and, in many cases, with former colonies. Their domestic political ideologies range from the extreme left to the extreme right, and their religious belief systems vary from Catholicism, Protestantism (in many variants), Islam and many more exotic ones, plus a substantial portion of atheism and agnosticism. In their daily lives, Europeans, living in free and pluralist societies, encounter a kaleidoscope of civil organisations such as companies, trade unions, political parties, churches and other interest groups. Their economies range from free-market systems in the north to more state-directed ones in the south (the Mediterranean) and the east (Central Europe). The EU people communicate with each other in 23 different 'official national languages' (acknowledged as such by the EU) and hundreds of regional ones. In France alone, one-third of the population regularly uses one of its eight recognised dialects.

In terms of *socio-economic statistics*, the variety in Europe is even more impressive [COM, Europe in figures]. The population size of the member state of Luxembourg is less than half a percent of that of Germany, but has the highest GDP per capita, two and a half times that of Portugal and five times that of Latvia. In general, there exist sharp contrasts in wealth between the relatively rich north-western and the poor eastern part of the EU, on a regional level with a ratio as high as ten to one, with the southern part (including Ireland) being roughly average. Rates of labour activity and unemployment vary widely across member states and regions. Employment rates for economic sectors show a mountainous landscape, with Greece and Poland peaking in agriculture (about 20% of the labour force), Germany in industry (about 40%) and the Netherlands in services (about 70%). Social security in Europe is a volatile variable, mainly due to the differences in domestic government programmes for income maintenance, health, housing and education. This description of social variety could be extended to a range of other variables, from urbanisation rates to leisure patterns, and from consumer behaviour to environmental interests.

Perhaps the most important, but certainly the least documented, is *cultural variety* [Halman and others, 2005; www.worldvaluessurvey.org]. In France, Belgium and Spain the dominant norms and values of social behaviour are relatively hierarchical or top-down, even inside small and decentralised units like family systems and sectoral networks. The new Central European member states, coming from a communist past, largely reflect the same pattern but show growing attachments to bottom-up networks. In Scandinavian countries and the Netherlands, national culture is more bottom-up, based on self-reliant networks. Portugal, southern Italy and Greece have a culture based mainly on family values, with elderly leadership and clearly defined loyalties. In the United Kingdom, culture is more centred on the value of free private life, also on the market, but limited by the rule of law. In Germany and Austria, orderly and predictable behaviour is a dominant value. These short generalisations of national cultures deserve, of course, a more detailed examination, but for the moment they suffice to underline the cultural variety. The cultural differences help to explain why the peoples of Europe have so little faith in each other. Except for the Italians, the Swedes and the Belgians, they put the most trust in their own countrymen then in the northern peoples and the least in the southern ones [COM, Eurobarometer, 1996, B 46-7]. In the much enlarged EU-27, trust in other nations is assumed to be even lower, so creating less cohesion and higher integration costs [Delhey, 2007].

Not least, there is a lot of *political variety*. Some countries have had a great imperial past inside Europe, for example Austria, Denmark, Lithuania, Poland and Spain. Other countries, such as France, Britain, Portugal, the Netherlands and Belgium, once built an empire with colonies outside Europe. Most of them, including countries like Bulgaria, Hungary and Greece, are very old states, while others such as Belgium and Germany are around150 years old. Slovenia has only existed since 1991. Many countries have a national memory of either long-term occupation by some neighbour (Ireland and the Central European states) or mere fragmentation (Italy, Germany). All countries have a multi-party system now, but with strong variations, such as proportional versus district-wise representation and presidential versus parliamentary government [Krouwel, 2003]. France and Britain have a centralist state tradition, as still reflected by the domestic position of their government leader. Others, like Germany, Spain, Belgium and Austria, have decentralised government, which is also on the rise in Italy, Poland, Hungary and some other Central European states that now show a restoration of state structures as they existed before 1939, the start of German and subsequently Soviet occupation. Due to their socio-economic and cultural differences, the various governments give expression to very different political interests and preferences.

All this variety is, of course, not unique to Europe. One can also find it in large geographical areas such as China, Brazil or the United States. These are already established conglomerate states. Their management problem is not to bring variety together but only to keep it all together. Europe is still in a *process of political integration*. Its first management problem is to bring the different parts together into a larger whole; keeping it together is its secondary agenda. It is precisely those differences causing cross-border irritations which pose problems of integration. Examples out of the countless many are the different taxation rules, subsidy practices or technical standards among the countries. Of course, in some cases variety is not considered irritating at all. Most Europeans tend to appreciate the varieties of music, cuisine or architecture as a non-irritating enrichment. The integration problem lies in the differences that do cause irritation. These can be anything, and may even include the way music is produced, the hygiene of the cuisine or the safety of the architecture. The management problem here is: how to solve the irritating differences?

Solving the Irritating Differences: the EU Method

Take the *gas hose*. By far the best, according to the French, is the 'Dormant' one: it has stainless steel helical tubing, moulded from a continuous spiral, with flare-type seals at the end and no covering. But the British believe they have a better-than-best gas hose: one with galvanised metal annular tubing, formed into concentric circles, and with a rubber covering. The real best one is the Italian gas hose, at least according to the Italians: stainless steel annular tubing, extendable and free of covering. The German, Swedish,

Spanish and any other gas hose is the best as well, according to its country of manufacture. The gas hose is just one example of variety in Europe, and numerous others exist, ranging from products and services to values and ideas.

So far the gas hose case does not cause any irritation. It only represents a difference, and this might continue to be the case for another fifty years. Some producers may even appreciate the difference, as this provides effective protection against imports from abroad. However, other interest groups in the private or the public sector may feel irritated and start to politicise the difference. Some producers may want to export their gas hose, to create economies of scale and to become the market leader in Europe. Consumer groups may demand a cheaper and standardised gas hose, health groups a safer one, and 'green' groups one that is more eco-friendly. Governments may want to save on inefficiencies. An irritation is born and may grow into a conflict. What are the potential solutions? There are five *traditional methods* in Europe.

(1) *Resignation* is the first one. The costs of resignation may be considered less than those of any other solution, so justifying living with an irritation for longer, just as those travelling across borders have to resign themselves to the irritation of different electricity plugs. Some may even count the blessings of a difference or accept it as a minor element on the balance sheet. Resignation may work for some time, as in the case of educational diplomas, which have different attributes and values in different countries. One day, however, an enduring irritation may become an obsession for which resignation no longer suffices.

(2) *Leniency* is a second standard solution. At least the irritation resulting from a difference may be dealt with by leniency, as a variant of tolerance. For example, the small country of Luxembourg irritates its neighbours by its practices in banking, being its major economic sector. For a long time, the neighbouring countries have accepted them leniently. Likewise, France and the Netherlands have become lenient regarding each other's different (and irritating) drug policy practices. A next step may be to equalise the differences as well. Concessions and the time involved are the costs of leniency.

(3) *The battlefield* is an old-style third approach to dealing with irritating differences. The histories of European countries are, indeed, full of wars with neighbouring states over all sorts of irritating differences. A victory may solve the irritation and equalise the difference. The method is, however, costly in terms of resources committed to it and only rational if the victor maintains the upper hand and can write off his war investments over a longer period. In hindsight, conventional wisdom in Europe since

1945 shows that this method is largely considered both inefficient and ineffective.

(4) *Imitation* is a fourth standard solution for irritating differences. Governments and companies may decide to follow what is called the best practice method. They adapt their position to that of the other(s), thus removing the difference and consequently the irritation as well. Many a national welfare scheme in Europe is based on such imitation, following the British 'Beveridge' or the German 'Bismarck' model [Flora, 1988]. Industrial companies easily adopt newly developed technology. Often they have to, due to the circumstantial pressures coming from an open and competitive environment. The costs of adaptation are real, but also beneficial and thus accepted.

(5) *Negotiation* is the fifth old method to resolve an irritation. A government or a company may enter into negotiations with those responsible for the irritating difference. Public treaties or private agreements can bring about the solution. There exist thousands of good examples, ranging from the Rhine Treaty to the standardisation of automotive parts. The method is based on an ad hoc approach, taking each issue separately. This may be inefficient if there are many old or emerging issues at stake at the same time, and ineffective if there is no sanctioning mechanism.

All these five solutions can make differences less irritating or even settle them. Together they form the old menu of integration practices with their limitations and disadvantages, as sketched above. The construction of what is now called the *European Union* (EU) aims to provide a sixth and better method to solve irritating differences. According to many, its machinery of common public decision-making with its capacity to safeguard solutions to cross-border conflicts by applying EU law, which always has priority over domestic law, is the very essence of European integration [Lindberg, 1970]. This EU method is, however, only applicable to policy areas incorporated in the treaties of EU, thus making the EU not so much a cultural community of shared values as a legal community of shared laws based on treaties.

The sixth method is not exclusive, as most of the older solutions are still applied. Neither it is undisputed, as Europeans disagree over every value, so also over the EU method [McLaren, 2006]. The EU is an open forum inviting cross-border resignation and leniency. It is a non-violent 'battlefield' in the sense that fighting takes place only verbally and on paper. The EU solutions to irritations are also flexible in their outcomes. Settling a difference and thus erasing its irritation as well is, of course, the most effective solution, exemplified by the many binding EU decisions on 'open markets'. Frequently, however, the effectiveness is limited by time, area, domain and other circumstances, and thus its promotion needs stimuli both from within the EU machinery, such as subsidies and package deals, and from outside, such as new complaints and crises. The 2008 financial crisis is only one example that shows a sudden reliance on the sixth method of European integration, now for the financial sector and mainly by OCM. The peaceful integration of the European variety proceeds step by step.

Not Member States but Member Countries

From the legal perspective, the national governments of the 'EU member states' negotiate every new treaty, which binds their country after its ratification by the electorate (through a referendum) or the national parliament. It would, however, be a misperception to see the EU as involving only national state governments. The EU is composed of member states, to be sure, but what are these?

Take the case of *France* [Elgie, 2003; Culpepper and others, 2006; Knapp and Wright, 2006]. It has the reputation of being the most 'statist' and most centralised member state of the Union, as illustrated by the saying *'Paris gouverne'*. The state intervenes strongly in French society, usually by way of specific and hard regulations. For almost any sector, trade or activity there is a detailed book of rigid codes. Through a *plan indicative,* long-term policies are developed and made. State banking and subsidies give the central government financial power over society. What is the state? It is largely the bureaucracy that issues the regulations and controls public finance. The leaders of this technocratic apparatus are not so much a closed group as a network, mixed-up with captains of industry and socio-cultural elites, with whom they have enjoyed a common education (the *grandes écoles*) and sometimes change of position (*pantouflage*). Major companies and associations can be present or represented inside the ministries by their membership of administrative *groupes d'études* or *comités*. Who is in charge of such a state system? The legal view is incomplete. State and society are partially overlapping and different.

Or watch *Germany* [Padgett and others, 2003; Timmins and others, 2007]. This member state is, even in legal terms, a federalised collection of sixteen *Länder* or regional states, each having its own government, parliament, bureaucracy and court. The umbrella state is less than one and a half centuries young, and encompasses all kinds of variation. Brandenburg is not the same as Bavaria. Like Europe at large, the German states have their more or less irritating differences with each other. At both the regional and the federal level, the governmental culture is mildly interventionist, with a preference for general and encouraging rather than specific and rigid policies. The regional governments can play such a mildly interventionist role through, for example, their *Landesbanken*. They also like to make long-lasting agreements with the influential interest groups from organised business, labour, consumers and environmentalists, the *Konkordanzpolitik*. In trade organisations, companies or neighbourhoods, comparable forms of *Mitbestimmung* (co-determination) exist. Social order is valued highly, hence the extensive provision of social security. Again: who is influencing whom? There is no major federal government policy without at least the basic consent of the leading decentralised governments and private groups.

Or consider, finally, the case of *Britain* [Judge, 2005; Bache and Jordan, 2006]. Here, the central government exerts moderate rule, shared with regional authorities and agencies. Their interventions in society usually have a more general scope (like in Germany) and rigid form (like in France). But all governments together have only a limited domain. Much is left to the private domain of market forces and competition. Developments of privatisation and deregulation during the Conservative years (1979-1997) enlarged and vitalised this private domain. Britain differs from consultation practices on the European continent, as the central government aims to keep organised business and labour at arm's length. The Cabinet, acting as the first committee of the House of Commons, likes to make its policies without compromising social consultations or co-determinations. It prefers the rule of law above the rule of compromise. These basics of governance have not changed very much since New Labour took over (1997). Once again: who is influencing whom? The UK looks like an open park with different public and private playing-fields.

The three country snapshots make clear that member states, widely seen as the crucial parts of the EU construction, are not identical to national governments. All countries have a government that is more-or-less both *fragmented* by different layers (regionalisation) and *limited* by the private domains. These two variables likewise have different values for all different countries at different times. The fragmentation is relatively low in France, Denmark, the Netherlands and the Central European countries (for now), but high in countries like Germany, Belgium and Spain [Flora and others, 2005]. The limitation takes many forms. The UK public domain is largely restricted to government officials, while that in France, Italy and Portugal is open to established interest groups from the business world in particular. In Germany, Austria and Sweden, the governments have their institutionalised negotiations with major private interest groups. In the Central European countries, the national government widely intervenes in society, including the private sectors, but sees its domain shrinking. In short, the general pattern is organised pluralism, which gives all public and private groups a limited domain and scope for influence at home.

The member states can best be characterised as *mixed public-private* systems. The government is only a part of any country's governance system, as the latter is a mixture of public and private organisations, such as ministries and companies. In between stand many hybrids or non-governmental organisations (NGOs), like trade unions and consumer groups, which by function and/or status may overlap with either the public or the private organisations [Hudock, 1999]. Between the public and the private organisations, mutual intervention exists. On the one side, government organisations intervene in private organisations, acting for profit or not. On the other side, private organisations intervene in what the public organisations of government do or leave. For this reason it would be better to rename the concept of member state into that of *member country*. Before we examine the consequences of this for the processes of European integration, we need to look more closely at the various patterns of relationships between the public and the private organisations as existing at home.

Domestic Patterns of Public-Private Relationships

For the sake of clarity, we will keep society split into two parts, the public and the private spheres, thus disregarding for the moment the many hybrids between them. Concerning the relationships between the two parts, we pose three important questions. Firstly, do they each have their own separate world or are they interdependent? Secondly, is the public sector dominating the private one or is the opposite the case? Thirdly, is the quality of their relationship antagonistic or friendly? The central variables behind the three questions are, in short, respectively: *domain, direction* and *affection*. If we limit ourselves, again for the sake of clarity, to dichotomised answers (the extremes of the three kinds of relationship), then we get six logically possible patterns. Jumping to conclusions, the answer to the first question shall be 'interdependency' and not 'two separate worlds', by which we shall end up with five both logical and relevant patterns of relationship, typified as follows [Van Schendelen, 1990].

(1) *Interdependency, no 'two worlds'*. True enough, in many countries many people take the position that both the public sector of government and the private one of business and NGOs must have or do have their autonomy, independent from each other, in short that the two sectors should be or are

two separate worlds. The normative beliefs certainly exist, as illustrated by popular values like privatisation and deregulation for the public sector and values like corporate citizenship and self-reliance for the private sector. Are the two sectors really independent from each other? There is not any empirical evidence that supports this position. For its income, support, information, effectiveness and much more, any public organisation is, directly or indirectly, highly dependent on the private sector, and vice versa. Therefore, public organisations want to intervene in the private domain, and they do as they like, as private organisations do in the public domain. This interdependency is, of course, not constant but variable, both across countries and in time. For example, the central government of France usually intervenes more frequently and more detailed in private organisations than its Irish counterpart. In Germany and the Netherlands, the public authorities usually undergo more interventions from private organisations than their counterparts in Portugal or Britain. All countries are mixed public-private systems, thus giving validity to the subsequent patterns.

(2) *Public interventionism.* This second pattern is one extreme of the core variable of direction. It refers to the interventions of government in the private domain through both its hard legislation, ultimately maintained by police and court systems, and its soft interventions such as subsidies, procurements, white papers, promises, privileges and more. These can have the positive variant of granting a desired item, or the negative one of refusing this. The outcome is that, in fact, every factor of, for example, a company's functioning, from production factors and processing to sales of products and services, is subject to some public intervention, except the factor of weather, which falls beyond government control. Many governments target their interventions most easily at the private areas with low mobility (big plants, farms) and/or high concentration (chemicals, the car industry). The factors and reasons behind public interventionism and its variations are manifold. It may be for managing some social issue like infrastructure, security, education, social welfare or financial crisis, but also be caused by, for example, government instability, imminent elections or technology. Every act of intervention in a pluralist society is, of course, always contested and not self-evident. Within governments, different ideologies and policy cultures compete with each other. Political parties extend their electoral competition to the realms of public decision-making. Bureaucrats may compete on budget, which encourages them to intervene even more. Much public intervention is, paradoxically, the outcome of pressures exerted by private interest groups.

(3) *Private interventionism* is the third pattern and mirrors the former.

Companies and/or citizen groups, together forming civil society, intervene in the government system, in order to protect or to promote their interests. A formal indicator like regulation in the former pattern is absent for private interventions. Only in a few 'corporatist' countries (especially Austria, to a lesser degree Sweden and the Netherlands) do the major social organisations of employers and employees have some formal say about the government's socio-economic agenda. The standard indicator of private interventionism is usually less formal and regards the behaviour of a private interest group as a pressure group, indicated by such activities as, in simple terms, 'exit, voice and loyalty' [Hirschman, 1970] or, in popular wording, the Triple F of 'flee, fight, flirt'. By acting in such ways, a pressure group tries to obtain a desired outcome from the public authorities. Private interventionism through pressure group behaviour can best be seen as a case of collective *participation in government*. As such it is, of course, again a variable and dependent on many factors, which can be downsized to four main categories [Milbrath and Goel, 1977]:

a. *capacities* to act, such as resources (size, budget, personnel), external support (coalitions) and skills;
b. *desires* to deal with threats and opportunities coming from or through government;
c. *compulsions* from competitions with other pressure groups or from its assessments that put the costs of action below its benefits and/or the costs of non-action;
d. *invitations* from government to participate as interest group or stakeholder.

Paradoxically, a governmental organisation is frequently a sort of 'meta-actor' behind these capacities, desires, compulsions and/or invitations. As part of its own competition with other public organisations, it tries to stimulate supportive actions from befriended private groups. The EU's Commission is famous for its open invitations to pressure groups [Greenwood, 2007], for example by its 'calls for interests', financial empowerment of groups and method of expert committees.

(4) *Public-private antagonism* is our fourth pattern, and it represents one extreme of our last core variable, affection. Indicators are distrust, evasion, insult and conflict. In most continental countries of Europe, much antagonism is more latent than manifest, due to a domestic culture of preferred harmony. Nevertheless, antagonism is a normal phenomenon everywhere. At some times it is caused by misperceptions and misunderstandings, yet is real in its consequences. At other times it is based on real conflict of inter-

ests, damage caused or misconduct. It can even be used as a bargaining chip in a negotiation game [Coser, 1956]. Public and private organisations can be antagonistic not only to each other but also to organisations of their own category, thus increasing the pluralism of the country. For example, on the issue of new railway infrastructure, a coalition of the Ministry of Transport, the regional authorities and the green movement can act antagonistically against a counter coalition of the Ministry of Trade, the truckers' organisations and the local citizens' groups.

(5) *Public-private partnership* is the fifth and final pattern, and it mirrors the former one. Mutual trust, co-operation, respect and harmony are its indicators. Public and private organisations feel happy with each other. The feeling may, of course, be the result of misperceptions and misunderstandings, but become real by its consequences. More commonly it is based on shared preferences, mutual dependencies and, in general, common interests. A partnership can also be a negotiating chip, even if it is only played through courtesy. This happens especially in the continental countries, where a partnership garners social approval almost by definition. Partnerships frequently remain, however, quite limited by time and place. For example, a local authority with land but without money can have a temporary partnership with an investment company for land development. More far-reaching cases are both the previously mentioned corporatism (like in Austria) and the state protection for companies seen as 'national flags' (like in France). By its creation of outsiders and losers, a partnership too can fragment both the public and the private sector. The result is once again an increased pluralism in the country.

The Europeanization of the Member Countries

The implicit assumption so far is that national public and private organisations remain inside their national borders. In reality they do not, especially not in the European area with its mainly medium-sized and highly interdependent countries. One indicator is the export ratio, which for Belgium is around 60% of its GDP while Germany rates around 25%. A ministry, company or whatever interest group can be more dependent on a foreign country than on its own. Every organisation or group has to cope with foreign public and private organisations and not least with the EU. All the above-mentioned patterns of relationship, characterising the mixed public-private member countries, can thus become relevant at this European level.

Of course, a small company or an ordinary citizen may consider this *EU level* as 'far away' and as belonging to another world. In objective terms, however, nobody can escape the interventions from the other countries and the EU. Every year the EU produces about 2500 new pieces of legislation, capable of overruling domestic legislation and creating many chain effects in the countries. From their side, ministries like Trade & Industry, big companies like Unilever, and NGOs like Greenpeace are regularly active pressure groups in other countries and at the EU level. With some parts of the EU, they may have an antagonistic relationship and with other parts one of close partnership. The same holds true for the EU units. A Directorate-General (DG) of the Commission intervening in a member country can develop both antagonistic and friendly relationships there. At the European level, there exists an even wider international context. Issues of, for example, agriculture, steel and financial services can be dealt with on global levels such as WTO (World Trade Organisation), WHO (World Health Organisation) and many temporary settings. All patterns of relationship can recur even here.

We have already observed that, at the European level, the EU is relevant as a *sixth approach* to the settlement of irritating differences among the member states. We also observed that a member state is not a homogeneous entity, let alone a monolith. In practice it stands for a fragmented and dynamic collection of public and private organisations, better described as a *member country*. These two observations can be linked now. An irritating difference between two countries is never a difference between two nationally cohesive coalitions of public and private organisations. It is always (without exception) an issue inside each country as well, both between and among its public and private organisations. On, for example, the EU liberalisation of postal delivery, all member countries tend to be divided. On both sides of the fight stand postal delivery companies, national ministries, consumer groups, trade unions and more. In the 2008 fight over the protection of Volkswagen against an open car market, the company was supported by its regional and federal government plus the trade unions, versus an alliance of the Commission, Porsche, the German employers' association BDI and foreign car makers. They all can air their preferences and disagreements over the issue within the framework of the EU. So they contribute to the europeanization of public and private issues existing at a domestic level. By raising them to the EU level, they make it mixed public-private, too.

This term or idea of europeanization has become increasingly popular in both public discussion and in the literature, but its definition is frequently implicit or loose and not yet well established. Some take it as a synonym for European integration or, in nasty wording, EU-ization [Fligstein and Stone Sweet, 2001; Kohler-Koch, 2003], others as a regional case of globalisation [Wallace and Wallace, 1996, 16-19]. Particularly dominant is the view that EU dynamics have become part of domestic policies and politics [Featherstone and Radaelli, 2003; Schimmelfennig and Sedelmeier, 2005; Graziano and Vink, 2007], which is so to say the downstream view, that goes from EU to the national systems and creates an impact on, for example, domestic social policies [Bache, 2008], public law [Jans and others, 2007] and urban government [Marshall, 2005]. The reverse view of an upstream of interventions from the national systems to the EU is seldom given equal attention but included here, as we define europeanization as the *increase of cross-border public and private issue-formation in Europe*. The core element is the transport of an irritation or an issue across state borders. The increase can take place not only by volume (more new issues), but also by content (more intensely contested issues). The definition deliberately, leaves open for research four questions about the process: (i) the source of europeanization, (ii) its direction at the starting side, (iii) the dependent variable there and (iv) its outcomes at the ending side.

The *source* can be one or more of the following four: a European or a domestic pressure group, either public or private. The source is, for example, the EU, a European federation, a national ministry or a regional trade association. On the same issue all different sources can be active at the same time, thus reflecting the plural divisions of Europe. Europeanization can occur in two opposite *directions*. Firstly, it can go from the European level, being another country or EU, to the domestic one, which flow is called the downstream. Secondly, it can start at home and be exported to another country or to the EU, which is called the upstream direction. In this case a domestic group influences the process of issue-formation in Europe. The *dependent variable* at either the European or the national level can vary from people's attitudes and behaviour to policies, institutions, regime values and constitutional arrangements in the public or private domain. The *outcomes* of issue-formation are left open here as well. They can be a binding decision or a policy proposal made by the EU or a private agreement among companies from various countries. Or the issue may remain as it stands, like the plug socket issue, or simply disappear, like the early 1990s HD-television issue.

Vectors of Europeanization

Elaborating upon our general concept of europeanization, we will maintain the two *central dichotomies* regarding the source: the national (or domestic) versus the European level and the public versus the private sector. Of course, every dichotomy has some grey area. For example, is an issue coming from the multinational company Siemens, headquartered in Germany,

VECTORS OF EUROPEANIZATION

Downstream Adaptation Model (E ──►N)

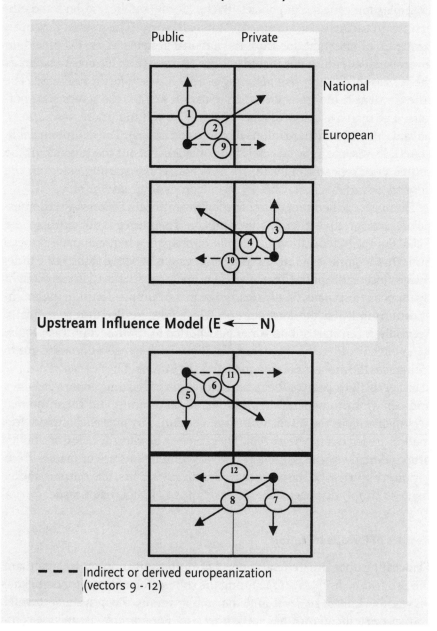

Upstream Influence Model (E ◄── N)

– – – Indirect or derived europeanization
(vectors 9 - 12)

Figure 1.1

a case that belongs to the national or to the European level? The realistic answer is probably: formally national, but practically European. If Siemens, further, creates an issue in close partnership with the German Ministry of Environment, does the case then belong to the private or the public sector? Although the two dichotomies are always less shaded than reality, we can fruitfully use them for analytical purposes, as they help to clarify the mechanism of europeanization. At least eight different vectors or carriers of europeanization can be distinguished: the four analytical sources multiplied by the two directions. They are presented in Figure 1.1 and outlined below. The first four cover the downstream from the European level to the domestic one that results in domestic (public or private) *adaptations* to European causes, and the other four the upstream from the domestic level that *influences* the European one. Viewed from the EU, the first four stream down from its output side and the second four stream up to its input side.

(1) *From the European public sector to the national public sector.* This is, for example, the popular idea of 'Brussels governs'. It has given rise to an enormous body of literature on domestic government adaptation to EU laws, which as binding regulations and decrees overrule domestic laws directly, and as directives still needing national implementation indirectly. Due to the treaties, a major focus of this literature is on market harmonisation and liberalisation. Soft EU interventions like 'guidelines' and 'memoranda', if freely adopted by national governments, fall under this vector as well, as do the treaties made by governments outside the EU framework, like the 1985 Schengen agreement on open borders.

(2) *From the European public sector to the national private sector.* Many decisions by European governments directly bind private sector organisations, whether profit-oriented or not. General examples are the many EU decisions regarding an open and competitive market. Specific examples are the EU regulations regarding safety and health in the workplace and those regarding emissions harmful to the environment. The Rhine Treaty, signed by national governments along the Rhine river, binds both those transporting goods and the companies on the banks.

(3) *From the European private sector to the national private sector.* Many private sectors have their European federations and institutions. For the food and drink industries there is the CIAA, for the trade unions the ETUC and for motorcyclists the FIM. Their manifest function is usually to influence the EU. This falls, however, outside our definition of europeanization, because no border is crossed here. Their most important latent function is frequently forming an internal agreement to which the members are expected

to be bound and to adapt. Without any public involvement, the agreement can europeanize the members back home. A lot of industrial norms and standards have been produced this way.

(4) *From the European private sector to the national public sector.* The federations and institutions referred to above may seek to influence national public organisations. This may happen through an open statement or a campaign. The European Round Table of Industrialists (ERT), for example, addressed its 1984 campaign for an open EU common market directly to the national governments, which decided accordingly in their 1986 Single European Act (SEA). Regarding the distribution of landing rights for air transport, the national carriers, united in the Association of European Airlines (AEA), have orchestrated since the early 1990s informal influences on their national ministries at home. European NGOs like Amnesty International frequently launch calls to national capitals for friendlier domestic policies.

Here we leave the vectors that stream down from the European to the national level and cause a national adaptation to the European level. The next four represent, conversely, national influences at the European level.

(5) *From the national public sector to the European public sector.* An obvious target here is the EU Council of Ministers. National ministers meet together in order to suggest, approve or reject proposals for new legislation coming from the Commission and possibly amended by the European Parliament. A semi-formal example is provided by the thousands of national civil servants that partially come from decentralised governments, meet in expert committees of the Commission and use this vector for squeezing their national government at home through the EU.

(6) *From the national public sector to the European private sector.* In 1998 the French government wanted to have its air defence industry Aerospatiale included in a European consortium with the British Aerospace and the German Dasa. To tempt these companies into an agreement, it even partially privatised Aerospatiale. Local governments can appeal to European companies to make a common cause, like local authorities in steel regions suffering from declining employment managed to do in 1995. Together with the major European steel companies and the trade unions, they established Caster, a public-private umbrella for steel interests, which fused with Reti in 2002 and is now called Eira.

(7) *From the national private sector to the European private sector.* Every membership of a private European federation involves this vector. As members of the EU Pharma Group (PGEU), all national professional groups of pharmacists discuss some of their issues within this federation. They try,

first of all, to monitor and to influence each other. The same sectoral approach is followed by thousands of other national private organisations, profit-oriented or not, from telephone companies to consumer groups. By making a cross-sectoral deal at home, they can even orchestrate their influence on more than one European sector. For example, the natural monopoly of the French TGV railway system in Western Europe strongly influences the time schedules of transport modalities in other countries.

(8) *From the national private sector to the European public sector.* This vector covers the many popular cases of EU lobbying by private companies and citizen groups. Another example is the thousands of private sector people sitting in expert committees of the Commission. Most complaints regarding unfair market behaviour are brought to the Commission by private groups feeling hurt. Multinational firms frequently approach foreign governments under the flag of their subsidiaries there, in order to orchestrate a pan-European symphony of lobby sound directed at the EU, as Philips tried to do in 1986 to gain EU protection for its 'infant industry' of compact discs, and in 2007 to get, conversely, liberalised import tariffs for its low-energy light bulbs made in China; in the latter case it succeeded in 2008, in spite of strong opposition from the German Osram. Frequently, fierce market competition is a major cause of this eighth vector. Take for example the pharmaceutical companies' push for the 2001 Tobacco Products Directive, at the cost of the tobacco industry, in order to create a market for their anti-tobacco products [Duina and Kurzer, 2004].

The Fuller Story of Europeanization

The eight different vectors are useful for a better understanding of the reality of europeanization. They represent eight hypotheses or stories of europeanization, thus stimulating the mental mapping for both research (description and explanation) and practice (evaluation and optimisation). For example, those who want to make their organisation *EU-proof* are usually focussed on the EU's rear flank, from which they receive the laws that demand adaptation of their domestic practices. Thanks to the vectors they now can broaden or even shift their focus to the EU's front side and try to get EU laws adapted to their domestic needs instead. The vectors form, however, a schematic model that can never tell the full story of any case of europeanization. Six realistic elements must be added: (1) public-private transactions not across borders, (2) the grey areas of the two dichotomies, (3) the connections between vectors, (4) the wider global level, (5) creeping europeanization and (6) rolling europeanization.

(1) *No crossing of borders.* In our definition of europeanization, all issue-formation by public and private organisations at only the national or the European level falls outside any vector. These events not crossing borders can yet be relevant for cross-border issue-formation. In Figure 1.1 they are labelled as indirect or derived vectors and numbered 9 up to 12. At the EU level, Commission and European federations (EuroFeds) often have regular communications and interventions. In 2003, the Commission called the EuroFeds of employers and trade unions to arrange more pension mobility (vector 9). From their side, the EuroFeds have as their major function the influencing of the EU institutions and stakeholders there (vector 10). In many countries, ministries at home ask private groups for information and support at the European level (vector 11). Very common is that a company or NGO observing a threat or opportunity coming from elsewhere in Europe asks domestic public officials to support its position at the European level (vector 12). Even events happening solely inside either the public or the private domain can be relevant for some European issue-formation. Domestic companies and NGOs frequently support or fight each other over action at the European level. Such events at only one level can be seen as side stories of europeanization: relevant, but not the main story.

(2) *Grey areas.* The two dichotomies are in real life not as clear as suggested. Many an organisation operates at both the national and the European level. The clearest example is the multinational company (MNC) acting in various countries and inside both European federations and EU expert committees. EU agencies are increasingly part of one network with national agencies. Many national ministries, decentralised governments and non-governmental organisations (NGOs) occupy positions at both levels as well. They may suffer from some schizophrenia between europeanization and domestication [Kassim, 2003], but nonetheless function across borders and take their issues with them. In 1987, UK Prime Minister Margaret Thatcher politicized this grey area by pleading for clearer separation between the two levels and, re-launching the old notion of subsidiarity, for the supremacy of the domestic level. The second dichotomy, between public and private organisations, has its own grey area. Well-known are state-run companies and company-run agencies. Many NGOs have grey shades as well, and as hybrids they may be called a quasi-NGO or QUANGO [Van Thiel, 2000; Beloe and others, 2003]. Some are government-organised NGOs, called GONGOs, and function as a hybrid public-private agency, institution or fake NGO sponsored by a government, as happens in fields like health, human rights, development and the environment. The EU Commission alone spends an estimated more than 1 milliard (US billion)

euro a year for enabling NGOs to participate at the EU level, which allocation of money the European Parliament has set at issue in the mid-2000s.
The antipode is the business-organised NGO or BONGO, such as any trade
organisation and the fake NGOs in such fields as health (patient groups),
transport and consumption. Parts of government and business create fake
NGOs for getting the friendlier face of 'civil society' and thus another vector
in hand, in short a better ticket to influence the EU. The parent of a fake
NGO takes the risk that its creation becomes unmasked or a monster that
eats the parent. NGOs can get even more hydra-headed. If they want to sit
on the government's seat, they become a government-interested NGO or
GINGO. By selling special products and services, as the simoniacal cleri-
cals did in the past and Greenpeace and Oxfam still today, they become
business-interested or BINGO. They usually do this for acquiring power or
money. These hybrid relations between the public and private domains
have become an issue in mid-2000s. The notions for separating the two are
privatisation and nationalisation.

(3) *Connected vectors*. The cross-border formation of an issue is seldom
carried by only one vector. Most cases of europeanization are caused by a
number of vectors connected in parallel or series. An example is the Deck-
er/Kohll court case. In the mid-1990s these two citizens (a Luxembourger
and German) had received medical services (from an optician and a dentist,
respectively) during their holidays in another EU country. Back home they
wanted to get the costs reimbursed by their public health insurance companies, which refused to do so. After their appeal to the Court, it decided in
1998 that medical services are not exempted from the open market, thus
should be re-imbursed, so breaking open the formerly closed national public health insurance systems. Many public insurance companies were not
amused and, as a side story of europeanization, approached their domestic
ministry. They also raised the Court decision with their European federations, such as the CEA. National ministries discussed the issue in the EU
Health Council of April 1998. Encouraged by the 1999 Amsterdam Treaty
chapter on public health, the Commission began to prepare proposals for
the liberalisation of the public health insurance market. The insurance
companies soon started to lobby. In this single case the first two adaptation
vectors and three of the four influence vectors have clearly been operative serially or even in parallel. All together they form only one episode of this case.

(4) *The global level*. Finally, there are the complexities and the dynamics
coming from the wider international or global level. For example, trade issues on bananas, beef and biotechnology were once incited and partially
settled in the EU, but in 1999 the three 'B's were put on the WTO agenda by

the US chief negotiator Charlene Barshefsky, so becoming global issues. She also looked for support from national governments and private companies in Europe, thus exploiting divided positions and useful vectors there. Some governments and private interest groups from the EU indeed supported the US against the EU, in order to change the EU policies that disadvantaged their interests. The reverse happens as well. Then, US state-governments and/or private interest groups, having lost in Washington, support the EU side at the WTO table.

(5) *Creeping europeanization.* Many stories of europeanization have important prologues. In policy fields in which the EU has few or no formal powers, such as education, taxation and financial services [Linsenmann and others, 2007; Borrás, 2004], the Commission often initiates an 'open co-ordination method' (OCM) for benchmarking current domestic policy practices and for 'learning from each other'. Any outcome is not legally binding ('soft law'), but in practice it often leverages hard law as part of the EU's downstream. This often happens in the upstream, too. Interest groups wanting to get their policy preferences included in EU agendas go around in different vector domains to gather support, and sooner or later the EU decision process usually follows.

(6) *Rolling europeanization.* Many stories of europeanization also have important epilogues. A downstream example is the EU's general competition law that has had a strong impact on many different sectors, now also including parts of health, education and housing. A single case like the Habitat Directive (EC 1992/ 43) on Preserving Nature has affected many policy domains, ranging from water management and town planning to road construction and archaeological excavation. Similar epilogues exist in the upstream, too. Policy co-operation on cross-border control once started as an initiative of five of the original member-states (except Italy) as the Schengen Agreement outside the EU framework in 1990. Under pressure from interest groups from trade, NGOs and governments, the agreement was included in the 1993 Maastricht Treaty (not binding the UK and Ireland) and has become expanded and intensified since.

The EU is clearly not the only chapter in the full story of the europeanization of its member countries. Nevertheless, it has become the single most important *source and direction* of the process of europeanization. The EU deals with all sorts of irritating differences between domestic public and private organisations from the different member countries. It has political, legal and other capacities to channel issues and to bring at least some of them to accepted outcomes. In academic terms, the EU is both a dependent and an independent variable of europeanization.

Influence Challenges from Europeanization

It is old wisdom that every organisation is never independent from and always more or less dependent on its *challenging environment* [Thompson, 1967]. This outside world is perceived as having two faces. One looks promising and full of opportunities, the other threatening and difficult. The permanently changing complexities of the outside world make adaptive and/or influencing behaviour continuously necessary, particularly regarding other organisations and groups acting as either friends or opponents, in short as *stakeholders*. Therefore, every organisation has to satisfy two selfish interests. At its input side, it has to acquire the means of operation it needs from the outside, for example budget, support, information and other resources, and at its output side, it has to deliver what is demanded from the outside, for example special products, services, support and other contributions. In this functional sense, every organisation is an interest group. This is not less true for a ministry or the EU than for a company or a group of citizens. In fact, many government officials act as just an interest group [Baumgartner, 2007]

Only with regard to its internal operations can an organisation act more or less independently, but this *autonomy* is not sufficient for survival, always limited and dependent on many properties such as type (public or private), resources (affluent or poor), reputation (good or bad) and particularly awareness (alert or sleepy). The more an organisation is conscious about its position in the larger world, the better it can exert its autonomy and do more than merely adapt to the good or the bad luck coming from outside. If it is alert, it can decide to influence the environment by pushing the opportunities and by blocking the threats. Paradoxically, an unfriendly environment of threatening public interventions or market competitions frequently sharpens this awareness better than a friendly one that tends to dull the reflexes and increase the risk of being caught by surprise and of losing leadership, income or function. No organisation is secure in this respect.

Since the rise of the EU, the vectors of europeanization enrich this old wisdom with a new experience, because every organisation in Europe now has a stronger cross-border dimension that makes Brussels, so to say, its new domestic capital. The vectors from the European to the domestic level create *challenges of adaptation*. They can bring good fortune in terms of new opportunities, for example for the export of products or for policy change at home. They can, however, also bring new threats and increased costs incurred through adaptation. They can no longer, as in the past, be easily filtered or blocked by the national state. The influence vectors, going from the domestic to the European level, create their own *challenges of influence*, having two different faces as well. They can create new opportunities, for example a more level playing-field or a specific EU decision as desired. Yet they can also create new threats, for example because they provide a comparative advantage to a competitor at home or abroad. The fight for survival, in short, is shifting from the domestic to the European level and requires a cross-border or European approach.

This influence approach at the European and particularly EU level is central in this book. Anticipating chapters 4 and 5, the major prerequisite is an open mind for the vectors of europeanization, which is a matter of three forms of preparation or homework. First of all, new facts and trends occurring in the European environment need continuous monitoring. The observations need, secondly, assessment in terms of threats and opportunities that always imply value judgements, derived from one's own values and objectives. They result, thirdly, in interests, which are chosen positions regarding facts and trends in the world around and are labelled as either threats or opportunities. In pluralistic societies, these interests are always contested by some other stakeholders having chosen different positions or interests, thus making interests practically synonymous to *issues*. This is true for both public and private interests, as a public interest is not an interest of a higher or lower order than a private one, but merely an interest of a public organisation like a ministry, agency or party, whereas a private interest is one held by a private organisation.

The more alert or conscious an organisation is in defining its interests, the more it is capable of survival in the challenging European environment. This alertness does not imply, however, that a public or a private organisation always has to influence that environment. As will be shown later, there are various situations in which adaptive behaviour is more rational than an effort to influence a growing threat or opportunity. This rationality can only be based, again, on a consciously prepared study at home, to be called the *preparatory homework*. In daily life, however, adaptive behaviour is frequently not the consequence of conscious homework but of precisely the opposite, namely the neglect of it. Then, due to its nonchalance, the organisation can only try to adapt to, in our case, the europeanization of its environment. Sometimes it may enjoy some good luck from a free opportunity or faded threat, but usually it suffers more from the bad luck of a missed opportunity or neglected threat.

If a public or a private organisation comes to the decision that officials or stakeholders have to be influenced on an issue, it changes from interest group into, as this is called, a *pressure group*. Acting in the European area, it can choose from the menu of vectors, which is even richer if it also considers the vectors that are not crossing borders and/or can be connected. The quality of a choice is, as usual in life, largely dependent on such qualities as expertise and intelligence that to a high degree can be organised by preparatory homework and thus is frequently absent. For example, if it wants to save an opportunity or to solve a threat, an easy-going pressure group wants to go to the source directly and to influence the stakeholders or officials that have caused the challenge. It behaves like Pavlov's dog. A more intelligent pressure group, informed about the many vectors, shall consider a change of the vector by connecting the initial one to a different level and/or domain. In response to the 1992 EU policy programme on the Single European Market (SEM), with all its threats and opportunities for competition, many MNCs reacted not by lobbying the EU, but by quickly exploiting their market [Calori and Lawrence, 1991; Mayes, 1992; Urban and Vendemini, 1992]. In the early 1990s, the European Federation of Largest Textile and Apparel Companies (ELTAC) followed the reverse route. Suffering from cheap imports from non-EU low-wage (child-labour) countries and wanting (high) price protection, it pushed this market issue successfully through the EU agenda by acting as a sort of NGO against child labour.

Old Influence Techniques and Lobbying

Trying to influence somebody else is as old as human life. For the promotion of its interests, every lobby group can choose from an old menu of traditional techniques Greene, 1998], such as the following selection that runs from sweet to spicy:

Seduction. Famous cases in the literature are Eve's apple in Paradise (Old Testament), the 'Ars amandi' and, for repair, the 'Remedia Amoris' (Ovid) and countless more [Greene, 2001]. Indicators of seduction are for example donations (maybe bribery in other man's eyes), flattery and politeness attuned to the taste of the other. Competitors may seduce better. In the EU, stakeholders and officials usually have a sack of fresh carrots within reach for luring others.

Reframing. It is not the text but the melody that makes the music. By reframing an issue so that it sounds nicer to others' ears, one may collect more support, game or other targeted prizes. A subsidy for overproduced food is difficult to get, but for the upgraded purpose of humanitarian aid it is much easier. Opponents then have to play the downgrade.

Persuasion. A strong belief may convince others, at least for some time. A classical example is the 'missionary enterprise' of the Jesuits who in the past have converted many people by 'marketing and selling' their belief system through persuasion plus some seduction by way of social benefits [Wright, 2004]. Many lobby groups act as persuaders [John, 2002; Mc-Grath, 2005-A], particularly the 'green' NGOs in Europe. Their opponents have to fight that belief system or start a counter-persuasion.

Argumentation. Scientific reasoning, based on logically sound inferences and empirically credible references, is the influence vehicle here. Among all asserted correlations there is, however, so far only one having the full value of 1.0, namely that between life and death, and all others are by consequence contestable and at least partially falsifiable. Argumentation can be useful in four situations: when important stakeholders are still hesitant (they might be won), when an issue is in an early phase (many have not yet taken a position), when an issue attracts publicity (the audience wants argumentation) and when it needs an upgrade (as a more general interest). In these cases it is, however, salesman's talk rather than science.

Advocacy. The informal variant is for example a mass media campaign, which is frequently used by NGOs and trade associations [Warleigh and Fairbrass, 2002; Johnson, 2008]. Semi-formal is the lodging of a complaint, for example by companies feeling hurt by unfair market practices and forwarding their complaints to the EU competition authorities. Most formal is litigation in court, under reference to existing laws. But there is always some room for counter-advocacy.

Negotiation. Making a deal with an important stakeholder or official is an efficient way to get an interest at least partially met. It is the game of mutual giving and taking (maybe with the force of blackmail) or, in commercial terms, of matching the sides of supply and demand (maybe under unfair competition). Within the EU, though, many others are always around wanting to interfere and at least avoid any deal at their cost.

Authority. With some authority derived from tradition, charisma or position, one can cheaply get others to do what one wants [Friedrich, 1963]. Then, one becomes a leader with a following. Particularly at the EU level, no source of authority is permanent and absolute, and neither is any following.

Encapsulation. By making a stakeholder or official generally dependent on for example some budget or a procedure, one may more easily get what one wants in a specific case. Many a BONGO or GONGO is dependent on the financial lifeline from its parent and thus wants to please the parent at least now and then. Through the use of procedures of decision-making, one may encapsulate befriended interest groups in privileged positions and opposing ones in subordinate positions, so creating a more convenient playing-field to one's own interest. The EU is full of encapsulation fights, to which we shall return in chapter 3.

Coercion. The ultimate example is the launch of a war, the 'ars belligerendi' as masterminded by Sun Tze in old Imperial China [Griffiths, 1963] and frequently applied in Europe thereafter. In modern times, officials can coerce interest groups and citizens by issuing legislation that is ultimately maintained by police, court and jail systems. The EU is ultimately based on coercive legislation. NGOs may set up a blockade or a hate campaign, as Greenpeace did against Shell in the 1995 Brent Spar affair. A company can threaten to move production to another country. Coercion regards, in short, the use of sticks.

All these (and more) traditional techniques of influencing a challenging outside world are still used in practice and frequently even in combination in either serial or parallel settings. Equally old is the question: *what choice is best?* Every choice has its advantages and disadvantages, for example in terms of costs to the user, effects on the people to be influenced and reactions from the wider environment. Choosing at random or arbitrarily is not a rational option, as a blunder can easily be caused and a boomerang effect received. If driven by the ambition to influence others, everybody has always to cope with substantial degrees of uncertainty. One rational solution for this is acting very prudently, step-by-step, avoiding points of no return, in short finding out by prudent trial and error. Another one is finding out in advance what is probably best to do, by studiously comparing the various alternatives on the menu, assessing for each the probable consequences to one's own position, the targeted groupings and the wider audience, and finally choosing the best course of action. Frequently both solutions are applied simultaneously and the metaphor of the chess-player is illustrative here [Simon, 1979], as every game of chess contains a countless number of alternative moves and consequences of each. Only amateurish players just go and see what happens. More rational ones are studious before the game and play prudently.

The modern concept of *lobbying* fits here [Thomas, 2004]. The word lobby comes from the Latin lobium, in medieval times lobia, which refers to a hall or vestibule in an important building. People wanting to get something done from the resident came in and had to wait in the hall, where usually other people were waiting with a similar purpose. By talking with these other people, now called stakeholders, they tried to collect information about the rules of the house, the resident himself, the other stakeholders and other affairs of potential interest. If permitted to visit and speak to the resident, they could subsequently push forward their request more attuned to his or her whims. In modern times the political sense of lobbying gained popularity thanks to the US Congress in the late 19th century [Milbrath, 1963; US/GAO, 1999]. Waiting in the hall or lobby of the Congress building, representatives of pressure groups tried to gather information from Congressmen and their assistants and ultimately to urge the Congressmen to vote 'yea' or 'nay' [Matthews and Stimson, 1975]. Over the course of time, this 'lobbying' developed from merely corridor behaviour to a broader and more sophisticated set of activities, ranging from providing information to organising mass publicity and giving political or even financial support. This latter activity sometimes developed into bribery and has given lobbying a bad name among many ordinary people, in spite of all the stricter regulations on lobbying in the US since the mid-1920s. In contrast, the old French word for the same place and activities, namely the 'anti-chambre', has kept its neutral meaning. In short, lobbying is probably as old as the traditional influence techniques mentioned before and maybe the second oldest profession in history, if not the first (dependent on Eve's tricks to get Adam eating).

We shall use the word lobbying here in its neutral or technical meaning and, by-passing many other definitions and labels [McGrath, 2005-A, chapter 2], define it as *the build-up of unorthodox efforts to obtain information and support regarding a game of interest in order to eventually get a desired outcome from a power-holder.* We will define a lobby group as a pressure group that acts this way; in chapters 7 and 8 we shall return to its contested meanings. Our keyword, unorthodoxy, needs firstly to be addressed here. Clearly enough, it falls outside orthodox (or institutionalised) patterns of behaviour, such as a right to pose a question or a request during a formal meeting. Such behaviour is frequently considered uncertain or even risky regarding its effects. By using unorthodox ways and means, the lobbyist can improve his/her prudent trial and error and/or studious investigations in advance, in short enhance the chances of final success. The ways and means of unorthodoxy have, however, no fixed contents, as they (like those of orthodoxy) vary with time and place. What is (un)orthodox in one country or period may be the opposite in another one. Each dichotomy has also inevitably a lot of grey areas, in our case resulting in degrees of (un)orthodoxy. A few EU examples can clarify this. The Commissioner who offers the Parliament's rapporteur a fine lunch in order 'to listen to' or 'to make sure things are in order' is clearly lobbying, but his official letter in reply to a request from the rapporteur has nothing to do with lobbying. Attending an organised hearing is not an activity of lobbying, but pressuring for its convocation or calling-off may be. Using a break during a hearing in order to deal informally with other stakeholders is certainly a case of lobbying. The letter or lunch used for social talk has nothing to do with lobbying, but every lobby-related letter or lunch is best opened with some talk first, in order to create a pleasant atmosphere for conducting business.

The main logic behind collecting information and support in unorthodox ways comes from the need to diminish the risks of applying an influence technique at random or arbitrarily, and thus to increase the chances of success. Lobbying aims to discover the risks and chances of an arena studiously and prudently, in order to avoid blunders and boomerangs. Although its specific ways and means of unorthodoxy vary with time and place, lobbying has four *general characteristics*. Firstly, information about stakeholders and their issues is preferably gathered in indirect ways, for example through their neighbours, friends and previous acts of behaviour. All this is done, secondly, highly informally and preferably without any footprints, because otherwise some point of no return may be passed. Thirdly, the lobbying is done silently, because information is gathered through the ears and eyes and never through the mouth, and also because sound tends to mobilise potential opponents. Finally, a charming supply side is pushed forward, for the simple reason that others are usually less interested in somebody's demand side and more in 'what is in for them', being at the EU level particularly specific information and support. These characteristics require a lot of preparatory homework and come close to classical diplomacy [De Callières, 1716]. It is also quite akin to Ovid's basics of 'ars amandi', according to which young people aged around twenty are usually perfect lobbyists by instinct, as most of them approach their 'target' indirectly, informally, silently and always charmingly; at a later age many of them lose that instinct, do the exact opposite and have to rediscover the basics of lobbying in private affairs. One of the finest examples of a great lobbyist is Niccolò Machiavelli, to whom we have dedicated the title of this book. Driven by a strong ambition to win and not to lose a game, he always tried to study a match carefully before it might start and to act extremely prudently during the match.

Lobbying the EU as Public Affairs Management

Every political system has its complexities that, if one wants to get one's fingerprint on its outcome as desired, require a lot of ambition, study and prudence. This is very true for the highly *competitive EU playing-field*. Many players, coming from both the country level and the EU institutions, want to promote their interests here on whatever dossier at any time but, divided as they are, they do so in different directions. This competition limits the efficiency and effectiveness of their efforts to influence. The old techniques have proven their limits a long time ago, as a few examples may clarify. Coercion, if based on established EU law and exerted by litigation in the Court, frequently takes a lot of time-costs with short-term effectiveness, as the opponents can cause a retaliatory boomerang. Encapsulation requires both a strong position of power and an affluent financial footing, preconditions which rarely exist. Advocacy leads to little more than counter-advocacy, as every barrister has an opponent, and thus easily leads to stalemate as well. Argumentation is as salesman's talk useful in only a few situations but seldom sufficient, as most lobby groups in Europe can produce another position paper with logical inferences and credible references, behind which are hidden the real values and interests at stake. Like in an ancient Greek drama, all characters may then be right in their argumentation and, unwilling to compromise, dead by the final act. Argumentation is even more useless, insofar as strong allies are already convinced, and difficult opponents are unwilling to become convinced. For influencing the EU one needs, in short, a targeted ambition, a proactive study of the playing-field and a prudent style of playing. Lobbying indirectly, informally, silently and charmingly helps to gather information and support needed for this.

In the search for an even more efficient and effective way of organizing all efforts to get desired outcomes from a complex political system, *public affairs management* (PAM) has become the new catchphrase [Harris and Fleisher, 2005]. The public affairs (or, in Latin, *res publica*) of an interest group refer to its external agenda. This is simply the group of interests that has to be protected or promoted by influencing the challenging environment. The decision to do so is considered as an essential part of general management. In the field of PA management, the term 'influence' is often replaced by 'management', derived from the Latin *manu agere*, which means something like 'directing by hand' or 'having a hand in the game'. Ironically, the term 'manipulation', coming from the same language (*manu pulare*), has almost the same meaning but has a much different melody. So far, the new catchword PAM might be seen as an upgrade of the old idea of lobbying or as a new label on a bottle of old wine. It contains some fine old wine indeed, particularly the common focus on 'trying to influence or to make a difference as desired', now framed as managing challenges from outside by solving perceived problems and/or taking perceived opportunities. In this sense there is no difference between a group that lobbies and one that applies PA.

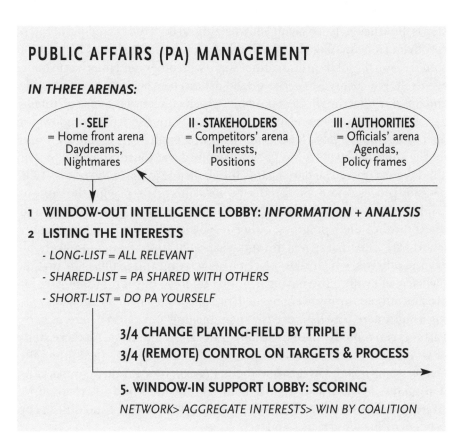

PUBLIC AFFAIRS (PA) MANAGEMENT

IN THREE ARENAS:

I - SELF
= Home front arena
Daydreams,
Nightmares

II - STAKEHOLDERS
= Competitors' arena
Interests,
Positions

III - AUTHORITIES
= Officials' arena
Agendas,
Policy frames

1 **WINDOW-OUT INTELLIGENCE LOBBY:** *INFORMATION + ANALYSIS*

2 **LISTING THE INTERESTS**

- *LONG-LIST = ALL RELEVANT*

- *SHARED-LIST = PA SHARED WITH OTHERS*

- *SHORT-LIST = DO PA YOURSELF*

3/4 **CHANGE PLAYING-FIELD BY TRIPLE P**

3/4 **(REMOTE) CONTROL ON TARGETS & PROCESS**

5. **WINDOW-IN SUPPORT LOBBY: SCORING**
NETWORK> AGGREGATE INTERESTS> WIN BY COALITION

Figure 1.2

Yet there is a lot of new wine in the bottle as well. The greatest difference between lobbying and modern PA management is the increased use of systematic methodology that must result in a more rationally organised 'ambition, study and prudence', as summarised in the stylised Figure 1.2 and detailed in chapters 3 to 6. As an appetizer we now sketch the five main steps of PAM. It all starts with the extroverted (*'window-out'*) monitoring of arising issues in the arenas of officials (who can decide 'yeas' or 'nays') and stakeholders (from whom support is needed), in short with the lobby for information or, better phrased, intelligence that comes from brains fed by senses. The resulting list of identified threats and opportunities or 'nightmares and daydreams' coming from outside is easily a long-list of over one hundred relevant interests, which is but a few percent of only EU's new binding decisions issued annually. The long-list serves as a database for intelligent selection, as its length makes it impossible to manage. The second step is the efficient (cost-saving) downsizing, to both the shared-list of interests that can be managed through other groups and the short-list that for some reason the lobby group cannot share with others and thus has to manage itself. For cost-reasons, the shared-list can best be the longest possible and the short-list the shortest possible, which efficiency is a case of 'intelligent laziness'. On every selected interest many more detailed window-out operations must follow, for the shared-list through flexible platforms and for the short-list by the lobby group. The third and fourth steps are preferably taken at once. The one regards the challenge to make the relevant EU decision process more comfortable to one's interest, by playing the game of Triple P (chapter 3); and the other both the sharpening of chosen targets and the control of their progress, either remotely (on shared-list) or directly (short-list). The final step is the organisation of support among stakeholders and officials, which takes place by networking and coalition formation ('*window-in*') with those having a similar interest, in short by lobbying for broader support in any event needed for realising a daydream and/or averting a nightmare. The logic of early shared-listing is evidenced here, as early partners can mobilise their own supporters and share costs. All these steps of window-out and window-in operations have to be managed internally ('*on the home front*'). On it the studious PA-expert or PA-desk supports its management board with getting both the outside world internalised by strategy and its interests externalised among stakeholders and officials by prudent influencing tactics and techniques.

Public affairs management is, indeed, more than a new label for old wine. True enough, the basic idea of PAM, namely that one has to be prepared studiously and organised prudently for a game or fight outside, is far from new. In the past the Chinese chief commander Sun Tze recommended this to his Warlord, as Niccolò Machiavelli did to Lorenzo dei Medici, the ruler of Firenze, and Ignatius Loyola to the Roman Catholic Church. They all considered the effectiveness (E) of any effort to influence the outside world as mainly dependent on both sufficient 'mass' (M) or support and superior intelligence (I), in short on the *formula* $E = MI^2$, to paraphrase Albert Einstein's one. Under PAM, however, the old wine is produced along a more robust and sophisticated prescriptive methodology, derived from both the logic and the experiences of winning games in a complex world such as that of the EU. The promotion of effectiveness is thus a matter of expertise, a word which can also stand for the symbol E of our formula.

This short appetizer of public affairs management and lobbying needs five nuancing comments from empirical observation.

Not the same as real influence. PAM or lobbying should never be equated with real influence. It is only an effort to create this, and hence it gives no guarantee of success. In academic language, the effort is neither sufficient nor necessary for success, but only helpful. The lobby group can always suffer a loss, and sometimes it can even be influential without doing anything, which is the anticipated influence [Friedrich, 1963]. Every lobby group can even rationally decide to abstain from lobbying on its own (on short-list) or through a platform (shared-list) in at least four situations: when it finds better alternatives such as at the domestic level or through the market; when it perceives that the officials anticipate its interests; when it considers the surrounding arenas to be so unpredictable that a position of wait-and-see is more rational; and when it considers the orthodox ways, through for example Parliament and Council, as sufficient. For assessing these situations PA remains necessary, however.

Interactive shuttling. The definition may suggest a one-way flow of actions, but this is only the initial pattern. In reality, usually a two-way flow and often multiple flows of communication and interaction exist between senders and receivers, and they include changes of roles and a multilateral shuttling of messages. The real pattern of behaviour frequently looks like a complex delta, full of side-streams, branches and channels [Deutsch, 1963]. Many stakeholders and also EU officials often play, even on the same dossier, the dual roles of both sender and receiver of messages.

Only few all-rounders. Figure 1.2 contains five main steps and, as will be shown in the chapters to follow, each of them contains numerous smaller steps to be chosen rationally from menus of options, based on logic and expertise. All steps require a lot of preparatory homework and field activities. Ideally, a PA expert is a master of all. Reality is much different. By far most PA experts are, for whatever reason and to put it mildly, specialised in only a few steps and skills, for example only representing the interest group, lobbying for information, making a long-list, running the PA-desk, studying issues or briefing its management. Only a very small minority can be said to be all-rounders. In a larger PA-team, those with limited expertise can complement each other and make the team all-round.

Only few full-timers. Many people partially or fully practising the essentials of PA management do so on a part-time basis, as a side-activity of another job such as general manager, civil servant, secretary of an association or policy analyst. Such a broader role-set can even positively contribute to their PA performance, unless their part-time PA work makes them less all-round or even less professional, as often happens.

Only few PA professionals. By far not all people trying to influence the EU put PA management into practice, as many still search their way at random or arbitrarily, as amateurs or cat burglars. Even all-rounders and full-timers, such as many Brussels-based PA practitioners and consultants claim to be, may score low on quality, which is our definition of professionalism, not that of occupation or time spending. The 'first league' of best professionals is marked by the quality of their PAM performances. Such professionals make double use of the order of Figure 1.2 by first studying the influence process backwards from the fifth to the first step and then managing it forwards from the first to fifth step. The EU Commission has a reputation for such backwards planning of its own precooking of the EU decision processes. To all this we will return in the chapters to follow.

Extra: The Growth of Public Affairs Management in Europe

The basics of PA management have a long history, older than its name. Our icon is Niccolò Machiavelli, who is famous for his ambition to win, his study of the arena and his prudence during the match. The modern basics come from two main sources. The first is *academic* and has two origins: business management and political science. This should not be surprising, because the relationships between business and politics or, taking it more broadly, the private and the public sector form the crux of any modern society characterised by mixed public-private governance. Since World War II, many US scholars have contributed to this field of study [Dean and Schwindt, 1981]. Those in business management took the perspective of business and particularly that of big companies and trade organisations. They took them in their dual roles of both a receiver and a sender of influence efforts, as business both influences and is influenced by its environment. Their basic question of research was how these organisations (can and/or should) cope with the threats and opportunities coming from that environment. They gave birth to the concepts of public affairs management [PARG, 1981]. Their colleagues in political science took the perspective of government and focused mainly on its receiver's role. Biased by the democratic belief that a government should not act as a pressure group against civil society, many political scientists implicitly denied the government's role as an influential pressure group. With regard to the receiver's role, they were able to draw on a large number of studies about private interest groups, pressure groups and lobby groups [Laurencell, 1979]. They questioned how government officials, elected or not, can and/or should cope with pressures and lobbies from the private sector. Their initial focus on the profit-oriented organisations was extended to NGOs later on. The two American academic origins spilled over into Europe via the UK.

The second main source is *practice*, again especially in the US after World War II. Due to a lack of formal training in PAM, many people in both the private and the public sectors simply had, and still have, to find out how best to cope with threats and opportunities coming from their challenging environment. Through daily experiences they collected empirical insights and wisdom, frequently resulting in 'dos and don'ts'. In the private sector, many joined peer group organisations, such as the *Public Affairs Council* (1954), so sharing their personal experiences with others. In the public sector, both at the state and the federal level, many officials particularly politicised the supposed threats from business lobbying. In an effort to cope with these, their governments frequently relied on the traditional technique of coercion and issued regulations, registration forms and codes of conduct regarding lobbying [US/Congress, 1977; US/GAO, 1999]. Again, it was the UK that became the first country in Europe to follow the US example in examining the management of public affairs. The first stimulus here came from the Labour government in the 1970s that proposed specific interventions in business, including the nationalisation of private companies. The second stimulus came, paradoxically, from the Conservative government of Margaret Thatcher. She wanted to create a sort of 'two worlds pattern' between the public and the private sector, and particularly to abolish the organisations representing labour and management [Grant, 1989]. Large UK companies felt compelled to follow the US example of PA management.

Thanks to internal and external developments, the small family of people interested and engaged in PA management in Europe underwent rapid *growth and spread* since the mid-1980s. On the internal side, first of all, the previously separate worlds of academia and business became better linked. In the UK the *European Centre for Public Affairs* (ECPA), founded in 1986 and originally based at the University of Oxford, became the major meeting place for both groups. From its inception it launched conferences, workshops and studies in the field of PA, now at the wider EU level. Another major British initiative has been the launch of the *Journal of Public Affairs* (JPA) in 2001, the first in this field. The second internal development has been the dissemination of PA experiences among both academics and practitioners in northwestern Europe. In academia, many more people study and research the practices of lobbying and PAM in Europe [Griffin, 2005; Coen, 2007; journal JPA]. In many more countries practitioners meet in peer groups for the exchange of experiences, so following the example of ECPA. In the Netherlands, four different circles of PA practitioners in big companies, public interest groups, trade associations and at the junior level have been formed since the mid-1980s, all four named and numbered after one of the country's many King Williams. Similar groups in Europe have now been established in France, Germany and Austria as well.

On the external side, the *changing methods of government* in many countries in northwestern Europe have become a major factor of growing awareness of the PAM potentials. Although happening a little later than in the UK, the pattern of change has come close to the British one. Many companies in Scandinavia and the Netherlands became unhappy with the government's politicisation of the economy in the 1970s and were subsequently surprised by a swing towards liberalisation, deregulation, privatisation and budget retrenchment in the 1980s [Van Schendelen and Jackson, 1987]. They could hardly control either change. They perceived the national governments as acting arrogantly, unpredictably and unfriendly towards business. Strong antagonisms started to arise. At the same time, new NGOs were born in the 1970s, particularly in the field of health and the environment, and had to fight for a position in their domestic political systems. Hardly invited but all the more driven by desire, compulsion and capacity, both those companies and NGOs subsequently searched for new ways to influence the domestic system, and many discovered PA management. In general, the combination of a closed government system and irritated pressure groups outside gives a strong impetus for the adoption of PAM. Another change came with the EU's launch of a Single European Market (SEM) in the early 1990s. Thanks to the previous changes at home, the private organisations in the northern countries could easily shift their PA focus from the domestic to the European level. More than their counterparts in the southern and eastern countries of Europe, they had learned already to lobby self-reliantly. They applied their experience of PAM at home resolutely to the then largely unfamiliar system of the EU.

Public Affairs Management Practices at the EU Level

Apparently, the EU is a most *appropriate system* for the application of PA practices and the common capital Brussels an excellent place for acting [Van Schendelen, 2008]. The EU machinery of common decision-making produces many new binding decisions every year that overrule any conflicting domestic legislation, to mention only this output. The system is clearly relevant to the countless interest groups having all sorts of backgrounds in the European area. Whether they appreciate that relevance or not is irrelevant for the appreciation of PA. The antagonists, even more than the protagonists of europeanization, should love the expertise of PA, because swimming against the stream requires more ambition, study and prudency than going with it. Anyhow, many interest groups want to influence this machinery, feel compelled or even invited to do so, and usually have a basic capacity to 'make a difference' somehow. In short, they can participate in the system. Disliking being a mere object of the adaptation vectors of euro-peanization, they want to be the subject of the influence vectors. Due to the variety of Europe, their interests will inevitably clash with those of others. In consequence, new issues are continuously arising. These pressure groups are willy-nilly the most manifest carriers of ongoing europeaniza-tion. By transporting their interests into the EU, they apparently consider the five old European methods of conflict resolution as either outdated or insufficient, and the EU method as more effective and efficient. If initially not yet so familiar with both the stakeholders from different countries and the EU officials, many groups tend to choose from the menu of influence techniques those that they used to apply at home. They still have to discover PA methods.

Nobody knows exactly or even by approximation *the total number* of inter-est groups and lobbyists that actively try to influence the EU system. A few sources give only rough and different numbers [Berkhout and Lowery, 2008]. The European Parliament (EP), having become aware of 'lobby density' [EP, 2003], has listed on its website (2009) almost 4300 accredited lobbyists, though double-counting means they represent a much smaller number of entities or groups. On its register (2009) the Commission men-tions about 1700 entities, no persons. In 2008 the EP and Commission decided to start a common register. Another source is the *European Public Affairs Directory* (EPAD, 2008) listing the interest groups having a perma-nent office in Brussels or nearby and comes to about 2400 offices. Their distribution is roughly as follows: European trade and professional federa-tions (35%), commercial consultants and law firms (14%), companies (12%), European NGOs in such fields as health care, the environment and human rights (10%), national business and labour associations (9%), re-gional and local offices (8%), international organisations (5%), think tanks and training institutes (5%) and Chambers of Commerce (2%). In addition, there are the permanent representations of the member-state govern-ments, around 150 diplomatic missions of foreign governments (such as from the US, Liberia and Turkey) and offices of almost all national parlia-ments, to mention only these. The EU clearly is an open area and Brussels an open city. Quoting Eartha Kitt, 'They all do it.' In the recent past, most interest groups felt particularly attracted by the EU policy fields of inter-nal market, the environment, health, agriculture, social affairs, research and development, and transport [Fligstein and McNichol, 1998], and there is no indication that this has changed much. Most groups come from the private sector, either profit-oriented or NGO, so reflecting also at the EU level their vast outnumbering of public organisations at home. Runners-up from the public sector at the end of the 2000s are decentralised governments, such as regional and local governments (particularly from Central and Eastern Europe) and domestic agencies such as on transport safety, food health and land registry.

All these numbers and figures, of course, only roughly indicate the presence of interest groups and lobbyists. They say nothing about how all-round, full-time and, ultimately, professional they are. According to survey data, most companies and federations have full-time staff of about six people, and consultancies have about ten people [EurActiv, 2009-A-B-C]. If we assume that the 2400 Brussels-based interest groups mentioned have on average a staff of slightly more than six people, we get as total staff for all about 15,000 people, a sacrosanct figure in public discussion. However, this is only part of *the fuller story*. The large majority of pressure groups are not permanently based in Brussels and only occasionally send somebody to this meeting place, when something of relevance to them is at stake somewhere. In addition to having different work to do, they may try for the rest of their time to monitor and to influence what happens there by remote control through befriended stakeholders. To give one number: roughly 100,000 experts attend the meetings of the about 2000 expert committees of the Commission. They represent their public or private interest group. The total sum of both all interest groups and all their representatives participating at the EU level only part-time and/or by remote control is really countless. Often even the officials of EU institutions, offices, agencies, committees and other parts of the EU machinery might be considered as at least part-time lobbyists based in Brussels.

But are all these interest groups and their people really applying smart PA methods, and thus *all-round and professional lobbyists* in practice? On this question, too, some indicative research is available. A survey among 91 regional and local offices shows that most are primarily 'listening posts', particularly for EU subsidies, and only hope to shape EU decisions but are rarely decisive actors [Marks and others, 2002]. A survey among 149 think-tanks shows that their large majority only produces studies and trainings from a domestic perspective, continuously fights for budgetary survival and has little firepower at the EU level [Boucher, 2004]. A questionnaire among 140 PA practitioners reveals that most of them do not have a formalised PA function and do not measure their PA performance, thus not presenting a high professional status of their public affairs [Com-Res, 2008]. My own experiences as a participant observer at the sender's side of many different pressure groups at the EU level are that, indeed, the large majority of their PA people are still far away from PA management. In contrast to Figure 1.2, they are busy with making introverted position papers that disregard the outside world of stakeholders and officials in the EU. They use their introverted long-list almost as a short-list, which inevitably exhausts them without much return on their efforts, and choose from the menu of influence techniques those they use at home. They may be ambitious, but fall short of a sense of study and prudence. Many have a modest ambition and feel satisfied with for example only profiling their organisation in the EU area (many regions and cities), writing 'fact sheets' (a lot of consultancies) or representing their organisation as an expert in an EuroFed (many companies and NGOs) or a committee (most ministries).

PA practices at the EU level are still limited by quantity and quality, but increasing. Private lobby groups from northwestern Europe have set the tone of PA management at the EU level. Thanks to the aforementioned domestic developments since the 1970s, they had gathered skills in PA much earlier than their counterparts elsewhere. They have become leading players inside the Brussels-based peer groups in PAM, such as in the *Society of European Affairs Professionals* (SEAP), the *Public Affairs Practitioners* (PAP) and the *European Federation of Lobbying and Public Affairs* (FELPA). There even exist Brussels-based national EU groups in PA, such as the Dutch *European Affairs Platform* (EAP). Most Brussels-based consultancies also have a northwestern and particularly British background. The same holds for the weekly newspaper *European Voice,* monthly ones like *Public Affairs News* and *EU Reporter* and the quarterly *Europe's World.* A Greek initiative is the weekly *New Europe* that also reports about developments in the member countries. French-orientated groups have followed Britain's lead by establishing in Brussels their own training centres, consultancies, peer groups and, particularly, information services such as the old daily *Agence Europe,* the website *Euractiv.com* (including a special section just on public affairs), monitors like *European Information Services* and *Europolitics,* and the (now British) *European Public Affairs Directory.* Regular surveys among PA people are held by *EurActiv* and the British *ComRes.* Major companies and NGOs from Italy, Germany, Nordic countries and Central Europe recently showed an increasingly active interest in EU PA management, and they are closely followed by critical (and frequently only moralistic) journalism at home that anyhow disseminates the message of lobbying and PA at the EU level there. Translations of this very book are another indicator of rising attention elsewhere.

There even seems to be a sort of *premier league* of Brussels-based EU lobby groups in development trying to manage their public affairs professionally. Usually, they have learnt their EU lessons through games lost in the past. Instead of giving up, they braced their nerves and body. Many had already tasted the honey of fewer threats and more opportunities, fewer losses and more wins. Now they keep their organisational windows open for going out and getting in. These rising professionals are, once again, not necessarily the same as those with either a permanent office in Brussels or a full-time job as EU lobbyist, acting commercially or otherwise, as nobody is excellent just by office or job profile. It is also true that some groups and people without a facility in Brussels and operating from elsewhere can be excellent players. The same may be true for the many part-timers on the EU playing-field. Nevertheless, the reputation of professionalism is frequently assigned to those with a facility in Brussels. They feel at ease there and learn from each other [Eising, 2007].

EU PA management is, of course, *no panacea*. If applied professionally, by careful homework (study) and fieldwork (prudence), it provides only better chances to win or, at least, not to lose an EU game. The professional PA manager operates by a set of norms or prescripts regarding, in our case, more successful playing at the EU level. Our approach, however, is not normative but advisory. Every interest group is free to manage its public affairs amateurishly, to follow its old preference for a traditional technique of influence, to solve its challenges by non-EU activities, to feel satisfied with merely getting adapted to EU outcomes, or to rely on the old non-EU methods of integration in Europe. However, if an interest group wants to improve its chances to create a desired EU outcome, then it had better practice the insights from public affairs management professionally. In this sense, our approach is advisory. The next step is to introduce the EU playing-field.

CHAPTER 2

THE PLAYING-FIELD: EU COMMON DECISION-MAKING

Deus Ex Machina

The interest group looking to influence the outputs of the EU machinery and its playing-field must understand how they come into being. This knowledge must be useful of course, which implies that it is true for what it claims to be (valid), not biased by research methods (reliable) and applicable in daily life (usable) [Lindblom and Cohen, 1979]. Otherwise the interest group cannot effectively lobby the authorities and other people inside, to obtain both information about their agendas (window-out operations) and sufficient support for realising its own targets (window-in operations). This chapter is about the playing-field or machinery that produces outputs and particularly decisions binding the member states. Knowledge of this also helps to identify relevant stakeholders around the machinery and to collect from them the equally valuable information and support, the focus of the chapters hereafter. What sort of machinery is the EU?

Not an ordinary system. The EU's set of operational functions differs from that of most other political systems, such as the member states [Almond and Powell, 1966]. It primarily has the function of producing common legislation binding its member states, also by its Court's adjudication function that overrules domestic courts; in these respects the EU is also not an ordinary international organization. Its second main function is that of a platform for interest articulation and aggregation from all sorts of domestic and foreign interest groups. Its administrative function is often mixed with that of the member states. By recruiting its people from all member states, it is similarly a multinational. It lacks the functions of mass socialization and communication as exist in national systems. The EU is not a union of widely shared values, and its few common mass media are mostly in English such as the BBC, *Financial Times* and CNN, which are atypical for European views.

Artificial and natural. The EU machinery was originally constructed by the six member states (France, Germany, Italy, Netherlands, Belgium and Luxembourg) that once made the 1958 Treaty of Rome and its forerunner, the 1952 European Coal and Steel Community (ECSC), in hindsight the pilot for the new method of integrating Europe better. Many new treaties thereafter, now among the 27 member states, regularly modify it [McDonagh, 1998; Beach and Christiansen, 2007; Luitwieler, 2009]. Two sorts of dynamics brought the artificial construct to natural life. One is the internal dynamic created by spill-over effects from competences used towards new agendas and decisions [Niemann, 2006; McCormick, 1999, 15-17]. For example, the 1987 SEA Treaty for a single market created internal dynamics forcing police co-operation, codified by the 1993 Maastricht Treaty. The other dynamic is the external one coming from interest groups which articulate and aggregate their demands to the EU. The story of 'EU-ization', once created by the vector of six national governments, is now written by all vectors of europeanization, and any new treaty is a mixture of modification and codification.

Skeleton versus Flesh-and-Blood. Treaties define the formal structure of the EU, such as its institutions, their competences and their procedures, in short its 'skeleton'. Its real functioning by 'flesh-and-blood' is often not so much in contradiction but simply different, as everything not forbidden by treaty is allowed. For example, in the Council of Ministers, formally the ministers decide upon proposals, but the real decision is made at the lower level of working groups mainly composed of national civil servants. Such differences between 'formalité' and 'réalité' are a normal fact of life in every system, as with any house reflecting both its architect and its inhabitants. New lobby groups frequently mistake the outside façade for the inner workings, and the formal powers for the real influence.

Every interest group looking to make a difference inside this machinery has to become familiar with its workings, which are so different from both national political systems and international organizations that it is called *sui generis*, a system without parallel. This can hardly come as a surprise as the machinery is not an organic but an artificial product, and has the age of an average sub-Saharan African developing state. It is surprising that, for already more than five decades, the creation of a machinery for integrating Europe better by the new method of common decision-making really has emerged from it, like a goddess called 'Europa'.

Our focus here is not on the broad concept and practice of European integration. It is limited to the *basic characteristics* of the machinery of EU common decision-making, particularly as it operates in practice. This is the playing-field for all PA management of EU affairs, the theme of this book. Our objective is also not to describe comprehensively the machinery's many aspects, issue areas, changes, causes and implications, covered by various textbooks [e.g. Nugent, 2006; Dinan, 2006; Hix, 2005] and diction-aries [McGowan and Phinnemore, 2006; Bainbridge, 2002; Dinan, 2000], if this objective would be possible for the changing and prismatic EU at all [Bellier, 1997]. For the PA management of the EU, it is seldom necessary to know all the ins and outs of, for example, voting points at the Council level, as their relevance depends on the specific situation. It is, however, crucial to know whether the Council takes a decision, how it does so and with what ef-fect. In anatomising the machinery, we shall pay less attention to its formal structure or skeleton than to its working practices or flesh-and-blood. True enough, the skeleton of formally established procedures, powers, positions and people may set serious limits on the flesh-and-blood practices, but this usually only happens when the machinery operates under serious strains and tensions, just as the physical skeleton can set limits on a tired body. Such moments are exceptional rather than regular. Usually, the EU bodies are energetic rather than tired, test their skeleton to any lengths and estab-lish different flesh-and-blood practices. Lobby groups, not being part of the EU skeleton and thus dependent on its flesh-and-blood, hence usually have a long-term interest in keeping the system relaxed and not strained or tense. Knowledge of the skeleton may help in setting limits they consider useful, but that of flesh-and-blood practices is truly crucial for influencing the EU.

The Skeleton of the EU Machinery

Its basic architecture goes back to four common beliefs of the original six member-state governments in the 1950s and laid down in the 1958 Treaty of Rome, designed for the European Economic Community (EEC) and pri-marily a treaty for economic co-operation.

Primary law above all. Any common decision must ultimately be based on treaty text, called primary law, which is concluded by the member-state governments and ratified by domestic procedure. So far more than ten treaties have been ratified; in this book we refer to them not by year of ratifi-cation but by effective date. To control any subsequent decision based on treaty text, called a secondary decision, the governments established their Council of Ministers. So they pooled part of their national sovereignty around their own Council's tables [Keohane and Hoffmann, 1991]. Treaty text specifies the decision-making procedures: by unanimity or qualified majority voting (QMV), the latter being originally about a 70% majority of voting points allocated to each government according to roughly the size of its population.

Autonomous Commission. The drafting of common decisions must be managed exclusively by a secretariat, now called Commission, independent of national politics. Its Board of Commissioners (the College) and its staff of civil servants is recruited from the member states. It also has decision-making powers of its own, being either assigned by treaty text, such as on competition policy, or delegated to it by secondary decision. They empower it to make binding implementing laws, which are largely produced through special committees, called comitology procedure.

Consultations. Both main political parties and major interest groups from the member states should be involved. This resulted in the establishment of both an Assembly of national parliamentarians, now called the European Parliament (EP) and directly elected since 1979; and for major socio-economic interest groups the Economic and Social Committee (ESC), two institutions which are asked for their opinion on planned decisions, as specified in treaty text (consultation procedure). These representative bodies are largely autonomous in their internal workings and decisions. Since the 1987 Single European Act (SEA), the EP has gradually assumed the much stronger position of co-legislator next to the Council (the codecision procedure).

Binding common decisions. The common decisions must legally bind the member states, as otherwise there is no new method of integrating Europe. For this purpose, the member states established the EU Court of Justice (ECJ) which in early rulings confirmed the general priority of EU law over national law. The common decisions being produced along either the secondary or the delegated way can have one of three different forms: regulations that fully bind directly, decrees that bind specific groups like farmers directly, or directives that fully bind indirectly through national acts establishing the tools to implement them before a deadline. All other texts, such as policy papers, guidelines and recommendations, are not legally binding.

Three remarks on *nomenclature* are useful. One is that the EU secondary route of common and binding decision-making should not be confused with the British secondary procedure that, by the absence of written primary law, comes after its parliamentary procedure and is in fact delegated procedure, a confusion created by many a British textbook. The second regards the new nomenclature for the EP's position, as arising in the text of the Reform Treaty, better known as the Treaty of Lisbon. It calls the codecision procedure 'ordinary legislative procedure' and the consultation one 'special legislative procedure'. The same treaty text, thirdly, defines secondary acts as 'legislative acts' and delegated ones as 'non-legislative acts', which are all legally binding. These labels bring the meaning of 'legislation' more in line with national grammar, where it usually stands for binding decisions produced by the national government and parliament (and where delegated acts are usually called 'rules'). Throughout this book we shall use both the old and new wordings, as both are still in use and interchangeable.

Since the 1958 Treaty of Rome, the member-state governments, whenever they agreed upon a new treaty, have often redesigned the skeleton by *modification or codification* of existing practices; the former really changes existing practices, and the latter formalizes existing changes. An example of the former is the 1987 allocation of codecision power to the EP; and an example of the latter is the now formalised position of the European Council. Most changes, besides, have not been radical but incremental or step-by-step, for example the 1999 Treaty of Amsterdam that 'improved' the 1993 Treaty on the European Union (Maastricht Treaty). Some treaties have taken bigger steps. One example is the 1987 SEA, which launched the policy programme on Single Open Market combined with preliminary codecision; and another is the 1993 Maastricht Treaty, which established the Committee of the Regions (COR) as the third representative body of regional and local politicians, and also brought sensitive policy domains like foreign-and-defence politics and justice-and-home affairs under modest europeanization by establishing special regimes under the Council (called Pillars II and III, making all other domains Pillar I).

The text of the *Treaty of Lisbon* contains some major changes as well, such as the following:

Council. The Pillars are abolished and their policy domains brought under the framework of co-operation with other institutions. On foreign-and-defence politics, the Council will act largely under the special legislative procedure of consulting the EP. The unanimity vote is replaced by QMV for many more treaty articles, covering a total of almost one hundred. After 2014, the QMV of voting points may (and after 2017 will) be replaced by the double threshold of representing at least 55% of Council members and 65% of EU population, thus preventing any majority of only big or small member states. The European Council will have its own President.

Parliament. An additional 40 treaty articles are brought under codecision. Upon proposal by the Council, the EP elects the President of the Commission. On the EU budget, it gets the final say over all expenditures, including the formerly compulsory ones on which it had no final say in the past. Its number of members becomes 750 plus its President as elected by the EP.

Commission. By additional decision (2008) every country keeps its Commissioner. The Commissioner on External Relations and the permanent High Representative chairing the Foreign Affairs Council become the same person, so-called the the the double-hatted EU Foreign Minister. The EP elects the Commission's President.

Court. It gets jurisdiction over specified matters of justice-and-home affairs.

National parliaments. If one-third of them objects against a Commission proposal for a secondary decision, the proposal must be reviewed, which procedure (called 'subsidiarity') anchors its older principle that holds 'no EU decisions on matters that member states can deal with sufficiently'.

In retrospect, the old skeleton has undergone continually changing forms. For the main institutions we shall now, with reference to Figure 2.1 (left side and middle), summarize the features of their formal structures, powers and procedures as developed over time.

The Skeleton's Main Components

The *Council*, hosted in the building of Justus Lipsius near Place Schuman, has undergone six major changes since its beginnings [Werts, 2008; Hayes-Renshaw and Wallace, 2006; Westlake and Galloway, 2004]. It developed, firstly, from a small group of six national governments, responsible for limited policy domains, into an extensive body of 27 ones responsible for a broad range of policies. It also developed, secondly, from a General Council of only Foreign Affairs ministers to three layers: the European Council of heads of government or state, the (combined) General Affairs and External Relations (GAER) Council, and eight specialised Councils, such as the Competitiveness Council and the Environment Council. All Councils are formally configurations of one and the same Council, as one God with many faces. Under the Lisbon Treaty, the chairmanship of the General Affairs Council and the Specialised Councils will continue to rotate among member states every six months, but the European Council and the Foreign (formerly External) Affairs Council will be chaired by nominated persons (the President of the European Council, respectively the High Representative who also belongs to the Commission for running foreign affairs). If a specialised Council fails to come to a common decision, the General Council of the ministers of Foreign Affairs and ultimately the European Council can take over the issue in order to reach a decision. The

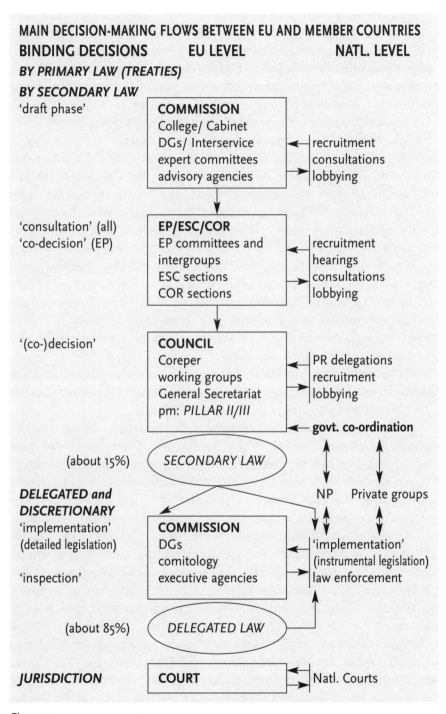

MAIN DECISION-MAKING FLOWS BETWEEN EU AND MEMBER COUNTRIES

BINDING DECISIONS   **EU LEVEL**   **NATL. LEVEL**

BY PRIMARY LAW (TREATIES)

BY SECONDARY LAW

'draft phase'

COMMISSION
College/ Cabinet
DGs/ Interservice
expert committees
advisory agencies

recruitment
consultations
lobbying

'consultation' (all)
'co-decision' (EP)

EP/ESC/COR
EP committees and
intergroups
ESC sections
COR sections

recruitment
hearings
consultations
lobbying

'(co-)decision'

COUNCIL
Coreper
working groups
General Secretariat
pm: *PILLAR II/III*

PR delegations
recruitment
lobbying

govt. co-ordination

(about 15%)   *SECONDARY LAW*

NP   Private groups

DELEGATED and DISCRETIONARY

'implementation'
(detailed legislation)

'inspection'

COMMISSION
DGs
comitology
executive agencies

'implementation'
(instrumental legislation)
law enforcement

(about 85%)   *DELEGATED LAW*

JURISDICTION   **COURT**   Natl. Courts

Figure 2.1

Council's General Secretariat (GS) of about 3,500 staff assists all Councils administratively. The political preparation by the Permanent Representatives (PRs), once with small staff from six member states, has thirdly, developed into a complex network of 27 PRs having about 1,900 staff in all (70 on average in 2009). Their high-level committee, called Coreper, has a formal position, two chambers (Coreper I and II), and under it, for preparing the dossiers, about 300 working groups largely composed of national civil servants plus PR staff. For some domains there exist special committees, such as COPS on foreign security, COSI on home security and CSA on agriculture. Fourthly, the formerly sole decision-maker, the Council, developed increasingly to codecision-maker alongside the EP. Its internal decision-making shifted, fifthly, from unanimity to increasingly QMV, and in specified cases even simple majority or, in academic catchwords, from 'intergovernmental' to 'supranational', the latter implying that every single member state can be overruled. Finally, the Council developed from deciding upon almost all dossiers, except those falling under the Commission's own treaty competences like on competition, to about 15% of all EU binding decisions, or about 400 dossiers out of now roughly 2,500 cases annually. The Commission produces the remainder of almost 85%, largely under powers delegated to it by secondary law. The Council can overrule part of these delegated acts by comitology procedure, to which we will return soon. Besides, based on treaty text the Council has some autonomous competences in sensitive fields like treaty formation, defence and taxation.

The *Commission*, headquartered in the Berlaymont building opposite the Council, shows the following six changed features [Spence, 2006; Nugent 2001]. Its College of Commissioners, firstly, expanded from six to twenty-seven members, each with a small personal staff, called the Cabinet and since 1999 selected from different countries. At all levels hierarchy is important. The President is in charge of the Commission's internal and external operations, such as the division of portfolios, the College's weekly agenda and inter-institutional affairs, for example on the EU budget and annual working programmes. Inside a DG the director-general runs several Directorates, and every director, several policy units. The Commission's apparatus, secondly, has grown from a few Directorates-General (DGs) to about 25 plus about ten Services, each led by one or more Commissioners. Some DGs and Services are more powerful than others, such as DG COMP due to its treaty powers, the Secretariat-General (SG) that serves the College and scrutinizes draft secondary proposals by impact assessments and the Legal Service, capable of blocking any proposal. By internal procedure, called interservice, cohesion among participating units and people is pursued. The number of staff, thirdly, has grown from about 300 statutory staff ('fonc-tionnaires') to about 25,000 and, if including external staff working for agencies or as seconded national experts (called ENDs), to almost 35,000 people (2009) consisting of managers at the highest level (5%), adminis-trators (AD, 33%), assistants (AST, 36%), temporary contracted or second-ed people (20%) and technical people (6%). From 1999 on, recruitment has shifted from national representation ('fourchette') to qualifications, or from 'spoils' to 'merits' [Bauer, 2008]. Internally responsible for policy are Managers and ADs, totalling around 12,500 people; the numerous ASTs, one-third of all personnel, are desk managers rather than secretarial staff. Compared to other bureaucracies, the Commission's statutory staff is tiny. The Dutch central government is five times larger and the US federal serv-ice, more than forty times. On average, a DG or Service has around 350 pol-icy staff and a policy unit less than twenty. The fourth change is the rise of agencies, from zero to almost 45 (2009), largely for monitoring, inspecting and advising (such as the European Food Safety Authority (EFSA) and the European Police Office Europol) and a few also for executing measures (such as on Public Health Programmes), mostly co-financed by the Com-mission and member states and located anywhere in the EU. A fifth change regards the EU budget that has grown to about 130 milliard euro (or US bil-lion, 2009) and largely (65%) comes from GNI-related contributions from member states, and for the rest from value-added taxation, customs and mi-nor sources. Almost 95% of expenditures are for external policy objectives, largely through structural funds like those for Cohesion, Agriculture, Re-gions and Social Affairs, and the remainder of about 5% on administration and half of this on the Commission, being another indicator of its minute format. To compare the total EU budget, fixed by treaty to less than one per-cent of total national GDPs: the Belgian federal budget is almost equal to it, and the 2008 US federal bailout of the mortgage banks Freddie Mac and Fannie Mae was three times greater.

Sixth but not least is the rise of *delegated legislation*, called non-legislative acts under the Lisbon Treaty (and in the UK, as explained above, 'secon-dary'). Its largest part is based on powers delegated to the Commission by previous legislative acts and made through comitology procedure, the re-mainder being treaty-based, as with competition or coming from the few executive agencies. Figure 2.2 presents the numbers of adopted binding de-cisions for five-year intervals since 1970 and the years 2007 up to 2008. It shows that now on average almost 85% of the EU's roughly about 2,500 newly binding acts annually comprise delegated legislation [Brandsma, 2010], which grew from almost nothing in 1958 when only treaty-based delegations existed. An important aside is needed here regarding the reliability and completeness of the data, as those published by the Commission's registers often fall short and thus allow different compilations [König and others, 2006]; the figure's data have been collected and checked by the referred author on the basis of original document registers. The delegated legislation is a normal phenomenon in the member states and often higher than the EU's 85% [Braun and Gilardi, 2005]. The Commission presents its proposals for more detailed legislation officially to about 250 special committees (together called comitology), largely composed of civil servants from member states, engaged in deciding upon these Commission proposals and headquartered in the Alfred Borchette building [Christiansen and Larsson, 2007; Bergström, 2005; Larsson, 2003; Andenas and Türk, 2000; Vos, 1999].

There are three main types of comitology. Advisory committees give only advice on proposals from the Commission, which has to pay 'its utmost attention' but has the last say. Management committees that manage a policy field like agriculture and regulatory committees that act as regulators can reject a proposal by QMV. In the management case, the Council can settle such a conflict by overruling the Commission by QMV ('blocking majority'). In the regulatory case, two variants of conflict settlement exist, roughly as follows. In the standard one, the EP deciding by absolute majority can ask the Council to block the Commission proposal by QMV, so giving the last say to the Council. In the other variant, called 'regulatory procedure with scrutiny' and existing since 2006 (2006/ C 255/02), the EP can overrule by the Commission and Council absolute majority, so giving the last word to the EP. The arrangements of conflict resolution indicate that the shift from secondary to delegated legislation stands at issue in particularly the EP that fears losing control and recently gained scrutiny power. Most directives, regulations and decrees are indeed cases of delegated legislation or, as called in the Lisbon Treaty, non-legislative acts.

The *Parliament*, located in its main Altiero Spinelli building at the distance from Council and Commission, has undergone many changes to its formal features [Priestly, 2008; Judge and Earnshaw, 2008; Hix and others, 2007; Corbett, Jacobs and Shackleton, 2007; Hix and others, 2003]. Firstly, since 1979 the Members of the Parliament (MEPs) are directly elected on a national party-political basis, which affords them direct mandate. Secondly, the number of MEPs increased from 58 in 1958 to 751 (750 plus their President) under the Lisbon Treaty, making it the largest in the world after the Chinese parliament. Due to the treaty, its plenary sessions take place in the French city of Strasbourg, which makes it a unique travelling parliament.

ADOPTED BINDING DECISIONS BY PROCEDURE AND TYPE 1970-2008

YEAR	SECONDARY CONSULTATION				CODECISION				DELEGATED				TOTAL	
	A	B	C	%	A	B	C	%	A	B	C	%	TOTAL	%
1970	76	24	256	40	0	0	0	0	166	2	364	60	888	100
1975	126	49	417	39	0	0	0	0	247	8	685	61	1532	100
1980	145	64	443	29	0	0	0	0	655	22	931	71	2260	100
1985	77	66	477	32	0	0	0	0	388	23	912	68	1943	100
1990	127	70	405	28	0	0	0	0	392	24	1110	72	2128	100
1995	129	38	263	12	6	10	0	0,5	384	34	2810	88	3683	100*
2000	192	44	194	12	16	34	16	2	487	39	2585	86	3607	100
2005	240	10	123	13	11	28	19	2	465	54	2022	86	2972	100*
2006	239	26	165	15	20	37	44	3	499	77	1808	82	2915	100
2007	219	5	121	15	16	18	21	2	447	53	1413	83	2313	100
2008	220	14	141	17	28	55	48	6	462	57	1149	77	2174	100

Legend: A= decisions, decrees/ B- directives/ C= regulations/ *= rounded total %.

Source: Brandsma, 2010; data compiled by author from Eur-Lex register of documents.

Figure 2.2

Its staff amounts to almost 6,000 people (2009). The around 200 different national parties holding a seat in the EP pose, of course, challenges of effective management engendering, thirdly, the creation of political groups which, if seeking entitlement for extra privileges (time, staff, budget), must have at least 25 members and seven nationalities now; most MEPs belong to such a group. The two largest groups are the christian-democratic EPP and the socialist S&D (formerly PSE), together holding potentially the absolute majority. The EP, fourthly, works mainly through about twenty standing and some temporary committees, each earning their competences and composition through plenary decision. The groups inside a committee assign dossiers for plenary decision-making to one or a few members (called rapporteur and co-rapporteur). The budgetary EP powers, fifthly, have always been strong in cross-national perspective, as until recently it had final say over both the total EU budget and the non-obligatory (mainly non-agricultural) expenditures, and under the Lisbon Treaty over all expenditures. Over the EU's production of secondary legislation, the EP powers, sixthly, have developed from, as shown in Figure 2.2, merely advisory (consultation) until the mid-1990s, to include also amendment and veto (codecision), the latter recently covering roughly one-quarter of secondary cases and expanded under the Lisbon Treaty. The codecision procedure goes through two readings plus, if necessary, a conciliation committee with the Council, and may require an absolute majority from the EP. On management and regulatory cases of delegated legislation, it has had intervention powers since 1999 and on part of the latter by scrutiny since 2006. On dossiers like enlargement and international agreements, the EP must give assent. In short, the EP has developed from assembly to parliament, with a hint of legislature now.

The most important other parts of the skeleton of EU machinery are the following. The *EU Court of Justice (ECJ)*, located in Luxembourg, has as its primary function to settle conflicts in specified treaty fields (not on foreign-and-defence policy) and to interpret EU binding decisions upon request, so being an additional 'legislator' [Nowak, 2007]. It has to base its judgments on treaty texts only, which inevitably brought it the reputation of being 'pro EU integration'. It suffers from a continuing overload of cases brought to the Court; its total staff is about 2,000 people (2009). To address the overload, the ECJ gets three layers under the Lisbon Treaty: the Court of Justice for major issues, the General Court for other issues and Specialised Courts for 'first instance' cases [Arnull, 2006; Nugent, 2006]. The first two layers have one judge from each member state, plus Advocates-General who assist. The unchanged authority of the Court is remarkable. Without an effective sanction (police and jail) system of its own, it manages to get its judgements largely accepted by civil entities, member states and EU bodies. The *Economic and Social Committee (ESC*, located in the Jacques Delors building near the EP can be said to be the body that has undergone the least change. Due to enlargements, it has acquired more members (344; 2009) nominated by the Council, but in its policy domain it still has only advisory (consultation) power. Its staff amounts to 700 people (2009). Under the 1993 Maastricht Treaty, it got, in the same building, a companion in the *Committee of the Regions* (COR), which is also an advisory body of 344 representatives (mainly elected politicians) from decentralised governments. It has its own staff of about 500 people (2009). Finally, a few other bodies exist, such as the *European Central Bank* (ECB), the *Court of Auditors* (CoA) and the *European Investment Bank* (EIB). Because they act at a formal distance from or, like the ECB, only in a specific area of the EU common decision-making machinery, they do not need further description here.

The EU's skeleton certainly remains in a process of change, as the enduring drive behind its evolution is the need to settle more or new irritating differences among member countries. This is reflected by the EU *policy expansion and intensification*. Its policy domains developed from simply encompassing coal and steel to almost the same broad policy landscape of member states. Figure 2.3 shows the expansion (+ sign) of EU policy domains by new treaty; every plus sign signifies time-intensified weighting, i.e. a double or triple plus. For example policy-making on competition, open markets and agriculture now fully or largely falls under the EU, while that on health, housing and civil liberties is still largely under national competence, and still other domains have some shared division of regime [Nugent, 2006, 388; Fligstein and McNichol, 1998]. The trend is a gradual shift from national to EU competences, in short EU policy intensification, as recently exemplified for consumer protection, cross-border crime and education. During such transitions, the Council often briefly assumes a privileged regime position, after which it steps aside in favour of the EU machinery or even delegation to COM. The 1993 Maastricht Treaty can be seen as a watershed between a mainly market-orientated EU to one that also covers fields typically the domains of government, such as defence, public health and migration.

The wider and more intense EU policy-making is only partially the outcome of new treaties. Much more happens that is not forbidden by treaty texts and thus offers a *menu of possible choices*, which mark the transition from skeleton to flesh-and-blood hereafter. One choice is between non-binding or 'soft' interventions like subsidies, benchmarks, open co-ordina-

OFFICIAL KEY DATES OF MAIN EU POLICY FORMATION

	1952-1957	1958-1972	1973-1985	1986-1993	1994-
Coal & Steel	+	+	+	+	+
Open Market	-	+	+	+ ('1992')	+
Competition	-	+	+	+	+
Euratom	-	+	+	+	+
Agriculture	-	+ (1962 EAGGF)	+	+	+ (MacSharry)
Transport	-	+	+	+	+
Regional Policy	-	+ (1957 EIB)	+ (1974 ERDF)	+	+ (Cohesion Fund)
Social Affairs	-	+ (1957 ESF)	+	+	+ (Social Protocol)
Developmental Aid	-	+ (1963 Yaounde)	+ (1975 Lomé)	+	+
Environmental Policy	-	-	+ (1973 Action)	+	+
Consumer Policy	-	-	+ (1975)	+	+
Monetary Affairs	-	-	+ (1979 EMS-ERM)	+ (1990 EBRD)	+ (ECB)
SM Enterprises	-	-	- (1983)	+	+
Fishing	-	-	- (1983)	+	+
Industrial Policy	-	-	-	+ (1986 R&D)	+
Energy	-	-	-	+	+
Education	-	-	-	+	+
Social Health	-	-	-	-	+
Security/Foreign Policy	-	-	-	-	+
Justice/Home Affairs	-	-	-	-	+
Member States	1952: 'Six'		1973: +UK, DK, IE 1981: +EL	1986: +ES, PT	1995: +AU, FI, SE 2004: +10 CEEC 2007: RO, BU
Institutional Reform	1952: ECSC	1957: 'Rome' 1967: 'merger'		1987: SEA 1993: 'Maastricht'	1999: 'Amsterdam' 2003: 'Nice'

Figure 2.3

tion and guidelines, and binding 'hard' ones like legislation and levies [Kurpas, 2008]. Another choice is between specific measures for a single sector, trade or item such as fishing, meat or compact discs, and general ones that apply to many sectors, trades and items, like competition and transport safety. A third choice regards policy-making by regulation, technically called 'positive integration' or interventionism, such as on agriculture and the environment; or by removal of barriers to free interaction, called 'negative integration' or liberalisation, as on open markets and education. A fourth choice is between full decision-making at the EU level or leaving (substantial parts of) decision-making to domestic layers ('subsidiarity'), as for the implementation of the European Agricultural Fund for Regional Development EARFD (COM 2005/ 1698) [Franchino, 2007]. A fifth choice regards the definition of 'common' policy either applying fully to all member states at the same time or to only a group of them ('enhanced co-operation') with different intensity ('opt-outs') or times ('exemptions') for the others and altogether resulting in 'variable geometry' or differentiated integration [Dinan, 2000]. Usually, the EU decision-makers quarrel over these choices when considering a common line for some policy issue, and create by compromise a mixture of choices. Since the 1990s, the choices made show an overall shift from soft to hard interventions, from specific to general measures, from positive to negative integration, from full EU regime to some subsidiarity, and from fully common to differentiated integration. The proportion of hard legislation is now up to the level of an average member state [Neyer, 2004; Alesina and others, 2002].

The treaties and their skeleton of EU decision-making thus allow much *creeping europeanization*. Paradoxically, in spite of all urgent calls since 2003 for a new treaty, in order to prepare the EU for the new enlargements, as otherwise the EU would become vulnerable to 'institutional paralysis', the process of europeanization has gone on as usual [Wallace, 2007]. The paradox is explained by the flesh-and-blood practices that can be unintended or intended. An example of the former is the spill-over from one formalised policy domain to another [McCormick, 1999], such as the effects from open markets on criminal behaviour which soon required cross-border police co-operation. An example of intended practices is the Open Coordination Method (OCM) for policies that, according to the treaties, largely fall under national competence, for which OCM works as a fishing net to get hesitant member states on board until a treaty basis is needed and codified. A recent case is the Commission's effort, after a call from the French Presidency in the autumn of 2008, to find common solutions for the crisis in the financial sector, on which the member states hold substantial national competences, partially pooled in the Basel Committee on Banking Supervision, independent from the EU. The Commission proposed in May 2009 (COM 2009/ 252) to set up two EU platforms without legal personality, one for systematic risk study and the other for financial supervision of financial institutes like banks, insurers and hedge funds. After strong opposition from the UK in the Council, a compromise was found, soon followed by more detailed proposals from the Commission pulling this policy domain into europeanization. It is the flesh-and-blood that matters now.

The Flesh-and-Blood of the EU Machinery

A lobby group reading the preceding summary may conclude that it has to target the Council in particular, as this body is formally in control of both the treaties and the binding decisions that follow. It would do better to read on and consider the work floors of the EU decision process, our chief concern from here on. The metaphor of 'work floors' represents the places where the work of decision-making is really done. Figure 2.1 (middle and right side) shows the main parts of the machinery with its work floors. Although decision-making is, strictly, only one early phase of the full decision-making process, we use it as *pars pro toto* that includes other phases like agenda building and inspection, to which we return in chapter 4. The skeleton may be a determinant of the EU work floors, but the *flesh-and-blood* makes them real. The same bodies are presented as in the skeleton approach, but are now regarded for their functioning in daily practice and showing different outcomes. Two differences of approach deserve attention first.

In the previous section, our key concept was formal power, as distilled from the treaties. From now on, the central concept is *influence*. We define it in terms of a relationship between two or more actors: A influences B if B's behaviour changes (either in accordance with the wishes of A or in any other direction) due to the behaviour of A [Dahl, 1991]. Like any relationship, influence is not a constant but variable factor, dependent on time, arena, intelligence, supply side and many other factors. In consequence, only repeated and controlled observations may permit generalisations in terms of patterns. Like any causal relationship, influence cannot be proven perfectly, but only in terms of plausibility. Formal powers can, of course, be a determinant of work floors or, in our terminology, provide potential influence. A hierarchically superior person or body may indeed really determine the behaviour of a lower-placed one. But reality is frequently different, as a lower-placed person or body may be the real influential force, due to key factors like expertise, support and gate-keeping. Lobbyists are the best-known example of persons usually having no formal powers and yet often exerting much influence. For measuring influence, formal powers have scant value.

Secondly, we reverse our starting point. In the formal approach, the treaties and thus the Council are the engine of EU decision-making, while the other bodies like the Commission and EP have more or less derived positions. In the work-floor approach, we focus on the EU decision-making process as it evolves from start to finish. The best metaphor for it is the initially *blank A4-format piece of paper*. At the end of the process this may be published full of text as a binding decision in the Official Journal. Filling in the paper usually starts in or around the Commission. Insofar as the Council has any say over a proposed decision, it usually gives this only as a last say at the end of the secondary pipeline, when the paper is already filled with text. In the many cases (around 85%) of delegated legislation, it rarely even has a final say. The difference between the skeleton and the flesh-and-blood, and thus the relevance of our metaphor, is illustrated by the saying among PA practitioners in the EU, whose daily job is to influence the machinery, that 'the most important people are not those who sign the decision, but those who write the text'.

The Polycentric and Multifunctional Commission

Except in two respects, the Commission is a rather normal bureaucracy, such as most member countries have [Kurpas and others, 2008; Spence, 2006; Nugent, 2006 and 2001]. One exception is its multinational and thus multicultural *composition*. In 2009, all member countries have to live with a Commission composed about 95% or more of staff coming from other countries, except Belgium (20% countrymen), France and Italy (both 10%). At all levels, the officials reflect by their different languages, customs, values and norms the variety of Europe, which far exceeds that of bureaucracies in federal countries like Germany or Spain. The apparatus is also an example of multicultural integration, stimulated by such factors as common location, pragmatic use of a few working languages (English, sometimes French) and basic *esprit de corps*. The second exception concerns the relatively *under-resourced* nature of the Commission in terms of budget and staff, as shown above. Due to its scarce resources the Commission has a strong appetite for information and support from the outside, to which we shall return below.

The Commission, appearing formally so hierarchical and united, operates in reality highly polycentrically. Viewed *vertically*, it has different layers. The President's style affects the College, as is exemplified by the contrast between Jacques Delors, who turned it into the engine of 'Open Market' legislation in the early 1990s, and José Barroso, who increasingly by-passed it to please the Council in the mid-2000s. The Commissioners, running a portfolio (policy area) and not a DG, often have to cope with various DGs that cover part of their portfolio, which brings many DGs the reverse challenge. As in any normal bureaucracy, inside a DG the substance of policy work is done at the middle level. Most important here are the *chef de dossier*, usually an Administrator (AD), the Assistants (ASTs) and the managing Head of Unit. They organise the draft papers for the Senior Managers, who normally make comments in the margin (and hence might be called 'marginal') but, of course, can have given instructions before. Drafts for secondary legislation first go into interservice, the euphemism for bureau-political in-fighting among the DGs, and often leak then already. The Legal Service is always involved, DG Budget and DG ADM if budget or staff is at stake, and Cabinets and Commissioners thereafter. The President can keep any proposal from the College's agenda, as José Barroso often did in 2007 regarding 'controversial' proposals such as on cross-border health-care (COM 2008/414) that could have disturbed the Irish, the EP elections and his chance of re-appointment; his gate-keeping resulted in a low EP workload in 2008. Seldom has the College really voted, as it searches for broad consensus, if necessary by package deal. On cases of delegated legislation, it usually mandates (by 'habilitation') the responsible Commissioner(s). The Commission's component parts have, in short, much room to manoeuvre.

Viewed *horizontally*, every DG has its own set of policy tasks and structures to realise them. However, usually this segmentation by policy sector does not fall in line with that of policy fields. For example, the europeanization of working hours for cross-bordering truckers falls under DG Transport, but is also an issue for DG Social Affairs, DG Internal Market, DG Enterprise and, regarding enlargement, DG External Relations. The result is frequently bureau-political in-fighting among these DGs and even inside a DG, as happened in 2003 inside DG MARKT when French opponents to the planned directive for Services on the Internal Market (COM 2004/2) published their deviant green paper on Public Services (COM 2003/270) that was soon withdrawn. Sometimes a DG succeeds in claiming a new policy area, as DG ENVI did in 1998 on Biotechnology, to the regrets of DG ENTER, DG AGRI and DG RTD; a few years later it lost it to DG SANCO. The Commission, in short, has a rather flat work-floor.

By taking a *diagonal* view, one observes structures and cultures that cross-cut horizontal layers and vertical units. Examples of such structures are joint working groups of Commissioners and high-level Director-Generals, mutually consulting Cabinets and DGs, and comprehensive impact assessments and policy reviews made by the SG. The most important cultural crosscut among officials is *double loyalty*, which may quadruple. Nationality has always been one [Page, 1997], as still applies to the recruitment of Commissioners and Cabinets, but is weakening at the lower level since 1999. A second variant is regional loyalty, as those coming from federal countries often feel loyalty to their region rather than state. A third variant is sectoral loyalty, as shown by the 'freaks' on health at DG SANCO, on the environment at DG ENVI and on farming at DG AGRI. Both regional and sectoral interest groups try to parachute their experts into relevant inside positions, for which the END positions provide an opportunity. Finally, there exist informal loyalties, based on personal characteristics such as education, age, friendship, seniority, hobbies and character [Christiansen and Piattoni, 2003]. The higher the number of loyalties and the more they crosscut each other, the more they all produce flexible networks. This seems to be the trend indeed [Geuijen and others, 2008; Trondal, 2008; Suvarierol, 2007].

The polycentric Commission also does much more than just drafting decisions and executing them after adoption. It operates, in fact, *multifunctionally*. Politically, it is the main aggregator of not only issues coming from public and private interest groups, but also their expertise and support, which is needed for drafting proposals able to gather substantial consensus among stakeholders. Administratively, it functions as the main supervisor of the enforcement of binding decisions, by taking for example supplementary decisions and setting up networks of EU inspectors that inspect domestic ones [Keessen, 2009]. Its economic function is to allocate discretionary (within its formal limits of budget and policy programmes) subsidies, tenders and procurements to interest groups. Managerial functions affect its internal apparatus and external information flow to the EP and Council, for example by issuing its annual working programme in advance, though it only covers part of its secondary planning. It also acts as plaintiff and adjudicator in certain policy fields, particularly on competition issues.

Legislation, however, can be considered the Commission's main function, for four reasons. On secondary legislation, firstly, it holds the monopoly on drafting proposals for new decisions. Through its edge on agenda-setting and gate-keeping, it has hidden veto power [Burns, 2004]. In most cases, the final decision is largely identical to the draft for its core text (starting after 'whereas'), as becomes evident from random comparison between most draft and final texts [Bellier, 1997, 110; Kassim, 2001, 15]. The widely amended exceptions to this pattern are so scarce that most insiders know them by name, such as the Reach Directive (COM 2003/ 644) and Services Directive (COM 2006/ 123 and the forerunners 2004/ 1, 2). Drafts that contain an anticipated influence of the EP and/or Council, such as on the annual budget often pre-fabricated by the Commission and EP versus the Council, only underline their decisive status as being much more than draft. On delegated legislation, secondly, the Commission sits firmly in the driver's seat, as the EP and Council hardly intervene in comitology effectively. In for example 2007, the Commission won agreement from comitology on almost all its proposed measures and could make them directly binding through the Official Journal. On the twenty cases of disagreement, the EP intervened four times (on development aid) and the Council sixteen times (mainly on genetically modified organisms or GMO), usually resulting in re-formulated proposals from the Commission (COM 2008/ 844). Thirdly, the Commission makes discretionary binding decisions, for example for awarding a subsidy or procurement, as mentioned above. Finally, the Commission produces (apart from non-binding 'soft law') a lot of supplementary legislation that re-interprets current law and is often presented as 'communication' to the EP and Council that, if not voicing objection, agree silently. Examples concern the allocation of slots to airports (COM 2007/ 704 and 2008/ 227).

The Commission, in short, is the EU's major legislator in daily reality. Some suggest, however, that much of its legislation is not by quantity but by quality of minor relevance, as it concerns mainly non-political, routine-like or technical details agreed upon by nominated officials, the *low politics that* differs from the *high politics* made by MEPs and Council ministers [Nugent, 2003, 241]. This may be true at face value, but there exists no objective criterion to assess the relevance of contents, as this has subjective value to everybody inside or outside. The level of the decision-makers is at any rate not identical to the relevance of the contents. For example, the 1989 Council Framework Directive on Safety, Health and Hygiene in the Workplace (EC 89/391) was regarded by many ministers and MEPs as a case of high politics, but mainly empowered the Commission to issue almost forty detailed directives through its Advisory Committee under comitology [Daemen and Van Schendelen, 1998]. Interest groups of employers and unions consider not the Framework Directive but these forty follow-ups to be the most relevant. Another example is the European Food Safety Regulation, adopted by the EP and Council in 2002 (EC 2002/ 178), that regarded it as 'high politics'. It contained, however, hardly any substantial decisions on food safety, as it was about delegation of powers to the Commission and its newly established Food Safety Authority, EFSA. The 'highest political' issue at the

Council level was the location of EFSA, in Italy or Finland. After the Council decision, the substantial decision-making could start under the flag of 'low politics' and thus at a distance from the EP and Council, to the pleasure of many involved interest groups. The devil is usually in the details, and so is the angel.

The Commission's Assistant Bureaucracy

As stated, the Commission is an exceptionally small bureaucracy. A policy unit has on average less than twenty policy staff. The Commission totters almost permanently on the brink of both volume and content overload. In order to manage this, it applies various solutions. On the one hand, it tries to reduce the overload, for example by setting priorities, combining issues and phasing policies [Deutsch, 1963; Easton, 1965]. On the other hand, it tries to expand its capacities in two ways: by *outsourcing* work to national governments (parts of implementation and inspection) and private institutes and consultancies (mainly research and advice) and by getting on board or *'in-sourcing'* people from the outside. This second way comprises four main techniques: hiring temporary personnel, setting ENDs to work, inviting experts from interest groups and organising public consultations. The first two fall under personnel policy. The third one has two variants: expert committees and comitology. The fourth technique intends to attract even more groups interested in the EU. The last two techniques are the clearest proof of the Commission's basic culture of permanent and intense consultation of stakeholders (COM 2002/744) or 'deliberative democracy' [Tanasescu, 2009] and shall be elaborated further below.

Most committees fall under the variant of *expert committees*, also bearing names like task force, scientific committee and interface [Van Schendelen, 1998 and 2003; Larsson, 2003; Larsson and Murk, 2007; Gornitzka and Sverdrup, 2008]. They belong to the Commission's drafting phase for both secondary and delegated legislation in a policy domain (first box of Figure 2.1), and are composed of experts representing an important public or private interest group, in short stakeholders. On its website, the Commission's SG has their register under construction. Their number, including subcommittees but without 'sleeping' ones, can be estimated at about 2,000 and the number of experts at about 100,000 people in 2009. A DG/Service has on average 57 committees, which is less than three committees per policy unit. The experts come from (roughly fifty-fifty) both public interest groups (central and decentralised governments) and private ones (business and NGO). A 'chef de dossier' (usually AD level) from the responsible policy unit recruits them from platforms like EuroFeds, leading stakeholders and by open 'calls for interests' on the EU website. Under this open method, the variety of the EU streams inside, which results in competitive settings that prevent policy cartels and, paradoxically, puts the 'chef de dossier' in the driver's seat. Exceptions to this open practice sometimes occur, such as the Scientific Group that prepared the 2001 Tobacco Directive and acted as a cartel of mainly 'health freaks'. All these experts, lacking any formal power whatsoever, only have semi-formal advisory status for the preparation of a green paper (defining 'the problem'), white paper (sketching 'the solution') and draft proposal. They do so on a part-time basis, for example once a month, and may get their marginal costs reimbursed (hotel, food, ticket), adding up to an estimated average of 50,000 euro for each committee annually. If they all would meet on average ten days a year, they would add to the Commission an expert staff equivalent to roughly 5,500 people.

The second variant is *comitology* acting in the delegated phase (lowest box of Figure 2.1) [Christiansen and Larsson, 2007; Bergström, 2005; Larsson, 2003; Andenas and Turk, 2000; Vos, 1999]. Their real number, including autonomous subcommittees, is not the official 250 but close to 450; on its website the SG presents the official register. They do have formal powers, such as advisory and regulatory ones. Usually, their members are supposed to represent their member-state government. In reality, many people from decentralised governments and private groups sit in comitology under the flag of national representative, thanks either to the secondary act that defined the committee's composition, or to their lobbying success in domestic politics or in the Commission. For example, by secondary act one-third of the Advisory Committee on Safety, Health and Hygiene in the Workplace comes from governments, employers and trade unions. Thanks to domestic politics, many experts from decentralised agencies hold the seat, not their ministry. Many private groups (profit-oriented or NGO) manage to wrangle a seat, too. As in expert committees, the member's main job is to reach consensus, but since the 2004 expansion, in management and regulatory committees they do this increasingly by QMV.

General observations for both variants of committees are the following [Van Schendelen, 1998 and 2003].

Old practice. Committees are an old European government practice, maintained by many positive functions. The first parliaments in Europe were, essentially, budget committees ('no taxation without representation') with experts representing citizens [Bisson, 1973]. They are a form of functional democracy that allows 'outstanding people', called representative experts now, to be consulted or to co-legislate. To the understaffed Commission, these people deliver at a bargain price excellent field expertise, articulation of support and aggregation of interests.

Influence. Both variants can be highly influential. By defining 'problems' and suggesting 'solutions', expert committees at least frame the policy climate in an area. Often they have a direct impact on the agenda and the proposals that follow. Sometimes they even draw-up the text for the Official Journal. In comitology's advisory committees, a major influence tool is delaying to the utmost; in management and regulatory ones it is the threatening with blocking QMV; and in all it is delivery of expertise and support, the latter by reaching consensus.

Fluidity. The formal distinction between expert committees and comitology is less relevant in practice than suggested by legalistic theory [Van Schendelen, 1998]. Often expert groups cast their shadow over delegated legislation, and comitology is consulted on secondary drafts. Some experts adhere to both variants. Many committee members are ignorant about their committee's formal status. Their interest is not formal power but influence, and the two are not identical. Powerful regulatory committees can lack influence, and powerless expert committees can be highly influential. The difference depends greatly on their images of expertise and representativeness, which they cultivate carefully but can be contested. Many experts, particularly those from central governments, behave as having free mandate rather than being instructed delegates [Schaefer, 2000]. The representative aspect of experts, particularly those coming from NGOs, has become an issue [Warleigh, 2003].

Chef de dossier. As shown by the figures mentioned on the outcomes of the internal process, the 'chefs de dossier' of the Commission practically run the work floors of committees [Lintner and Vaccari, 2007]. Usually, the person manages the consensus formation and is most prepared to accept the outcome. Many secondary proposals and delegated decisions are not the product of bureau-politics inside the Commission alone, but the outcome of political shuttling with committees, with the 'chef de dossier' in key position.

Proliferation. The number of both variants of committees continues to increase. An example is the 1976 Waste Management Committee now accompanied by about twenty other committees in this field [Van Kippersluis, 1998]. Many factors contribute to this. To serve new member states seeking committee positions, a committee is split or subdivided. New issues give rise to new committees. For example, the 1990 comitology committee on GMO has eight autonomous subcommittees, officially counted as one, for new specific issues. Lobby groups often push proliferation, as this helps to obtain a seat somewhere. All proliferation causes the single committee to lose influence, but all committees together to become increasingly the influential work floor of the Commission.

The fourth technique that the Commission applies for in-sourcing relevant groups is *public consultations* [Tanasescu, 2009]. Old variants, still in use, are those with institutions like ESC and COR, and irregular hearings and meetings of stakeholders. Nowadays the online consultations are booming, from nine in 2000 to 130 in 2006 and, since the 2006 e-Participation Initiative, to around twenty simultaneously in 2009, each with a short deadline and usually open to citizens, private groups and public authorities. The Commission applies them in its early policy planning, sometimes even before a green paper and often as a questionnaire attached to a communication or report regarding preliminary impact assessments and policy ideas on controversial matters, for example Public Access to Documents (COM 2007/ 185). Referring to the report 'An Integrated Maritime Policy' (COM 2007/ 575), the consultation has coined the new catchphrase *blue paper*. On its website the Commission (SG and Your Voice in Europe) publishes a list of current and finished consultations, the latter usually including responses and information about the next steps to be taken. The growth of online consultations is stimulated by the Commission's desire to consult groups and people beyond the circles of established groups that attend committees, and to reduce the proliferation of these committees. The satisfaction with the new tool varies. Established stakeholders have started to complain about its open-endedness, their free delivery of information without much chance of influence, and the influx of new challengers. The EP and some member states express mixed feelings about the Commission's increasing consultations in their 'backyard' [Bouwen, 2007]. 'Chefs de dossier' signal doubts over the sometimes enormous workload of handling the numerous responses and regret that stakeholders cannot be brought to negotiation online, as this can only happen in direct meetings. To them the online tool is not an alternative but a supplement to committees, as it produces even wider responses.

Intermezzo: The Commission as Smart Lobby Group
The understaffed Commission can, in short and with reference to Figure 1.2, be assessed as *the most intelligent lobby group*. It organizes its information or intelligence lobby, which is indispensable for its own efficiency and effectiveness, not by going window-out on its own, but by openly inviting different stakeholders to come along and to respond. Their controversies are housed in deliberative arenas. In committees it chains the stakeholders

in parallel settings, with their interests connected in series, from the one to another meeting, so promoting a compromising mood among them ('one always wins and one always loses something'). From public consultations it gets even more checks and balances of information. Even financially, it stimulates groups to establish new platforms, so creating new supply lines [Coen, 2007]. Similarly, it stimulates the bundling or *engrenage* of domestic bodies into an EU network [Leonard, 1999], in fields such as food safety, competition control and banking, which often develop into an EU Agency it can more easily influence. It organizes the tendering of policy problems, solutions and proposals among ever more stakeholders and, paradoxically, thanks to all the competition, it usually comes to sit in the driver's seat. Its 'chefs de dossier' operating this way are like PA managers, all acting as an extensive and flat PA desk. In return for small investments on reimbursements and management it can, with 'intelligent laziness', monitor many interest groups, collect information, test the feasibility of its ideas and influence the participants window-in directly. In return, it also gets a substantial and high-quality assistant workforce, which helps to depoliticise issues in Cartesian (rational, scientific and technical) fashion and, after countless participations and consultations, to legitimise its proposals and decisions in front of the EP and Council. Most interest groups accept the invitations willingly from their side, as these provide low-cost channels to influence each other, the Commission and, ultimately, the Official Journal. All this is much different from most national practices that allow entrance to only a few stakeholders and are not structured parallel but sequentially and with their interests not linked but distinct. In its intelligent approach, the Commission is smarter than most member states [Lord, 1998, 29].

The Parliament's Influence Role

The roughly ten *political groups* in the EP are more or less loose networks of about 200 sister parties from the member countries, and as such contributing to European integration [Judge and Earnshaw, 2008; Steunenberg and Thomassen, 2002]. They are steering rather than working platforms. The two largest groups, the christian EPP and the socialist S&D, command an absolute majority in theory and often in practice. Between 1979 and 2004, cohesive voting by these groups increased from on average 82% to 91%, with the other groups at lower increasing rates and altogether with national voting on the decline [Hix and others, 2007], also after the 2004 expansion [Hix and Noury, 2009]. Perfect bloc voting remains an exception on policy issues but not on power issues ('housekeeping'), such as regarding externally the Commission and Council, and internally the allocation of chairs and rapporteurships. The high group cohesion seems rather miraculous, as the MEPs are not easily socialised due to their national mandate, their high turnover of around 15% during term and 40% at election time, the weak disciplinary instruments of their group (except on assigning positions) and the cross-pressures from both other national parties inside and domestic interest groups outside, which circumstances could make them trustees with free mandate. Explanations for the miracle are the common need to get a very big parliament organised; the groups' control of important EP positions; and the competition among the groups for winning in plenary. The steering power of the political groups is anchored in the EP's own Rules of Procedure and the 2007-09 reports on Parliamentary Reform from its high-level working party.

About twenty EP standing *committees* plus a few temporary ones provide the main work floor, each being a kind of micro-parliament for a specific policy field [Corbett and others, 2007]. Their composition roughly reflects the groups' proportional share in the EP. MEPs can have more than one committee membership. The size of committees, on average about 50 people but with a wide range [McElroy, 2006], requires further downsizing that is done by assigning a rapporteur for every major dossier on the committee's agenda and, if the dossier covers more committees or is huge in contents and volume, one or more co-rapporteurs. They are all closely watched by 'shadow rapporteurs' from other groups. All told, the key MEPs on a dossier number on average around ten people plus their assistants. They are intensely lobbied by interest groups, including officials from the Commission and the PRs. Their task is to prepare a resolution acceptable to the majority of the committee and finally the plenary body. They do so in a usually informal and, in anticipating demands, proactive way. The role of rapporteur on secondary legislation is a scarcity, given the current 2,000 or so cases per full term (five years of about 400 cases each) and the number of MEPs, (on average about three cases per MEP), but disproportionally held by German and Dutch members of the two larger groups [Kaeding, 2006].

Part of the work floor is also formed by the around fifty *inter-groups*, which have no formal status at all and thus cannot act on behalf of the EP. They are governed by an agreement among the political groups that, in return for some facilities, requires inter-groups to be composed of at least three political groups, to disclose financial interests and to publish their membership. There exist about 20 registered inter-groups and even more non-registered ones. Inside the EP, they all act as an interest group of MEPs who share some common interest or concern, such as on disability, Roma rights or family protection. People from outside, representing an interest group, can join inter-group meetings. The common objective is to push the interest onto the EU agenda through a resolution to be accepted by the plenary EP. However, like any other 'own initiative', this cannot formally bind the Commission or the Council as there is no Commission proposal. Yet, it frequently influences them. Often the Commission feels sympathy for such new issue-creation and may stimulate it. With usually a time lag of about four years, the issue then appears on its official agenda, which makes inter-groups effective U-turns for official agenda-building. A famous example of success is the inter-group on Animal Welfare [Corbett and others, 2007, 189].

The case of inter-groups illustrates that the *EP's influence* can be far larger than is suggested by its formal powers, which are largely limited to the about 15% secondary legislation and particularly its smaller proportion under codecision. The codecision process began with its forerunner in 1995 (16 cases) and, due to treaty changes, has grown to one-quarter of all secondary cases in 2008 (or six percent of all binding decisions) [Brandsma, 2010]. Codecision powers are, indeed, not only powerful in theory but can also be influential in reality. According to the EP's own statistics (exceeding those in Figure 2.2), almost 500 codecision dossiers, including about 3,800 amendments, were tabled for plenary vote in 2004-2007. Of these dossiers, 71% were concluded in first reading, similar to the conciliation procedure, 23% in second reading and 6% in third reading, the 'conciliation' among key people from the EP, Council and Commission (the trialogue or triangle) behind closed doors [Rasmussen, 2008; Williamson, 2006]. In only a few cases so far has the EP finally vetoed a proposal under codecision, for example on Voice Telephone, Biotechnology and Port Services. The potency of the second and third readings casts its shadow clearly, as the Council agrees with the outcomes of most first readings. The EP has spent most of its plenary time, however, not on codecision dossiers (11%) but on non-binding reports from Commission and Council (23%) and its own initiatives (22%). Most codecision dossiers, moreover, come from only a few DGs like TREN, ENTR, ENVI and SANCO and fall under the few related EP committees. If formal powers would equal influence, then the EP would have been non-influential before 1995, and, as it exerts codecision powers over about one-quarter of secondary cases up until the Lisbon Treaty and almost half thereafter, would still be so on most dossiers since 1995. In various ways, however, the EP's influence can far exceed its formal powers and has always done so [Van Schendelen, 1984]. Pushed by civil interest groups, it has always been a major creator of EU issues and agendas, particularly in policy fields like social affairs, the environment and consumer affairs. Even under consultation, the EP can exert real influence by making use of other resources, for example by linking a dossier under consultation with that under codecision or other treaty powers, mobilising lobby and media support vis-à-vis Council and Commission, and profiting from dissension inside the Council. On budgetary matters it often has common interest with the Commission. Frequently, it forces a gentleman's agreement with the Commission (like on firing Commissioner Cresson in 1999) or the Council (like the 1994 *modus vivendi* on comitology).

Like the Commission, the Parliament behaves *polycentrically* and *multifunctionally*. It provides supportive MEPs, groups and committees for almost every issue or interest. The decision to assign a dossier to one or another committee or rapporteur may strongly determine the policy outcome. The risk of contradictory decision-making is balanced by discursive deliberations at all levels, which keep the EP representative for the variety of Europe. It enjoys much room to manoeuvre as, different from national parliaments, it is the single parliament in Europe that cannot be dissolved and is free from the Trojan horse of a government-controlled majority. Jointly with the Commission it often acts as a lobby group in favour of europeanization, although 'EU-scepticism' is rising among MEPs now. Many MEPs launch new policy ideas, contribute to the EU agenda formation, negotiate with Commission and Council, scrutinise their activities and act as barristers 'in first instance' on proposals from the Commission. They frequently belong to the influential players of the EU machinery. No surprise that many lobby groups come along. Decentralised governments and private interest groups in particular show intense lobby activism on rapporteurs and use other MEPs as 'assistant lobbyists' for questioning the Commission and Council, and for (re)framing issues and agendas. They find the EP to be the most open institution, followed by the Commission and last by the Council, the oyster of Brussels.

ESC and COR: More Influence than Power
In the *ESC*, three groups of socio-economic interests meet: employers' organisations, trade unions and various others like consumers, farmers, the green movement and SMEs. They are consulted on secondary Commission proposals that concern them, according to treaty texts, regard them. They can also issue recommendations on their own initiative. As a Grand Committee, the ESC comes close to an advisory committee under comitology: its advice has to be given the utmost attention, but not necessarily any response. Its logic of influence is similar. As long as its expertise and representativeness are acknowledged, it may exert influence far exceeding its

weak formal powers. The main influence factor is the formation of sufficient consensus. The ESC is an active committee. Currently, it produces almost 200 reports upon request and another 50 on its own initiative annually [General Report, 2008]. They comprise varied domains, such as the environment, agriculture, social affairs and transport. The real work floor exists at the level of sections and subcommittees, led by a chairman, assisted by the bureau and, for every dossier, a rapporteur.

Although its own reports praise its *influence* on EU decision-making, outside observers are more reserved [Van der Voort, 1997]. They see the ESC as rarely having an observable direct impact on Commission proposals. Its influence is more indirect and mid-range: by reframing the policy climate, issue or agenda in the secondary process. The main explanation for a lack of direct impact is that the ESC has difficulty in building consensus on concrete and specific issues. It produces much output, but the contents either sum up the diverse views or suggest consensus at an abstract level. The main reasons for this are its internal divisions, challenges to its expertise and representativeness and strong competition from other institutions. The employers' and workers' groups have their strong divisions both with each other and internally, such as those between members from rich and poor countries. Many use their ESC position for primarily monitoring the opponents and for blocking their preferences. Thus, they exert a negative rather than positive influence, find this better than an uncomfortable consensus and target their positive lobbying at the Commission, EP and their governments.

Much of the same can be observed for the *Social Dialogue*, a procedure that is distinct from the ESC as it has had its own legal status since the 1993 Maastricht Treaty, and only concerns employers' organisations and trade unions, the 'social partners' [Smismans, 2004]. About twenty committees and some informal groups do the real work inside. If they come to an agreement, either generally or for a specific sector like construction or road transport, they can formally break the Commission's exclusive privilege to propose legislation and, after adoption by EP and Council, they can implement the decision on their own, two entitlements which stand for corporatist-like self-regulation under EU public law [Gorges, 1996]. Since 1993, they have managed to produce a few laws in this way, such as the 1996 Parental Leave, 1997 Part-time Work and 1999 Fixed-term Contracts Laws, and also many solemn texts phrased in abstract terms without specific proposals, such as on disabled people, vocational training, and employment. Because their core problem is to come to a common proposal, the Commission has helped them in this since the early 2000s, so informally regaining its privi-

lege of drafting texts. Once adopted by the EP and Council, the social partners implement the laws, such as the 2002 Tele-working, 2004 Work-relat-
ed Stress and 2005 Equal Opportunities for Men and Women Laws. The social dialogue at least contributes to policy framing, europeanization in this
field and self-implementation of a few laws. Besides, it helps the social partners to monitor each other better, so providing a place for (window-out) information lobbying. Usually they each prefer to target their (window-in) influence lobby at the Commission, EP and national governments, as
happened on the 2008 Working Time proposal.

The other Grand Committee *COR* is in several respects comparable to
the ESC. It too has an advisory position only, same size, similar work-floor
operations and a high level of activity. Five differences are its young age
(1994, after the Maastricht Treaty), regional focus and background, composition of mainly elected regional politicians, internal dominance by political groups like in the EP and its reputation of influence, as underlined by its
impact on new treaty formation [Bindi, 1998]. Under the terms of the treaty,
it must now be consulted on secondary Commission proposals affecting
decentralised government, such as subsidiarity, cross-border co-operation,
budget and territorial cohesion. In addition, COR has its own-initiative
agenda with a broad variety of interests, from environment to employment
and public procurement. That COR has been rather successful in reaching
internal consensus and external impact is not self-evident. Those first four
differences with ESC can be seen as beneficial resources. As a young body,
COR is full of ambition, its regional focus gets tail-wind from growing regionalism in the EU [Telò, 2001; Loughlin, 2001], its politicians have close
links with party colleagues in the Council and EP, and its political groups
give it the image of a second EU parliament, as kind of the *Bundesrat* next to
the *Bundestag*. Of course, these influence resources may not last. One internal issue is that members from federalised countries like Germany, Belgium and Austria can, due to domestic politics, take positions on all layers
of the Council and hence have less interest in a strong COR that may challenge their position there. Anticipating the Lisbon Treaty, COR now wants
to develop closer co-operation with the EP, which will have to consult it
on more codecision dossiers. The new treaty also allows it to go to the Court
on issues of subsidiarity and consultation. In the past the Court (Constanza
ruling 1988/133) strengthened the position of decentralised government.

The Council: More Power than Influence

Formally, the Council is the body that acts as the gate-keeper of binding
decisions, by both allocating powers through treaty formations to institu-

tions, and deciding upon proposals based on these powers. The flesh-and-blood story is very different, as its treaty formations are increasingly subjected to many outside forces, and its final say over decisions based on treaty text has even more limited impact. Only a small part (the 15%) of the blank A-4 format paper that results in binding decisions ends here, and much less starts here. The Council now is a *polycentric* and *multifunctional* institution, as the following main observations show [Naurin and Wallace, 2008; Hayes-Renshaw and Wallace, 2006; Westlake and Galloway, 2004].

The Council operates as a *multi-layered* construct. The European Council meets a few times a year to discuss internal or external crises, settling complex issues and launching policy ideas. Crucial for its effectiveness is consensus among France, Germany and the UK, which is seldom easily reached and requires many negotiations that often fail [Tallberg, 2007; Beach and Mazzucelli, 2007; Warntjen, 2007; Elgström, 2003]. The GAER Council, next to the European Council, has managed two agendas so far: ·the one on general matters like conflicts arising inside or among the Specialised Councils and the other on external relations and defence; under the Lisbon Treaty the two will be split, the one to be run by the General Affairs (GA) Council and the other by the new Foreign Affairs (FA) Council, chaired by the double-hatted High Representative. The Specialised Councils are the terminus of secondary legislation and each meet only a few times a year, except the almost monthly Agricultural Council. Among them there is a sort of caste system, with the Economic and Financial Council (Ecofin) starring and the Youth Council closing the league. Under the Lisbon Treaty the GA Council and all underlying layers remain chaired by a member state that rotates every six months and that closely co-operates with the previous and next chair (troika), during which time it can subtly influence agendas, meetings (about 1,500 per half-year) and minutes. If a Specialised Council meets an internal stalemate, it can return the dossier to Coreper or forward it to the GA Council for solution. Usually, it prefers the former rather than the latter, as it loses control over what the GA does. The General Secretariat (GS) runs the household, administers activities and contributes to the Council's autonomous policy domains, but on the latter it is often overruled by political bodies like the Presidency, Coreper and COPS [Christiansen and Vanhoonacker, 2008].

The real Council work is done at the lower levels of *Coreper and working groups*. The almost 300 working groups (about 170 standing ones and 100 special and ad-hoc ones) are functionally comparable to the Commission's expert committees but act on broader policy domains and are limited to secondary dossiers [Häge, 2008; Fouilleux and others, 2007]. Officially they consist of domestic civil servants from both the capitals and the PRs but, dependent on domestic politics and lobbying, people from decentralised governments and private groups can sit behind national flags; Austria and Denmark exemplify the former and Germany, where these seats are distributed by the Bundesrat (Länder House), the latter. Working groups explore, according to the required decision procedure (unanimity, QMV or other), the political feasibility of a legislative proposal. They mark them as positive (Roman numeral I) or negative (II) and send them to Coreper, which gives them a final check, forwards them as A-point ('settled) or B-point ('unsettled') to a Specialised Council and usually follows their pre-marking. The A-points are in the large majority, mostly concern legislation and are rubber-stamped in a minute at the start of the next Council meeting. The minority of B-points are brought under Council discussion, mostly remain unsettled and return to Coreper in the hope it will be settled as an A-point later on. Only a very small minority of B-points are both formally and really decided by the Council [Häge, 2008; Hayes-Renshaw and Wallace, 2006, 53; Van Schendelen, 1996]. On delegated legislation the Council seldom intervenes and has so far never done so decisively.

The Councils are *formalising rather than deciding* bodies for many reasons. The most general one also applies to capitals, where ministers rely on preparatory layers before cabinet meetings as they, falling short on technical expertise, would run high risks of blunders if they act otherwise. Specific EU factors are at least threefold. Firstly, a Council meeting with 27 'flags' around the table is unmanageable as a discussion forum, as one round of four-minute statements by each 'flag' would take about two hours and require rigid formalisation. Secondly, a Council's composition is usually unstable as, due to dynamic domestic politics, often one-third of its ministers are replaced during the year, so making this layer unsuitable for ongoing negotiations. In the Council, the dominant culture, thirdly, is still the search for broader consensus and not the efficient counting of votes or voting points. The first QMV ever was taken on the Banana Trade dossier in 1992, five years after its introduction [Pedler, 1994]. On average (1994-2002) about 80% of legislative acts pass by consensus, with only very few 'flags' voting against (mostly Germany, Italy) or abstaining from voting (mostly Germany, France) [Hagemann and De Clerck, 2007; Heisenberg, 2005; Mattila and Lane, 2001]. After the 2004 enlargement the rubber-stamping of decisions became even more common [Naurin and Wallace, 2008]. Ministers usually prefer quasi-unanimous agreements and not QMV or veto, as the latter would reveal lost positions; sometimes they need such a loss, however, for domestic purposes and/or creating nuisance value in the Council, as the Dutch did twelve times in 1998 for getting their 'money back'. The multi-layered preparation of Council sessions is one response to the ministers' incapacity to decide. A second response is the growing informalisation of the Council process counter-balancing its formalisation. Most Councils now also hold informal meetings discus just to current issues without formal decisions, and many countries now initiate ad hoc platforms for precooking coalitions, such as the Baltic States (Nordic agenda), 'Sparing Six' (freezing the EU budget), Aachen Group (public health) and Barcelona Group (Mediterranean issues). In the preparatory working groups and Coreper, the formal procedures and informal negotiations have their balance, as the countries' representatives here shop around for coalition partners, usually with a preference for big countries from the North.

In three respects the Council is a strongly *fragmented arena* [Naurin and Wallace, 2008; Meerts and Cede, 2004]. Firstly, it exhibits many internal competitions among all layers and players, often on formal competences and usually solved by wheeling and dealing [Lewis, 2000]. They occur between the European Council and GAER (on foreign crises and general affairs), among the Specialised Councils, among Coreper and specialised bodies like COPS and COSI, and among working groups. Under the Pillar structure existing until the Lisbon Treaty, the Council was often so strongly divided on both Foreign Affairs and Defence (Pillar II) and Justice and Home Affairs (Pillar III) that it failed to agree upon its agenda, let alone its common position, and allowed the Commission to submit proposals informally. Another example is the aforementioned dossier on GMO trade and production, which held issues of agriculture, health, research, industry, development, employment, the environment, external relations and more and thus could have been handled by numerous different working groups and half the number of Councils, but went to the Environment Council and its working group. The choice for a particular working group and Council is an important determinant of outcomes on the matter, as in transport the tracks may determine the destination. Secondly, there is much inter-institutional competition. The clearest case regards legislation by codecision, on which the Commission is in the driver's seat, the EP is co-legislator and the Court can intervene upon request; usually the Council accepts the outcome of the EP's first reading. A source of inter-institutional conflict is the asymmetry of work division among the institutions, on which each is autonomous. In 2008, a proposal from DG SANCO on the prohibition of cancer-causing substances in pesticides was handled by the Agricultural Council, which declined it, thus upsetting the EP. Thirdly, many domestic conflicts continue at the Council level, often due to asymmetric work division, now between EU and at home. An example is the aforementioned case of pesticides that in many countries falls under the Ministry of Health but was handled in Council by the ministers of Agriculture. Germany, having ministers at also the provincial level, often shows up in Council meetings with several different ministers who distrust each other. The Competitiveness Council has even earned the nickname of Mickey Mouse Council, as 50 to 75 different ministers from the 27 member states may fly in and out to discuss an item on the agenda.

The Council member states, once having created the current EU and acting as managing proprietor, have undergone a transition *from managing directors to shareholders*. They still have a final and mostly formalising say over the secondary proposals, which is not unimportant as otherwise there is no binding decision. It is close, however, to the final say of an Upper House or Senate that has the last but seldom the decisive word. In 2001, German Chancellor Gerhard Schröder proposed to codify this change and to redefine the Council as a sort of EU *Bundesrat*. Another comparison is that with a company in which many decisions, proposed by a different executive board (Commission), are taken by 27 shareholders (Coreper and Council) together, which of course hardly works efficiently and effectively. In addition to formalising some decisions, the Council has other functions. Firstly, it discusses the leftovers from Coreper (B-points), usually resulting in openings that contribute to ultimate consensus. Secondly, at the end of Council meetings ministers can, under 'various other points', raise new points and, through (non-binding) declarations, memoranda and recommendations, contribute to EU agenda-building. The Council, thirdly, functions for playing home politics, for example to satisfy the national parliament or to bypass and overrule another ministry at home. On the latter aspect, the Environmental Council has acquired a reputation, as it often engineered formalised decisions that highly surprised other ministries at home. These limited functions are those of shareholders rather than managing directors, a role that is now left to the Commission.

The transition does not cease. The Council member states seem gradually to be evolving further *from shareholders to stakeholders*. Standing on the sidelines as shareholder, they have to. Increasingly, they are pressed by their national parliament to become more proactive on the Commission and are by-passed by lobby groups from their pluralistic country, which oppose their government's position, and lobby the Commission and EP earlier. Many more single ministries try to influence the Commission early, either through their own civil servants or through befriended lobby groups.

Many PRs, until recently focused on Council negotiations, start to lobby both the Commission and their national MEPs. Some Councils now act as a group of stakeholders, as in the autumn of 2008 the Environmental Council did by making an early deal on CO_2 Emissions Trade with the EP's committee on the Environment against the Commission, the Competitiveness Council and some member states like Germany. In the Council, at the end of the secondary pipeline, these parts of governments acting as stakeholders try to reap the fruits they sowed. Centripetal forces still balance these centrifugal ones. Coreper and the GS try to keep all decisions coherent. Coreper, GAER and European Council tackle stalemates among and inside Specialised Councils. By co-ordinating ministries at home better, national governments try to avoid more exportation of domestic fights up to the Council level. All this and more may slow down the Council's evolution towards meetings of stakeholders that compete internally, lobby other institutions and fight against opponent groups from home. Centripetal forces seem to be on the winning side, however. Particularly driven by their competition with other interest groups at home and abroad, the few national ministries already lobbying the Commission and EP pro-actively attract even more followers. Their effectiveness greatly depends on their capacity to apply public affairs and lobby professionally, to which we return in the following chapters. To give one indicator, as long as their own civil servants on the work floors of the Commission often act as self-instructed trustees, they still have a long way to go [Schneider and Baltz, 2005; Trondal, 2004].

Some Other Decision-Makers
The *Court of Justice* is frequently a major EU decision-maker [Cichowski, 2007; Arnull, 2006; Nugent, 2006]. Its decisions on cases brought to trial are formally binding on the parties involved. By their precedent-setting, they become a full part of EU law. The Specialised Courts handle hundreds of cases a year, mainly of three types: appeals from private parties against Commission decisions such as on subsidies and competition; citizens' complaints in new policy fields like health, insurance and taxation; and disputes involving EU personnel. Under the Lisbon Treaty the new General Court will get its workload both from the Specialised Courts as cases on appeal and directly from private parties (individuals, companies and organisations), national governments (including national courts) and EU institutions. The German government leads the pack in Court cases. An example of individual cases is that of Mr Decker and Mr Kohll regarding their public health insurance abroad, mentioned in chapter 1. National courts, asking

for an authoritative interpretation of EU law, bring about half of all cases. For the Commission, the Court procedure is the main touchstone for its enforcement of competition law, over which it has its own authority. Parliament and Council sometimes go to Court if they believe that their treaty-based powers and/or position are not sufficiently respected.

The three layers of the Court frequently act as an *engine of europeanization* for two reasons. The one concerns the formal contents of its decisions which, following the treaty texts, tend to be in favour of European integration. For example, its 1978 Cassis de Dijon ruling ordered the free circulation of goods, as this was laid down in the 1958 Treaty of Rome but was kept dead letter. The other reason is that the Court often functions as an alternative and indirect route to secondary legislation. Usually, this route is taken when the Council, whose members did approve the treaty texts in the past, cannot come to an agreement on Commission proposals based on them, such as that regarding free circulation of goods. A Court ruling then gives a strong green light to the Commission to make new proposals 'as ordered by the Court', which the Council then tends to accept [Nowak, 2007]. A recent example is the directive on Environmental Protection by Criminal Law (COM 2007/ 51), which the Council first opposed and then after a Court ruling approved in 2008. The Court is highly effective in getting its decisions accepted by contesting parties, which comply either voluntarily or under pressure from the domestic legal system that acts as annexe to it. Even member-state governments, being in the past the most reluctant to accept Court decisions, usually comply now [Nicolaides and Suren, 2007]. In the 1993 Maastricht Treaty, the Court received authority to impose financial penalties. In July 2000, the Greek government, disregarding EU environmental laws, was the first to be fined 20,000 euro for every day it continued to do so.

The *Court of Auditors* (CoA) can act as a decision-maker as well. In fact, it is another fine example of the paradox that weak formal powers, in this case in the field of financial inspection, can run parallel to real influence in the longer run. Its usually critical reports on EU revenue and expenditure can formally be left unread by the Commission and Council, or be taken as read by the EP, which has to sanction the Commission for its financial behaviour. In reality the CoA's criticisms and recommendations often fuel the EP's agenda with regard to the operations of the Commission, and contribute to decisions made at a later stage. The 1999 fall of the Santer Commission started with the critical CoA report on the 1997 budget, for which the Parliament refused to give discharge in December 1998.

Finally, there are the special *Institutions, Bodies and Agencies* for specific policy sectors. The European Central Bank (ECB) provides the most institutionalised example, with its own operations on common monetary policy-making. The Bilbao Agency for Safety and Health at Work exemplifies a monitoring agency connected to DG Social Affairs. The EU Ombudsman can inspect policy decisions in the case of a citizen's complaint. Whatever their formal status is, they all can influence EU decision-making, for example by influencing other EU authorities, making use of their discretionary and/or delegated powers or getting mass media involved. They also prove that the distinction between decision-making on the one side and implementation and inspection on the other is really artificial. Implementation is continued decision-making at an operational level, and outcomes of inspection that almost always show some gap between legal norms and reality usually feed back into new EU issues and agenda formation. New decisions are then taken by the responsible Body or Agency, the Commission (delegated legislation), the Council and EP (secondary legislation) or the Court (jurisprudence).

The EU Playing-Field in Helicopter View

A popular question is *who rules the EU?* In the skeleton approach, the Council looks to be the dominant institution, followed by the Court, the EP and lastly the Commission, positioned as service apparatus. If the Council formally acts by unanimity and if inside it the few big countries are most dominant, the question is answered with the academic catchword of intergovernmentalism. In the flesh-and-blood approach, the answer is almost the reverse, as here the rank-order goes from Commission and Court to EP and Council, an order with the catchword of supranationalism. In both approaches there is, however, not really a single answer to the question. The skeleton shows many changes over time, such as the EP's growing codecision, the Commission's delegated powers, the Court's jurisprudence and not least the Council's loss of powers to other institutions. Besides, already in the 1958 Rome Treaty, a number of internal checks and balances were built in, such as the Commission's own competences, the Court's adjudication and the privileged position of smaller member states in the Council. Such internal checks and balances have been strengthened in the meantime. For the EU's flesh-and-blood it is impossible to give one single answer to the question, as there is much variation by policy domain and even by dossier for each domain. Positions and patterns of influence are always variable, as they depend on various qualities of both those who try to exert influence and those who undergo these efforts, which qualities are relative according to circumstances. Ultimately, every case of EU decision-making gives its own answer to the question. Only by aggregating many cases can one come to a sort of overall answer. Aggregation methods from political science, such as before-after comparison, process analysis and reputation measurement [Dahl, 1991], allow an overall answer but with many exceptions. The answer is that in the production of most binding decisions, usually the Commission exerts the strongest influence, followed by the Court, the EP and finally the Council, COR and ESC.

Another popular question regards the *balance between the EU and member states*. In the skeleton approach, the member states' power positions vary with the position of the Council and their voting position inside. If member-states have ever had sovereignty at all [Krasner, 1999], they have increasingly lost much of it to the EU. At the Council level their independence, equality and veto power are declining the three main indicators of sovereignty [Morgenthau and Thompson, 1985, 331-2]. In the Council they need much support from other governments and institutions to get their wishes granted; they are treated unequally by voting points and thresholds; and they can more easily be overruled by QMV than say 'no'. Also on the second question the skeleton view gives no simple answer. In the flesh-and-blood approach, the influence of member states is not equivalent to their national governments' position in Council, but taken as the outcome of any effort from a member country to influence EU decisions. Then, a single ministry from a country can be highly influential in a policy domain, as can a decentralised government, an NGO or a business, and particularly if it forms a coalition that crosses sectors and borders. The second question can better be rephrased to address the balance between the EU and member countries. The answer then depends on the public affairs (PA) and lobby qualities of the component parts of a member country and the circumstances under which they operate. It is never one single answer, but always as many as the number of active stakeholders. This theme is addressed in the chapters to follow.

Although there are no simple and easy answers to the two predominant questions, it is possible to typify the EU playing-field in a few catchwords that can promote a better understanding. We take the following four: relevance, complexity, dynamics and manageable or open to influence.

(1) *Relevance.* As relevance is a subjective category, interest groups value the final or arising outputs and outcomes of the EU differently, ranging from 'heaven' to 'hell'. Initially, most of them see a daydream or nightmare possibly arising, as the decision may strengthen or weaken their position in their policy area or commercial market. At a more general level, they also

tend to prefer the EU method as a one-stop shop for solving irritating differences in Europe that always occur and may need solutions, rather than any of the five old methods. The EU method has its own relevance, which can be measured threefold: by the volume of formal decisions (Figure 2.3), the creeping europeanization before them and the rolling europeanization thereafter. Measuring the total 'weight' of EU laws on member countries is already difficult for the formal output [König and others, 2006], but really impossible for the creeping and rolling effects. One can better try to find a domestic policy domain still without any EU impact.

(2) *Complexity.* Considering its atypical design and workings, the EU skeleton and even more its flesh-and-blood may appear complex, like a labyrinth in which one easily loses one's way. The EU machinery is strange indeed. On its input side it is highly open and informal through its endless absorption of different experts, interests and lobby groups from member countries; on its output side it acts legalistically through its multi-layered enforcement of EU laws; and in between it pragmatically transforms different inputs into common decisions by negotiations among many competitive stakeholders. Numerous groups from the pluralistic societies add more complexity to it by their role-playing inside and around the institutions once constructed by their governments, like inhabitants adapt their house to their needs. The term 'complexity' is, however, a value judgement too, made by those lacking in understanding, just as any machinery is complex to the layman but not to the mechanic, and as any foreign political system looks complex to a tourist. Apparently, many people are still 'tourists' in the EU. In contrast, informed stakeholders hold a different judgement: thanks to complexity, any desired outcome can be acquired in different ways (multicausality) and the same way can lead to various desirable outcomes (multifinality). The precondition is knowledge of the machinery's workings.

(3) *Dynamics.* A popular party game among EU watchers is to name the five most important recent EU changes. Unable to agree, they end up with a long list that includes shifts of formal powers, intensified policy domains, regionalisation, enlargements and much more. The EU machinery looks like a trampoline on wheels, moving both up-and-down and faster and slower [Stacey and Rittberger, 2003]. The speed of codecision-making by EP and Council is, according to statistics of the Commission (SG, 2007), 12 months for the first reading that completes 71% of dossiers, 22 for the second one (23% cases) and 29 for conciliation (6% cases); on the last the Council takes the most time, on average 18 months. The most delaying factor in the years 1984-2003 is the Council's controversial B-points and the

main accelerating factor, the increase of QMV there [Konig, 2008]. Many national capitals take more time for their transposition of EU directives than codecision does [Haverland and Romeijn, 2007]. EU delegated legislation goes of course faster than secondary, as the Commission handles the former primarily alone. Major causes of dynamics from inside are skeleton changes, spill-over effects and flesh-and-blood practices and, from outside, enlargements and new issues imported by lobby groups. Perhaps the best indicator of EU dynamics is that every EU handbook needs revision after a few years. The dynamics are of no surprise to insiders. They watch trends like institutional reactions to both new spill-over and trend-setters like DG AGRI, the frontrunner of europeanization. Trained stakeholders take dynamics as opportunities that enable them to take chances to their benefit. Knowledge makes the difference.

(4) *Open to influence.* The Commission has a record of welcoming stakeholders to participate in preferably cross-sectoral and cross-national settings. Next-best are the MEPs and most PRs, which hold their doors open for single groups from their own country. The Council is the least open and its members are usually only in their capital for a few established groups at home. The same rank-order applies to their transparency and accessibility of documents, making the Council the oyster of Brussels, even more closed than Nordic capitals which, due to domestic laws on access to documents, leak many Council documents. No surprise that most groups prefer to sow their interests inside the Commission. Due to Europe's pluralism, its openness almost automatically keeps stakeholders from outside competitive inside, so bringing its officials into the driver's seat. Of course, there are many limits to efforts to influence the institutions and people inside successfully. They range from those at the receivers' side of lobbying and the competitors to the home front of every lobby group. Widening and using these limits demands intelligence and knowledge and belongs to the substance of following chapters.

Extra: Wandering Scholars

If knowledge about the EU playing-field is so important as sketched above, one might expect many useful (valid, reliable and applicable) insights from academic experts. Usually, however, they (too) disagree over their insights and, like the wandering scholars in the Middle Ages [Waddell, 1952], search according to their own best view. Other academics voiced their *widespread dissatisfaction* in the recent past, so creating almost consensus in disguise. To quote a few EU scholars: 'imprecision of theory' [Schmitter, 1996, 137], 'we, the prisoners of our concepts' [Wallace, 1990, 19], 'the crisis of legal studies' [Shaw, 1995], 'the many either...or approaches' [Wallace, 1997], 'the near-chaotic state of theorizing' [Chryssochoou, 2001, 193], 'the tribalism of specialisms' [Jørgensen, 1997] and '(the Council)...is incompletely addressed' [Heisenberg, 2008]. One cause of differences, at least with time, is the prismatic and ever-changing character of the EU, 'which wrong-foot extant theories' [Hooghe and Marks, 2008]. Here we focus on three causes that belong to the academic world.

Firstly there is the difference between the *disciplines* or 'bodies of knowledge' that, so far, have made the largest contribution to the study of the EU. The two oldest are international law and international relations. The lawyers describe, explain and assess the EU mainly as ruled by primary law or treaties. They keep their focus on the formal institutions, procedures and powers, in short the EU skeleton. Scholars in international relations describe the EU as a regional case of multilateral foreign policy-making by state governments [Howell, 2000], focus on the negotiations among these governments and regard the EU as being led by the Council. In the mid-1970s, political science appeared as the third major discipline, at first borrowing much from international relations and later on developing its own concepts and theories [Wiener and Diez, 2009; Pollack, 2005; Chryssochoou, 2001; Rosamond, 2000]. In their study, most political scientists shifted their focus (dependent variable) from EU integration to decision-making, broadly taken as the process of converting the inputs from the countries, including interest groups and citizens, into more or less binding outputs (like laws and policies) [Hix, 1999, XIII]. Such differences by discipline are fair and enlightening, as they result from different starting-points. We will continue by focusing solely on political science.

Secondly, academics follow many different *approaches* that can be broken down into three categories: conceptualising, grand theorising, and mid-level approaches [Nugent, 2006, part V]. To the first category belong old concepts derived from domestic politics, as if EU politics is more of the same, and either analytical ('what is') or normative ('what should be'), such as sovereignty and federation. New ones, among others, are multilevel governance [Kohler-Koch, 2003] and consociation [Taylor, 1996]. In the second category figure many grand theories, each assuming one coherent set of driving factors and again ranging from analytical to normative, such as (neo)functionalism, institutionalism and supranationalism, and new ones like constructivism and historical institutionalism [Eilstrup-Sangiovanni, 2006]. The third category of mid-level approaches can overlap with the previous two, but its claim is less general and more modest by its focus on specific settings or cases of EU decision-making. An old example is the three-fold reinterpretation of the same few decisions [Rosenthal, 1975], and more recent ones are those on policy networks [Fligstein and McNichol, 1998], transactional exchange [Sweet and others, 2001] and, of course, lobbying the EU [Coen, 2007]. Such differences in approach are not necessarily fair and enlightening, as they come from one discipline or body of knowledge that should bridge them, the sooner the better.

Thirdly, differences of *methodology and methods* cause a lot of differences of opinion. Many academics have the strongest appetite for constructing new theory, from which they deduct reasoned expectations (hypotheses) to be tested later or by others. If tested, almost always the validity, being the essential ingredient of usefulness, appears to be fragile. No surprise that one theory follows another, any theory is amended after testing, and all together illustrate wandering scholarship. The weakness of insufficient validity can only be solved by more and better empirical research focused on indisputable fact-finding. This is arising, but mainly as a by-product from deductive theory and by study of EU documents, such as those on comitology [Brandsma, 2010], legislative output [König, 2008] and lobbying [Coen, 2007]. Scarcer still is open-minded field research by interviewing people or participant observation, for getting either new ideas and hypotheses (inductively) or testing them (deductively). Early examples are the MEPs' views on lobbyists [Kohler-Koch, 1998] and the functioning of committees [Van Schendelen, 1998]. The third cause of differences is least fair or acceptable, as it concerns disciplinary idiosyncrasies rather than the EU.

In spite of all their differences, the political scientists display some *common traits and trends*. The older ones from Europe share some beliefs on the EU: deductive over inductive reasoning, integration rather than decision-making, skeleton over flesh-and-blood, importance of national governments rather than civil society, theory construction above empirical research, general rather than specific statements and evaluation above explanation. The younger academics increasingly adopt opposite beliefs and take the fragmented state of EU studies for granted or even as a rich mosaic [Wiener and Diez, 2009; Peterson, 2001; Rosamond, 2000]. As three new trends, they also push mid-level study, empirical research and field methods, for getting both inductive insights and deductive tests. Their approach in fact follows the example of older American scholars who, long before the birth of the EU, had gathered much empirical knowledge of their 'multi-country' US by mid-level empirical field-research. Many Americans took the lead in applying this to the study of the EU, such as Ernst Haas

[1958], Leon Lindberg [1963], James Caporaso [1974], Glenda Rosenthal [1975] and Leon Hurwitz [1980]. Some even tried to synthesize or amend old grand theories and concepts [Moravcsik, 2000]. Journals reflecting the new trends are the *Journal of Common Market Studies* (JCMS), *Journal of European Public Policy* (JEPP) and *European Union Politics* (EUP).

Our approach comes close to theirs, with two differences. We take the fragmented state of current knowledge as normal regarding a fairly young, unique and changing system and support the trend towards empirical research, also by field methods and at mid-level. One difference is that we prefer this knowledge also to be useful and hence to be both scientifically sound (valid and reliable) and applicable to questions about the EU's flesh-and-blood [Heisenberg, 2008]. The second difference is that we want to rely also on PA professionals and lobbyists as being informative sources for coming to better knowledge about the EU. Every day these people have to find ways and means through the EU machinery, and so they collect useful experiences and discoveries. This information is not yet tested knowledge, but can greatly help to develop better insights inductively and, as even one single piece of information might refute a theory, test academic views deductively.

EU Playing-Field and Public Affairs Management

Returning to our four catchwords that typified the EU playing-field in helicopter view above, we shall now draw general conclusions for the sake of interest groups seeking to influence the EU. The catchword of relevance implies that the EU has a potentially or really interesting supply side for many public and private interest groups. On their own demand side they feel attracted to it, so becoming influence vectors of europeanization. This is, in a free world, not different from the birds and bees that, according to the Jewel Akens song, are attracted by the flowers and the trees in the garden. Even more so than in nature, there is on the EU playing-field too little bread and honey for too many birds and bees. The logical result is usually *strong competition* among coalitions of officials from inside and stakeholders from outside. Due to the proliferation of lobby groups from many more countries, the competition gets even stiffer. Many issues persist as a drama of fights and stalemates. The Official Journal that continuously publishes new common decisions proves that sufficient consensus can often be reached over the distribution of a scarce value. This outcome is almost a political miracle and seldom explicable by a dominant position of a single or a few officials and stakeholders, just as one bird seldom takes the most from the garden. Dominance can happen (threaten to) on the EU playing-field, but usually it is counter-balanced early. Even if some category of interest group, such as technical experts or NGOs, is seen as dominant in a field for a while [Michalowitz, 2007], then it usually remains competitive internally.

The EU's openness to influence, being another catchword, basically comes from a match between two demand-and-supply sides. The Commission and EP want to receive useful information and support from interest groups and are prepared to give them chances of influence. The interest groups demand such chances and are willing to supply information and support in return. The two sides set negotiations into motion among coalitions of interest groups and officials and result in compromises that are formalised by officials [Elgström and Smith, 2000], mechanism which largely explains the aforementioned miracle. The metaphor of *political market* helps us to understand this mechanism. When two groups provide both a supply and demand side to the other, they together stand for a market on which a negotiated deal can be made, being the match between the two demand and supply sides. This consensus formation does not work differently from price formation on the commercial market. One may, of course, criticise any consensus as being a compromise that falls short of rational (effective, efficient) decision-making, as is often done by selfish English groups that, due to their culture in which a compromise comes close to 'disgrace', want to win all. The criticism has had its parallel in the old economists' debate about 'the right price' (pretium justum), brought to closing by Adam Smith [1776] who pointed out that, under the precondition of open competition (market pluralism), the match between demand and supply sides results in the most rational price. Similarly, for the EU playing-field (political pluralism) the formation of consensus through compromise can be seen as giving the best possible outcome.

The EU's seeming complexity and dynamics, our other catchwords, are helpful rather than disadvantageous for decision-making by compromise, as they provide *ways and means to influence success*. Thanks to complexity, the labyrinth always offers a way to a desired destination, and thanks to dynamics the trampoline always moves to a better moment. The flesh-and-blood of the EU machinery allows every interest group to be optimistic that, one way or another and sooner or later, on any issue their demand and supply can match those of officials and result in a compromise, the decision. Not surprisingly, most PA experts familiar with the EU machinery are optimists about possible outcomes, like scientists searching for findings [Popper, 1945]. Proactive professionals may even try to make it more complex and dynamic, thus setting at a distance the more amateurish players who, in contrast to them, often complain about losing their ways and missing their moments.

This contrast unveils the missing ingredient of influencing the EU playing-field with a good chance of success: *useful intelligence* drawn from collected information [Johnson, 2006]. The best points for tapping information and feeding one's own intelligence are the following.

Watch early. Monitor and study early debates and non-binding texts proactively, as any new policy line starts here. Identify 'chefs de dossier' and their manager(s) and assistants before the person starts to write a blue, green or white paper, and also key people from other DGs capable of interfering as partners or opponents.

Work floors. Find the potentially relevant expert committees or other platforms that assist the 'chef de dossier'. If the text is for secondary decision, identify the relevant EP's committee(s) and inter-group(s), ESC's and COR's work sections and the Council's working group(s) and, if for a delegated decision, the comitology in charge. Focus particularly on key people inside and around there. They always come from different countries and have both common and different interests.

Various. Watch the interservice procedure inside the Commission, the Agencies that can play a role at either the input or output side of decision-making, the PRs acting as a voice of their government, and the Court that can act as legislator. Not least, watch attempts to change a specific playing-field by Triple P (see next chapter).

The former is but a very short summary of the main tapping points of information inside the EU machinery, and every point already requires a lot of window-out lobby. The ambitious interest group has to broaden it to the level of the numerous other stakeholders interested in the same issue or dossier, and not least to the level of its home front. For all three levels, it must studiously keep the information updated, transpose it to intelligence and make it useful for the window-in support lobby needed for getting the EU decision outcome in the desired direction. All these activities that start with information are a matter of *PA expertise* to promote effective lobbying, the basic E of our formula $E = MI^2$. No surprise that such a big PA agenda, outlined in Figure 1.2, needs most of the other chapters of this book. In the applied political science of lobbying the EU, with a desired outcome as a dependent variable, the interest group's PA expertise is the independent summary variable that differentiates the most between winning and losing. Even the best expertise meets its limits, however. The ambitious and studious interest group must hence also lobby prudently and become an all-around PA expert like Machiavelli. How this prudency creates an EU variant of Darwin's Law, under which the most expert lobby groups have the best chance to survive, and whether this still meets criterions of democracy, are questions for the last two chapters.

CHAPTER 3

PUSHING THE BUTTONS OF 'BRUSSELS'

Managing the Crucial Variables

The ultimate goal of public affairs management (PAM) is to achieve a complete victory in a supposedly interesting game. Such an achievement requires winning in three arenas: the EU, from which one has to gain the desired outcome; the stakeholders which have to deliver substantial support; and the organisation at home for sufficient backing. In real-life, the chance of such a full score is low. Competition in the EU is usually extremely strong and hard. EU officials act under many cross-pressures, competitors hold the belief that it is at least in their common interest to prevent one player from gaining too much, and groups with different interests at home may feel threatened if one achieves a full score at EU level. Every lobby group, therefore, has reason to be satisfied if it has won the game only partially and/or has maintained its position in the fighting arena and/or has kept the home organisation on his side. These three – *compromise, respect and backing* – might be seen as second-class prizes to win, but they are in reality frequently valued as the highest attainable and thus as satisfying achievements. They give a prolonged licence to operate. Of course, a lobby group may lose as well by not being party to the compromise, getting disrespect from others and/or losing backing at home. But as long as it lobbies ambitiously, studiously and prudently like Machiavelli, it seldom runs this risk. In short, the full score is normally only a daydream to all lobby groups, while the severe loss is usually the nightmare that only befalls the amateurish groups. Both dreams have their positive functions for the professional, too. Without the daydream of becoming the complete winner, and without the nightmare of ending up as the complete loser, no sportsman can ever hope to become a great and competitive player.

The definition of a *desired outcome* from the EU is, of course, up to every lobby group and can be anything. The main field of desires is usually legislation, because this is expected to be binding on those whom it concerns and to supersede domestic laws, although both effects are not always perfectly realised, thereby resulting in no guarantee either to win or to lose through EU law. An interest group lobbying on legislation may desire, for example, a change of either secondary or delegated law, a new Court decision or the granting of an exemption to a rule. Equally desired may be a derived act of legislation, such as the allocation of subsidy or levy, the granting or withholding of a procurement, and either the launch or postponement of an inspection. It may even appear to be mere detail: a deadline, sanction, annex, word, definition, number, comma or whatever else is considered relevant by a player. Whether the other players consider such a desire irrelevant or silly does not matter. Due to the lack of objective criteria to distinguish between relevance and irrelevance, every value is always a relative and subjective affair. A desire that seems silly to others may even have the great advantage of attracting less competition from those others. Other outcomes rather than legislation may also be desired, such as support for one's cause, change of an agenda, seats in committees, crucial information or financial favours. From other stakeholders a lobby group can desire such items as respect, information, support, network, burden-sharing and even favours unrelated to the EU, for example a commercial contract or co-operation on policy, and from groups on the home front more backing and resourcing. An exhaustive catalogue of desires cannot be made.

The desired outcome is, of course, not necessarily a positive one from the EU decision process, longed for as a daydream. It may also be a negative one, feared as a nightmare and targeted as never being realised. A studious lobby group always has desires in stock for both daydreams and nightmares. Such a *non-outcome* can be the rejection of a legislative proposal, the delay of a decision, the fading away of an issue, the jamming of the decision-making machinery and anything else that produces a desired non-event. In fact, the more competitive an arena is, the more the influence behaviour is directed at preventing the undesired outcomes rather than promoting the desired ones. On a competitive playing-field, being complex and dynamic as well, it is often easier to bring a fear to death than a dream to life, as every single player simply has more nuisance value than pushing power. No lobby group, however, can only play the negative game as it would become an outcast then, and hence it has to push for some positive outcomes as well. This may be a nuisance in a friendly disguise, for example the desire to get a policy area reviewed, a stakeholder's consultation broadened or an impact assessment extended. By implication, lobbying the

EU has nothing to do with being in favour or against Europe, European integration or policy europeanization, but only with the promotion of one's selfish interest at the EU level. If this interest is in line with a current trend, one can take the opportunity of lobbying at low costs, but if it goes counter, one has to fight the threat at high costs. Swimming upstream always takes more energy than downstream. The most intelligent lobby groups try to set the trend by early agenda-building.

The positively or negatively desired outcome is, in other words, the dependent variable of EU PAM. All sorts of pressure groups hold this ambition. Some multinationally organised companies (MNCs) and NGOs may have the strongest reputation for successfully realising the ambition, but many other groups do not different by ambition and equally so the EU officials who want to score as well and as such play dual roles, as both receiver and sender of lobby messages. The big question is *how to successfully realise ambition*. Many of the countless factors of success are variables, and many of them are manageable by PA ingenuity. In this chapter we shall apply this basic insight to the arenas of both EU decision-makers and competing stakeholders. We shall conclude that the single most crucial independent variable of lobbying is the intelligence or expertise of managing the variables that determine both arenas. Effective influence is, however, seldom a straight line between the intelligent player and the final decision-maker. For influencing 'Brussels', one has to push many buttons both serially and in a parallel setting, which taken together may connect the desire to the decision.

The Manageable Machinery: General Approaches

Thanks to the characteristics of the EU playing-field, there is no shortage of buttons to push. In fact, there is an oversupply compelling one to make an intelligent selection, as otherwise one may push the wrong button, lose momentum, shake up competitors, hit a dead end, make a short circuit, irritate officials or cause whatever damage to one's interests. Before one can make the best choice, one has to become familiar with the menu of existing or potential buttons. In the following we distinguish between three general categories: the *actors to approach*, the *factors to use* and the *vectors to create*. The actors are the people who contribute to the making of a decision, the factors are the determinants of their decision-making behaviour and the vectors are the newly created factors that may carry an intended influence on that behaviour. As with every menu, ours too is limited and not exhaustive for all potential items under the three categories. In an ever-changing machinery there is, besides, always room to find and develop new actors, factors and vectors. Our objective here is to make the reader systematically more aware of and familiar with the many buttons. Taken together, they form in academic speak the intervening variables of influencing the EU machinery, which can often easily be applied thanks to their multicausality (many causes) and multifinality (many consequences). This is a matter of knowledge and creative management.

Actors to Approach

Which actors are crucial in the making of an EU decision? The answer depends, of course, on the dossier, arena, procedure, setting, time and many other circumstances. In the flesh-and-blood of EU decision-making, some patterns and configurations are discernible. The metaphor of the *A4-format* piece of paper, starting blank and ending up full of text in the Official Journal, remains helpful here. Much paper, of course, may never get a final and authoritative signature and, as such, may have been the object of successful blocking actions. Every authoritative decision, however, starts out as a first draft on paper and is then subject to pressures pushed successfully. As stated in the preceding chapter, those who draft the decision are frequently more important than those who finally sign it. Our question therefore is: which actors are, not formally but actually, usually the major contributors to the paper that may carry the final decision and thus can best be approached?

In almost every case of EU decision-making, people inside the *Commission* play a crucial role. Usually they drive the flow of secondary legislation, frame the substance of both delegated and discretionary decisions, prepare the yearly work-programmes, enjoy the habilitation freedoms, make the bulk of supplementary decisions, and to some degree even contribute to the formation of both primary legislation and Court jurisdiction. For every DG, key people are usually the chef de dossier and the levels of Managers and ASTs, the in-sourced experts in committees and otherwise, the staff of other DGs and Services able to intervene through the interservice procedure, and the people at the level of Cabinets and College. For every dossier of relevance the ambitious lobby group must try to identify the names of these civil servants and the affiliated people in an early phase, and also their potentially relevant backgrounds (like policy position, education and career) and idiosyncrasies (private values and hobbies). This is not simply for one DG but also for the other DGs with an interest in the outcome. On for example an issue of food production, a lobby group must study not only DG AGRI but also, for example, DGs as SANCO, MARKT, ENVI and TRADE. All this lobbying for information or intelligence and finally sufficient support is clearly a lot of work that, in order to save costs (more efficiency) and to personalise a contact (greater effectiveness), can best be organised at the level of a platform of befriended stakeholders. Frequently, the most difficult is the information lobby regarding comitology committees, being the oysters of the Commission. After all information-gathering work, the lobby group will discover that inside the usually internally divided Commission it has many potential friends and enemies, which frequently have their own policy family or network, not only inside the Commission but also connected to befriended interest groups in various member countries. After their identification, the lobby group can start to mobilise the friends, to disarm the enemies and to approach them wherever they live.

The key people of the *EP*, *COR* and *ESC* are first of all, at the organisational level, the rapporteur, the co-rapporteur(s) and their shadows; secondly at the supervising level the chairmen of the committees (or the intergroups and sections) and the co-ordinators of the political groups (in EP and COR) or interest groups (in ESC); and thirdly, at the operational level their staff members and assistants doing lots of substantial work. The total number of key people involved with a dossier is in each of these three institutions usually around twenty. In practice they make the plenary resolution. Under the consultation procedure their impact may be limited to both the timing and framing of the issue or agenda, but this can be decisive for the final result. Insofar as the MEPs occupy a codecision position, they can also formally intervene in secondary legislation and, to a limited degree, in the delegated one. All members of these three institutions have their feet planted in domestic public or private organisations. Here too, the ambitious lobby group has to identify the names of its partners and opponents inside in an early phase and also their personal characteristics, including their footing in domestic public or private organisations through which they can be approached. All this work may seem easy once a secondary proposal breaks through the surface. Yet this moment comes not early but late. During the Commission's drafting, the ambitious lobby group should try to identify the players who come next. Otherwise it gets difficult to take the edge over competitors and is not really ambitious.

At *Council level* the most relevant actors are, first of all, those who determine the Council position, being the national civil servants sitting in the working groups under Coreper and in some special committees like SCA and COPS. They make the bulk of the Council decisions (A-points) rubberstamped by the ministers. They all are appointed nationally, even if coming from a decentralised or private organisation, and can be influenced in their member countries. Secondly, relevant too is the staff of the Council's GS, which handles the dossiers 'administratively', being often a euphemism for all sorts of manoeuvring. Particularly in times of a weak Presidency, this staff takes over some of its roles, such as scheduling the meetings and thus arenas, pushing issues up or down, arranging logistics, drafting conclusions and proposing solutions. Thirdly, the members of Council working groups are relevant to be identified and, as they work and live in their member country, be contacted there for debriefing and inspiration or briefing. Even the Council, being the oyster of all 'Brussels' institutions, can be opened by the studious and prudent lobby group.

Thanks to the polycentric and fragmented character of the EU, *many more officials* can usefully be approached. At the Court, the advocates-general and the referendaries usually have a strong impact on the Court's decisions, which in their turn influence the Commission. The researchers at the Court of Auditors offer a similar back-door access. The inspectors of inspection agencies are useful for the identification of a difference between norms and practices of implementation that always exists and can be used for getting an issue back on the agenda. The jurists of each institution's legal service are influential advisors to their high officials. By changing their mind they produce different advice. The translators convert legally binding decisions usually composed in English into all official languages, but no two of them have fully identical semantics, and a small change of translation can make a big difference. High-ranking officials frequently play important 'meta-roles' in decision-making, for example by dividing work, assigning positions and allocating resources. By approaching them, one may change an arena and get, for example, another DG, expert group, EP commission, rapporteur or Council working group to be formally in charge. Even a small change can make a big difference for the outcome, as a minor change of course can divert a ship miles away from its original destination.

Other important actors to approach are *the stakeholders* not formally belonging to the EU, such as other pressure groups at both the EU and domestic level. For example, the Brussels-based PRs, MNCs and NGOs have their established links and networks with parts of the EU machinery. Regional governments, units of national ministries, trade organisations and citizens' groups frequently have their own linkages between home and EU as well. In addition, many people hold positions at intersecting points of various networks to which they belong and can be approached from different sides and be used as carriers of interests. Since every country is always divided over every dossier, one can always mobilise domestic pressure groups to influence, for example, a national position in the Council in the desired direction. A potential gold-mine is the person sitting as expert on an expert committee for drafting a decision, a Council working group for secondary cases and in comitology for delegated dossiers, thus covering all dossiers in a domain of policy. People with the same domestic identity often meet informally, as the Irish do in their Brussels pubs Kitty O'Shea and Wild Geese. Many people also play relevant roles outside the EU, for example in non-EU countries or at the level of the OECD, the WHO or the WTO, three platforms that often influence the EU outcomes and thus can be used as a U-turn to EU decision-makers. Also the EU officials, often having their own agenda and ambition to score, can be approached in their secondary role of stakeholder lobbying for not only their own case that may fall under the official EU agenda, but also for their personal one linked to a special sector, region or interest. The lobby group has only to discover these personal interests of any official.

There is, indeed, no shortage of actors to approach for collecting information and ultimately support. Plenty of them are available and, as no single actor is decisive, many of them are needed by every ambitious lobby group. From a lobbyist perspective this fragmentation of power is better than a concentration would be, as it is easier to win many friends than a single Ruler. Most actors on the playing-field have, besides, their own relations and networks there, which helps to get 'the snowball rolling' from one befriended contact to a wider network that crosscuts institutional, national, sectoral and other borders. Every lobby group has thus, in theory, all reason to remain optimistic about its chances to create a desired outcome. The real puzzle of its PA management is to select the most useful actors to approach, the best connections, the precise timing, the correct approach, the right balance between stick and carrot and much more that is important for bringing ambition to success. This puzzling by study and prudence is treated in the chapters to follow.

Factors to Use
The number of relevant EU actors may be numerous, but is modest in comparison to the total sum of factors affecting their behaviour. Every interest group can make use of factors, just as a green farmer exploits the natural conditions for growing and flowering to his advantage, or as a shopkeeper uses market opportunities of supply and demand to make his family wealthy. Manipulating factors of behaviour is certainly more sophisticated than approaching actors. The increasing competition among EU stakeholders produces this sophistication and makes it a current trend. From the long list of factors useful for promoting a desired outcome, we select the fol-

lowing ones, gathered under four categories: cultural, formal, operational and decisional.

Cultural factors. Those who make a decision on whatever issue need sooner or later policy concepts defining aspects of the issue, policy values framing the decision in a specific direction and regime values governing the process. Due to the diversity of Europe, there are no concepts and values that have common meaning or acceptance, and thus they are open to lobbying. In 1999 there appeared to be no common concept or definition of 'chocolate', which was needed since some chocolate companies in some countries tried to get banned from their market the products from foreign competitors they considered fake products misleading the consumer. To the stakeholders such a situation is either an opportunity or a threat, dependent on both their current position and their strategy for the future. The Belgian chocolate industry took it as an opportunity to reposition itself as a producer of pure product, and it lobbied for a strict definition (high percentage of cocoa) and, as policy value, for labelling (to inform consumers). The final decision was made accordingly, after which the regime of 'open market' solved the issue. New concepts and values come and go like the wind: if it is friendly, one can hoist the sail, and if not, one can at least try to steer a middle course. The Commission is a main producer of such concepts and values, frequently carried by green books and communications, which to attract broad initial support are usually phrased in abstract wording to provide room for lobbying at a concrete level thereafter. Examples of such new policy values in recent decades are health, solidarity, sustainability, cohesion, growth and security. Intelligent lobby groups try to sail with any wind. For example, in the 1990s some pharmaceutical MNCs like Glaxo-Wellcome promoted the WHO recommendations against the use of tobacco that resulted in EU legislation under the flag of public health, which created a market for their new anti-nicotine products [Duina and Kurzer, 2004]. If hungry for EU subsidies one can best, far before lobbying for money, first lobby for adoption in the next cadre-programme another policy objective or criterion that is more profitable to one's interest. Examples of new regime values, launched in recent decades, are subsidiarity, transparency, proportionality, impact assessment, better regulation and reciprocity. Smart lobby groups use them for pushing a daydream or blocking a nightmare and, like squirrels do in the wood, for dragging their interests to a better arena. For example, subsidiarity is often used for slowing down EU environmental or social policies, transparency for hindering efficient negotiations and reciprocity for retarding an open gas or railway market.

Formal factors. The skeleton of the EU decision-making machinery can work as a determinant of its flesh-and-blood and thus is full of potentially useful factors. Because treaty texts provide room for interpretation and the EU process law regarding legislation is not yet well-established, the choice of procedures is open to lobbying. For example, according to the treaties taxation is, with a few exceptions like VAT, a national competence, but under the different names of a levy and a duty, a financial imposition may fall under EU competence. This manoeuvring room stimulated green groups to lobby for EU duties on polluting consumption like air traffic in 2008. For the outcome of a decision-making process, it may make a big difference whether the process is based on either the one or the other Treaty article, follows the secondary or the delegated procedure, positions the EP under consultation or codecision, requires unanimity or majority from the Council, is dealt with by the one or the other Commission DG, EP committee or Council working group, assigns the implementation to EU civil servants, national bureaucrats, regional authorities or private organisations, or whether a decision gets the formal status of a non-binding guideline or binding decision. By linking formal factors in a series, one gets repeated opportunities for blocking or pushing. Then a lobby group feeling hurt by a Commission proposal for secondary legislation can use the EP to appeal against the Commission, the Council against the EP and the Court against all of them, as the German government did on the 1993 Banana Case [Pedler, 1994] and on the 1999 Tobacco Case.

A change of the Treaty, which is *the mother of all procedures*, may provide many threats or opportunities, dependent on a lobby group's interest position. After nearly twenty years of stalemate, the first directive on works councils for multinational companies came through in 1994, thanks to the 1993 Maastricht Treaty's provision of Council QMV on this matter, and the anticipation on this by the Commission, together with the trade unions federation ETUC [Van Rens, 1994]. By making use of the 1993 Social Protocol, the Commission and ETUC managed to push more co-determination in such companies in 1997 and to get the directives on parental leave and part-time work passed. Both the 1999 Amsterdam Treaty and the 2003 Nice Treaty changed a number of procedures, as they expanded the codecision one to, among others, food and transport policy and moved civil law issues from Pillar III to Pillar I, thus creating easier arenas for lobby groups. There is also lobby anticipation to Treaty change. In 1998, the EP decided to delay its proceedings on the Water Framework Directive until after the Amsterdam Treaty went into effect. In 2005 lobby groups, including EU officials, anticipated the possible adoption of the (failed) New Treaty of Rome, by trying to speed up or slow down dossiers for decision-making. In 2007-08 the

Commission's President José Barroso gave full priority to the national ratification of the draft Treaty of Lisbon and, wanting to avoid any risk at the Irish referendum, made use of his power to halt temporary all potentially controversial Commission proposals. Lobby groups wanting to delay whatever proposal from the Commission in 2007 only had to pump up some controversy. In 2008, green lobby groups opposing a Commission proposal regarding poultry meat falling under the Standing Committee on Food Chain and Animal Health (SCoFCAH, part of comitology) tried to delay this process, as they knew that under the Lisbon Treaty their befriended EP would have scrutiny power to intervene on the matter.

Operational factors. For their daily operations, the EU officials are highly dependent on material resources such as staff and budget, and less tangible ones like information and support. Such factors can make a big difference for the desired outcome. The under-resourced Commission has no alternative to opening its doors and calling-in a great number of inexpensive and excellent experts, which is an opportunity for interest groups. When lobbying for a piece of law, subsidy or procurement, they can deliver the Commission what it lacks, particularly specific information and support. Some Commission units may, of course, have more or fewer resources than others. In 1995, the DG Social Affairs, unit V, had to call off meetings of its Advisory Committee on Safety, Health and Hygiene, due to lack a of means at the end of the year. The members from organised management, fearing more labour laws, welcomed the delay as an opportunity, and northern unions regretted it [Daemen and Van Schendelen, 1998, 135]. Similar imbalances between workload and resources may arise in the EP, the Council and the Court. The EP's Friday session in Strasbourg, had a low turnout of MEPs and was therefore abolished in 2000 and became a case of underload, making it simpler to get resolutions adopted by simple majority, much to the pleasure of the lobby groups. Overload by either volume or content distributes threats and opportunities among lobby groups as well. The Commission's proposal on Reach (COM 2003/644) regarding 'dangerous chemicals' gathered the exceptionally high amount of about 1700 proposals in 2005 for amendment in the EP, overload which an helped to annul their large majority, to make the proposal more friendly to industry and to put the responsible DG ENVI in ward of DG ENTER.

There are many more operational factors, three of which deserve special attention. One is *friendship*. In the multicultural EU, the daily operations are frequently quite dependent on this. Actors tend to like or dislike each other, for whatever reason. By using friendship as a tool, one can further a desired outcome. A DG civil servant may then be prepared to raise an issue with a friend in another DG, an EP committee or a Council working group; and a MEP may mediate with party friends in Commission, COR, Council or even at home. Secondly, there is the personal *ambition* of an actor. Almost everybody wants to score with a dossier and to further their careers. By paying a person and his/her principal a compliment, a favour may be received in return, as courtesy usually repays in a comity of politics. Thirdly, there is *language*. Any binding decision is usually produced in English and published in every official language. Many a key word goes into translation without common definition, and no two languages have fully identical semantics, as a few examples will show. In the 1999 dioxin case (on polluted animal food), the French farmers could claim that the sludge they used (as such forbidden, but undefined in the text) was not sludge but fertiliser. In the euro-zone there is no common word for the English 'vigilance' that the ECB can issue in specific situations. For the word 'control', English has many near-synonyms like scrutiny, surveillance, supervision and oversight, which many other languages lack. Since 2002, the semantics of 'packaging' have been under continuous redefinition. In 2008 the Court had to solve the question of whether leaked oil falls under 'waste' or not (C 188/07). A clever lobby group makes use of language differences and always checks various translations on its EU website. In 2006, a Dutch trade association in fruits and vegetables found that in the Council Directive regarding Harmful Plants and Plant Products (EC 2002/89), composed in English, the 'operational overheads' of the phytosanitary inspection to be paid by importers (Article 13d) had been translated into Dutch (and German) as 'fixed costs', which is a much higher amount of costs; DGs SDT (translation) and SJ (legal services) can correct such an error.

Decisional factors. On every issue some stakeholders and officials are in favour of a common decision and others are against, thus there is always some room for pushing or blocking a decision or a policy as desired. As long as a dominant side is absent, every outcome is a matter of give and take or decision-making by compromise. For successful negotiations, at least two factors are essential. Firstly, one's demand regarding an issue at stake has to come on the agendas inside the EU's dealing rooms, because otherwise it cannot be taken into account. Hence, ambitious groups lobby for a position in, for example, an expert committee as this provides some control over the agenda. Secondly, one has to offer something of interest or advantage to important officials and stakeholders around, because without an interesting supply side, one will be neglected or opposed. By using green and white papers as sort of marketing tool, the Commission has developed a sophisticated method of both discovering the demand sides of important stakeholders and then making its supply side more attractive. Smart lobby groups always like to know the nightmares of other stakeholders, as this enables them to offer cheap remedies or to threaten more. In early 2000 Oxfam, an NGO lobbying for poor countries, found that pharmaceutical MNCs were reluctant to provide cheap medicines against HIV and Aids to poor countries out of fear of the re-import of the low-priced products to the rich countries. Their remedy became a regulation with a re-import prohibition (EC 953/2003). The use of decisional and other factors clearly requires much study and prudence.

Vectors to Create

The number of useful factors may be countless, but the number of potential vectors is as unlimited as human creativity. While in the factor approach the lobby group makes use of existing factors that can influence stakeholders and officials, it creates new ones in the vector approach. Vectors are newly constructed carriers or factors, comparable with the use of chemicals or GMO technology by a farmer or with the manipulation of supply and demand by a shopkeeper. The conditions under which stakeholders and officials operate are changed and constructed so that they increase the likelihood of getting a desired result. Of all three approaches, the vector method is by far the most sophisticated and becoming a trend-setting example provided by the smartest players. Major cases of cultural decisional, formal and operational vectors are the following.

Cultural vectors. Policy concepts, policy values and regime values provide excellent vectors. A different concept and even indicator can already earn one a trophy. In 1994, the wealthy Dutch province of Flevoland managed to receive a subsidy of more than 150 million euro from the regional fund ERDF by excluding from its poverty indicators its most wealthy commuters. In 2008 the Commission, wanting to earn less annual criticism of the Court of Auditors about its expenditures, proposed a new concept of 'tolerable risk of error' (COM 2008/866). Vector examples of policy values come from the German beer industry that feared an open beer market in the 1990s. Referring to its *Reinheitsgebot* of the Middle Ages, it first promoted the value of public health and, after this failed, that of the environment, by demanding that every empty bottle or tin should be repatriated to the country of origin, so imposing high transport costs for importers from abroad. In the early 2000s, the European textile producers, organised as ELTAC (now EuraText), promoted the policy value of children's rights, to get rid of cheap textile imports from the Third World that widely uses child labour. The Commission often pushes a regime value like OCM for europeanizing a policy domain that is weakly anchored in Treaty text, such as taxation, spatial planning or police co-operation, as an elegant means to catch reluctant stakeholders in the EU net. In the 1990s, the UK government was suspected of promoting EU enlargement ('widening') merely as means to hamper the trend towards a more supranational Union (its 'deepening'). Those wanting to delay or halt EU decision-making can do so by pushing regime values like impact assessment, transparency and subsidiarity. At the start of his Council Presidency in 2008, the French president Nicolas Sarkozy proposed publishing the minutes of the European Central Bank (ECB) meetings, so hoping to stimulate more political control over the ECB, an old French desire. The protection of a national interest is forbidden by treaty, but if called general interest it may be allowed. Creating such a concept or value is intended as a catapult towards a desired outcome. As a way of argumentation it is salesman's talk. The real art is to launch the next spectacular concept or value, as fresh and attractive as the young lady Lorelei of German legend; to this we shall return in chapter 6.

Formal vectors. Ranking tops here is the creative (re)interpretation and reframing of formal procedures and powers, as laid down in treaty texts and formal agreements. Such documents refer almost usolely to general issue areas like agriculture or health and seldom to specific issues, such as a new type of margarine that lowers cholesterol, by which they provide room for creative lobbying on procedures that should apply, for example those under agricultural or health law. Every fight over EU decision-making is ultimately not general but specific and may be won by bringing the specific issue under a different general label and thus under different procedures, powers and actors, and altogether a friendlier Commission DG, EP committee or Council work group. The arenas of agriculture, the environment or consumer affairs may indeed result in different outcomes for Unilever, the food producer seeking market admission for that new margarine in 1999 and obtaining this from DG SANCO in 2004. Regional lobby groups can make creative use of the tension between EC Treaty article 10 keeping national governments liable to the EU and the Court's 'Constanza' ruling 103/88 that attributes responsibility to decentralised government. Other popular procedural vectors involve the lobby on legislative procedure (secondary or delegated), the position of the EP (consultation or codecision), the voting in the Council (unanimity or majority) and the ways of implementation and inspection (European or national). At the end of the 1990s, the German government claimed that the Commission's draft Tobacco Ban Directive (EC 2001/37) was wrongly based on (then) article 100a of the EU Treaty and should have been based on article 129, which does not permit a ban at all, and this position was upheld by the Court, besides advising the Commission to apply article 129, thus leaving Germany a won battle and a lost war. Inspection vectors can be found under the notification procedure obliging governments to notify the Commission about their new domestic laws, and this enables lobby groups to hinder a competitor. All this requires much study, after which one usually finds room to manoeuvre. The Commission is frequently an expert on this. In 2007 and 2008 it sent to the EP and Council through communications (2007/704, 2008/227) its re-interpretation of article 8 of the 2004 Regulation (EC 2004/793) on slots in air transport, so replacing new secondary legislation with supplementary legislation.

Formal vectors can be created in even more *ingenious settings*. For the sake of simpler risk assessment of new food products, Unilever lobbied in 1999 (in 2003 successfully) for the establishment of a brand-new European Food Safety Authority, which like its US counterpart would act as a one-stop agency replacing the mess of current procedures. Another example concerns the internal tracking of a dossier, on which every institution is autonomous. Lobby groups know that those who control the tracks also have much control over the destination and are keen to lobby for or against a switch of tracks between the one and the other institution. In the late 1990s the health movement managed to move all responsibility over tobacco dossiers, once falling under DG AGRI, from DG ENTER (then INDUSTRY) to their bastion DG SANCO and to get it assigned inside EP and Council to the health officials there; on such logistics the health movement has been clearly superior to the tobacco industry. If a Commission proposal to a regulatory committee of comitology does not get sufficient support there, it must be forwarded to the Council and, if this has had a codecision position before, to the EP, which institution(s) then can overrule the Commission by (qualified) majority within a limited time; otherwise the Commission is the winner. An ingenious lobby group can win its case by first getting the Commission's proposal on its line and, if the committee is not positive, by creating strong divisions inside the Council and, if necessary, the EP, as French lobby groups managed to do on the free trade of transgenic maize in 1996 [Bradley, 1998; Töller and Hofmann, 2000].

Operational vectors. Many lobby groups exploit the EU officials' demand for special expertise, reliable information and solid support. The dream is to become their sole supplier of such scarce items, so encapsulating the official. By increasing their workload by volume or contents, one can more easily meet their demand. Making available or parachuting experts as staff members inside an institution is often done by lobbies from industry, farmers and the green movement. In 2001 the Dutch Ministry of Transport managed to get one of its experts nominated to the staff of the EP's Transport committee. At the Commission's management level, lobby groups can play 'meta-games', such as getting tasks and resources shifted from the one to another unit or outsourcing to a consultancy firm under their scope. Friendship, ambition and language again provide special vectors. *Friendship* in political settings is a diplomat's show of understanding and charm that most receivers appreciate, whether they are partners or opponents. Background information about the hobbies and lifestyles of high officials is for sale at some Brussels consultancies. One can serve the personal *ambition* of an official by, for example, promoting career opportunities or delivering good publicity. In the Babylonian EU, *language* is a crucial vector. To work in one's own language gives an advantage, as does preventing the opponent's language being used. One can try to get a loose or narrow translation of a word, as this may give room for manoeuvring afterwards or may destabilise a competitor. In 1991 Dutch Frisia Dairy was enraged by an EU decree prescribing in the Dutch text metal instead of carton packaging for milk products, which would oblige it to rebuild machinery. Finally the Commission qualified this to be a mistranslation of the word *boîte* (French working text) that was meant to refer to any sort of packaging, but according to Frisia Dairy it was a trick of mistranslation engineered by the French, their main competitors on the dairy market. Interest competition can heat up a fight over words. At the Council Summit of December 2007, the governments of France, Germany and the 'southerns' strongly opposed the view of Britain and the 'northerns' that trade agreements be based on 'reciprocal' instead of 'mutual' advantage, obscuring the real fight that the former word forbids protection of domestic industry and employment and the latter does not forbid and thus allows it.

Decisional vectors. A great vector here is the creation of a strong and preferably cross-sectoral coalition. In 1995 the steel regions managed to do this by bringing together local authorities, trade unions and steel companies under the umbrella of Caster, now Eira. A variant is the set-up of a BONGO or GONGO, such as the 2004 new EuroFed of Purple, the Peri-Urban Regions Platform Europe, set up by regional authorities thirsting after subsidies for urbanised areas. Setting-up a real or fake NGO is frequently useful, as it provides a finer title to operate and can yield subsidy and projects from the Commission for covering some fixed costs, by which the NGO can not only outbid commercial competitors on tenders by charging only variable costs (the fixed ones being subsidised already), but also influence the Commission through its report. Intelligent lobby groups also like to exploit newly arising issues and preferably dramas, such as terrorism in 2001 and food shortage in 2007, as these are usually followed by attractive budgetary allocations. Another game is the creation of a new decision-maker. In 2003 D/ Energy of DG TREN, after meeting opposition in the Energy Council for its proposal on Gas Market Security (EC 2003/55), managed to win as a compromise a new advisory committee under comitology by which it can take measures in emergency times. A different game is to raise or lower the intensity of an issue, so changing the outcome. In 2004 the chemical industry, organised in the ad hoc Alliance for a Competitive European Industry and wanting to get rid of the Reach-proposals from DG EN-VI, lobbied successfully to get an impact assessment first, so delaying the dossier. For assessing public support for new agenda-building, the Commission frequently uses its mass-survey Eurobarometer, as in 2007 on the use of cannabis that revealed wide majority support against this in the EU-25 [COM, Eurobarometer, 2007, 66] and under the Lisbon Treaty may soon result in proposals to limit it. In order to achieve a better compromise, a lobby group can majorate its demand, pay concessions, push or block an exemption, combine with another dossier (package dealing) or split a dossier, in short manipulate many parts of its demand and supply side. Great examples of dossier splitting are the treaties of Amsterdam, Nice and Lisbon, each containing many leftovers from their predecessor.

In order to bring the wide gap between ambition and success down to manageable size, the creative engineering of actors to approach, factors to use and vectors to create requires ever more proactive study or preparatory homework. This starts best with *proactive thinking* regarding actors, issues, time and many other conditions, as briefly indicated at the end of chapter 1 (Figure 1.2: from activity 5 to 1) and to be described in detail in the next chapter. By thinking backwards from the best possible (desired and realisable) end-result of lobbying to what has to be done from the beginning, the lobby group tries to engineer the most efficient and effective settings, so hoping to gather more anticipated influence beforehand. This PA work is not something done by amateurish lobby groups that score high on nonchalance and thus risk by definition, but only by professionals conscious of the possible causes of any event and prudent of the many consequences of any action.

The Meta-Game of Triple P

The pious wish for free and open competition on the market is well-known, where every producer or merchant yet dreams of becoming the monopolist.

As long as all merchants acting on freely accessible markets have the same ambition, they all end up as competitors indeed. However, thanks to their smarter buying and selling techniques, some may be successful in gaining a stronger position in their market, which thus becomes less open. On the EU political market, the behaviour of players is not much different. Many interest groups piously claim to love a level playing-field, but privately they almost all dream of a most unlevel playing-field, with themselves uphill in a sort of citadel and their opponents in a weak position downhill. The really level playing-field is only their next-best preference, much better than a downhill position.

The game of *Triple P* is intended to make a playing-field more lopsided by changing its regime. In this smart game, the lobby group tries to place, like pickets in the field, the friendliest *persons* in the best *positions* in the most beneficial *procedures*, establishing a position in an uphill citadel filled with powerful sticks that save on delivering carrots. As long as the EU process law is still in development, there is much room for this special game. The game must be played long before the match on substance (the ball) starts. Triple P is a most proactive and coherent meta-game that prearranges or re-arranges the playing-field in advance and thus limits the competitors' range of action. Those who have succeeded in arranging the field more to their comfort enjoy the great chance of subsequently scoring the ball when the real match begins. It is like playing billiards by *bricole*, and comes close to the proactive variant of the old technique of encapsulation. Every treaty formation is in essence a Triple P game that places pickets on policy fields, anticipating the years of fighting on substance. Both Commission officials and French lobby groups are often leading players in this game. When others start to argue over the substantial contents of an issue, they have already prearranged the playing-field and limited the other players' radius of action by their early settling of procedures, positions and people favourable to their cause. The meta-game of Triple P requires a systematic and coherent selection of vectors to create, factors to use and actors to approach, to be connected in a series and/or parallel setting. Its rich menu is regularly enriched with new discoveries (Figure 3.1). The game can be played in every arena, the EU (any institution or part of it), the stakeholders (for example inside a EuroFed) or domestically (inside the home organisation). Here we shall focus on the EU.

The First P, *procedures,* is not different from our category of formal factors and vectors, as far as they prearrange or rearrange the field. By getting a benign procedure applied to one's issue, one automatically gets a distribution

THE META-GAME OF TRIPLE P

P1: PROCEDURES AND PRINCIPLES, SUCH AS

- CONSULTATION OR CODECISION OF EP
- UNANIMITY OR (Q)MV IN COUNCIL
- COMITOLOGY, SUBSIDIARITY, OCM
- DEFINITIONS, REVIEW CLAUSES, DEADLINES

P2: POSITIONS, SUCH AS INSIDE

- COMMITTEES, WORK GROUPS, INTER-GROUPS
- COM DG, EP COMMITTEE, COUNCIL SG
- COUNCIL CHAIR, THINK TANK, EUROFED
- INSPECTION AGENCY/POLICY CONSULTANCY

P3: PEOPLE, SUCH AS

- BEFRIENDED COMMISSIONER, CABINET PEOPLE
- FRIENDS AND STAFF IN EP, ESC, COR
- COURT MEMBERS AND REFERENDARIES
- COM OFFICIALS (STATUTORY, SECONDMENT)

Figure 3.1

of formal powers that are fairly likely to protect one's interests. The benign procedure may be secondary, with the EP having codecision powers or not, and Council voting by unanimity or majority, delegated procedure or whatever other procedure is considered to be beneficial. The best choice requires a lot of preparatory homework, as in a game of chess. The issue may even be reframed in advance, so that it makes the benign procedure more suitable. For example, in the 1990 EU tender for food supply to Russia, French lobby groups in the meat trade managed to include in the tender conditions a definition of the size of cans for potted meat that were normal in France but strange to their Dutch rivals, and they won the tender. Under the First P there is, of course, much room for issue reframing as well. National market protection, as such formally forbidden, might be preserved through different procedures resulting from its reframing in terms of health, security, the environment or 'general interest'.

The Second P of *positions* is a mixture of formal and operational factors and vectors. The lobby group now tries to acquire directly or through friends (indirectly) crucial positions in a procedure of EU decision-making, like the position of chairman or rapporteur of a relevant EP committee or Council working group, and at very least to prevent opponents from getting such a position. The best position is frequently not the top of the formal hierarchy but one that confers daily control over the issue. French pressure groups have a traditional appetite for positions of chairman, and in doing so are often more formalistic than pragmatic [Legendre, 1993]. Their northern competitors often feel happier with low-key positions as *apparatchiks* who control the work. A position in a supervisory board close to a consultancy firm contracted by the Commission can also provide control over the advice given. The reframing of an issue can be part of the Second P game. Since the early 2000s, green lobby groups have managed to get various issues of agriculture, transport and trade reframed as issues of sustainability. So they obtain positions close to their friends in DG ENVI, where the proposals are prepared.

The Third P of *persons* is a mixture of mainly cultural and operational factors and vectors regarding actors found to be crucial. A friend or an associate in a relevant position in a beneficial procedure can give the finishing touch to the ball in the real match. Highly valued is the old friend who already shares values and perhaps interests and thus hardly needs a cultural massage. New friends can be won by stressing common values and creating common interests, based on the dossier and strengthened by personal characteristics such as policy preference, background or career. A good friend in a relevant position can distribute material resources such as staff and budget, and less tangible ones like information and support as desired. When the real match starts, the other stakeholders hardly have an alternative to coming along and offering a deal. A lobby group can always find a friend in, recruit from or parachute into all institutions and units and at all levels. On their recruitment and promotion, part of personnel policy, they frequently have fights with others, which gives them a personal agenda that might be met. By pushing such issues as representative versus merit recruitment, one can arrive at totally different outcomes of personnel selection.

The Triple P meta-game usually has a *bad reputation* among the players who are in a downhill position. They consider the covert framing of an arena before the match starts as unfair, Kafka-esque and sneaky. They grumble over the devilish manoeuvrings regarding such abstractions as procedures, positions and people in charge and say they prefer to play the real game on substance directly and openly. Many lobby groups making that sort of complaint are only sore and bad losers. Once they understand this meta-gaming, they often start to apply it and to appreciate its sophisticated efficiency and effectiveness. The aggression is then reassessed as a professional skill, the Kafka style as an interesting composition and the snake as part of the Paradise, worthy of enjoyment. In fact, there is hardly anything new about the Triple P game, as it is classical behaviour that can be found in, among other places, the politics of Rome, the Catholic Church, the Ottoman Empire and the Florentine republic [Loewenstein, 1973; Reese, 1996; Wright, 2004; Stout, 2005; Machiavelli, 1513]. At the EU level it simply has new applications. One paradox, encouraging to less smart players, is that the higher the number of lobby groups playing this meta-game, the lower the chance that a single one can prearrange the playing-field solely for its own benefit. Another paradox is that most lobby groups should feel familiar with the Triple P game, as this is quite common in most domestic systems, being much less open than the EU system. Anyhow, if a playing-field is unlevel, the cause may be that the lobby groups being down-hill have been nonchalant in their lobbying for a level field, their next-best preference, and at least have been ineffective. They pay by the higher risk of losing the substantial match that soon follows and should blame not the smarter others but only themselves for this.

Many examples of a Triple P game can be given. One is the 2002 *European Food Safety Regulation* (EC 178/2002), adopted on the eve of the fifth enlargement and in Central Europe widely seen as trick to keep their 'less safe' food products from the Western markets. This text of about twenty-four double-column pages does not contain any substantial decision on food safety and is, as a real Triple P text, only about definitions, objectives, principles, procedures, delegation of powers, bodies in charge and people to be recruited, including the set-up of the European Food Safety Authority (EFSA). After its adoption by Council and Parliament, the substantial match started under the Commission's delegated legislation, supported by the EFSA's Management Board that included persons from the French re-tailer Carrefour and the Anglo-Dutch producer Unilever, two of the lobby groups which pressed for this regulation. Another example of Triple P is the 2001/37/EC *Tobacco Directive*, proposed by DG SANCO in closed shop with anti-tobacco lobby groups, connected in series to both the EP's Health Committee and the Health Council, and having as its main contents the delegation of legislative powers to a regulatory committee (comitology) consisting of almost only 'health freaks'. A third example is the COM 2003/622 proposal from DG ENVI, an outcome of 'green' lobbying via the international route of the 1998 United Nations 'Aarhus Convention' [Bugdahn, 2008], that would give 'entitled' (green) lobby groups *privileged access* to information and participation, in short an uphill position. Opponent stakeholders, being sharp this time, achieved a milder compromise from the EP and Council, but in 2008 they still had to fight over the interpretation of wordings. A fourth example is Giscard d'Estaing's presidency of 'his' *Convention* that resulted in the 2005 pre-draft Constitution for Europe. As the composition of the Convention (third P) had been decided by others, he could only play with the first and second P, and he did this ingeniously [Tsebelis and Proksch, 2007]. A final example is the 2008 EU agenda-setting regarding 'the protection of *unaccompanied minors* in air-traffic', engineered in a closed triangle by DG JFS, police organisations and the NGO Child Focus, the latter presenting both sponsored research findings and precooked policy proposals on this matter to a televised meeting with invited stakeholders, so legitimising official EU support to selected proposals.

To the Central European farmers, the pro-tobacco groups and all other stakeholders having to fight an uphill battle from a downhill position for some time, we have *two consolations.* The first is that, according to standard EU legislative practice, there will be a review after about five years, which offers them a chance to recover and to realise if a win can be only temporary, so can a loss be too. The second consolation is that for achieving recovery, they as well can make use of Triple P. As they can hardly conquer by direct attack a citadel overlooking the surrounding fields, they have to do so indirectly, for example by positioning their troops in strategic places around the stronghold, trying to gain control over its supply lines and launching new mobilising values, such as consumer freedom and mental health in the current tobacco case. Attacking indirectly, they can rearrange the playing-field more to their advantage and beat the old citadel. The continuing battle therefore becomes a competition between different sets of Triple P and not of two teams around a single ball.

Structural Trends in the Management of EU Affairs

On the EU playing-field the countless public and private lobby groups have one thing in common: the ambition to win or at least not to lose a game relevant to their interests. They try to achieve this by one or more of the three aforementioned general methods on actors, factors and vectors. One trend is to combine the first method more often with the others, for example by playing the meta-game of Triple P. There are more specific trends. The major outcome of all change is an increasing *variation in lobbying.* Many

EU stakeholders show increasingly different preferences, approaches, resource lines, management forms, networks, lobby styles and the like. The major cause of it is their increased amount and intensity of competition. For the logic of this we refer to the previous chapters: the more the lobby groups smell relevant 'flowers and trees' in the EU policy gardens (supply side), the more they will act as 'birds and bees' trying to gather nectar (demand side) that is scarcer than in nature (competition). In addition to this deepening of the lobby competition, there is also a widening of it, due to the EU expansions and the growth of non-EU stakeholders. Their growing presence on the EU playing-field indicates the strength of the general factors behind their participation: strong desires, sufficient resources, irresistible compulsions and seductive invitations [Milbrath and Goel, 1977]. All together, their presence begins to overcrowd the playing-field at particularly the Commission, EP and Council, to limit the efficiency and effectiveness of lobbying and to require new responses. The following three specific trends can be seen as, at least partially, such responses. As always in sports life, these trends are set by a few players and more or less followed by many others. The few are apparently the quickest to learn and the most innovative.

From 'National Co-ordination' to Self-reliance

In the past the individual lobby groups wanting to influence EU decision-making preferred to take, as a matter of course, some national route to Brussels. At their micro-level, they contacted their national associations (meso-level) that stood at the crossing of routes to both their EuroFeds and central government (macro-level). The latter felt happy to try to collect all sorts of domestic interests, to co-ordinate them by both a procedure and some central office, and to defend the selected interests at its Council level. On the national playing-field, every government ministry thus had a triple position: as public interest group of its own (micro), as a sort of public association for interest groups in its policy domain (meso) and as participant in both its central government co-ordination procedure and at Council level (macro). For a long time its third role made some sense, as most EU decision-making then was still secondary legislation with, until the 1987 SEA, a veto position for the national minister in the Council. Thus, with the help of its central government, a domestic lobby group could at least block an undesired EU decision. With a few exceptions like the MNCs and the agricultural associations, most lobby groups lacked any experience and infrastructure for cross-border lobby activities. They felt uncertain and looked for help from their central government. This feeling has largely disappeared in the fifteen old member-states, but still exists in the new member-states.

Although all central governments still maintain such a procedure for 'national co-ordination' at the highest level (Cabinet, Prime Minister or President) [Kassim and others, 2000 and 2001; Wessels and others, 2003], they have found that it has become a 'quagmire' [Peters and Wright, 2001] or 'Byzantine mechanism' [Schneider and Baltz, 2005] that takes many players, interests, conflicts and time. Since the early 1990s, central governments hardly co-ordinate their own level effectively, not to mention the rest of their society, [Van Schendelen, 1993]. In usually only four cases they at least try to co-ordinate their influence on the EU, as part of their upstream vector: (a) if for upcoming Council meetings the national voting position has to be formalised, (b) if the national parliament pressures for a common position on some issue, (c) if there are heavy interdepartmental conflicts over an issue and (d) if the government still holds veto power in the Council. Even in these cases the attempt at co-ordination often comes closer to the creation of coherency between different views of ministries on paper than to the co-ordination of their behaviour, and thus it largely remains *symbolic co-ordination*. Besides, the rest of society is hardly invited to participate, making it not 'national'. The specialised ministry usually frames the voting position for the Council long beforehand, during the Commission phase. Most national parliaments receive symbols of coherency like solemn statements, promises and considerations rather than indicators of co-ordination. Conflicting ministries frequently prefer their common interest not to become co-ordinated centrally. Only in the case of a Council veto position can the central co-ordination, if attempted, be really effective in blocking an undesired outcome, but not for pushing a desired one. Due to the power of veto, the blocking could however also be achieved without co-ordination.

The growing new practice can be summarised by the catchword *self-reliance* [Van Schendelen, 1993]. Public or private pressure groups may like to co-ordinate others actively, but they abhor being co-ordinated by others passively. Those having a specific interest increasingly prefer to act on their own. This is the case with all sorts of interest groups, even those that otherwise preach co-ordination. Many trade associations wishing to co-ordinate their members prefer to bypass their national umbrella, and units of ministries often find their way to Brussels long before informing their co-ordinating office. Ministries of Foreign Affairs, which in most countries are charged with the dual task of both central government EU co-ordination and their foreign policy-making, frequently act self-reliantly at the EU level on their second concern. Already in the early 1990s, even from France, formally a most centralised country, more than one hundred interest groups, including units of central government, escaped their central co-ordinating office SGCI (under the Foreign Ministry), since 2005 re-positioned as SGAE (under the Prime Minister), by setting up their own lobby office in Brussels [Legendre, 1993], discretely called 'information bureau'. In most countries national co-ordination is now almost only requested by the national parliament wanting to bind the government formally, by the leading ministry wanting to control other ministries and by mass media smelling conflicts.

The trend of self-reliance, found among all sorts of interest groups, justifies the view that the EU is not a collection of member states but of member countries. The trend can be explained as a rational response of lobby groups to the challenge of finding more efficient and effective *road-mapping or navigation* from home to EU, particularly for the following four reasons.

(1) *Domestic divisions* on every EU issue is the natural state of affairs in every member country, more nicely phrased as pluralistic or democratic. The country or society always contains many more varied interests than the state alone, and the latter more than the central government which is internally divided. Where no 'national' interest exists, defined as 'shared by all at home', there cannot be 'national' co-ordination. No domestic lobby group can trust that its central government will back just its interests. By denying pluralism at home, a central government willy-nilly stimulates many domestic stakeholders to look after their EU interests self-reliantly. By excluding decentralised governments and private lobby groups from its co-ordination, the central government legitimises their self-reliance even more.

(2) *The benefits* of national co-ordination can only exist if the Council plays a crucial role and if the central government's position can make the difference there. As shown in the previous chapter, the Council usually plays a formally decisive role in only the last phase of about 15% of EU legislation. Under the QMV voting practice, a single member state rarely makes a difference anyhow. In the drafting and delegated phases of EU legislation, the position of central government is even weaker.

(3) *The costs* of national co-ordination can be enormous. A public or private lobby group relying on it runs all the risks of, for example, losing its case already there, mobilising opponents early, diluting its interests with heterogeneous other ones, being too late in the Commission phase or missing a rising European coalition.

(4) *The alternative benefits* of self-reliance usually outbalance both its costs and the cost-benefit ratio of 'national co-ordination'. This refers to the aforementioned factors of participation at the EU level. Every lobby group can get presentation or representation there. Competitors on its market or policy domain, frequently being already there, compel it to follow. The

Commission and EP really welcome well-prepared lobby groups.

This quadruple logic of self-reliance, based on considerations of efficiency and effectiveness, applies not only to the macro-level of central government, but also to the meso-level of national associations and even to the micro-level of public or private lobby groups. In the *open and free* European countries almost every specific interest group has the real option of self-reliance, by escaping some overarching structure or by-passing it silently. Rarely can the parent or sister organisation prohibit this effectively. For example, a central government has few legal means to keep domestic lobby groups at home, because private groups are free to move around and decentralised governments (regions, cities, agencies) usually possess some legal autonomy, which in federalised countries like Belgium, Germany and Spain is 'constitutionalised' for regions. Figure 3.2 gives a helicopter view of the main routes from home to the EU playing-field, with arrows indicating the upstream direction.

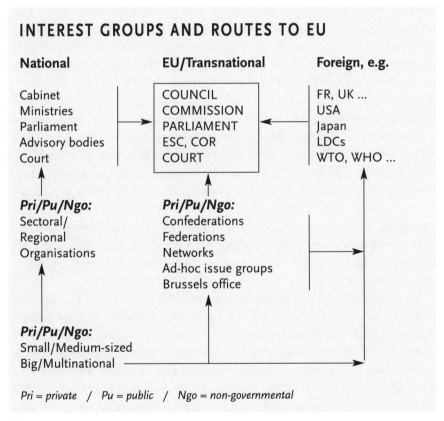

Figure 3.2

The menu of main routes consists of the following three:

1. *The national route* used either up to the meso-level of domestic associations and/or into the central government that is asked to transport the specific interest into the EU. This route is still used for the few dossiers falling under Council unanimity and by poorly informed or desperate lobby groups pleading for government help.

2. *The transnational route* to the EU, usually by way of membership of some cross-national platform, such as an ad-hoc group, informal network, homogeneous European federation (EuroFed) or heterogeneous confederation, necessary for aggregating and shunting the many different interests, and sometimes backed by a Brussels office. Except for national ministries, almost all domestic lobby groups use this route for gathering information and support intensely.

3. *The international route* that runs from home or a transnational platform via organisations in different countries inside the EU or elsewhere (like WTO, OECD, US, Japan, less developed countries/ LDCs) that can influence EU agendas and decisions. MNCs with global trade issues and NGOs on development, health and environment are smart users of this route via, for example, WTO (bananas, steel, sugar, textiles) and WHO (tobacco, pharmaceuticals), with the EU and the US as major negotiation partners, rendering lobbying in both Brussels and Washington relevant.

The road-map of Figure 3.2 is clearly full of lanes, junctions and round-abouts that can be used for *efficient navigation*. Into the EU lead many routes, usually without any dead end. Most lobby groups that leave the old national route take the transnational one first, usually by becoming a member of a platform there. From here they can also take the international route, as is frequently done also directly by multinational MNCs and NGOs with strong positions in various countries inside EU and elsewhere, and thus able to optimise their road-mapping even more. In daily life, the lobby groups' navigations or uses of the road-map allow the following observations, even for trends.

(1) *Multiple routes.* All main routes are used in practice. The national route is still used as well, but seldom exclusively anymore. If domestic lobby groups believe this route may support their case, they take it selectively and as supplementary to the transnational route. Many multinational lobby groups use all main routes, in series and parallel, thus also the many junctions and roundabouts. They practice multi-level public affairs: in their home country, different countries, on the global level and the EU.

(2) *Deviant governments.* Central governments still tend to go directly

from their national capital to their European one and particularly their Council building, Justus Lipsius. Single ministries tend to bypass most domestic stakeholders, such as decentralised governments and private interest groups, even when many of the latter hold strong positions around and inside the Commission and EP. They also seldom have a sort of EuroFed for the aggregation of their interests, but sometimes rely for this on bilateral meetings and largely on their Council meetings, including working groups there. Only a few take the international route to the EU.

(3) *Reversed arrows*. Running up is the reversal of some arrows in Figure 3.2. The one at the upper left, between central government and the EU, is in reverse the route to squeeze the government at home by lobbying at the EU level for new legislation that overrules domestic law. Another example is the arrow between domestic associations and the world of EuroFeds, which in reverse increasingly makes the former subsidiary to the latter. Particularly big-sized companies and NGOs, if direct members of such a EuroFed, cause this reversal.

(4) *Road mapping*. The general factors of participation at the EU level differentiate road-mapping as well. The desires, capacities, compulsions and invitations can all lead to a specific, personalised choice of navigation. This partially explains why the best established and often multinationally organised lobby groups, usually scoring high on all factors, tend to use so many routes in parallel and in series, and why so many lobby groups from new member states still largely rely on their standardised national route.

(5) *Intelligence*. As an essential part of any lobby, road-mapping should not be done at random, but as the outcome of much window-out intelligence or preparatory homework. Only then one can identify the best routes with the least obstacles and most support, navigate efficiently and effectively and arrive at a desired destination. Smart navigation is like intelligent shopping and should be prepared at home. Most lobby groups, however, are still rather nonchalant about road-mapping and simply take the route they see or are used to.

From Individual to Collective EU Action

Every lobby group would love to be the single player on the EU playing-field, but this is only a daydream. Even in the old Community of six member states interest groups always had to compete, also in a niche of a policy sector, but their number was clearly smaller then than now. Individual lobby action can in theory still be effective for blocking unanimity dossiers at the Council level but, as governments seldom really use their veto, it is hardly so in practice. Pushing for a positive decision in either the Council or other bodies requires collective action. In each niche of a policy sector, the number of competitive interest groups is presently so high that collective action is necessary more than eve . The pressure group may fly alone from home but, arriving near the EU playing-field, it usually has to become part of a *flock of birds*. It may still contact people around or inside the Commission, Parliament or Council individually, but such action is done for supplementary window-out monitoring and window-in negotiations on its interests that differ from the common ones. The latter are pushed by a collective approach through a body with common ears, eyes, face and tongue. As such, a coalition with other stakeholders is increasingly necessary. Anyhow, any lobby group can best anticipate it by early shared-listing, and as such getting returns on this for longer.

The factor providing the impetus for more collective action is the *logic of influence* [Schmitter and Streeck, 1999], which to some extent is related to the size of a political system. At the local level even a medium-sized interest group may have sufficient mass and weight to present its interest to officials. But at the regional, national and EU level, it needs to create more mass and weight in order to attract attention for its interest. In fact, it has to make the symbol M (weighty mass or sufficient support) of our PA-formula $E = MI^2$ (chapter 1) adapted to the relevant system. It does so by acting collectively: the single bird joins a flock of similar birds. In addition to this factor pushing collective action, there are pulling factors as well. Stakeholders around are always looking for those with similar interests and useful resources in order to join forces. Commission officials, wanting to interact with lobby groups at low costs of volume and content overload, prefer to do so not at the individual but at the aggregate level, and can even subsidise such group formation [Greenwood, 2007, 18; Broscheid and Coen, 2007]. Every lobby group has, in short, to puzzle about the optimal composition of a European platform or flock to join [Spencer and McGrath, 2008, 79-83]. This optimum is a subtle balance between homogeneity and control. With similar birds (homogeneity) the issues are shared, but the interests may be extremely competitive. As easy as the building of a common agenda is, the decision-making about it is as difficult because any outcome can change market or power positions. With different birds (heterogeneity) there is usually little community of issues and interests, by which the formation of a common agenda easily results in endless waffling or long-listing without effective scores. In the first instance most lobby groups prefer homogeneity, usually on a sectoral basis, with their direct competitors around the table. In addition they want to keep control over the collective action. Multinationally organised companies and NGOs frequently have a capacity of direct control

[Coen, 1998], but the large majority of lobby groups remain dependent on remote control via their domestic umbrella extended to the EU level.

The model for collective action is the more or less homogeneous European Federation or *EuroFed* [Greenwood, 2007], although many EuroFeds have become less homogeneous since the enlargements from EU-15 to EU 27. Groups with some specific interests in common meet together in such a transnational umbrella close to the EU machinery, as shown in the middle of Figure 3.2. Variants of it are the more heterogeneous confederation, the informal network, the specific ad hoc coalition and, as it is called, the European House with stakeholders sharing logistical facilities, such as the Renewable Energy House. Besides, many groups establish their own Brussels office, not only for supplementary window-out operations and window-in fine-tuning but also for control over their umbrellas. The national houses like Austrian House and Czech House have a similar function in providing a common office for their domestic regions and agencies. Most EuroFeds and their variants have a basically similar organisational form. There is a General Assembly with the national associations and sometimes also major individual organisations as members. Stakeholders from outside but active inside the EU like US companies and Turkish associations can frequently be members as well. The Assembly appoints the members of the Executive Board, supported by an Executive Committee and usually a small Secretariat or Bureau (mostly about six people). Through their preparatory work groups and procedures, the Committee and Bureau, usually the main players [EurActiv, 2009-B], push for the adoption of common positions. Many umbrellas suffer, however, from fragile vitality, due to shortcomings of sufficient homogeneity, experience, leadership, focus, following, prestige, cross-nationality, resources and stability [Greenwood, 1995, 44-7; EurActiv, 2009-B]. The management of a EuroFed clearly requires the highest PA skills internally.

In spite of such fragility, the collective platforms usually exert, as evidenced by casestudies [Greenwood and others, 1992; Mazey and Richardson, 1993; Pedler and Van Schendelen, 1994; Greenwood, 1995; Wallace and Young, 1997; Greenwood and Aspinwall, 1998; Pedler, 2002] and surveys [EurActiv, 2009-A-B-D], many of the following functions for their members:

– *providing a cross-national platform* for meeting, watching and listening to each other, in order to find out 'what there is in it for me';
– *common agenda-building* by aggregating the different interests of the members coming from various countries up to a long-list;
– *common decision-making* regarding the agenda, particularly the down-

sizing to and target-setting for both the shared-list and the short-list;
- *getting a more European face*, without which the lobby at the Commission is only a case of national attire or folklore and thus almost without any chance of success;
- *organising weighty mass* for an economic sector or policy domain, which title of representation is an influence asset in the eyes of the EU officials;
- *dividing the work of lobbying* (and saving on its costs), particularly by a common PA-desk and using technical experts from members for fine-tuned communication (expertise, language) with relevant EU officials;
- *serving as shopping centre* for pre-cooking both the aggregation of interests and the selection of stakeholders inside, if necessary for setting-up a separate ad hoc platform;
- *influencing the EU*, particularly by parachuting technical experts into the Commission's committees, attracting cross-sectoral supporters and negotiating window-in;
- *doing other business*, as competitors around the table are also useful after the meeting for making a market deal or policy initiative unrelated to the EU but interesting at home.

Of course, there is much *functional variation* among EuroFeds and even more among other variants of collective action. For example, the more heterogeneous a cross-national platform is, the less it functions as decision-maker for lobby actions and the more as a shopping centre for ad hoc coalition-formations. Like in air transport, most lobby groups use such a main port as means to switch to a preferred hub. Collective platforms have some disadvantages too, such as dilution of one's specific interest, internal dissent followed by stalemate, dependency on the platform for the quality of lobbying and, not least, distrust that in the end the gain is for a competitor and the pain for oneself. Therefore, only naive members of a common platform fully rely on only one platform. Intelligent lobby groups take safeguards, for example by using multiple routes, making multiple stops at different umbrellas, taking a strong position inside and installing a Brussels office. For them, a platform like a EuroFed is merely one route or means of influencing the EU, among many more. Anyhow, the positive functions or advantages of collective action are widely seen as outbalancing the negative ones or disadvantages. In fact, a good alternative is absent, not only because the shared-list method is the most efficient and effective, but also because the officials on the receiver's side of lobbying want to have this. Particularly the Commission officials require a cross-nationally aggregated interest, while single MEPs and Council people may be willing to support a national interest but can only push this through if colleagues from other countries receive the same preference, for which a cross-national approach is needed. On the receivers' side, there exists also some criticism of collective platforms, particularly for not sufficiently keeping promises of information or support, a lack of reliability that is usually caused by their internal instability [Warntjen and Wonka, 2004, 48].

The EuroFeds and their variants are a *voluminous phenomenon* of more than one-thousand settlements near Brussels [Broscheid and Coen, 2007; EPAD, 2008]. Companies and associations in pharmaceuticals meet in EFPIA, chemical ones in CEFIC, small- and medium-sized enterprises (SME) in UEAPME and food-producers in CIAA. NGOs, including GONGOs and BONGOs, have countless platforms that range from consumers' group BEUC, employers' umbrella organisation BusinessEurope and trade union confederation ETUC, to all sorts of social movements, from child care and environment to citizenship and development [Lahusen, 2004]. Many regional and professional groups have an EU body and face as well, for example steel regions in EIRA, big cities in EUROCITIES [Antalovsky and others, 2005], architects in ACE and journalists in AEJ. National police organisations have their FIEP, transport police TISPOL, agencies on shipping inspection ParisMou and those on car registration EReg. An umbrella is, however, seldom representative for the whole of the sector. There exist, for example, about 15 EuroFeds dealing with construction, 20 with packaging, 40 with environment and 75 with chemicals. Many of them are not broadly European for their sector, but limited to, for example, only southern or Teutonic countries or are area-specific, such as for some type of chemicals or the environment. In short, almost every domestic lobby group can find a European platform, even a fragile voluntary group such as on breast cancer for which there is EuropaDonna. There is only one big exception: national ministries are practically absent in the world of EuroFeds. Almost all take the Council as place for meeting ministries from other countries, whose main function of formalising secondary legislation in its end-phase is hardly compatible with most aforementioned functions of a EuroFed. By incident only, the Ministries of Defence, insofar as they belong to NATO located north of Brussels, have a cross-national platform useful for EU action. Since the mid-2000s, there has been a rapid growth of informal meetings initiated either by a Council and thus open to all ministries, or by a few and only open to them, such as the 'Sparing Six' on budget reform, the CEMT of some ministries of Transport and the Baltic Group. Sooner or later such meetings might develop into a full-fledged EuroFed.

The world of collective platforms is, not surprisingly, full of change. One major trend from the recent past is the rise of EU BONGOs and GONGOs, such as the EACF (a consumer's platform set-up by air-transport companies) and TISPOL (transport police, sponsored by the Commission). Another one is their supply of technical experts to the Commission in return for free tickets for seats in committees. A third one is their embedding in multiple routes for influencing the EU. In addition, *three new trends* can be observed.

(1) *Going cross-sectoral.* Many lobby groups search for a broader 'weighty mass' of support and use their platform(s) as a shopping centre for allies which can help to set-up a broader cross-sectoral ad hoc network. One cause is the increased heterogeneity of many EuroFeds since the new enlargements; another is the Commission's appetite for broader interest aggregation beyond sectoral borders. An example is EACEM, the EuroFed of the consumer electronics industry, whose major members (including Siemens, Thomson, Philips and Nokia) created such ad hoc coalitions with, among others, trade unions (on labour conditions), publishers (on intellectual property) and customers (on standardisations). The construction costs of such cross-sectoral ad hoc coalitions may be high but are limited in time, while the return on investment is considered better [Pijnenburg, 1998].

(2) *Subsidiarisation.* Most EuroFeds have been set-up by national associations but, according to a sample of 170 EuroFeds, one-third of them now accept (for financial reasons) major individual organisations as direct members [EurActiv, 2009-B]. The direct members then get better control over not only the EuroFed but also their national association(s). Through the former they can instruct the latter on its domestic agenda, setting as another new trend the subsidiarisation of national associations, often to the detriment of minor members like SMEs. According to a sample surveyed, most companies are members of two EuroFeds and almost half of them of more than five [EurActiv, 2009A]. Examples of direct membership are the CIAA (food products), the ECF (construction industry) and EPEE (energy-saving products). Some major regions and cities follow this trend by relocating to the building of CERM, the confederation of associations of local and regional authorities. National associations usually resist this trend when pressed by their major members and some, like BusinessEurope, with success.

(3) *Multi-level lobbying.* Many MNCs and also NGOs in the fields of the environment and health are increasingly connecting their multi-level lobbying inside the EU to the global level [Eising, 2004; Van der Heijden, 2006]. Through major countries and organisations they try to push or block decisions on, for example, trade issues (WTO), health (WHO) or the

environment (Aarhus Convention) and, serially or parallel, to get the EU committed to the outcome by laying it down in EU laws. An example is the World Business Council for Sustainable Development WBCSD, formed in 1995 by about 200 companies from twenty sectors, in order to influence the UN decisions on Climate Change, like the Kyoto Protocol 2005 and the planned post-2012 Climate Change Agreement. By implication, some early phases of EU legislation start much earlier and far away, so taking less alert stakeholders by surprise.

From Ready-made to Tailor-made Action

Until the 1980s, the individual lobby group usually showed little variation in its EU lobbying. Acting relatively *ready-made*, it took the traditional routes to its domestic umbrella and/or ministry and trusted on this linkage to the relevant EuroFed and/or EU institution. It hardly differentiated its approach for different issues, stakeholders and dossiers. From the side of the EU, there was equally little variation in responses to lobby groups that by number were as small as a village. At that time, much legislation was secondary and based on unanimity; the phenomenon of comitology had just been coined. Among the old Six existed a fair amount of common understanding. Inevitably, the lobby groups similarly reflected in their EU behaviour the characteristics of their association (sector, size, composition) and government, such as type of regime (presidential or parliamentary), structure (central or federal) and size (large or small). Such government-related differences of behaviour still exist, particularly in the new member states that often have lower scores of both self-reliant behaviour and membership of EuroFeds. Increasingly, they are being replaced by country-related differences that show more variety, such as rich versus poor countries, 'Catholic' versus 'Protestant' administrative cultures and industrial versus agricultural countries.

As a consequence, all differences are becoming less clear-cut, making each of them less dominant and the domestic factors of lobby behaviour more varied. The interest groups acting more self-reliantly and discovering the world of EuroFeds demonstrate in their behaviour even less the imprints of their government or country and more those of their own organisation and allies. They are *pushed toward tailor-made* rather than ready-made lobby actions. They reflect, first of all, their organisational traits, such as size (large versus small), sector (industry versus services), focus (profit-oriented or not) and status (private versus public), and, secondly, their specific interests on current issues. This trend ensures that two multinational food producers or two public health insurers from the same country may behave quite differently on the EU playing-field. The same may be true for two food-policy units from the same central government, one belonging to the Ministry of Health and the other to that of Industry. In spite of their similarities of nationality, public accountability, control by politicians, bureaucratic procedures and food domain, they behave differently in the EU.

As far as there exists one single determinant of EU lobby behaviour, it is more and more the perceived relevance of an EU arena *pulling toward tailor-made lobbying*. The perception may start as a Pavlovian reaction caused by old domestic culture and structure, but seldom remains so among the self-reliant lobby groups that assess a new EU arena as either a threat or an opportunity and develop a plan of action. If they want to interfere on the EU playing-field, they try to construct an efficient route to the EU and to develop an optimal coalition there. Arriving at the EU side, they make their choice from the rich menus of actors, factors and vectors, including the meta-game of Triple P, and also from the oversupply of multiple issues, stakeholders, access points and routes available there. They set the trend from ready-made towards tailor-made behaviour. As such they behave like the self-reliant chess player. Kasparov does not play in a standardised and thus predictable way, but always varyingly and thus surprisingly. Even more than the chessboard, the EU playing-field requires a tailor-made approach, simply because it offers a countless number of options. Here there is no limit on time, players or rules, and there is even not just one ball or one referee. An EU match is potentially infinite.

Even lobbying styles become tailored, so producing more *campaign variety*. For example, the formal request to the Commission or the Parliament is increasingly shaped by preceding semi-formal activities through expert groups or inter-groups and even more by informal lobbying. As in marriage, the desired support is usually gathered informally, subsequently safeguarded by a semi-formal engagement, and formalised only at the successful end; reversing this order will bring bad results. Support from somebody else, which is usually led by the question, 'What's in it for me?', is not gained by one's demand side (which is better kept secret for some time) but by one's supply side adapted to the other's demand side, even if it is only a showcase of charming flattery. The intelligent and prudent lobby group tailors its own profile, usually beginning not with a high profile, but low-key and quietly. This style is less upsetting to the desired partner and causes less alarm to competitors. The high profile is kept in reserve for emergency situations. A relevant person is not simply approached directly but indirectly, such as through a trusted contact, a friendly coalition, an authoritative mediator or another effective U-turn. All this (and more) tailoring requires much study and prudence in advance and during any game. It serves the ambition of escaping the overcrowded arena of competitors and pushing the buttons of Brussels more efficiently and effectively, in short, to achieve greater success. We shall return in the next few chapters to this professionalization of EU lobbying that results from the third trend. First we will present short country profiles of EU lobbying that show variations of imprints.

Extra: Country Profiles of EU Lobbying

Self-reliance, EuroFeds and tailor-made lobbying can be taken as catchwords for the three new trends that result in the conclusion that generalisations about, for example, French or Spanish EU lobbying can hardly be made. Yet, frequently the question is posed whether there still exists something like a national approach to EU lobbying. The answer requires synchronic comparison. The problem, however, is that thorough comparative research on the national styles of EU lobbying hardly exists. Only a few studies give some insight. In the mid-1960s, the styles were qualified [Spinelli, 1966] as 'the easy and smoothly operating Belgians, not making too much trouble'; 'the most difficult and obstinate Dutch, distrusting their southern neighbours and niggling about the most minute details'; 'the opportunistic Italians, with their fine sayings and lazy doings, and more obsessed with Rome than Brussels'; 'the dedicated Germans, wanting to reacquire esteem and acting with great sense of primordial duty'; and 'the ambivalent French, being both antagonistic and constructive, sending their best officers, and holding them to co-ordinated instructions'. The modest Luxembourgers were overlooked. In fact, Spinelli based his qualifications mainly on the behaviour of the six member-state governments at the Council level. Another study [Van Schendelen, 1993] described the trends towards self-reliance and tailored actions for different countries, broken down into public and private players. The many studies that compare countries on their adaptation to the downstream of EU decisions provide supplementary insights useful for our upstream focus [Rometsch and Wessels, 1996; Meny and others, 1996; Hanf and Soetendorp, 1998; George and Bache, 2001; Kassim and others, 2000 and 2001; Wessels and others, 2003; Bulmer and Lequesne, 2005]. In addition, there are a few studies based on the views of practitioners in the field, as recorded in interviews [Kohler-Koch, 1998] and memoirs like Spinelli's above, in addition to single country studies to be mentioned below. Because of the lack of systematic research, the following summary of country profiles can only be a tentative sketch, to the best of our knowledge. It is limited to the member countries and thus leaves aside the EU lobbying from outside the EU, for example from candidate countries such as Croatia, Turkey and the western Balkan states [LaGro and Joergensen, 2007], non-EU European countries such as Switzerland and Norway closely connected to the EU by bilateral treaties [Church, 2006; Archer, 2004] and US companies [Winand, 1998]. Our focus is on the three structural trends above and on major alleged characteristics of behaviour. It is divided into three sections: the five old larger countries, the ten old smaller ones, and the twelve new ones of Central Europe.

The Five Old Larger Countries

French interest groups have an old reputation of acting under co-ordination by the central government, in particular its SGAE office that succeeded the SGCI in 2005 and now falls under the Prime Minister. Part of this reputation is dubious. The large-sized SGAE (in 2007 employing 183 people, largely at management level) is partially an internship programme for young graduates from the *hautes écoles* on their way to the ministries and agencies. Its main product is not co-ordinating EU actions but making different policy views more coherent on paper and so instructing the French PR in Brussels (with more management staff), out of the belief that effectiveness will follow [Guyomarch and others, 1998, 53-60]. This bureaucratic approach to EU affairs takes much time, which is rationally managed by planning early and storing memory, two outstanding qualities of SGAE. However, conflicts between the *Elysée* (President), *Matignon* (Prime Minister) and *Quai d'Orsay* (Foreign Affairs) often weaken even coherency, especially in times of *cohabitation* when the first two have a different party-political colour. French ministries, agencies, companies, regional authorities, professional groups and other interest groups tend to perceive issues at the EU level differently and, paying lip-service to Paris, go to Brussels self-reliantly, even by setting-up their 'information bureau' there, as stated before. The main exceptions to this rather pluralist pattern are the issues falling under the President, such as security, Treaty reform and a few others. However, the old power patterns inside France have been rapidly changing since the mid-1990s, through both constitutional change and trends of decentralisation and privatisation, which provide more EU lobbying room to decentralised governments and private sector groups [Elgie, 2003; Culpepper and others, 2006]. Common among many French groups is that they are driven by well-organised self-interests [Drake, 2005; Grossman, 2007]. Agriculture, with its many small farmers, is run by strong umbrella associations. Industry, from chemicals to utilities, is highly concentrated and run by multinationals. A *pantouflage* (circulation) of leaders gives major companies close connections with ministries in Paris and often even a special desk and funding there, although this is in decline now. NGOs and trade unions largely lack such a privileged position.

At the EU level, most French interest groups prefer positive rather than negative integration and specific rather than general legislation. Lobby groups in external trade are frequently biased in favour of *mercantilism* (market closed for imports and open for exports). Centralised political planning, with strong input from experts and led by a hierarchy, is still popular, but now at the lower level of the acting lobby groups. Inside the EU machinery, originally of French design, the French usually turn the Triple P game into an art form, particularly regarding the formal actors, factors and vectors. A special unit of SGAE supports the ministries in getting their people nominated as high officials in procedures they have engineered before, treating Brussels as another Paris. But often they mistake this meta-game for the end game, by attaching more value to the formal setting than to the practical outcome. Critical reports about French lobbying at the EU level have recently been published by the National Assembly (under number 1594) in 2004, the Chamber of Commerce of Paris (report Karpeles) in 2005, the Ministry of Economy, Finance and Industry (report Dassa) in 2006 and the State Council (document 58) in 2007. This self-criticism concerns failures at the EU output-side, such as loss of power, declining subsidies and Court procedures, all due to French nonchalance at the EU input-side, where many French officials rigidly stick to their introverted plan of action and neglect the tailoring of their lobbying. Their behaviour is often formal, demanding and, in the final phase, loud and direct and thus not very effective and much unlike their style in their old *anti-chambre*. They are more inclined to apply traditional influence techniques like encapsulation and coercion than modern PA techniques, although the latter is slowly arising as shown by new PA circles like the AFCL.

British interest groups are marked by self-reliance. There is a Cabinet Office for EU Affairs, but it has fewer than ten staffmembers, circulating among the ministries. In addition to its standard preparation of the UK voting position in the Council, it works mainly for settling interdepartmental conflicts and for special interests of the Prime Minister. The number of such conflicts is usually small, because the last thing quarrelling ministers want is interference by the Cabinet. The special interests of the Prime Minister are frequently inspired by party politics, not to say the survival of the party as the EU is a sensitive issue-domain at home. Strongly voiced Cabinet demands usually concern domestic values such as sovereignty, subsidiarity, rebate (return on financial contribution) and open market, all indicating the low interest of this 'awkward' country in European integration [George, 2000; Geddes, 2004]. The practice of self-reliance was encouraged under the Thatcher cabinets, as a side-effect of her general ideology of privatisation that kept interest groups responsible for their EU affairs. The central government applied this belief internally, for example by setting-up a personnel policy for its civil servants ('no career in London if no experience in Brussels'), which has become a model for many other countries.

This *privatisation* of EU management has prompted many UK interest groups to apply modern PA management they had discovered at home in the 1970s, earlier than elsewhere in Europe, and to develop their own EU routes, alliances, agendas and entrances. When the UK government did not participate in the EU Social Protocol and the EMU, it found British trade unions and financial organisations (the City) among the EU lobby groups that opposed the UK and supported EU social and monetary policies [Giddings and Drewry, 2004; Bache and Jordan, 2006]. Many UK companies, regions and NGOs have given birth to new EuroFeds, and Birmingham has been the first city ever to establish a lobby office in Brussels. Usually the British prefer negative rather than positive integration, general rather than specific legislation, and hard rather than soft law, bringing them frequently in opposition to French desires. They have also stimulated the birth of EU agencies and regime values as 'better regulation', the latter officially for improving EU policy-making but in practice also for re-launching issues and delaying policies. Their lobby style is often at least partially tailor-made: informal and indirect during agenda-building, but visible and demanding during negotiations. They like to create nuisance value, even if they have no interest in the issue at all, in order to get compensation for their support to a compromise (which in the English language is an unpleasant word). Partially as a result of their feelings of discomfort with both the formal institutions and the semi-formal work floors, the British lead in PA consultancies.

German interest groups in the EU often show the imprints of their decentralised state (called 'federal'), their sectoralism and the economic weight of their organisations [Maull, 2006; Green and others, 2007]. The country has not one government but, coming from twenty-five during its empire, sixteen (the regional *Länder*) plus the Federal one in Berlin now, all fully equipped with their own ministries, parliament and court. Like a smaller-sized EU, the country is more a community of laws than of values, formalistic more by consequence than by cause and accustomed to multi-level relationships. This makes it feel at ease in the real EU. The federal government has always followed a pro-integration course and, probably caused by the memory of wars, it did so in a very compliant way, not giving expression to its economic and demographic weight; since 1998 the post-war generation, starting with *Kanzler* Schröder, behaves more like other governments. The German regional governments are frequently less EU-minded than their central government, and less than most regions in other countries, as they fear to lose their strong position towards Berlin to a stronger 'Brussels'. They all have a Brussels office that they use also for watching both each other and the federal PR there. Through their *Bundesrat*, the *Länder*-controlled federal 'Upper House', they take the German seats of the Council working groups for dossiers falling under their competence at home. All ministries at the two levels tend to cherish the *Ressortprinzip* of rigid sectoralism, deepened by their *Expertenkultur*. Due to its internal disagreements, Germany is represented in many Council meetings by more than one minister and/or has to abstain from voting or to reject a proposal, and subsequently ends up resorting to the Court. National co-ordination is, in short, more a German daydream or nightmare than a reality. The implementation of EU decisions at the decentralised level at home is another common problem, resulting in a lot of infringement procedures. In short, the upstream and downstream to and from the EU are full of domestic veto points [Dyson, 2003].

German private lobby groups usually prepare their EU positions self-reliantly and thoroughly, drafted by many experts and signed by a hierarchy of chefs, much like their ministries. They usually prefer to further their interests first via a German platform on a sectoral and/or regional basis, and/or a public-private partnership *(Konkordanz)*, and from here to a European platform and finally the EU institutions. Many also have an office in Brussels. Due to their multiple internal deliberations among experts and chefs, again like their own governments, they frequently arrive late on the playing-field, fall short of tailor-made lobbying and thus are dependent on more formal approaches in the end-phase of EU decision-making. With British-style negotiations they have difficulty; the German word for offer means not supply but sacrifice. Their lobbyists in the field usually have limited mandate, meaning they have to wait for new instructions from headquarters, while the EU match is going on. Demanding and vociferous behaviour is, however, seldom a characteristic of German lobby groups. In many cases, this is less a result of a tailor-made approach than of their fortunate position in the middle between the French and the British regarding issues of positive versus negative integration, general versus specific legislation and hard versus soft intervention. Since the early 2000s, the country has shown growing interest in PA management and the set-up of PA platforms.

For *Italian* interest groups, self-reliance is less a choice than a necessity, because the country has had since 1946 a new Cabinet every year on average and thus no stable central government [Bull and Rhodes, 2007; Cotta and Verzichelli, 2007]. The fragile state is fragmented by the *partitocrazia* of volatile party politics, regional antagonisms and strong competition between big companies. It suffers from a fragile legal system, corruptive practices and clientelism. The government, since 1870 mostly the forefront of twenty regional republics gaining in power with every change of the constitution, is more or less kept together by the formalistic bureaucracies of 'Rome'. Here the President's Council, the Ministry of Foreign Affairs and the Ministry of European Affairs cover EU affairs officially, and thus no one body does in actual practice. Other ministries have their own EU operations, as do regional governments, major associations and most multinationals. Finding that the central government takes too much time with formalities and hardly achieves EU successes, they all prefer to be self-reliant, out of necessity. The private interest groups usually operate through their domestic umbrellas, like *Confindustria* for business, that are linked to EuroFeds. About 120 Italian front-offices *(antennas)* in Brussels represent regional and local governments, industrial sectors, companies, institutions and NGOs [Raffone, 2006].

On the input side of the EU machinery, the Italian interest groups and particularly the ministries have the reputation of more words than deeds, except for the collecting of subsidies. Frequently, they are absent in the EU drafting phases, applaud whatever the EU decides and, if working inside the institutions, live with their minds planted in their network *(apartenenza)* of Italian politics. The country's record of implementing EU laws is usually one of the poorest in the EU, even on the correct spending of subsidies. Since the early 2000s there has been, however, some change in the air [Franchino and Radaelli, 2004]. The tighter inspection practices of the EU have begun to make Italians on the EU input side more alert. Yet the report on those 120 Brussels offices assesses their quality as mainly poor: locked in domestic and not EU logic, weak on strategy and tactics, fragmented on interests and amateurish. Some regional and sectoral groups from northern Italy increasingly set the example of professionalization now. They play the EU game not only with charm, informality and secrecy, so reflecting old virtues of their domestic politics, but also by making sophisticated alliances, such as the public-private coalition between the region of Piemonte and its main company Fiat or that of, as it is called, the 'horizontal' axis running from the Lyons region in France to the state of Slovenia, with the region of Lombardy in the middle. In 2004 the Commission concluded a Tripartite Agreement with the Italian central government and the government of Lombardy on the implementation of transport mobility rules, the first agreement ever between the EU and a regional government.

Spanish pressure groups in Brussels reveal their own mixture of domestic features, particularly that of traditional versus modern ones. Coming from centralism under Generalissimo Franco until 1975, Spain has become one of the greatest success stories of modernization thanks to the third enlargement in 1986 [Magone, 2008; Closa and Heywood, 2004]. It is now a German-like federal state of seventeen more or less autonomous regions, all with a facility in Brussels. Both party politics and formalistic bureaucracies like those in Italy characterise the central government in Madrid. As in France, most public and private interest groups rely on the EU for experts and approvals from chefs, with *coherencia* on paper as the ultimate criterion of success. The main example of active EU lobbying is the *Junta de Catalunya*, the first ever with a regional office in Brussels. Some recently emergent multinational companies in sectors like banking and telecom have become active on EU affairs as well. The many small-sized interest groups start their collective action at home through numerous domestic umbrellas that go the long route to Brussels self-reliantly.

On the playing-field in Brussels, Spanish lobby groups are notorious for arriving late, particularly at the Commission level. Like the Germans, they spend too much time at home. Unlike the Italians, they remain committed players, keeping their words more in line with their deeds. Often discovering new proposals for legislation at a fairly late stage, they tend to resort to the next-best game of the *exemption lobby*, which is largely a Spanish innovation of EU lobbying and common practice now. Not wanting or able to block the proposal, they try to attach an additional article giving Spain an exemption to the rule for a number of years, as happened on the 1997 Telecom Liberalisation Directive. Like the Italians, they do not comply with the law but, unlike them, they manage to make this vice legal. Another Spanish speciality, also a next-best game and an exception to their slow behaviour, is the *subsidy lobby*. Many regional and sectoral lobby groups tailor their actions in this area. Frequently low-key, indirect, charming and informal, they try to influence the Commission by Triple P on the objectives and conditions of the subsequent subsidy programmes, so increasing their chances of milking more euros. Spanish negotiators at the Council level, mainly coming from central government, frequently exhibit however the exact opposite styles, making them unpopular here.

The Ten Old Smaller Countries

In the past, major *Dutch* public and private interest groups, believing that their small-state position is best protected by the Commission and not the Council, and that their welfare with an export ratio of about 55% of GDP is most dependent on an open market, held a utilitarian preference for more supranational and negative integration [Van Schendelen, 2002]. In 1992, both left- and right-wing political parties became critical of EU integration, and this attitude had an effect on the Cabinet (always a fragile coalition), central government and the citizens that rejected the draft Constitutional Treaty in 2005. The interest groups have numerous domestic umbrellas linked to EuroFeds, in which Dutch people disproportionally run secretariats that give power over agendas, meetings and budget. They feel at ease on EU collective platforms. Most act self-reliantly, many have a Brussels office, and a minority is a direct member of EuroFeds. Trendsetters are Dutch multinational companies (like Unilever, Philips) and some NGOs (environment and labour). Many decentralised governments and SME umbrellas followed their example. Dutch people working in EU institutions score low on nationality [Suvarierol, 2007]. Although in Europe the country is second to the UK on adopting PA management, most groups have difficulty with tailoring their approaches. The Dutch in the EU often see their demands as a generous offer to Europe and so have earned the reputation of being spontaneous, direct, loud, impatient and, as apparatchiks, semi-formal when lobbying on their long-list and often with free mandate, in short amateurs. Belonging to 'the first republic of Europe' (Montesquieu), they see courtesy as intrigue. By such behaviour, many Dutch experts on an EU work floor often upset their PR. The travelling lobbyists often turn their living at about two hours from Brussels into a disadvantage, by arriving in the morning and leaving in the evening, thus neglecting all informal networking. Their PR has since 1994 been eccentrically located in a Brussels suburb near the highway leading homewards, but in 2010 it will take offices near Place Schuman.

The *Belgian* and *Luxembourger* interest groups belong to young states. Belgium has a low sense of nationalism and unstable central government [Swenden and others, 2006]. Due to their high export ratio (about 65% of GDP), the two countries usually give strong utilitarian support to open market integration, except Luxembourg for its banking (protected). Their behaviour can best be characterised as 'pragmatism', the academic word for lacking a clear pattern of behaviour. They can afford to behave so because, living at an extremely short distance from Brussels with its lobby density [Van Schendelen, 2008], they can hardly escape informal networking, and they enjoy the overrepresentation of countrymen at almost all levels of the Commission, roughly one-fifth of all personnel. Due to their language issue at home, most Belgian groups are organised at only the regional level and along this line linked to EuroFeds. The three major Belgian regional governments (Flanders, Wallonia, Brussels) have their own people inside the Belgian PR, and their ministers circulate in Council meetings. The governments of Belgium and Luxembourg are French-styled party-politicised bureaucracies, driven by experts and bound by formalistic chefs. Their internal distrust makes private groups distrustful, too. Their behaviour looks tailor-made: informal, silent, indirect and charming. They are well-known for taking free rides on stronger foreign lobby groups, but this free-riding is mainly the result not of PA skills but, due to the lack of it, out of necessity and thanks to their 'Catholic' nose for opportunities. In 2006, the Flemish government set-up the public-private desk VLEVA for supporting its interest groups in the EU.

The *Nordic* countries (Denmark, Sweden, Finland) score high on nationalism, decentralisation and open market orientation, although Finland has met this profile only since its liberalisation from Soviet control [Raunio and Tiilikainen, 2003]. Their pressure groups have many conditions in common. Brussels is far away, which is a hindrance for frequent and intense informal networking. Lobbying at the EU level is under critical debate, so indicating only partial acceptance. Their few multinational firms such as Carlsberg, Scania and Nokia apply PA methods. Most small-sized interest groups approach Brussels only indirectly via their domestic association, public-private network and their PR. Their governments hardly intervene in their lobby behaviour, except when their national parliament uses its power to instruct a minister on the national vote in the Council; the Danish parliament has started the now common practice of a parliamentary desk in Brussels. The value of parliamentary democracy is often at odds with that of EU success, as an instructed minister can hardly negotiate. To solve this problem, the new trend is that the government drafts the parliament's instruction. Coming from wealthy countries that appreciate welfare, the Nordic groups inside the EU usually support careful spending and both social and environmental policies. Their 'Protestant' culture of transparency and accountability makes them supporters of such regime values at the EU level and means their capitals leak much information from inside the Council, otherwise the oyster of Brussels. By keeping their words in line with their deeds, they have the reputation of predictability, which may reduce their lobbying effectiveness. Tailor-made behaviour comes from only the few multinational companies and national umbrellas. Interest groups from central government, however, often excel in direct, formal, vociferous and demanding behaviour, especially at the Council level.

Irish, Portuguese and *Greek* interest groups have, of course, many differences of their own. Not least among them is the Irish reputation for saying 'no' to Treaty change, which is stimulated by its domestic constitution that prescribes a referendum for this. On policies, most Irish groups have strong interests in the issue areas of industry, trade and open market [Coakley and Gallagher, 2004], while those from Portugal and Greece prefer protected agriculture and small enterprises. Irish groups act highly informally and via public-private networks, often led by their few MNCs. They meet in, for example, their Irish pub Kitty O'Shea in Brussels, which functions as a sort of informal PR for all Irishmen. Portuguese and Greek groups come from much more formalistic societies. Their governments like to control their ministries and to intervene in the private sector, which by the absence of MNCs lacks counterweight. Without sufficient size and other resources, most private groups can hardly act self-reliantly. For the remote control of the EU, they are dependent on their domestic government and umbrellas often linked to that government [Pari, 2003]. Their governments put more effort into the production of coherent position papers at home than in lobbying in Brussels, except on the Council level. The three countries have, however, much in common too: they are small-sized and at a far distance from Brussels; clientelistic party politics and rising regionalism fragment all three; their people usually play a marginal role on the input side of the EU machinery, thus relying much on their Council position; like the Spanish they keep their focus on lobbying for both exemptions and subsidies; they have achieved a great reputation for milking structural funds; their records on implementing EU legislation and subsidies as required are weak. In tailoring their actions, the Irish are more politic than the Portuguese and the Greek, especially by acting informally, charming and low-key, as they do at home. All three countries are largely unfamiliar with PAM.

Austrian pressure groups, finally, are stigmatised by national corporatism, the academic euphemism for being held together by distrust. Believing in formal authority, they see the Council as decisive, and many hold positions inside the Austrian PR, partly for observing the others there from the federal level, the nine *Länder* governments, the organisations of employers and workers, and major business groups like the Chamber of Commerce and banks. This unique PR, entitling the members to sit in Council working groups, is the Austrian innovation of EU influence practices, though hardly followed by other countries. Some other lobby groups have their own desk in Brussels or sit in the Austrian House. Various government units at both the federal and the *Länder* level try to co-ordinate all Austrian public and private groups, thus nobody does. These units, in their turn, often receive instructions from the formally powerful parliaments at both levels, causing the same tension between domestic democracy and EU effectiveness as in the Nordic countries. MNCs, which might act as trend-setters in lobbying, are absent. Broader group formation at home is difficult and time-consuming by mutual distrust. Consequently, many groups often arrive late in EU processes. Since some have their own links with both the EU work floors and EuroFeds, there is a rising trend toward self-reliance, particularly among the regions. Tailor-made actions remain exceptional, but on many EU dossiers Austrian groups are part of the winning coalition. The main cause is that, like the Germans, they frequently hold centre positions that lie close to the final compromise. An example is the EU policy of protected farming, at issue between countries like the UK and France, but under the flag of Sustainable Agriculture adopted and approximating the Austrian practice of farming. As in Germany, attention for PA-methods is growing.

The Twelve New Central and Eastern European Countries

Systematic observations of EU lobby behaviour are scarce for the twelve Central and Eastern European Countries (CEEC), from the Baltics in the north to Cyprus and Malta in the south, which joined the EU in 2004 and 2007, respectively, than for the fifteen older members. The following is largely based on some general books [Grabbe, 2005; Schimmelfennig and Sedelmeier, 2005; Epstein and Sedelmeier, 2008], specific country studies, articles, lobby cases, reputations on the playing-field, personal experience and general background data [Circa, 2008]. Easy generalisations cannot be made. The countries show a lot of *differences*, of course, such as in size (the village-state of Malta versus big Poland), language (eleven different ones), age (old empires like Poland, Lithuania and Hungary versus the brand-new state of Slovenia), recent history (the 1956 uprisings in Hungary and Poland, the 1968 one in (then) Czechoslovakia, the 1993 separation between Czech and Slovakia), regionalism (arising in Poland and Hungary, similar patterns existing before 1939), ethnic composition (with the special cases of the cross-border Hungarians and the Roma), economic sectors (industrial Hungary and Slovakia versus agricultural Poland and Lithuania), foreign conflict (Cyprus with Turkey) and political system (parliamentary Estonia and Czech versus presidential Poland) [Krouwel, 2003].

Yet many of the new members also have *common characteristics*. Except for Cyprus and Malta, they have all been under occupation by first Germany and then the Soviet Union from the late 1930s until the late 1980s. Except for Slovenia (established in 1991), they all have had some form of independence before, even if only for a short time (Baltic states) or under protectorate status (Slovakia). Their people show a great sense of nationalism and sovereignty and many cultural differences between generations. According to socio-economic data (DG ESTAT) and compared to the old fifteen, all countries score high on poverty, dependency on family assistance, unemployment, cheap labour, reliance on agriculture, lack of MNCs and low exports to the EU. Their economies are highly informal (untaxed payments) but are undergoing rapid transformation towards Western economic practices. They score high on educational quality and (until the 2008 financial crisis) economic growth and better balanced government budgets; many countries are trying to get prepared for adopting the euro, while Cyprus and Malta have joined already. Some countries also score high on corruption, for which reason the Commission froze EU subsidies to Bulgaria and Romania in 2008. The political systems of the ten formerly communist countries show a rapid transition from totalitarian to limited government, from one-dominant party rule to multi-party, from dependent agencies and courts to independent ones, from old to new policy and regime values like privatisation and decentralisation, and from old to new political personnel. Personalised party-politics, volatile electorates and weak coalitions (with, for example, a new Polish Cabinet almost every year) all indicate the fragility of the political transition. The CEEC's europeanization is still proceeding rapidly, as shown by first country studies [Sepos, 2008; Papadimitriou and Phinnemore, 2008].

In their *lobby behaviour* at the EU level, the countries also have much in common. Firstly, the countries that regained independence from foreign occupation are ambivalent on europeanization ('no Brussels instead of Moscow'). Both their citizens and politicians frequently express a preference for subsidiarity rather than EU laws and even, except regarding subsidies, for sovereignty rather than subsidiarity. Secondly, as their business landscape is very flat (hardly any big companies) and their decentralised governments are in an adolescent phase, most interest groups at home are heavily dependent on their domestic capital. At the EU level, thirdly, their central government is largely focused on the Council and its Brussels PR, as it has still only a few people inside the Commission, the expert committees and comitology. Only for dossiers falling under unanimous Council voting can this dependency perhaps work for obstructing decision-making, as the Polish Kaszynski-twin government tried to do during 2005-2007. One effect of this is that their central government has to play second-best games such as lobbying for exemptions and subsidies. Another effect is that at the Council level it frequently has to fight an uphill battle against Western stakeholders that included their interests in the Commission's proposal, and often does so with a lot of demanding, noisy, direct and formal exposure. A fourth feature is that, due to unstable domestic politics, their policy positions at the Council level are frequently also unstable, as ministers tend to come and go and their policy positions with them. Fifthly, the countries have some very common policy interests, particularly on agriculture (less food safety legislation and more subsidies), free movement of workers (export of cheap labour) and security (their borders with Russia, Belarussia and Ukraine); for the last interest some states, such as the Baltics, have set up a regional alliance. In early 2009, on the eve of the Council Summit, nine of their heads of state met informally to join hands on more financial assistance to CEECs.

The aforementioned *trends* in lobbying in the old fifteen states are already becoming visible in the twelve new ones as well. More and more interest groups, particularly from decentralised governments and business, travel now and then to Brussels or have already established their offices there. The Polish air-carrier LOT has been a trendsetter in this rising trend of self-reliance, while the regional governments of Hungary took early training in 'how to escape Budapest' in 2001. In 2008, about forty lobby groups each from Poland, Czech Republic, Slovakia and Hungary were present in Brussels, a total of 160 groups representing about 40 percent business interests and the remainder in fairly equal portions professional groups, NGOs and decentralised governments. The national co-ordination of domestic interests is, as a result, more at issue at home, and is probably over its peak now. Many lobby groups attach much value to EU lobbying (although its name is still often mistaken as corruption) [McGrath, 2008], are critical about the lobby support from their government, have become members of EuroFeds, and lobby self-reliantly for financial assistance and supportive coalitions [Borragán, 2003]. Inside and via these EuroFeds they gain familiarity with both the more tailor-made styles of lobbying and the backdoors of EU institutions (on which ten countries got pre-training in communist times), particularly on the work floors of the Commission that actively encourages their participation. Scoring high on their ambition to win or at least not to lose a game, the various lobby groups from CEECs show a great eagerness to professionalise by preparation (study, Triple P) before and by prudence (tailor-made actions) during the game. Many attend EU lobby training sessions in Brussels or at home and are starting to apply PA methods [Schneider, 2007].

Professional EU Public Affairs Management

The country profiles show that the first two of the three new trends in EU lobbying are more or less visible everywhere. Self-reliance and collective action are becoming the rule rather than the exception, with a time-lag for CEECs. The third trend of tailored lobbying is still fresh, but increasingly visible among MNCs, some NGOs and a few decentralised governments and parts of ministries, again with a time lag for CEECs. The growing belief is that in any EU arena ready-made lobbying does not make sense, and that tailored behaviour is necessary and can be much improved. Its catchword is *professionalization*, which stands in contrast to amateurism, and the professional should, again, not be confused with the full-time lobbyist or consultant, who may behave amateurishly, too. They all have their ambitions, but the professional lobbyist is led by conscious and targeted behaviour (study, prudence), while the amateur behaves like a lobby tourist ('flying-in and flying-out', or FiFo) and returns home with only souvenirs from Brussels.

The professional in PA management at the EU level is capable of identifying more options for behaviour and can optimise choices that score better on effectiveness (goal realisation) and efficiency (cost-benefit ratio). The PA expert fine-tunes the approach of actors, the use of factors and the creation of vectors, if necessary as the meta-game of Triple P. All this 'pushing the buttons of Brussels' is only a necessary means, as the objective (dependent variable) remains the winning of the desired game or, as next-best pay-off, an encouraging compromise, respect and backing. The single most important factor (independent variable) of lobby success, *political intelligence*, can always be improved by professionalization. This requires both intelligent homework and tailor-made fieldwork or, in different catchwords, window-out lobbying for information and window-in for support or, even shorter, study and prudence. In the formula $E = MI^2$ it is the I that counts double. One can compare this with the thinking of Kasparov before any game and any move of a chess piece. The rationales behind the movements are comparable: the difficulties of the game (complexity and dynamics) require proactive thinking; the outcome is seen as highly relevant, since the prizes are so interesting; and the increasingly strong competition gives birth to a 'premier league' of smart players. Darwin could have rephrased his law in terms of the survival of the political fittest here. The difference is made by political intelligence.

Regarding the fieldwork, intelligent lobby groups frequently puzzle over the question, *'What action is better?'* For example, is it better to strive for supranational or intergovernmental EU decision-making, to have co-ordinated or self-reliant units, to politicise or depoliticise an issue, to enter a standing or a flexible alliance, or to behave actively or passively? The amateur player hardly considers such dilemmas or solves them dogmatically or at random, while the professional's answer to the question is: *'It depends'*. The next question, then, is: *'On what?'* This is a matter of preparatory homework regarding crucial variables, many of which can be managed to create the desired outcome. These variables are countless, as they include all sorts of actors, factors and vectors. The amateur may see this infinite menu of options as a confusing problem and may prefer to play at random. The professional, however, sees it as an opportunity for creating greater effectiveness and efficiency, because it provides more ways and means to the desired outcome and enables optimisation of the fieldwork. Tailoring the fieldwork is also full of questions that need consideration, regarding both oneself and other players, such as *'Who acts why, for what, to whom, on what, how, where, when and with what result?'* They apply to all lobby groups, including the EU officials.

These questions of professional EU public affairs management are summarised in Figure 3.3, with a breakdown for the key activities of homework and fieldwork. The figure can be seen as composed of modules for learning.

PROFESSIONAL PUBLIC AFFAIRS MANAGEMENT

QUESTION	HOMEWORK: ANALYSING	FIELDWORK: ORGANISING
1. WHO ACTS?	the internal organisation	improving the organisation
2. WHY?	threats and opportunities	choosing the strategy
3. FOR WHAT?	menus and options	determining targets
4. TO WHOM?	finding crucial actors	building relationships, networks
5. ON WHAT?	selecting issues, dossiers	bargaining
6. HOW?	methods and techniques	LOBBYING
7. WHERE?	route planning	bringing partners together
8. WHEN?	time and agenda-phase	timing, agenda-building
9. & RESULT?	process evaluation	learning, improving

Figure 3.3

The player at *Kindergarten* level has only an emotional approach to some perceived event (or non-event) and only one question: how to promote or to prevent that event? Without further thoughts, the player is fascinated by the last catchword, 'lobbying', on the sixth row and immediately tries to lobby other people on the field or the corridor and to open some door, usually a revolving door. Then the learning process starts. At *primary school* level the player begins to wonder about reality and to pose a range of questions (the first column of the figure). Advancing to *secondary school*, the player believes he or she understands the world and even knows how to improve it. Quick answers are provided (third column). If a clear strategy is needed, it is made within three months. If a network is needed, it is quickly made; with whom, it hardly matters. The player becomes a doer, full of energy, spending great resources, but hardly scoring. A few players go on to the *university* level. They learn to think about all options for playing and about the best choices to make (middle column). They think about ways of doing better. Others take them more and more as an example to follow.

The various questions in the figure have been placed in the sequence that most lobby groups follow in practice. They start with questions regarding their own organisation (Q 1-3), followed by those regarding the arena, including the issues and stakeholders involved (Q 4-5), continue with questions related to precisely tailored lobbying, locating and timing (Q 6-8) and regularly pose the question of whether the desired result is close at hand (Q 9). This sequence is certainly not necessarily logical or politico-logical, not to mention that it may be wiser first to try to understand the world around one before taking a position and to make also the sequence dependent on the specific situation. In any event, in daily practice all questions are usually on the table at the same time and remain so. In our *educational approach* here we shall discuss the questions from the perspective not of what is usually done but of what is usually wiser to do. In the next chapter we shall first focus on the questions regarding any EU arena's stakeholders and issues (Q 4-5), in chapter 5 on the EU public affairs agenda inside the home organisation (Q 1-3 plus 9) and in chapter 6 on the external fieldwork, including the optimal choice of lobby styles, location and time (Q 6-8).

CHAPTER 4

MANAGING THE EU ARENA

Whom to Lobby in an Arena and on What?

Following up on the end of the previous chapter, we shall spend this chapter primarily on the extroverted window-out scanning of the EU pipelines, which are full of potential daydreams and nightmares, in short relevant dossiers that go through an arena full of critical stakeholders. After the introduction of arena-analysis, we shall outline the method of scanning first for a single arena, making clear how an arena can best be identified. Thereafter we shall present the 'quick scan' for getting an elementary overview of many more dossiers comprising the long-list. In order to demonstrate that all this preparatory homework is only a necessary means for successful window-in lobbying, we shall subsequently anticipate chapter 6 and present as appetizers 'best lobby practices' based on such homework and also a case-study. In chapter 5 we question how the lobby group can downsize its long-list to both a short-list and a shared-list, and can best get organised for the window-out and window-in activities.

An arena is not a physical place, but the virtual collection of all stakeholders, including EU officials, together with their interests-at-issue regarding a specific dossier at a specific moment. Our leading question now is *whom to lobby in some collection of stakeholders and issues, and on what?* The simple-minded lobby group, at no higher than 'secondary school' level and still amateurish, will regard this question as superfluous. It knows what it wants to get from EU officials and finds their names and addresses in some EU directory. Then it approaches them as directly as possible and tries to convince them that their best response is to comply with its demand soon. If it gets a refusal, it will probably make a lot of noise, on both the national and the EU scene, and launch a second strike, now joined by a number of 'friends' gathered in the meantime. It may also get some advice from a semi-amateurish or semi-professional group already with some experience on the EU playing-field. Then it may follow some rules of thumb, such as that the best actors to approach are one's national PR officials, one's countrymen in the EP and one's regional friends inside the responsible Commission DG, and that the best way of approaching them is to invite them to a free lunch or something similar.

The professional lobbyist, perhaps observing that lunch, may consider this more charming, informal, quiet and indirect approach as preferable to the confrontational one, but also as poorly engineered for its composition (only domestic friends) and sequence (making trouble first). The professional also knows that in the open and competitive EU arena, the best way to lobby always *depends on the specific situation*. The professional investigates, first of all, the broad concept of 'the situation', which is taken today to be a synonym for arena, and breaks it down into at least the four components of stakeholders, issues, time dynamics and arena boundaries. By collecting information on them and setting its brains studiously to work, it gathers useful intelligence by which it can identify its friends and enemies (or partners and opponents), the issues at stake, the time aspects and the differences between the insiders and the outsiders. All this is a matter of window-out preparatory work or, as called here, homework. Then it may come to know whom to lobby on what issues most effectively and efficiently. Subsequently, it applies the best practices of managing an EU arena and its four components, in order to build up broad window-in support for its targets. Then even a formal, demanding, noisy and/or direct approach may be the best possible in a specific situation. All this puzzling regarding an EU chessboard may be seen as logical, not to say self-evident. However, in daily life most lobby groups still behave more amateurishly than professionally, and apparently consider the quest for useful knowledge non-essential. Nevertheless, in the past it took three waves of intellectual PA thinking among mainly US scholars before it became established in theory and among professionals.

The Predecessors of Arena Analysis

The first wave may be called *ruler analysis*. It is the oldest and most classical one, and in many companies is still reflected in the management name of 'government relations' instead of 'public affairs'. In this old approach a group or, at the lowest level, a citizen may have a strong interest in the outcome of some political decision-making and may want to influence the authority formally entrusted with making the decision. To this end, it tries to collect useful information about the highest official in charge, in order to increase the chance of success. In the old days the King or the Prince was the highest ruler to be approached. In his *Il Principe*, Machiavelli gives both free advice to his ruler, Lorenzo dei Medici, on how to survive politically and, more implicitly, a code of conduct to his fellow citizens on how to approach Lorenzo successfully. More recently, until the mid-1970s, US scholars had studied interest group behaviour particularly for its impact on the formal ruling institutions such as the Congress and the President [Key, 1964] and on the elected officials such as the congressmen [Milbrath, 1963; Scott & Hunt, 1965]. Examining the safety of private investments in foreign countries, US scholars also developed the study of political risks coming from changes of rulers there [Coplin and O'Leary, 1976 and 1983; Gigerenzer and others, 1989]. Another American scholar applied the ruler analysis to the EU [Gardner, 1991] by equating 'effective lobbying' with knowing the idiosyncrasies of its highest authorities. This type of knowledge is certainly still necessary, but it is also insufficient. Its weakness is the assumption of political hierarchy or central rule, neglecting the presence of both negotiable issues and stakeholders intervening from outside. In modern jargon it is only actor analysis, limited to the top officials. Many French lobby groups still belong to this first wave of PA.

The second wave is described as *issue analysis*. It started in the late 1960s, as a chapter of ruler analysis, under the flag of policy studies. Authoritative institutions and officials came to be placed in a dynamic perspective, namely as producers of public policies. They make their choice, called policy, from a surplus of more or less contested specific facts, values and/or solutions, in short from a menu of issues [Heath, 1997, 44 and 84]. American scholars have linked the study of policy-making to that of interest groups from business [Bauer and Pool, 1960; Bauer and others, 1963]. Others, subsequently, broke the concept of policy down into issues and presented their issue analysis as a tool, called issue management, to interest group managers [Brown, 1979; Kingdon, 1984; Buchholz, 1990; Frederick and others, 1996; Heath 1997]. They also made a key distinction between opportunities and threats, which are assessed as issues with a positive and a negative effect, respectively on the specific interest group. US-educated people within the EU [Andersen, 1992; EC Committee, 1994] were soon promoting this approach. In many cases the issue analysis remained closely linked to the ruler analysis, resulting in the study of issues inside, for example, the US Congress [Hojnack and Kimball, 1998] and the EU Commission [Emerson and others, 1988].

One chapter of issue analysis has become most popular: the *dossier life cycle* of an issue. A contestation or dispute over a specific fact, value, instrument and/or solution may start out silently, unnoticed or widely considered to be futile. At some point it may emerge into the institutional arena and attract public attention in the form of a bell curve: rising boisterously, achieving some settlement and sinking to slumber or death [Tombari, 1984]. A similar biography may apply to a set of connected issues, called a policy dossier. This dossier life cycle helps us to understand the dynamics of an issue and is summarised in Figure 4.1, which outlines its different phases, separated by barriers, and presents as a bottom-line for each barrier the most important parts of the EU machinery. It begins with the rise of a 'social problem' (phase 1) that may attract mass public attention and then, overcoming the first barrier, can achieve the status of a political problem (phase 2), whereupon it may pass the second barrier, be placed on the official agenda (phase 3) and, overcoming the third barrier, become subject to decision-making (phase 4), after which the decision may be implemented (phase 5) and finally be inspected for its effectiveness (phase 6). This life cycle has a stylised order here, but in reality it may run highly erratically, and include feedback, loops, such as problem-setting by the inspection. Anticipating chapter six, its real life may be like that of a human being and thus, for example, suffer an early death, never get wide recognition or be gone with the wind. Viewed in retrospect, however, every established policy has more or less followed the life history of the cycle and survived like an *éminence grise*. All this knowledge, derived from issue analysis, is necessary as it helps to understand the ups and downs of an issue or dossier inside the institutional arena. It is not sufficient, though, as it takes the life cycle as an affair among only EU officials and views other stakeholders from outside as only senders of messages from the outside, thus neglecting their dynamic and interactive interventions. In reality, many lobby groups, smelling a threat or opportunity, try to influence the course of an issue actively by levelling or raising a barrier in an early phase or, even more proactively, by re-framing an issue and by re-arranging the process by Triple P. Mass media too can play a role inside the arena, domestic ones particularly in the first and the last phase, when the issue is perceived or newly created by EU policy; and (the few) European mass media mostly in the middle phases, when high-level EU officials stimulate great attention. Stakeholders from outside the institutions, and their window-out and window-in activities for every phase and barrier, should be part of a realistic arena analysis.

The third wave of research is *stakeholder analysis*, which took hold in the US during the mid-1980s [Freeman, 1984; Carroll, 1989; Alkhafaji, 1989; Huxham, 1996]. A stakeholder is broadly defined as another player affecting the performance of an interest group or, in turn, being affected by this group [Mitchell and others, 1997]. A stakeholder is thus an interest group as well, one that holds a stake or a position in an issue area. In a pluralist

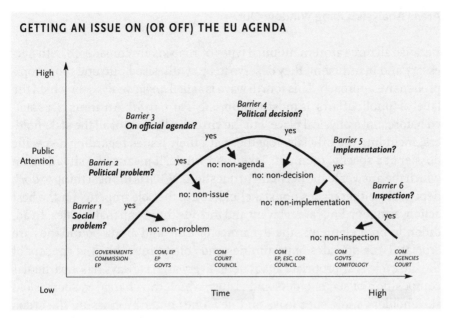

GETTING AN ISSUE ON (OR OFF) THE EU AGENDA

Figure 4.1

society, a lobby group always has to cope with a variety of stakeholders with an interest in the same issue or the same dossier. The study of their behaviour is, technically, a multiple-actor analysis. Stakeholders want to push their own interest and to block any opposing interest. They intervene in both the policy process and in the relationships between competitors and officials. Usually adopting a position during the life of the dossier at stake, they may become either a supportive partner and even friend or a reluctant opponent and even enemy, and join a coalition. Others remain ambivalent or indifferent, as a result of either mixed feelings or of calculated negotiation behaviour [Savage and others, 1991]. There may even be simulating stakeholders, who give the impression of having an interest in the matter, but who in fact only want to build up nuisance value to be used regarding a different matter; many English lobby groups have earned a reputation for this skill. At the EU level, the stakeholder analysis is applied both by many practitioners and in a few EU lobby case studies [Pedler and Van Schendelen, 1994; Greenwood, 1995; Wallace and Young, 1997; Pedler, 2002]. All this knowledge is still useful and necessary, but its strength is also its weakness, by its suggestion that the decision outcome is essentially produced by the interplay among stakeholders only.

Arena Analysis: Going Window-Out

Because all three aforementioned types of analysis are considered both necessary and insufficient, they deserve to be synthesised into one more comprehensive approach. This fourth wave is called *arena analysis* for which the label of 'public affairs' is most appropriate [Parg, 1981]. An arena is, as stated before, not a physical place, but the virtual collection of all the stakeholders, including the officials, together with their issues regarding a specific dossier at a specific moment. Taken as a whole, it means 'the situation' on which the answer to the permanent question, 'What is the best thing to do?', depends. Neither issues nor stakeholders are the sole impetus for the best action, although both are relevant and include the group that lobbies. In addition to both elements, the dynamics of time and arena boundaries are crucial. Time provides opportunities and constraints, thus the concept of the life cycle is appropriate again here. Every arena always has a particular composition of stakeholders and issues, which can change as soon as old stakeholders and issues leave and new ones enter by crossing the arena boundaries, which thus must be researched carefully as well. Of course, it is the perception of both the situation and one's own interest that drives behaviour.

In order to avoid incomplete and false perceptions, an *extroverted* study of the situation is necessary, as free from preconceived judgements as possible. Adults who are framed by their values, experiences and perceptions from the past usually have greater difficulty with this than youngsters with their open minds and curiosity. The extroverted discovery of the situation, contained by the metaphor of 'going window-out', is indispensable for arriving at an overview of the situation that is outstanding by quality (reliability, validity) and quantity (completeness). Only then can a lobby group see in advance the many different stakeholders in the arena, their many different interests in the same dossier, the opportunities and constraints of time and boundaries surrounding them, and particularly its own fragile position in this complex and dynamic arena. With such organised intelligence from the onset, it might be able to organise sufficient support or mass for its interests and to manage the arena with a good chance of success or effectiveness, to realise the formula $E = MI^2$. Its difficulty is shown by the many EU lobby groups that are merely driven by their preconceived perception of the situation, usually limited only to their selfish interest and to a very few stakeholders related to the same interest and with neglect of time and boundaries.

Arena analysis is thus aimed at the acquisition of *realistic insights* regarding a specific arena on a dossier, not as a goal but as a necessary means for achieving better arena management. It brings together all window-out intelligence (the upper arrow of Figure 1.2), not performed only once like taking a photograph, but repeatedly like filming the battlefield before and during the fight. The description of the arena should precede its analysis, resulting in intelligence needed for any action. All this preparatory work for every arena each time usually takes a lot of energy, as simple games with low complexity and dynamics seldom exist. A level playing-field is difficult for all, as stakeholders, issues, time and boundaries are not fixed but flexible. An unlevel field may be not so difficult for the insiders on top, but difficult to maintain in the longer run, while those in the downhill position may have a reversed view of its difficulty. It is, however, not the EU skeleton but its flesh-and-blood that matters. Even a seemingly simple game that falls under Council unanimity decision-making, such as Treaty formation, can be complex, as many stakeholders from other institutions and from outside may try to intervene in informal ways or via side-dossiers. In contrast, not all games of Commission-driven secondary legislation are necessarily difficult, as the 1992 Slots Case shows [Van den Polder, 1994]. Thanks to their early arena study, national air carriers like Lufthansa and Air France could, as insiders in an uphill position, proactively mobilise 'their own' ministers in the Transport Council and easily protect their private distribution of landing rights (slots) against EU intervention demanded by new carriers like Virgin and Lauda Air. In short, arena analysis requires a lot of work and resources, but usually much less and with better results than any lobbying without it. As in equally complex and dynamic games like chess or war, proactive investigation and critical reflection are the best investments, usually making the difference between winners and losers.

Describing an Arena

What is best to do in lobbying depends on the situation. Believing this, the studious lobby group wants to know in what sort of arena it is before it starts any action. By going mentally and physically window-out and setting its radar to work, it tries to collect useful information about the four main components of any selected arena: the relevant stakeholders, issues at stake, time dynamics and arena boundaries.

Stakeholders
The serious lobby group really wanting to win an EU game starts with drawing up an *inventory* of all stakeholders, including the officials on the matter

and, of course, itself. They all are players or actors which can affect or be affected by its performance and, because of this, might intervene. In this chapter we assume that the lobby group has cohesion and stable objectives; in the next chapter we will challenge this assumption. The inventory is not biased towards only friends or enemies, or towards only formal entities. It is like military reconnaissance: all warriors on the field are taken seriously for their weapons and thus respected, according to the etymology of the Latin verb re-spectare, looking back at armed people. On a specific dossier a Greek group of farmers or a Lithuanian ministry may be as relevant as the French President or a Commission expert. Even non-EU players may have to be taken into account, such as the Thai exporters on the tapioca dossier, the Central American countries on bananas and the World Trade Organisation (WTO) on external trade liberalisation. For example, lobby groups from Switzerland, which is formally not a member of the Union but in practice strongly dependent on EU decisions, belong to the most important stakeholders in policy areas like transport, pharmaceuticals and banking [Sciarini and others, 2004].

All this may sound trivial, but in daily life most lobby groups fail to perform well in this first step of arena monitoring. Common *mistakes* are the following two. One is to be biased when making the inventory. National ministries tend to neglect both local governments and private interest groups and to consider the EU arena as an intergovernmental field of battle. Many a business group neglects the intervening role of some national ministry or decentralised agency. On the other hand, NGOs are often comparatively good at unbiased scouting of an arena. Secondly, many lobby groups deify stakeholders, putting them in, for example, 'the British position', as if such a stakeholder ever really exists. Instead, every country is pluralistic and thus always divided regarding every dossier. At best, there may be a statement from the British Cabinet or Prime Minister, which is frequently only perfunctorily supported by the national ministries and even less by other groups in society. In reality, they all may go their own way. The same holds true for the position of, for example, Greenpeace, Siemens or the Commission. Accurate scouting requires that stakeholders be inventoried at the lowest relevant level, even if this is just a person or a unit. An unbiased and specific inventory usually results in a long-list of stakeholders, especially in the early phase of a game. In later phases its length is usually reduced to only a few coalitions. At any rate, no information that is potentially relevant in a later phase should be lost at the start.

Subsequently, the identified stakeholders must be assessed in terms of *relevance*. A relevant stakeholder is one who is expected both to intervene actively and to possess sufficient influence capabilities to become effective. The stakeholders are, as it were, placed along at least two continuums: one ranging from active to passive and the other from strong to weak [Mitchell and others, 1997]. Regarding the first continuum covering key variables of participation as discussed in chapter 1, it is not enough to include only the stakeholders who are obviously participating. Many others may be active in an indirect or hidden way, for example via a caretaker, or they may become active soon. The second continuum covers their resources for influence, such as expertise, skills, affiliations, personnel, reputation, networks, budget and other assets [Schlozman and Tierney, 1986]. They indicate the stakeholder's potential to become an influential player. Potential influence should, however, never be equated with real influence, as an army with many resources is not necessarily victorious.

Finally, a sort of *rank order* of stakeholders should be made. Most relevant are the primary stakeholders, identified as both prone to action and potentially highly influential. Those being assessed as remaining passive and/or falling short of sufficient potential influence can be taken as stakeholders of secondary importance. They should not be deleted but placed on a memory list as, in another phase in the life of the dossier, they may join the primary group, and the reverse may happen as well. The drawing up of the inventory of relevant stakeholders clearly requires a lot of intelligent monitoring. The smartest stakeholders will try to play both passivity and impotence, like a cat seemingly sleeping on the roof but really watching the birds. The most assertive stakeholders, suggesting they can hardly refrain from strong action, may be like barking dogs that do not bite. One can even make a typology of stakeholders, such as those assessed as irrelevant, dormant, potential, demanding, dominant, dangerous, dependent and definitive [Mitchell and others, 1997]. The outcome of all this preparatory homework is merely a reasoned estimate, but this is much better than nothing. It enables one to take prudent measures with regard to every major stakeholder [Hunger and Wheelen, 1998, 112].

Issues

Every stakeholder is driven by his own interests, which are chosen positions on issues arising in his environment, usually caused by new facts, changing values and proposed solutions to problems. The positions represent daydreams and nightmares regarding the arena at stake on, in our case here, the EU playing-field. The stakeholder likes to promote and to preserve the daydreams and to prevent the nightmares. A chosen position always contains a confrontation between cherished values and perceived facts.

How a stakeholder comes to a chosen position or to the definition of his interest, and how he can arrive at a better choice or definition will be part of the next chapter. The focus here is on the *identification of the interests* of the various stakeholders in an arena. In pluralistic societies every perceived fact, cherished value and proposed solution is always contested and contestable by others, as they contain subjective elements. For this reason interests, positions and issues are practically synonymous in the field of lobbying. In the EU practice of decision-making by negotiations and compromises, a professional lobby group has to know precisely which different positions there are on a dossier and for which conflicting interests they stand. With this information, it can take solid sides, by getting primary stakeholders interested in its position and so becoming part of the final compromise. This relevant information is necessary but never sufficient for getting the desired or satisfying outcome. Without it a lobby group has a low chance of such an outcome and remains dependent on sheer luck.

Again, this may sound trivial and self-evident. All the more surprising, then, that most lobby groups fail to acquire this type of knowledge. Introverted, they live in their own world, see the EU officials as the formal and only rulers and interact with a few befriended stakeholders only. Subsequently, they frequently make two big *mistakes*. The first is one of arrogance: believing that their chosen values and perceived facts are perfectly right, they expect that sooner or later other stakeholders with different interests shall join their 'excellent' position. They may even become proselytizing and enforcing, two variants of a Holy War to which there is usually no successful end. The second mistake is one of naïveté: still believing they are right, they may come to the conclusion that those not sharing that position must be wrong. They are like the theatregoer who thinks the other members of the audience that evening must either share his opinion about the play or be stupid. Many spectators, however, see the same play from a different position, interpret it differently and go home with a different lesson from it [Cherry, 1966]. Likewise, different stakeholders may be perfectly right on their different positions, simply because they cherish different values and perceive different facts. For example, the draft directive on Laying Hens (COM 1998/ 135), promoted by NGOs on animal welfare and aimed at allocating more space and comfort to laying hens, was seen by industrial egg producers as bringing additional costs, by traditional farmers as a comparative advantage, by suppliers of better cages as new business, by trade unions as worsening labour conditions and by northern governments as an expenditure to support their industrial farmers, and those are only five out of many more stakeholders. If they would all be introverted players, then the game ends in a classical tragedy in which all heroes feel they are right and end up dead. The professional lobby group respects the relative or subjective backgrounds of values, facts and solutions in pluralist society and wants to identify and understand them in order to develop an interesting supply side before the negotiations. The amateurish group, lacking respect for the positions of others, can hardly develop an early and interesting supply side needed to get its demand side accepted.

The identification of current issues is, indeed, not at all easy. It is particularly difficult to identify the *real positions* of the primary stakeholders. Their official statements can never be taken at face value. The smartest players can disguise their internal divisions, remain silent or cover their real interests. The many amateurish stakeholders may hardly have a solid position. Behind their interests, then, stand badly reasoned values and poorly perceived facts. The discovery of the real positions clearly requires a lot of knowledge and understanding about stakeholders. As in diplomacy, one has to monitor their internal arenas at home, their dominant values, their perceptions of reality and the forces behind them that may change them. From this information the intelligent lobby group may deduce their real interests or positions. Knowing that on every dossier every stakeholder always has more than one real interest, a daydream or a nightmare, it can find even more room to manoeuvre. Assessing these various interests of the other stakeholders as friendly, hostile or indeterminate, it can build a coalition among the friendly ones, launch a fight over the hostile ones and take time or give cheap support regarding the indeterminate ones. It can even make a trade-off between friendly and hostile interests and so come to a package deal. Such preparatory homework can even be used for other dossiers and thus create wider room for package dealing. The five stakeholders mentioned on the Laying Hen Dossier, all being involved in many more EU dossiers as well, might have been included in a broader package, thereby settling almost any current issue among them. It is all a matter of knowledge first.

Time

Every EU arena continuously changes with time. The professional lobby group is conscious of the relevance of *time analysis*. From general experience it knows that in the early phase of a dossier's life, normally many stakeholders and issues are at stake; that during the dossier's life most stakeholders become part of a larger coalition and most issues part of a package; and that in the end-phase of an EU decision process usually only two groups remain, the proponents and the opponents of the proposal, and only a few issues are left, such as 'the envelope' (who pays the bill), the date it takes effect and any exemption demanded. The professional group also knows that the dossier's life is only partially regulated by procedures setting deadlines for, for example, public consultation, codecision, inspection and review. Usually the next phase starts after a barrier has been passed in a sufficiently supported way. In its own rhythm of time, a difference perceived as irritating by some in Europe is elevated to the EU playing-field, adopted on an official agenda, challenged by other stakeholders, mixed up with different issues and maybe dossiers, processed into the EU machinery and, finally, decided upon, implemented and inspected, or perhaps not all that is happening. During the dossier's life, some stakeholders act under pressure; others have all the time in the world. Those in a losing mood want to delay, those in a winning one want to speed up. Time, in short, distributes constraints and opportunities.

All this is general wisdom, which the professional group demonstrates when it, for every new situation, studies the time dynamics precisely in order to fine-time its lobbying activities. Most lobby groups are, however, nonchalant about time in an arena and thus make many *mistakes*. They enter their arena when the dossier gets much public attention, which is frequently halfway through its life cycle. Most dossiers, however, hardly get any public attention, as they fall under delegated legislation and thus are missed altogether. The nonchalant groups are often too late to seize upon a growing opportunity or to stop a growing threat at its birth. They only notice different players and issues after they take position or take shape. If they take a photograph of the arena at all, they easily mistake it for the film. They are hardly aware of coalition building and package dealing occurring, hope to meet formal deadlines at crunch time or even later, and easily misperceive the urgency of any state of affairs. In short, they can hardly act effectively, leave alone proactively. Delaying or speeding up the process is beyond their capacity. Their lobbying is like fighting one fire after another, directed at preventing only the growth of current threats, not its occurrence or breakout. In contrast, professional groups have updated protocols within reach for immediate and flexible responses to various types of serious threats, such as Unilever applied to the 2008 financial crisis.

The *calculation of time* is clearly not easy. The dossier's life cycle remains an abstraction of reality, to be updated at any time. Competitors playing Triple P can make the early phase of problem definition full of implicit decision-making that is subsequently binding. The early framing of the Laying Hen Dossier as a problem of animal welfare strongly determined its outcomes. The phases of implementation and inspection may certainly be full of substantial decisions at the detailed level. Many stakeholders consider them to be the most relevant ones as 'both the devil and the angel are in the details'. The best attitude toward time is to remain alert and prudent. The professional group regularly updates its inventories of stakeholders and issues, links them to formal deadlines if these exist, reassesses a newly found situation in terms of time constraints and opportunities, and tries, if necessary, to delay or to speed up the process. It can, however, be misled by even smarter stakeholders who suggest that there is either all the time in the world or no time left. By verifying this, it may avoid being misled by, in fact, its own insufficient intelligence. Even if all this time knowledge is based on an estimate, it is still much better than nothing. It enables intervention to be more carefully timed and less haphazard.

Boundaries
As an arena is permanently changing over time, it is also always changing in composition. Therefore, the studious interest group explores the *arena boundaries*. Seldom are they fixed or closed. Usually, every stakeholder can introduce new issues, and every issue can attract new stakeholders. Formal arrangements that determine the composition of an arena can be subject to Triple P. A dossier that attracts wider public attention usually attracts new stakeholders and issues also, as often happens in the formal decision phase of the EP and Council, observed by many journalists. The aforementioned Laying Hen Dossier started as a mini-arena on animal welfare, subse-quently attracting attention from egg producers, importers of non-EU eggs, trade unions and more stakeholders, each raising their own interests, contesting those of others and attracting more new players and issues. Stakeholders can also leave an arena, for example because they see another dossier or arena as more promising, and then they take their issues with them. Such volatility of the arena boundaries is normal for every open society, and no different from any interesting garden where animals searching for food come and go.

Most lobby groups neglect the arena boundaries. They consider the composition of an arena to be static like a photograph, and hardly pay attention to stakeholders and issues that disappear from the arena, or they forget to notice those that enter. As a result, they seldom care about the causes and the consequences of this *boundary traffic*, which may be highly relevant for their own position as well. Due to this lack of understanding, they can hardly anticipate future issues that will take them only by surprise. Pro-active action, aimed at attracting new stakeholders and new issues or at re-moving old ones, is almost beyond their mental scope. In the Laying Hen case, the animal welfare groups should have tried to keep the boundaries closed and to anticipate the potential entrance of farmers, importers and trade unions.

The professional lobby group explores the volatility of the arena boundaries by monitoring those who enter or leave and their interests with them. From these *traffic statistics* it tries to deduce useful intelligence for improving coalitions, negotiations and time scheduling. Proactively it can try, if needed, to pull in new supportive stakeholders and issues and to get rid of old annoying ones. It also broadens its homework by including adjacent dossiers or arenas, as any overlap can be used for either stimulating cross-traffic or erecting roadblocks, in short for pushing or blocking another combination of stakeholders or issues. Knowing that growing public attention to a dossier is the single most important determinant of attracting new stakeholders and issues, it is therefore prudently keen to keep silent. Only in a dreadful emergency situation will it make noise in order to prevent immediate loss and to enjoy the immediate effect of new stakeholders and issues delaying the current decision-making process. All such fine-tuning is dependent on the quality of the boundary analysis. Even if this is only based on estimates, it is much better than nothing. It can make the difference between winning and losing.

The Satisfactory Description

Two short cases first. One is the *1992 Dossier on High Definition Television* (HDTV). In the early 1990s, the European consumer electronics manufacturers, organised as EACEM and including companies like the French Thomson, Dutch Philips and German Bosch, demanded from the EU both a legal standard and a big subsidy for R&D on HDTV [Verwey, 1994; Cawson, 1995]. Soon they received personal support from the DG R&D Commissioner Filippo Pandolfi, once a board member of Olivetti, and a promise of 850 million ecu (now euro). But in 1992, they appeared to have ignored opposing stakeholders with different interests, such as broadcasters (fearing the costs of rebuilding their studios), satellite companies (offering a competitive alternative) and consumer groups (against compulsory purchase of new television sets). The mass media, smelling the sensation, finally helped to bury the dossier, the standard and the subsidy. In hindsight, the companies realised that better preparatory homework could have prevented this failure. The other case concerns the 2004 development of the *Radio Frequency Identification Device* (RFID), a new high-tech barcode with great efficiency potential, such as rendering most retail cashier personnel superfluous. Before going to lobby for the introduction of RFID, some European food retailers like the French Carrefour and Dutch Ahold first made a prudent arena study and found that the new device would raise issues of, among others, environment (hazardous substances, waste), privacy (consumers' data protection), health (electro-magnetics), competition (RFID's costs prohibitive to SMEs) and unemployment (more than 50% of personnel) and, of course, would mobilise the stakeholders behind them. With foresight, they decided not to lobby (yet) and to leave this to others, such as the producers.

Clearly enough, the description of the four components of any arena requires a lot of information that is neither readily available quantitatively (completeness) nor qualitatively (reliability, validity) and which thus has to be collected and improved. In the EU there is no shortage of useful sources for collecting specific information on our leading question here: 'Whom to lobby in an arena and on what?' Major ones are listed in the upper part of Figure 4.2 and explained as follows.

(1) *Desk research.* Internet is a major tool. The EU website, being more open than most national government sites, informs about much that is in the EU pipelines, but not everything by far. On their sites, the national governments provide information about their own positions, and a few, such as the Swedish, due to domestic transparency rules, can be even more open about particularly the Council than the EU site is. National newspapers provide additional information and can be consulted through sites like eufeeds.eu. Many established stakeholders currently have their own website, and search engines like euractiv.com collect many of their documents. A potential gold-mine of information is memory, as many arenas are recurrent and many stakeholders and issues with them, history which only has to be stored and read again. Corporate memory as laid down in archives is, however, usually poorly organised, except in France where such information from past fights is considered most useful for future ones. The SGAE is famous for doing this.

(2) *Debriefing friends.* Every lobby group can make use of other groups that share its interests and, once it has identified them, it can try to download their information. Collective platforms find one of their major functions just in the sharing of costs and benefits of monitoring. After some time, every lobby group can find informants both inside EU buildings and among stakeholders, including media, thanks to a match of characters, interests and/or backgrounds (like passport, education or hobby). For its own information needs, the Commission makes wide use of its countless insourced experts and, additionally, academics and consultancies. Lobby

groups can put in efforts to debrief befriended people among them, and their own technical experts.

(3) *Visiting the corridors.* Much information, however, is not available in sufficient quantity or quality from the sources mentioned above, and has to be gathered and checked by going around the corridors, the classical 'lobbying'. Usually, the most important source is the Commission, as it does not publish most pre-drafts of its texts, particularly not those under comitology, and thus has to be visited directly or through the aforementioned friends indirectly. On secondary legislation, the PRs, which act on the crossroads between their national ministries and all other national capitals, can be very informative, but only a few are helpful. Journalists often get easy access to high EU officials competing for 'good publicity' and can, if trusted, be used for asking for or checking information, in exchange for a scoop later. Other relevant aspects are also the conference meetings in separate rooms of hotels around Place Schuman, where stakeholders meet on a running dossier, often together with EU officials. The corridors around such rooms are the modern 'lobia'.

An ambitious lobby group will not, however, only search for information within the frame of the dossier at stake, but go beyond and try to broaden its mind by an *open search* with the help of techniques, such as those mentioned in the lower part of Figure 4.2 and briefly clarified here.

(1) *Comparative study.* By studying a more or less similar (homomorphous) dossier, it can find new solutions to issues at stake. For example, on an issue like working hours, falling under social affairs, lobby groups in the fields of hospitals, retail, road haulage, fire & rescue and manufacturing can all learn from each other's dossier on this matter, as this usually reveals useful similarities and differences.

(2) *Hindsight wisdom.* By evaluating a recent game using the question 'Which surprise should we have seen coming?' a lobby group can come to hindsight wisdom, useless for the past game but most useful for monitoring the next game astutely. Well-organised memory yields a real reward here. There is always room for improvement and, as the costs of shortcomings have already been made, this is gratis, as the HDTV companies learnt.

(3) *Pilots.* A popular technique in Brussels is to organise, by invitation, a conference, seminar or round-table just for the sake of getting varied insights into some domain of issues, such as on 'cisgenetic fruits', 'district heating and cooling' and 'transatlantic services', to name just three of countless more being held in 2008. Variants of this technique are the launch of a debate in newspapers or online, two channels that have the ad-

MAJOR SOURCES AND TECHNIQUES OF ARENA MONITORING

TARGETED SEARCH:
1. DESK RESEARCH REGARDING:
WEBSITES: EU, COUNTRIES, STAKEHOLDERS, SERVICES
MEMORY (PERSONAL AND CORPORATE)
NEWSPAPERS
2. DEBRIEFING BEFRIENDED KEY PEOPLE IN:
COLLECTIVE PLATFORMS
INSTITUTIONS AND AGENCIES
COMMITTEES, INTERGROUPS, WORKING GROUPS
EU ASSESSMENTS (ACADEMICS, CONSULTANCIES)
ONE'S OWN ORGANISATION (TECHNICAL EXPERTS)
3. VISITING THE CORRIDORS OF:
EU OFFICIALS
STAKEHOLDERS
JOURNALISTS

OPEN SEARCH:
1. COMPARATIVE CASE-STUDY
2. EVALUATION: GETTING HINDSIGHT WISDOM
3. PILOTING CONFERENCES, SEMINARS AND MEDIA DEBATES
4. LAUNCHING BALLOONS AND RUMOURS
5. ROLE-SIMULATION GAME
6. OPEN NETWORKING
7. BASIC EU KNOWLEDGE

Figure 4.2

vantage of producing even more varied insights, but also the disadvantage that they can less be controlled and so mobilise early undesired opposition.

(4) *Balloons.* Even more challenging is the launch of balloons or rumours through, for example, a befriended MEP posing a question or a medium publishing a report. The objective is to solicit reactions from stakeholders who believe it is all serious. This technique requires, of course, the anonymity of the real sender, much fine-tuning and great prudence.

(5) *Simulation.* Every lobby group might easily organise internally a role-simulation game, in which the participants play very different roles that include EU officials and devil's advocates and during which every player wants to win. The outcomes are frequently spectacular, not only for their richness of information but also for the better understanding of even the greatest enemy.

(6) *Open networking.* The old technique of just going around, like in classical diplomacy and lobbying, for watching and listening and without any specific target in mind, is still an enlightening technique and almost always brings new insights that are useful for specific situations.

(7) *Theoretical knowledge.* Since the EU machinery of common decision-making remains seemingly complex and dynamic, it makes much sense to study the causes behind it in order to understand better their consequences for the room to lobby. Theoretical knowledge is a search machine in itself.

A lobby group may consider the exploitation of all these sources and techniques of information gathering, aimed at getting a useful description of the four arena components, to be costly and troublesome preparatory homework. Such a group should make *better calculations* of effectiveness and efficiency, such as follows below.

– Lobby action without preparatory homework usually creates the biggest troubles, as one may miss relevant stakeholders, crucial issues, better moments and boundary traffic. The comparative costs of losing the game usually exceed those of homework.

– After preparatory homework an arena may look more complex and dynamic than before or without it, but that is reality, and this insight is the greatest reward from homework. Thanks to intelligence, one can win in a difficult arena more than in a simple one, just as one may profit more on a difficult rather than on a simple market.

– As time goes by, all the homework becomes easier. At the end of a fight there are usually only two major stakeholders, namely the coalition in favour and the one against, and only a few hot issues, particularly 'the envelope' (who pays the bill), the date of entry and a possible exemption. Soon one can also determine which stakeholder is merely a comedian, a passive cat on the roof or a barking dog.

– The sooner and better a lobby group starts its homework, the earlier it will identify stakeholders with the same interests and with useful for the shared-list approach, including the sharing of the costs of scanning and monitoring. The possibly mutual competition is usually not in the gathering of information (window-out) but on the use of it (window-in), a hurdle which can be solved during the process.

– The most intense homework has only to be done on the short-list which, as will be explained in the next chapter, should remain really short. In the next paragraph we shall present the less intense 'quick scan'.

– The many sources and techniques of arena scanning also produce a great spin-off for the window-in activities, beyond the objective (in fact the means) of getting better information for playing successfully. Once it has a trusted relationship with an official or stakeholder, the lobby group can often easily go from debriefing to briefing, from window-out to window-in, from information to influence.

No lobby group, however, is capable of getting a perfectly complete (both quantity and quality), valid and reliable insight into the state of an arena at a specific moment. As in a game of chess [Simon, 1979], this is beyond human reach, sometimes due to practical circumstances, such as the volatility of an arena or simply lack of time, and fundamentally to the extremity of the norms of completeness, validity and reliability. Besides, no information source or technique is watertight. Often, the search for the best is the enemy of the better and the good, and thus one should *optimise rather than maximise* here, too. By critically reviewing the norms, one can come to satisfying next-best solutions. Completeness can be considered a utopia anyhow. Because of the absence of fixed arena boundaries, there is no stable criterion of completeness. As every historian knows, a complete description can be approximated only for an extremely short period, and even then it remains a daydream. Validity, meaning that one finds what one seeks, is always a problem. For example, the perceived weight of a stakeholder is only potential and not yet proven by its real impact. Reliability, so that an observation can be taken as factual, can be considered equally impossible to realise perfectly. Among the stakeholders there are always some who only feign an interest, who remain silent like the cat on the roof or who bark like seemingly vicious dogs, so misleading the observer. An observation can, besides, be outdated to-morrow, for example when a stakeholder reassesses a threat as opportunity or vice versa, and thus redefines its stake in the dossier. Because of such practical and fundamental obstacles to perfection, every lobby group has inevitably to accept optimal or satisfactory next-best insights.

The satisfactory description has at least *two bottom-lines*. One is the reasoned estimate, being the educated guess regarding the composition of an arena to the best of one's possible knowledge. This is no license to easiness, as the most intelligent competitors usually increase the level of ambition and are, so to say, one's best friends in ambition. The reasoned guess only protects a lobby group against searching for what is beyond reach, practically or fundamentally, but not against the necessity to do its utmost to gather the best possible insights, as otherwise a competitor will take the edge. The second bottom-line, still at a high level, is the repetition of the homework by one or more other observers in a parallel setting for the same moment in time (duplica) and/or in series for a later moment (replica). The duplica gives the better photo, and the replica the better film. By setting several observers to work on the same duplica or replica one gets, thanks to their intellectual competition, usually much better insights, as they will deliver different observations and their good reasons for them. They only have to start a dialectic exchange of arguments to arrive at higher collective wisdom. Therefore, a small team, if available, can best be split first into individuals each doing the same arena study and then be brought together to exchange observations. The replica is essential for observing changes in the arena. When observing a new stakeholder or a new issue (or the disappearance of an old one), one should question whether this has happened due to arena dynamics or to shortcomings in the previous homework. In case of the latter, there is room to improve the use of information sources and techniques.

The Quick Arena Scan

The most thoroughly prepared homework, described above, is needed for dossiers a lobby group has selected for its short-list. However, when it makes the long-list of more-or-less relevant dossiers, follows the dossiers on its shared-list or is under time pressure for its short-list, the group might rely on a *quick arena scan*. This is a simple two-dimensional matrix, with the left-side vertical axis representing the stakeholders and the upper-side horizontal axis the issues involved (Figure 4.3). It is, in fact, no different from what most people do in their minds when they are thinking about an arena. They consider only the major players and the key issues. The mind has, however, a limited capacity for considering many stakeholders and issues at the same time and also for storing the collected insights. It is already far better to write them down on a paper napkin, but this may be lost in the shuffle. The best thing is to put the quick scan on a computer spreadsheet or grid. The rationale behind it remains unchanged: if one wants to enter a challenging place like a battlefield or jungle, it is better first to know its structure and composition. Without a general overview first, no insight will follow. The quick scan can often produce a sufficiently complete and reliable helicopter view of the best ways to proceed at calculated risk.

On the vertical *stakeholders axis* there is endless room for listing all sorts of stakeholders, even with breakdowns made at the lowest relevant level, for example a government unit or a person. The criterion is whether they can become relevant warriors in the arena. The scanning lobby group can put itself on top; in the next chapter we shall question whether its position is sufficiently clear or has to be made subject to an internal arena study, to compare with the external one here. The other stakeholders can be grouped into

DOSSIER HOMEWORK

Dossier 1 : .... (2 and ff = agenda analysis)
Moment t : .... (t−x .... t+x = time analysis)
Analyst A : .... (B and others for control)

STAKEHOLDERS	Issues involved	
	1 2 3 4 5 6 7 8 n...	
Own organisation		
National - public and private - sectoral - cross-sectoral - regional - others: media, etc.		
Foreign - governments - sectoral - cross-sectoral - regional - others: media, etc.		→ select items for trade-offs
Transnational - COM (DGs, agencies) - committees - EP, ESC, COREG - COREPER, council - Court - EuroFeds, NGOs - others: media, etc.		→ identify coalitions for or against

↓ assess their actions
 + potential influence
 = relevance
	↓ assess relevance of issues and make for ↓
	
	 unfrienfly columns: loss scenario
	 friendly columns:
	     win-win/free ride scenario
	 undetermined columns:
	     negotiations scenario
		↓ other
		 dossiers
		 and
		 players

Figure 4.3

three categories. Firstly, there are the domestic stakeholders with an interest in the same dossier as well. Examples are national ministries, private companies, NGOs, trade unions, regional interest groups and others. As interested players, they may try to intervene on the dossier already at home, in order to enjoy its opportunities and/or to eliminate its threats. Secondly, there are the foreign stakeholders, of course with possibly the same breakdown as those at home. They may come from both EU and non-EU countries, including global platforms like the WTO. Those from outside the EU can be as active and effective as those from inside, and have their linkages with the EU regardless. Thirdly, there are the many stakeholders inside the EU machinery, ranging from Commission officials and experts to Parliament rapporteurs and Court referendaries.

On the horizontal *issues axis* there is endless room for registering the interests or positions of the identified stakeholders regarding all contested facts, values and solutions. For every different issue they are grouped by column. If necessary, every issue can be split into more, which only results in even more columns, and every issue on top of a column should be defined in precise terms indicating what is in dispute. On the HDTV dossier, the issues on top might have been labelled as 'an EU standard', 'subsidies to the producers', 'studio compensation' and so on. The issues must be registered not from only one's own position but particularly also from that of every stakeholder, this being the crux of extroverted monitoring. In the cells, where the two axes intersect, one can register for every stakeholder the estimated position on any issue in a simple and digital way, by putting in the cell for example a plus sign (+) if a stakeholder is assumed to support the issue as defined at the top; a minus (-) if one observes that the issue is perceived as a threat; a plus-minus (-/+) if one believes that a stakeholder is wavering or ambivalent on the issue and thus can go in both directions; a zero (o) if a stakeholder has really no position; and, if no positions at all are observed, the cell is left empty. Of course, one can also apply shaded scores, ranging from for example +5 to -5 that express the intensity of a stakeholder's preference.

This simple arena description in order to identify potential partners and opponents on one dossier at a specific moment is indeed not substantially different from what every person can do in his mind, on a napkin or on paper. However, the *computer grid* is, once the preparatory work has started, much superior to old-fashioned techniques, especially for the following sequels to the work.
- *Memory*. It helps to save data for longer time, to include updates and to study trends in the arena. The outcomes of replicas (at another moment,

second line on top of matrix), which replaces the still photograph by moving film, can easily be added.

- *Checks.* By organising one or more duplicas (by other observers, third line on top), one can identify their differences and push critical discussion among them to get sound agreement.
- *Key stakeholders.* To every stakeholder on the vertical axis one can add a measure of relevance, defined by their probable action and potential influence, which allows a closer study of primary stakeholders without losing information on the others.
- *Key issues.* On the horizontal axis one can mark the issues assessed as probably real and prominent, and not fake and fading, and also make a closer study of that hard core, without losing potentially relevant information on the other issues.
- *Blank areas.* Empty and zero cells, indicating that a stakeholder seemingly or truly has no interest, which is often soon forgotten when working only in the mind or on paper, remain under useful observation as sooner or later they can go on to play a role.
- *Broader views.* To the two axes one can easily add unexpected findings from the exploration of the arena boundaries. This is a matter of rotating the two axes. Then, one always finds more dossiers and issues of interest to stakeholders, and when researching the latter one also finds more interested groups. The new dossiers can be recorded on the rows on the right side, and the new interest groups under the columns on the bottom. They can all be used at a later moment for both new package-dealing and coalition-formation. Frequently, a game is won by this use of what has been beyond the boundaries before.

Analysis for the Action

After this preparatory homework, Figure 4.3 is full of observations. Like Kasparov one is watching the chess-board, and now going to think about transforming, information into intelligence, by analysing the perceived arena, so squaring the I in $E = MI^2$. By *vertical analysis* of the stakeholders, the studious lobby group can rationally discover room for action on every issue on the horizontal axis. Starting from the top with its own position, it can always arrive at one of three assessments of the situation it is in; this we shall do now by using the metaphor of wind and weather or 'political meteorology':

- *Tailwind.* Its own position on an issue, either plus or minus, may be widely shared by most stakeholders or the primary ones. For its interest the

wind, in short, is blowing friendly and promising as a tailwind. Most likely its preference will shine through during the competition with other stakeholders and be approved by the EU officials.
– *Headwind*. It may also be, however, that most other major stakeholders have an opposite preference and hence do not share its position. Now it feels an unfriendly and cold headwind. The chance that its preference will prevail is low to zero. It has, so to speak, a dead horse in the column.
– *Unclear wind*. The lobby group may also observe that in a column most (primary) stakeholders hold positions that are indifferent (o), ambivalent (-/+) or still blank. Thus, mainly unclear side-winds are blowing now, or there is no wind at all. The column is indeterminate, the game open and the outcome unpredictable.

The *horizontal analysis* of the rows reveals the great surprise that every stakeholder is always open to negotiation. In its row it has pluses (daydreams) that it wants to score and minuses (nightmares) it wants to eliminate. A smart lobby group can always negotiate with every stakeholder by supporting or opposing each of them and, if required for package-dealing, by raising another dossier identified as relevant to that stakeholder as often happens. A lobby group that complains, it cannot negotiate effectively with some other stakeholder, almost certainly has badly prepared or even neglected its homework. In the HDTV case, the producing companies could have negotiated with their opponents if they would have known their different interests beforehand. The costs of doing good homework are clearly much lower than those of misperceptions. An intelligent lobby group gets the highest pay-offs on issues brought in by competitors and not crucial to itself, as it can cheaply give highly valued support (like a cigar from another man's box) and start its offer for negotiations.

One can also make a *diagonal analysis*, which is the helicopter view. The order of both the horizontal and the vertical axis is nominal and thus may be changed. By reordering, one can bring both the pluses and the minuses together into aggregates representing the potential coalitions in favour of or against a single issue, or the full dossier. Sooner or later most stakeholders will discover these coalitions as well, but a studious interest group can see the potential coalitions long before and anticipate them by smart actions. These potential coalitions are, besides, of high quality, as they are based on common interests and thus more solid than those based on, for example, common language, tradition, passport or location. The helicopter view provides two further pieces of interesting information. Firstly, no potential coalition is perfectly unified. Thus there is always some room for undermining an opposing coalition, just as there is always a need for strengthening one's own. Secondly, every coalition is always a uniquely mixed collection of public and private interest groups, which includes some national and local governments, NGOs, business groups, non-EU stakeholders and Brussels officials. One always acquires many more useful routes and entrances into the EU system, while erecting road-blocks for opponent access.

Finally, one can add the *diachronic analysis*, which is an assessment of trends over time or, to use our metaphor, the film instead of the photograph. On a computer grid one can easily store the history of the arena and acquire two benefits. Firstly, one can check one's previous analyses and expectations, such as regarding boundary traffic, coalition formation and package dealing. The more one is surprised, the more one can and should improve the descriptive homework. The second benefit is insight into the next development of the dossier's life cycle within the arena. During the process most stakeholders will take a clear position, filling in their previously ambivalent or empty cells. Many stakeholders will come together, settle their mutual issues and combine their interests somehow. Others may fail to do so and become vulnerable to isolation. As time goes by, the two axes tend to become much shorter, but the friction between the remaining stakeholders and issues grows more intense as well. This often happens when the dossier enters a new phase, for example on the eve of the Commission's proposal, the Parliament's report, the Coreper's A-points or the start of an inspection procedure. The lobby group with diachronic insight can, if required, reposition itself in plenty of time, not reactively but proactively.

Pro-Active EU Arena Management: Window-In

The integrated and research-based analysis of an arena is, again, not a goal but a means to better action on the playing-field, to lobby window-in more successfully. Due to the complexities and dynamics of the arena, the action has to be reasoned and precise, thus be based on good preparation. Thanks to the complexities and dynamics, the investment in homework can bring great rewards. It gives major comparative advantages over the competitors who have neglected their preparatory work and act as amateurs seeking gold without inspecting the ground beforehand. Thanks to their homework, the studious lobby group can always see reasonable options for both trading-off issues and forming coalitions. Of course, it has to constantly update this work, based on new information and reflection, readying fresh options for tomorrow. Many a lobby group may be embarrassed by the luxurious paradox of *embarras du choix*: seeing so many attractive options, it struggles to decide what is the best thing to do. In such a case it should feel happy with the better choice and not search for the best choice, being the enemy of the better, as optimising a choice is usually more rational than maximising it. The worst situation is one without much choice at all, such as in the simple arena of a fight with one's spouse over the single issue of the next holiday's destination, when he wants to go north and she to the south; and the best solution is to lengthen the two axes of the matrix by inviting more people to join and by raising more issues among them, as then in any event an optimal solution will become possible. The proactive, research-based management of the EU arena can be described now for both the short and the long term. The only difference is the room to manoeuvre, which increases if there is more time.

Short-term EU Arena Management
The principles are based on the four components of an arena, each containing a basic dilemma. Firstly, there is *stakeholder management*. This contains the dilemma of whether to exploit both one's own strengths and the opponents' weaknesses or to reduce one's own weaknesses and the opponents strengths. In the EU arena, once again, the defensive strategy is usually both easier and less risky than the offensive one, in the same way as one survives an ambush on a battlefield better by improving one's shelter than by launching an attack. But by remaining under shelter, one gets something like a 1914 trench war, where nobody wins the battle. The second principle regards *issue management*. Here the main dilemma is whether to push both the opportunities to oneself and the threats to the opponents or to block both the threats to oneself and the opportunities to the opponents, in short to play either offensive or defensive again. In the EU arena, the blocking strategy is usually easier and less risky than the pushing one, just as one controls one's car on a slippery road surface better with the brake than with the accelerator. Thirdly, there is the dossier's life cycle or *time management*. This brings the dilemma of speeding-up or delaying the EU decision-making process. The delaying strategy is usually easier and less risky than the accelerating one, just as it is easier to keep one's balance on a slow-moving rather than on a fast-moving treadmill. However, if this goes slow, more competitors can leap on as well. Finally, there is *boundaries management*. This involves the dilemma of whether to widen or to restrict the arena boundaries. Here, the narrowing strategy is usually easier and less risky than the widening one, just as one negotiates more effectively in a small group than in a mass meeting. However, the stakeholders and issues left out may become disruptive at a later stage.

Easiness and low risk are, however, not necessarily the best criteria for deciding about the lobbying 'to whom in an arena on what'. A bias towards easiness and low risk often results in poor rewards. The lobby group accepting big trouble and high risk may become either the winner, taking almost all, or the victim of its own greediness by losing successively the desired outcome, respect from others and backing at home. Many EU lobby groups prefer moderate troubles and risks. They see a good chance of winning little bits as more attractive than the bad chance of losing almost everything, even if the latter may include the small chance of winning the big prize. The rationality behind this trouble and risk avoidance is usually their interest in many more dossiers than just one. The sum of many small but easily and safely obtainable prizes is seen as more attractive than the big prize, with greater trouble and with a high risk of severe losses.

The question remains of whether such avoidance of trouble and risk is really rational. Frequently, the standard practices of blocking, defensive, delaying and restrictive behaviour are nothing more than *rules of thumb*. Once a dossier or issue area has been selected as highly relevant, to which we will return in the next chapter, the rational choice of acceptable troubles and risks should not depend on such popular and unscientific rules, but on the situation in the arena. Three main types of situation have been distinguished above: friendly or promising, unfriendly or endangering, and indeterminate or unpredictable. These labels should not be taken as absolute but, as for any assessment, as relative because every arena can have varying degrees of difficulty and risk and therefore requires permanent prudence. For example, a friendly arena is one perceived as having more friends than enemies, containing benign rather than difficult issues, promising better rather than worse moments and being less unpleasant than the outside world, as having a relatively favourable tailwind blowing. It may still not be heaven, but it could be much worse. Instead of the full arena, even only part of it may be friendly, for example one category of issues and stakeholders. Every arena type thus requires specific management of the stakeholders, the issues, the moments in time and the boundaries, all together fine-tuned fieldwork (chapter 6). The *best practices* for the general management of the three main types of situation are derived from the logic of PA management and can be summarised as follows (Figure 4.4).

BEST PRACTICES OF ARENA MANAGEMENT

If the arena is then, best is:	FRIENDLY	UNFRIENDLY	INDETERMINATE
GENERAL MANAGEMENT	keep status quo	change situation	influence components
STAKEHOLDERS MANAGEMENT	secure support take free ride	divide opponents approach waverers	maybe argumentation negotiate
ISSUES MANAGEMENT	keep issues high block others	compensate the loss reframe the issues	reframe the issues try a balloon
TIME MANAGEMENT	speed up	delay	wait and see
BOUNDARIES MANAGEMENT	keep restricted	expand the arena	wait and see

Figure 4.4

In a mainly *friendly* arena (or section of it), the wind is turning into a tail-wind or already blowing supportive. The general strategy here is to keep the situation as it is and to harvest the fruits. The interest group can confine itself to a few securing actions. The identified friendly stakeholders with a primary status should be brought together, and be bound to common action on their common interests for optimising the M in $E = MI^2$ [Knoke, 1996]. From among the many supporters, one can best select a strongly influential player for both taking the lead and providing a free ride. The potentially opposing coalition(s), which always start out fragile, can be undermined by pumping up some of their internal issues and by seducing some of their influentials to defect. To keep the tailwind up to strength, one should distribute new evidence regularly and precisely that supports the benign issues and counter-evidence that blocks counter-issues, but without overkill. As the wind is blowing nicely, time management can best be directed at keeping the speed of the decision-making process high. The arena boundaries should not be widened but kept restricted to, as much as possible, the friendly stakeholders and issues already at hand. In this situation it is best to lobby very silently, as sound tends to attract new stakeholders that bring in new and maybe less friendly interests, which would delay the process. If, however, on the eve of a crucial moment in the decision phase, even more support is observed among the mass public, publicity can cause victory.

In a mainly *unfriendly* arena (or section of it) the wind is unpleasantly turning into a headwind or already blowing cold. A clear case is the down-hill position in an arena with the opponents uphill. Here the general strategy is to stimulate a change in the situation. The strong coalition(s) of opponents can best be divided by stirring their internal issues as revealed by the homework. This also shows which opponents are wavering and maybe open to argumentation, persuasion or negotiation. They might leave their coalition and thus help to turn the wind. On the unfriendly issues one can best try to find compensation for those assessed as probably lost. There is no good reason to lose with empty hands: as every win has its costs, every loss can bring its benefits. Even a dead horse may have a market value, especially among the amateurs who believe it is still alive. Alternatively, one can start to lobby for an exemption, to avoid the loss in the short run. More advanced is the search for such a reframing of a difficult issue that it will attract more support. Time management must be directed at delaying the decision-making process, for example by urging the need for extended impact assessment and consultation. A delay will, most probably, temper the cold wind and retard the expected loss. The widening of arena boundaries can also make the tide friendlier. New issues and new stakeholders delay the process, give more options for combining issues and create new coalitions. Here it may be rational to make some sound that usually attracts new stakeholders and issues at low costs, but this should be done through indirect channels that hide the sender. An uphill fight is not a lost cause, as many best practices are useful here, too. One only has to lobby differently, just as a sailor can proceed under headwind by sailing differently. In military terms, easier than the army positioned uphill, the troops that stand downhill can move around, build up an army and attack the lifelines of the enemy.

A mainly *indeterminate* arena (or section of it) has increasingly or primarily either side-winds (mixed positions) or no wind at all (empty cells). In case of *side-winds* the general strategy is to turn them into friendly ones. Most important here is the management of stakeholders and issues. In this indeterminate situation many stakeholders look for information and support and appear to be open to negotiation. They might accept argumentation regarding the disputed facts, values and solutions and be brought onto one's side by pleasant behaviour and compromises. A little bit of issue re-framing (salesman's talk) may be enough, in which case one tries to push better sounding interpretations of the facts, values and solutions at issue and to block those from the opposing side. Preferably indirectly, through befriended stakeholders, mass media or any other U-turn, one can also try launching a balloon in order to test reactions. There is no good reason to speed up or to delay the decision-making process. That depends on the turn of the tide, which is still to come. The same is true for either widening or narrowing the arena boundaries. There is sufficient room for playing inside the existing arena and no need to change it, unless the homework indicates that its widening will bring in mainly benign issues and stakeholders, or that its narrowing will repel mainly the difficult ones. In general, the better practice here is to wait and see alertly and to invest the saved energy in double scenario homework, in order to be better prepared for either the friendly or the unfriendly wind, one of which will arise anyhow sooner or later.

The other indeterminate variant, in which *no wind* is blowing, usually occurs only in the earliest phase of a dossier's life, when issues are still in formation and stakeholders absent or just arriving. The general strategy here is to mobilise support for one's own preferences. This, too, is mainly a matter of managing stakeholders and issues. Most stakeholders with empty cells will remain passive on the issue and might, like those who fake empty cells, be more open to direct deals than to argumentation. Conversely, the same applies to one's own empty cells on which one is indifferent and which can be used as free gifts, like another man's cigars. Issue reframing may help to convince others that their interest is shared. If others do so, this requires a lot of checking, as they may play comedy by feigning indifference, so trying to get free cigars. In this indeterminate situation it is hardly logical to speed up or to delay the process, or to change arena boundaries. It is better to follow a wait-and-see approach, combined again with double scenario homework. If, however, one is under time pressure coming from, for example, the organisation at home, it is better to launch a few trial balloons, so trying to get the wind to rise. In order to conceal the weakness of time pressure, one must do so only indirectly.

The *best practices* are clearly different from the rules of thumb mentioned above, which advocate blocking, defensive, delaying and restrictive behaviour. In a friendly situation, the action should be directed towards pushing one's coalition and issues offensively, speeding up the process and keeping the arena restricted. The first three rules of thumb are better not applied here, but only in an unfriendly situation. The fourth rule on boundary management should be applied in reverse in this situation. In an indeterminate situation it is frequently better to wait and see. The popularity of those rules of thumb among EU lobby groups suggests that many of them consider both their arenas and the areas beyond the boundaries to be unfriendly. Another interpretation is that they have neglected their homework and, without reflection, are simply relying on popular but unjustified rules of thumb. If so, they are behaving not professionally but amateurishly. The two interpretations are not mutually exclusive. In fact, the more unprepared a lobby group is, the more unforced errors it makes, and thus the more it feels itself to be in an unfriendly situation. From the aforementioned criteria of easiness and low risk, such an amateurish group suffers, paradoxically, the greatest troubles and highest risks. Rational risk avoidance must be based on a risk assessment study only. The lobbying based on rules of thumb should be replaced by prudent behaviour, based on best practices derived from continuous preparatory study. Notwithstanding all this, every lobby group can make mistakes that are not necessarily unforced ones. Some may be caused by imperfections of the preparation due to, for example, the volatility of an arena, others by the organisation at home, and even more by stakeholders lobbying in a smarter way, as will be shown in the next two chapters.

Long-term EU Arena Management

The long-term management of an EU arena has both *an early start and a late finish.* So should the preparatory work. The earlier one starts with it, the sooner one can possess in-depth insights regarding the arena allows one to play proactively. This sounds self-evident, but is often hard to realise in practice. There is usually an imbalance between (scarcely) available resources and (manifold) pressures from current games. Early preparation as a method of fire prevention can contribute to a rebalancing, as it reduces the chance of unforced errors and so saves on resources. The higher efficiency and effectiveness of window-in fieldwork clearly remain the sole objective of and the only justification for the early preparatory work. The arena has to be monitored continuously, even after its formal ending as a political game. It is never completely over: the losers may take revenge; a win may turn into a loss in disguise; unforeseen side effects may open new arenas and mistakes may have a boomerang effect. After the official decision, more dossier phases can come or create spill-overs.

The long-term approach to EU arena management yields three more advantages other than those contained in the short-term approach. First of all, one can *fine-tune the dossier phases.* In every phase there is usually a different demand for action. When, for example, an issue is becoming irritating to many more interest groups, the EU officials develop a special need for information relevant to the definition of the underlying problem. Through early preparation, a lobby group can supply the information that not only may bring the official problem definition but also the solutions thereafter closer to its interests. In the decision phase, both the officials and the other stakeholders have less appetite for information than for support. Again, through early preparation, a lobby group can select the most efficient and effective type of support. In its long-term management the lobby group can even consider an integrated process-oriented approach rather than a phased one. The homework then anticipates the future, and the action is organised backwards, into the present. An example is the aforementioned Air-Transport Slots case, with its backward action by the national air carriers at Council level against the proposals from the Commission.

Secondly, the long-term approach permits more than the proactive management of the impending stakeholders, issues, phases and boundaries. One can also apply the *general influence approaches*, as outlined in the previous chapter and applied there primarily to the EU officials. The actors' approach, focused on those who really make a decision, can be extended to every stakeholder, such as a EuroFed and a member inside. More sophisticated are the approaches based on factors and vectors. Their cultural, formal, operational and decisional variables can be equally relevant for any stakeholder, issue, phase or boundary. For example, the vector of issue reframing can change an enemy into a friend, shorten a phase and move a boundary at will. The Triple P game, with its prefabricated procedures, positions and people, now applied to collective platforms, can make the arena situation friendlier in future. All these approaches should contain covert sticks and overt carrots and a lot of poker play in disguise, and therefore require early and continuing study, permanent prudence and proactive management.

The third advantage of the long-term perspective is the possibility of *scenario management*. This starts with homework on the basic question of mental mapping: 'What can happen if x-y-z occurs and what then is the best course of action?' [Van der Heijden, 1996; Ringland, 1998]. A scenario is based on logical and/or empirical relationships between the independent variables x, y, z on one side and the possible outcomes or dependent variables on the other. The alleged relationships should meet the tests of relevance, consistency and possibility, but not of probability. In the field of EU arena study, the core variables are stakeholders (including the officials and one's own group), issues, time and arena boundaries. One can add such intervening variables as factors and vectors, or the components of Triple P. The outcomes are a few coherent scenarios or 'possible futures', to each of which one can pose the general question: *If this happens, what then is the best course of action?* More specific questions are enlightening too: *What is the best course of action, if...* (for example) this or that stakeholder disappears or changes his position? if a particular issue is traded-off or reframed? if a potential coalition achieves or loses cohesion? if the arena becomes widened or restricted? if the process is speeded up or delayed? if, regarding a stakeholder, a particular (cultural, formal, operational or decisional) factor is influenced or vector is created? if a Triple P game is played differently? Such questions are particularly useful in indeterminate arena situations.

By creating scenarios, a lobby group opens different windows onto possible futures. A grand example is the five possible Futures for Europe at the end of the 1990s, respectively called 'Triumphant Markets', 'One Hundred Flowers', 'Shared Responsibilities', 'Creative Societies' and 'Turbulent Neighbourhoods' [Bertrand and others, 1999]. They are not assumed to be probable. The least advantage they offer is *mental preparation* for the future. Someday a possibility may become more probable, and then the lobby group will be less surprised than it would have been otherwise and be able to use the scenario analysis for arena planning. This is no different from the thinking of the chess player, who wonders what will happen if the opponent moves one or another piece. The great reward from scenario study is that one can consider possible actions for possible futures and so turn scenario analysis into scenario management. An attractive possible future, at present still a daydream, might be promoted or managed in such a way that it becomes self-fulfilling, whereas a horrible possible future, at present only a nightmare, might be turned into a self-denying possibility. The precondition for scenario management is, of course, the early and ongoing study of both real and possible arenas.

Extra: The GMO Food Arena

Food is permanently at issue in the EU. A few issue dimensions out of many more are traditional food versus industrialised (processed), fat (causing obesity) versus light, fast versus slow ('tasteful'), regionally protected versus open-market produce, subsidised versus non-subsidised, healthy versus harmful (diseases) and produce containing genetically modified organisms (GMOs) from biotechnology versus those without. Every dimension has its variants with very different underlying interests. For example, GMO has variants called red (medical, health), white (industrial enzymes) and green (food), and the last, on which we focus here, differs for transgenic (different genes) and cisgenic (same genes). In the field of food, ranging from research and production to trade and consumption, the EU has always been so full of irritating differences that at present, most food laws operative in the member-countries come from the EU. In this broad issue domain, mostly Commission DGs are involved, such as on general matters COMP and MARKT, and on specific ones AGRI for subsidies, restitutions and quota, SANCO for food health, ENTER for industrial processing, RTD for research, TRADE for global trade and WTO affairs, REGIO for land use and DEV for food support to poor countries, to mention only these. The EP and Council play their role on secondary legislation and, under much pressure from Poland and other CEEC countries that want EU food policy more attuned to their needs, on agenda-building. The Commission, however, is the key-player, since most legislation in the field of food falls under delegated legislation, while the Court intervenes in both types of legislation. A milestone in the EU was the adoption of the 2002 Food Safety Regulation (EC 178/2002) and its establishment of the European Food Safety Authority. A major indicator of the overall relevance of the EU food domain is that this holds the biggest proportion of EU spending, expert committees, comitology ones and lobby groups of any kind. Now we shall focus on a part of the GMO arena in the early 2000s, when Prince Charles of the UK qualified its consequences for food as 'Frankenstein food'.

In February 1998, the Commission's DG Environment, Nuclear Safety and Civil Protection, which stood for consumer protection, proposed to revising the old Directive 90/220/EC on the deliberate *release into the environment of GMOs* to the EP and Council. Its objective was a stricter regulation, but not a full prohibition of the research, the production and the trade (both external and internal) of GMOs. In June 1999, the ministers of the Environment Council reached an informal, non-binding agreement mainly on procedure: any acceptance of GMOs for experimental or market releases must be based on both risk assessment and a decision by a competent authority and must meet special standards of risk management, monitoring and public information (such as labelling). France, protective of its traditional farming, wanted a full moratorium on further admission of products with GMOs (so far eighteen had been admitted) that the Council took as 'no further admission, unless no risk', with UK, Ireland and Portugal abstaining. In October 1999 the EP, being less rabid than the Council and acting under codecision, adopted 39 amendments, all directed at regulation without full prohibition of GMOs and almost all accepted by the Commission. In December 1999, the Council included four other principles, being precaution (no admission, if risk), traceability (regarding the origin of GMO products), authorisation period (a maximum of ten years) and the need for global agreements ('Biosafety Protocol'), and it formalised its previously informal position accordingly, now with France, Ireland and Italy abstaining. In the second reading, the EP and Council kept disagreeing, after which by conciliation procedure the compromise included the principle of labelling ('let the consumer decide') and lifting the moratorium, and so the proposal became law in March 2001 (EC 2001/18). As usual, the text held many provisions for detailed delegated legislation by the Commission, with the EP and Council at a distance, such as concerning admissions, traceability and labelling. As the devil (or the angel) is often more in the details (misleadingly called 'low politics') than in the framing text of secondary legislation (called 'high politics'), new conflicts lie in wait. Indeed, the next conflict came as early as May 2001, when the new DG ENVI (headed by Margot Wallström) presented its drafts on traceability and labelling and its new policy value of environmental liability (not limited to GMOs only), and proposed to set minimum levels of permitted GMOs immediately. The new DG SANCO (headed by David Byrne), however, claimed the competence on labelling and took the position that maximum levels should be set by comitology in due time. In the meantime, the Commission said it would consider ending the moratorium.

Between 1998 and 2001, the whole dossier has been a clear example of *many cleavages* inside and between the Commission, the EP and the Council. The three bodies primarily functioned as forums of conflict between numerous different stakeholders from inside and outside, and hardly as bodies to promote cohesion. The Commission was particularly divided by its DGs, their Cabinets and even inside them. While DG Environment was sitting in the driver's seat, DG External Trade (for settling GMO issues with the US), DG Industry (for economic growth) and DG R&D (for new technology) wanted to hit the brake pedal. DG Agriculture was divided between traditional and modern farming, and DG Consumer Affairs (the forerunner of DG SANCO) between consumer benefits (price, quality) and safety (health). In the EP, the environment 'freaks' got strong support from the Green Party and, inside the committee on Environment, the driver's seat, while all other groups were divided. In the Environment Council the ministers disagreed among each other. Instead of making decisions, they quarrelled about principles and procedures, their resort of Triple P. Many ministers had to cope with domestic cleavages as well, particularly among ministries, industrial groups and NGOs. Not surprisingly, at the end many issues had to be left unsettled and, as part of the conciliation compromise, became delegated to the Commission that then won this Triple P game. The politicised dossier collected a gathering of lobby groups from outside, each closely connected to the different stakeholders inside the three institutions. To cut a long story short, those groups soon became reduced to two main coalitions: the anti-GMO and the pro-GMO one.

The *anti-GMO movement* was led by Greenpeace and included lobby groups from the health, religion, ethics, animal welfare and development aid camps. It also received support from traditional farmers (averse to new technology) and retailers (fearing consumer protests). Now nestled within DG Environment and the EP's committee, the anti-GMO movement had experienced a tailwind before. The 1990 adoption of the old directive had turned out to be a hard pill to swallow for the industry. It became a classic Greek drama, full of ideological conflicts and power-plays between different Commission DGs, EP committees and Councils, but gradually with the officials on environment getting the driver's seat [Gottweis, 1999; Patterson, 2000]. The 1996 acceptance of transgenic maize proved to be a Pyrrhic victory for the traders [Bradley, 1998], with Italy, Austria and Luxembourg refusing to implement the decision. The 1998 Biotechnology Patent Directive (EC 1998/44) narrowly passed, after fierce opposition from inside the Commission (DG Environment), the EP (across parties), and the Council (from Denmark, Austria and the Netherlands). Opposing this directive, Greenpeace had constructed the European Campaign on Biotechnology Patents (ECOBP), and soon it could use this as a springboard for its campaign against the 1998 proposal on the release of GMOs. To strengthen the arising tailwind, it mobilised public opinion at both the national and European level. Mass media smelled and fanned the fires of public fear for 'Frankenstein food'. The anti-GMO coalition got its edge when the dossier came under control of their friends in DG Environment and those in the EP and Council. It applied and enjoyed the Triple P game. Seeing that the arena was turning friendly, it tried to speed up the process and to keep the arena restricted to its issues and allies. It applied the best practices of arena management rather professionally.

The *pro-GMO coalition* lacked a cohesive platform but was led by Europabio, a EuroFed of companies interested in biotechnology, particularly the red variant for pharmaceuticals (like GlaxoSmithKline). Europabio was not against regulation of GMOs, but wanted it to be based on sound risk assessment, permitting research, enabling consumers to choose and keeping trade competitive. Major food companies (like Unilever) shared this approach and, as their EuroFed CIAA was divided on the matter, started to cooperate with Europabio. Soon they found that companies and patients in the health business tend to consider GMO risk to be an opportunity rather than a threat, and they came to occupy an almost isolated position. From stakeholders in their chain (farmers, retail) and in other trades using GMO (like chemicals, beer, meat and feed) the food companies hardly got any support. Only a few DGs (Industry, R&D and Consumer Affairs) and some MEPs (Socialists and Christian Democrats) gave some support. Most national governments took shelter from this issue area. Noisy and aggressive support from US seed-producers like Monsanto and Cargill soon proved to be more hindrance than help. Mass media fanned the flames. The headwind calmed a little bit in 2000, when the EP plenary rejected the most contentious amendments, the Commission presented its package deal including the lifting of the moratorium, and the Council agreed with a delegation of powers to the Commission. For Unilever, this came too late: in May 2000, it decided to end, for the time being, the production and trade in Europe of products containing GMOs. Three months later the Swiss giant Novartis followed this example. The food companies were weary of feeling that they were on the lower side of an unlevel playing-field. However, they should not have been surprised. The previous EU decisions on the 1990 Directive, transgenic maize and the Patent Directive had shown them a mounting headwind that made the Commission, preparing its 1998 proposal, an open forum for conflict. All this was widely known, and should have stimulated the food companies to become better prepared for the headwind. Instead of the exit option, companies like Unilever could have applied the best practices of surviving in an unfriendly arena, for instance as follows.

A good *stakeholders analysis* could have revealed that the opposing coalition was far from unified. For example, the green movement was divided into a polemic European faction and a moderate Third World faction that considered GMOs as the poor man's 'cheap fertilizer', better than chemicals. The health movement, partly organised in the European Public Health Alliance (EPHA), was divided into a 'caring' and a 'curing' faction, the latter acknowledging the benefits of GMOs for patient groups. Other stakeholders had taken ambivalent positions, such as the consumer organisation BEUC that was not against GMOs, but concerned about consumer safety and price-quality ratio. Traditional farmers were only partially orthodox green peasants, averse to new technology, the rest were small farmers fearing stronger competition. Multinational food retailers, such as Carrefour (France), Sainsbury (UK) and Delhaize (Belgium), were divided by market competition with both each other and alternative retailers like health food stores. Last but not least, the Commission, EP and Council were notoriously divided over the whole dossier. In short, the advocates of GMOs had strong enemies but also many potential friends around, and could have strengthened their own position by undermining the fragility of the opponent coalition, by seducing ambivalent stakeholders to indifference or even defection, and by creating a better collective platform of their own, without indifferent stakeholders like pharmaceutical companies or aggressive ones like Monsanto.

Proactive *issue analysis* could have provided many clues for all that. At an early stage, the food companies could have promoted the controversial issues among their opponents, such as the poor man's fertilizer, medical benefits, price-quality benefits for consumers, crop benefits for small farmers, and market opportunities for health food retail. Then they would have restricted their opponents' room to build a broad coalition around the issues of environment and safety and reframed them as, for example, global nutrition, agricultural development, public health, consumer welfare, economic growth, quality employment and environmental savings. Then they also might have found better loss-compensation than the lifting of a moratorium that had no legal basis at all, for example EU research subsidies for low-risk GMOs or a simplified admission procedure for new food products. Shortly after the game Unilever did push the latter successfully, not for its GMO interests but for its GMO-free new margarine that lowers cholesterol. In the new 2003 European Food Safety Authority, it even managed to secure the chair of the Management Board.

In an unfriendly arena, one should try to delay the process, as one is still alive as long as love is not yet hanging. The companies should have made a better *time analysis* for finding smart delays. For example, on the disputed GMO benefits for Third World countries, the companies could have lobbied in those countries, and at DG DEV for a round of consultations with developing countries; via Europabio, they could have mobilised patient groups to lobby for exemptions that complicate the process. The menu of delaying techniques is really not short, as it ranges from actors to approach, factors to use and vectors to create. For example, the companies could have elicited new research to confuse some opponents, challenged the Treaty basis of the Revised Directive or evoked an early complaint from the WTO, all that not for its own merits but as a means to win time. With anticipation, the companies could also have created a more cohesive platform of their own in good time, without companies like Monsanto wanting to speed up the EU decision process for having its new GMO products admitted, and thus dividing the Europabio camp and helping their enemy.

By *boundary analysis*, the companies could have created their last safe resort. In such an unfriendly situation they should have striven for a widening of the arena. By provoking new issues and stakeholders, they might have won at least more time and at most more benign issues and stakeholders. They could have reactivated, for example, the issues of stagnating employment and global competitiveness that need innovative technology. That might have brought to their side the trade unions and the socialist parties fearing loss of employment to US producers. Even DG Social Affairs and DG Industry might have joined this coalition actively. The companies could also have demanded that the precaution principle (if risk, no admission), if adopted, should be applied, as a matter of legal fairness, to totally different policy areas as well, such as to transport, chemicals, regional development and, not least, traditional agriculture. This might have brought many new stakeholders into the arena for fighting against the principle. The companies could even have linked their interests to the Agenda 2000, being decided in March 1999, on which the issues of employment and growth stood central.

All the foregoing recommendations are hindsight wisdom, useful for learning and anyhow illustrating the room to manage an unfriendly arena. Since 2002 much has changed. The EP has kept its moderate position, but DG SANCO (David Byrne) came to sit in the driver's seat on the food domain and took the lines of traceability and labelling. DG AGRI (Franz Fishler) wanted controlled experiments with GMO in agriculture rather than a full prohibition. DG RTD and DG ENTER joined the troops actively on research and production. To open the EU market to new US GMO crops, the US government continued its pressure through the WTO and directly on European governments in the Council. In September 2003, the Commission proposed its moderate regulations on GMO food and feed authorisation (EC 2003/1829) and traceability and labelling (EC 2003/ 1830) to the Parliament and Council. True enough, its crucial Standing Committee on Food Chain and Animal Health (SCoFCAH, comitology) often votes against Commission proposals, based on EFSA expertise, to allow new GMO crops and so enables Parliament and Council to overrule the Commission formally but, as always the case so far, neither the EP nor Council could produce a majority against these proposals and hence they all let (according to the rules of comitology) the Commission win and admit new GMOs willy-nilly. At the end of the 2000s, the wind has clearly shifted in a friendlier direction, particularly thanks to the EFSA's scientific approach to GMOs, the decline of the ECOBP alliance, friendlier reframes like innovation, stronger positions of GMO protagonists inside the EU, US pressure at the WTO level, the 2007 issue of 'food shortages' for which GMO can be a solution, and the change of public opinion towards moderate acceptance [Heslop, 2005]. Frankenstein has been exorcised, at least for a while.

Arena Analysis: Necessary Means, No Sufficient Goal

The short exercise on the GMO food arena is no magic show but an example of the utility of thoughtful arena analysis for finally managing an arena more successfully. It also illustrates the many reasoned options obtainable through systematic descriptive and analytical homework. Professional lobby groups consider this preparatory work as necessary in order to find sound answers to the question of *'whom to lobby in an arena on what'*. They can now see the best practices for window-in lobbying, as illustrated by the GMO case. Semi-professionals limit the homework to studying only a few stakeholders and issues and perhaps some moments, and take the arena boundaries as set, thereby failing to match the performance of professionals. Amateurish groups that take into account little more than a few EU officials, their own desires and usually a decision-making moment at a late stage of the game hardly have a chance of winning. Yet, like any sporting achievement, preparation is only the means and not the objective or, in academic words, it is a necessary but not a sufficient condition for success. Even after the best preparation, at least four factors may contribute to losing a game regularly, a set sometimes, and perhaps a match.

Firstly, inherent to every complex and dynamic situation there is always a degree of *uncertainty*, caused by a less than perfect quantity and quality of information and an inevitable dependency on next-best solutions. The volume of both observations and options makes their all-round processing mere howling at the moon, as for the game of chess that is simpler than the game of an EU arena. Every player decides to the best of his knowledge, but the level of knowledge may vary significantly. The smallest margin can, however, be decisive for the outcome, like a few balls in the match point in tennis. The management of uncertainty is, in other words, the management of best possible knowledge, including chance and opportunity. Every player, secondly, can have some *bad luck*, even if this is only the good luck of a competitor. It may come from some special information or support. In the 1992 HDTV case, Commissioner Filippo Pandolfi, personally in favour of this technology, was the embodiment of luck: good for the producing companies and bad for the opponents, and when he left in 1994 the luck reversed. Good or bad luck is, however, seldom a message from heaven or hell. Often it can be (or could have been) foreseen by good homework and scenarios. Thirdly, the *chance of winning* is a factor. The best prepared and most excellent player at the low side of a mountainous playing-field can have less chance of winning than the amateur player entrenched in an uphill bastion. In the 1998 GMO case, the food companies found they had a downhill position. Chance, however, is not a metaphysical category. By studious homework it can be noticed and responded to through appropriate measures that improve and stabilise chance.

Finally, an otherwise professional lobby group can lose a game and even its reputation, if its *home organisation* has become disorderly or in bad shape. Even when all its preparatory homework for an arena has been carried out excellently but is not taken at home as input for strategy and mandate for action, then it cannot create a winning performance. In general, when the home organisation has no sufficient capacity for arena management, lacks a clear strategy, leaves its targets undefined or does not learn from its mistakes, whether forced or unforced, then it will bring even its best professional to despair instead of high performance. This is the theme of the next chapter.

CHAPTER 5

MANAGING THE HOME FRONT

Who Is Lobbying, Why, for What and with What Result?

In this chapter, the lobby group is the *unit of analysis*. It may be the Siemens company, an NGO like Animal Welfare, the EuroFed CIAA (food industry), the Warsaw local government, the Regional Affairs Ministry of Italy, the AmCham in Brussels, the Commission or any other established organisation of either a public or a private nature, and based either inside or outside the EU area. They have all been formally established, but have semi-formal or informal layers that exist either internally or externally and may also be relevant for consideration as a lobby unit. Internally, any part of an organisation can behave as a lobby group, for example a company's division, a ministry's bureau, a Commission DG, a DG's unit, an EP inter-group, a section of an NGO, or the junior staff of MEPs. Every established interest group participates in external networks and platforms that might develop into lobby groups as well. They may take place as an ad hoc coalition, cross-sectoral platform, interface between industrialists and officials, Irishmen's club, meeting of French and German officials or a regular dinner among ministers from applicant member states. The formally established interest group, however, remains our focus for the leading questions here regarding internal organisation, strategy, targeted agendas and evaluation, in short for getting insight into 'who is acting, why, for what and with what result?', as summarised in Figure 3.3 and placed on the left-hand side of Figure 1.2.

The simple-minded lobby group answers the questions before they are posed. It takes its self-image as self-knowledge, its motivation for the action as self-evident and its objectives as clear enough. It divides the results into two categories: the losses are to be blamed on others, and the gains come from its own performance. In daily life it will continually blame others and whitewash itself. In contrast, the professional group knows that its internal affairs are always an incomplete puzzle, its motivations uncertain and its objectives full of dilemmas. It divides the causes of both its losses and its gains into either its own behaviour and/or outside (f)actors. It aims to strengthen the *causal relationship* between its behaviour and the targeted results of lobbying by improving its internal PA organisation. Many PA officials spend more than half their energy on improving the home organisation, the remainder spent on EU officials and competitors. Their own organisation is often the most difficult arena, called the home front, requiring much ambition, study and prudency.

Our approach is, once again, not normative but *advisory*. There is no good reason why a lobby group or even a citizen should not be allowed to act in a simple-minded or amateurish manner. It may be in a situation that sufficiently justifies this. But if it wants to create real chances to influence its challenging EU environment, then it must europeanize, by taking the EU arenas as sources of inspiration for the early improvement of its home front. For this reason, chapter 4, on managing the EU arena, preceded this chapter. No lobby group can ever get a desired outcome from EU decision-making by an introverted focus on its own inner world, as this would block its window-out and -in. It has to adapt its organisation, strategies and agendas to EU constraints and possibilities permanently by allowing required variability and flexibility within its internal affairs. The ambitious lobby group is also eager to learn all the time from both its own experiences and those of others. These differences between amateurish and professional behaviour remain our focus.

Organisational Assets for Lobbying

From the general literature [such as Milbrath and Goel, 1977; Kobrin, 1982; Schlozman and Tierney, 1986] and the aforementioned case studies of EU lobbying, one can distil four main assets or qualities that differentiate strongly between amateurish and professional behaviour: sufficient cohesion, useful knowledge, basic resources and skills, and a good image. Of course, they are distinguishable but not separate from each other. An ambitious lobby group should permanently improve them by, again, optimisation rather than maximisation.

Sufficient Cohesion
In the previous chapter we assumed, for the sake of simplicity, that a lobby group acting on the divided EU playing-field is internally cohesive. *Cohesion* we define here as the end situation of both coherency of preferences and co-ordination of actions. The assumption of cohesion is usually false.

Under normal circumstances every group is internally divided, with its members arguing for their chosen facts, values and solutions. In short, it has its internal issues, which become manifest through different preferences and divergent actions at its informal, semi-formal and formal layers.

(1) At the informal level exists the *pluralism* of the group members with their different values and interests, and the larger the group, the greater these usually are. Within a multinational company or NGO, people differ in their behaviour according to, for example, their age, education, religion, ambition, nationality, language, expertise and position. Within a EuroFed there is usually a pluralism of members differing according to, inter alia, national origin, managerial style, market position and organisational strategy. Every Commission DG has a multitude of civil servants who differ in, for example, expertise, national or regional background, character, career aspirations, policy beliefs and loyalty patterns. A regional or local lobby group often has its differences among people in the administrative units and the political level. Such pluralism can fragment the larger organisation and transform parts of it into self-reliant lobby groups that act externally on their own.

(2) At the semi-formal level the *variety of role expectations* is normally the main cleaving factor. Staff and line people tend to have different expectations regarding each other's contributions, which may cause misunderstandings and conflicts between, for example, the legal affairs staff versus that in public relations, and the people in one product line versus those in another. A company like Philips, a DG like External Trade, an NGO like Greenpeace or a EuroFed like ETUC is, at the semi-formal level, normally an amalgam of different sets of role expectations, based particularly on functional and territorial divisions. The amalgam can easily and centrifugally cause self-reliant behaviour from the constituent parts, including the establishment of new external networks.

(3) Even at the formal level of an established organisation, internal cohesion can normally never be assumed. The formal division of *tasks and duties* already makes the organisation internally divided. The Commission's DG Agriculture and DG Development have a real conflict of interests regarding meat exports to poor countries like those in the African Sahel, as the one DG has to promote the subsidised exports by European farmers and the other has to prevent them in order to protect the Sahel farmers. In an NGO, the steering committee, the bureau and the plenum have different formal positions, which can easily conflict. In most countries, the national Ministry of Transport has formal responsibility for both railway and road transport and is thus internally divided about the values of public versus private transport.

All such internal divisions are so *normal* for a lively organisation that it is an abnormal or unnatural state of affairs for them to be absent. If there is full and spontaneous cohesion at all layers, then something must be seriously wrong inside due to, for example, a crisis emanating from outside, internal despotic rule, or simply a malfunctioning of people and units neglecting their different values, roles and duties. The natural state of internal divisions can even be seen as richness. Its pluralism makes the organisation better adapted to the pluralism of the European environment, its variety of role expectations generates more dialectical dynamics internally, and its different task allocations create a strong stakeholder inside for every formalised value the organisation holds. Even their centrifugal forces can be potentially healthy for external operations, as they may increase the organisation's capacity for flexible and rapid responses to EU challenges, for cost-saving self-reliance of the constituent parts, and for prospective antennae and protective shields.

The richness of internal divisions should neither be minimised nor maximised, but *optimised*. The economy of EU lobbying starts at home. Minimising the divisions by strict orders to obey creates high risks of losing the rewards from internal divisions and of becoming vulnerable at the top. Only in abnormal crisis-like situations, when all hands need to be on deck, could this be justified. Under normal circumstances, however, such an enforcement of both coherence and co-ordination makes the organisation introverted, takes up a lot of scarce resources such as time and initiative, and puts a premium on obstruction. Maximising the richness of diversity should also be avoided, because a deeply divided organisation cannot act effectively outside. Competitors who have done their homework well might fan the flames of the internally dividing issues and so paralyse the organisation, and EU officials cannot take seriously an interest group with cacophonous or even contradictory voices, such as those that came from the government of Malta regarding its membership request (in favour in 1993 and 1998, but against in 1996). Only 'sufficient' cohesion is needed, but this optimum is, inevitably, always a delicate balance between internal support and external effectiveness, and it has to be found anew each round [Kobrin, 1982].

The big question, of course, is how to achieve sufficient cohesion. Here too, *preparatory homework* should drive the internal fieldwork. The internal arena can best be monitored in the same way as the external arena, outlined in the previous chapter and summarised in Figure 4.3. For any EU dossier, the internal stakeholders can be listed, such as the people doing the monitoring, colleagues in the office, those in other staff and line offices, main executives and, if applicable, key people in the country units. Their issues and positions should be described realistically. One person can be made responsible for this homework, for example the PA officer, the secretary or a board member, but the better result comes from the simultaneous involvement of a few people or small groups, the duplica method described in the previous chapter. Multinational companies (MNCs) often question their key people in the product divisions and country units about their views on an EU dossier, who then inform the PA manager about the internal arena. In government organisations like ministries and agencies, people frequently voice their differences spontaneously on paper or orally, which is less efficient, as positions on paper are hard to change, and spoken statements are easily confused and confusing.

Subsequently, this homework has to result in the *building of sufficient cohesion*. Its formation must balance the assessed internal and external arenas and is the starting point of strategy development, to be discussed below. There is, of course, a lot of variation by type of organisation, to which we will return in the extra section below. Even domestic culture can be a factor. If cohesion is mainly constructed top-down, as is frequently the German practice, then the cohesion is highly formal, requires a lot of signatures and time and tends to be poorly anchored [Nutt, 1999]. Dutch and Danish organisations, by contrast, have the reputation of favouring a bottom-up approach, which includes staff and line units and even work councils. The more bottom-up, the better the cohesion can be anchored at the informal level, but the costs of internal compromise and hence time are frequently the price to pay. British organisations usually rely on mid-level managers for cohesion, under approval from the top. Whatever the style, internal lobbying is always required, both window-out for monitoring and window-in for getting commitment. The final test of sufficient cohesion lies in the outside world and concerns the capacity to deliver what has been promised to stakeholders and officials there.

Sufficient cohesion is necessary but often not achieved. An organisation can remain substantially and seriously divided on an EU dossier, even after a Teutonic top-down intervention. In the case of *enduring dissent* the organisation can best remain passive on the dossier, in order to avoid boomerang effects. For this reason, heterogeneous EuroFeds like BusinessEurope usually have to abstain from taking positions on specific dossiers on which their members have conflicting interests. If dissent develops into an almost permanent and paralysing cleavage, then the dramatic step of really splitting the organisation should be considered. In the mid-1990s, the Philips company became internally deeply divided on the EU dossier regarding the imposition of copyright on compact discs. Its music-producing unit Polygram wanted this, but its CD-rewriters production unit was strongly opposed. In 1998, Polygram was sold to the Canadian entertainment company Seagram, thus resolving the internal cleavage. In a voluntary association such as a EuroFed, dissatisfied members usually anticipate such a dramatic decision. They simply start an ad hoc coalition or a new EuroFed. In 1990, most European car manufacturers left the EuroFed CCMC because the French Peugeot group PSA continued to block a common position regarding the EU dossier on car imports from Japan. They formed the new ACEA in 1991 (with, ironically, PSA joining in 1994) [McLaughlin, 1994].

Useful Knowledge
A second characteristic of the professional lobby group is the acquisition of knowledge useful for getting the desired EU outcomes. The amateurish group is easily satisfied with its own impressions and perceptions of reality, or it simply follows the wisdom of its leadership. Of course, the professional group is not an epistemic or academic faculty. It sees the acquisition of knowledge not as a primary objective, but only as an essential means for the realisation of its EU targets [Lindblom and Cohen, 1979], which requires knowledge about both oneself and the arena.

The most critical category of knowledge is *self-knowledge*, which requires a balanced insight into one's own desires and fears on the one side and one's own capacities on the other. These desires and fears must have a better basis than the random collection of daydreams and nightmares. In a self-conscious lobby group, they are assessed after much window-out monitoring, as described in the previous chapter, and followed by a critical match with internal preferences, which has to be in balance with the capacity for action. The group has to know realistically the state of its internal variety of informal values, semi-formal role expectations and formal tasks and duties, which all exist behind its official façade of unity. It must also be informed about resources and skills at its disposal and, not least, about its image in the eyes of other stakeholders. The whole matter of self-knowledge is so essential in EU lobbying that we will return to it in the next paragraph.

The second category of required knowledge is *arena knowledge*, as discussed in the previous chapter. For every major phase in the life of the dossier at stake, it must comprise at least the primary stakeholders, including the EU officials, with their issues and their preferences. The lobby group has to become familiar with the arena boundaries, because otherwise it cannot exploit new stakeholders and outside issues. In addition, it has to assess every time the precise nature of the arena and the direction of the wind blowing there or not. With the help of a PA expert, it can obtain all this 'software' knowledge from the sources mentioned in Figure 4.2, and add to this the 'hardware' of the EU machinery, such as the important institutions and their components (chapter 2) and the manageable actors, factors and vectors, including the Triple P game (chapter 3).

In spite of all efforts to collect useful knowledge, even the most professional group can only act under *limited knowledge*, as concluded in chapter 4. The required information about one's own organisation is, like that about the external arena, never complete or fully reliable. Uncertainty is the lot of every lobby group, but of the amateur more so than of the professional. The latter has the ambition and expertise to improve the quantity and quality of information continuously, but is also aware of the costs of maximising it and therefore wants to optimise. Being more conscious about the relativity of its desires, the professional group is also more capable of reconsidering its strategy and observing a new option or opportunity, for example a different dossier, a better moment or a friendlier stakeholder. It knows that also the competitors and EU officials have limited knowledge and that often the marginal difference of knowledge is most crucial and the final test of optimisation. In order to cover this crucial margin, the professional group, paradoxically, tends to overexpose its uncertainty, while the amateur one frequently camouflages its uncertainty by a show of self-confidence.

Optimal Mix of Resources and Skills
Resources are the organisation's tools for survival. They are not fixed assets in permanent possession, but have to be acquired and constantly kept in good condition. A tool can be anything that contributes to effective and efficient participation in EU politics. Even the strong desire to influence the process or the nuisance value acquired during lobbying might be seen as a resource. A more common tactic is to limit the concept to an organisation's *capacity for action*, and not include the categories of desires, compulsions and opportunities [Schlozman and Tierney, 1986, V]. Even then it remains a broad and dynamic concept. Sufficient cohesion, useful knowledge and a good image, all taken here as indicators of professionalism, could be presented as important resources as well. In both the aforementioned case studies and the limited research in the field [Kohler-Koch, 1998; Wessels, 1999; Koeppl, 2001], the most frequently mentioned resources are, however, expertise, networks, external positions and financial means.

(1) *Expertise* comprises not only the useful arena knowledge mentioned above, but also the self-knowledge and the expertise of managing an arena. The latter has both a technical and a political dimension. In the EU system

of compromising decision-making, every big fight, for example regarding health conditions at the workplace, tends to be rapidly split up into many technical issues, such as regarding the noise or the radiation coming from a machine. A lobby group must have the technical expertise to deal with such issues. Political expertise is required for finding the terms of their settlement, which is primarily a matter of lobbying for support. Most interest groups have plenty of technical experts within reach, but fall short of political or, more precisely, public affairs experts. The Commission and the EP usually show a reversed imbalance, as they excel in political expertise but fall short of technical expertise, and hence have to insource the latter via expert committees or inter-groups or by inviting experts to come along.

(2) *Networks* are crucial in the pluralistic and fragmented EU area for bringing together the different stakeholders. Most important is the informal network, because this is the precondition for the development of a stable semi-formal one, such as an ad hoc coalition, which in its turn is a precondition for the formation of a formal organisation, such as a EuroFed. A formal platform without a stable semi-formal layer falls short of authority and can only survive artificially, for example thanks to a privileged legal position. Many a Council session is just such an artificial platform providing a privileged position to the national government. A solely semi-formal network without an underlying informality can easily lack stability and create its own misunderstandings, as frequently happens in Commission committees [Van Schendelen, 1998].

(3) *External positions* are seen as crucial, because they link a lobby group to the networks of stakeholders and to the EU machinery. The position may be that of an ordinary member of a EuroFed or an EU expert group, who sits around the table, monitors the others, voices a few comments and uses the seat mainly as a means to improve his self-reliant plan of action. It may also be that of an informal leader, such as a big multinational in a fragmented EuroFed full of small and medium-sized enterprises (SMEs). A formally empowered position is not necessarily better than a merely informal one. It is not formal power but influence that matters, and the former, with its obligations of accountability, can even hamper the latter. In many a case, it is better to be the secretary running the apparatus invisibly than the formal chairman attracting all the attention. Particularly useful is the accumulation of positions. Some lobby groups have managed to position the same person as secretary of a EuroFed, expert on a committee, member of an inter-group and representative in a working group. By contrast, the civil servants of the Commission for the most part do not hold positions somewhere else.

(4) *Financial means* are, due to the costs of EU lobbying, frequently

claimed to be important resources as they enable the group to hire better resources such as staff and office and thus to create better chances of success [Coen, 2007; Eising, 2007; Greer and others, 2008], although others are sceptical about that claim [Beyers and Kerremans, 2007]. There is no reliable or complete information on the size of PA budgets at the EU level. There seems to be much variation, as some sources show. Almost half the EuroFeds of any kind have an annual budget of less than 100,000 euro, which covers a few staff members and some office space [Greenwood, 2007, 17], while those from business are estimated at a mean budget of one-and-half million euro [Eising, 2004, 234]. NGOs range from less than 500 euro for some Polish ones to multi-millions of euro for Care International [Belou and others, 2003, 18]. Regional offices have on average an annual budget around 200,000 euro [Marks and others, 2002, 11]. A survey among 140 diverse PA practitioners shows that in 2007 their budget increased by around ten percent on average [ComRes, 2008]. The definition of costs remains, unspecified in all sources however, and may vary from full to marginal and from gross to net costs. Some cost items, such as for expert-group work, are usually reimbursed by the Commission, which also sponsors many NGOs directly or by granting projects to them. Many lobby groups have a joint office and staff, and divide the costs among themselves. Even the concept of 'poverty' is not easy to measure, as Shell looks rich and Greenpeace poor, while both are rich if all the volunteers of the latter are capitalised [Maloney and Jordan, 1997]. Nonetheless, in 1998 Greenpeace was able to spend 70 million euro, mainly on political action [*Financial Times*, 20-09-00], which is much more than the public affairs budget of any known EuroFed or MNC.

In practice, the four resources can sometimes be interdependent and substitutive. For example, expertise can be derived from one's, network, be the result of acquiring a position or be bought from a consultancy. A strategic position inside the EU machinery may make networks or finances redundant. A popular belief among mass media is that financial means can produce all other resources. In reality, however, expertise, positions and networks are often linked to a particular organisation or person and as such are not freely for sale on the market. Therefore, one cannot conclude that one single resource is absolutely the most important one, although PA expertise may be, relatively speaking, the key resource, as this gives the ultimate trade-off in lobbying by its provision of information and support. However important all resources may be, many professional EU lobby groups shift their lobby investments *from resources to skills*, which can be defined as meta-capacities for developing the capacity for action or, simly, as meta-resources. Then it is not the possession of expertise, networks, positions and budgets which is seen as crucial, but that of the skills needed to acquire them at the right moment, in the right place and with the optimal mix. An example is Unilever's Crisis Prevention and Response Toolkit, developed in the mid-2000s for improving its managers' skills to anticipate and cope with any sort of downturn. It soon proved useful during the 'financial crisis' of autumn 2008. The logic behind this emphasis on skills is two-fold: skills rather than resources make the difference, and they are more cost-efficient. Taking care of, for example, a resource like a network is an extremely time-consuming affair. The homework can reveal in advance which optimal mix of resources and skills is needed for the fine-tuned fieldwork on a dossier in hand. The final test takes place, again, in reality.

Two different skills deserve special attention. One is the ability to remain cool and calm during a game of lobbying, in short *unagonized*, in spite of all the tricks played by opponents. Whatever happens during the game, a lobby group must always remain concentrated on its target in the arena, like the football player challenged by various tricks (spitting, scolding, tackling) must keep watching the ball only, as otherwise the ball is lost. This difficult skill of remaining unagonized gives a highly competitive advantage. The second special skill regards the *research and development (R&D)* for useful new resources. In daily practice, many available resources hardly make a difference, because they are widespread or do not match the need in a specific case. The art is to develop new ones that surprise competitors and attract EU officials, thus truly making a difference. In theory anything, even making a virtue out of necessity, can be used as a tool of effective EU lobbying. Recent real-life examples are networking through electronic media (like blogs, YouTube and Face Book), 'inspiring' accountancy firms that work for the Commission, multi-level lobbying via the US or WHO and establishing a fresh BONGO or GONGO. From its side, the Commission has developed new Triple P tools, such as the open online consultation and the impact assessments. New tools may be found by trial and error or by imitation, but by R&D the lobby group can be the first to take the lead. They are ultimately the product of PA expertise.

Good Image
The fourth characteristic of a qualified lobby group is a good image. Stakeholders and officials feel easily attracted to groups with a good image rather than a bad one. The notion of image has two main dimensions, the first being its *good reputation in general*, which stands for both importance and

trustworthiness. By being seen as important, the group can avoid being overlooked and can have an anticipated influence on the others, even if it remains passive [Dahl, 1991]. There are, of course, different forms of importance. At one extreme, the lobby group is seen as having the power of, for example, a veto position (such as at the Council level) or a strong nuisance value (a blocking minority in a EuroFed). At the other extreme, it is sympathy among a wider public that makes the lobby group important. In the 1990s, NGOs promoting environmental issues ranked high on social sympathy. In between power and sympathy stand the variants of authority, prestige and respect, as enjoyed by the European Round Table of Industrialists (ERT) and the Economic and Financial Committee (EFC, formerly the Monetary Committee). The image of trustworthiness is the necessary addendum to importance. The lobby group must be seen as one which can be trusted to make a deal, because it has a reputation of credibility for its words, loyalty to its promises and predictability for its subsequent actions. The best trust is based on a common interest, but cultural traits can solidify it [Grant, 2003]. Without trustworthiness, even the most powerful or sympathetic group may have a limited appeal, as it may be considered a monster or comedian to be blamed rather than trusted. After its 1995 campaign against the Brent Spar, Greenpeace became distrusted for its false information. In 2008, German car manufacturers earned the Worst Lobby Prize, awarded by NGOs like Spinwatch, for their 'biased information' on CO_2 emissions. However, trustworthiness without importance is even worse, as it makes the lobby group a helpless lamb for the wolf.

The professional lobby group always cares about its general reputation. It wants to be perceived as important and trustworthy, as the resulting goodwill decreases its costs of lobbying and increases its effectiveness. The more anticipated influence it enjoys, the less it has to lobby. The more respect or sympathy it enjoys, the more easily it can obtain a place around a table of interest. The more it is seen as trustworthy, the more comfortably it can come to a deal. A good general reputation is no gift from heaven but the product of careful *reputation management*, requiring a lot of preparatory homework, as otherwise there is no chance of improving the impressions of importance and trustworthiness others hold. Merely launching solemn statements, subsidising social needs or confessing social responsibility is insufficient, if indeed even necessary. If such activities have no solid impact at the EU level, then they are useless. If they contrast with daily reality, they can even return as boomerangs, which is the risk run by every GONGO or BONGO that covers a selfish interest of government or business. Good preparatory work, including reputation measurement [Fombrun and Van Riel, 2007], can reveal extra room for creating the impression of being more important and trustworthy than others. Competitors doing their homework may, however, unmask such impression management as hypocritical, the old Greek word for theatre.

The second dimension of a good image is the *specific supply side*. The amateurish lobby group easily mistakes its own demand side, laid down in a position paper that advocates its preferences, as an attractive supply for stakeholders. The professional group, by contrast, tries to meet the demand side of the primary stakeholders and to supply what makes them feel happy. By facilitating such an exchange, it can make a deal. Many stakeholders primarily want to receive support, as they feel weak on the competitive EU playing-field and need to join a coalition. Commission officials have a strong appetite for detailed and reliable information regarding facts and trends in reality, and private lobby groups, often having the information edge over governments, can supply this. Commission officials also want to get a transparent aggregation of different interests by way of a EuroFed or a cross-sectoral coalition. This saves them from doing the work of aggregation themselves, while the transparency unveils both the views behind the scenes and some clues to dividing and conquering if needed. In return, they are expected to supply privileges such as a desired draft proposal, a financial favour, a better procedure, another deadline or a strong position inside. High-ranking officials and politicians have an insatiable appetite for good publicity through the mass media, in return for policy information and leniency. All this is usually true, but the best items for supply and exchange are always precisely attuned to the issues and the stakeholders in the current arena at a particular moment. They are different for the friendly, unfriendly and indeterminate situations. The clues come from the preparatory work.

Strategy: Why Lobbying?

The ultimate objective of a lobby group is to achieve happiness by scoring a target as a means to strengthen its ultimate objective, such as its licence to operate or improving its balance sheet. External circumstances and developments always challenge that sense of happiness. Perceived problems and expected threats may be called negative challenges, while perceived blessings and expected opportunities can be seen as positive ones. In popular wording, they are the nightmares and the daydreams, and as such they form two sides of the same coin of any challenge. In Ancient Greece, this coin was called a 'problem', literally a rock that was thrown into the sea by playing gods and could endanger ships on one side and provide shelter on the other. Today, 'a problem' no longer refers to the coin but only to its endangering side. The dual objective of EU public affairs management is, however, still inspired by the Ancient Greek idea: to solve the negative challenges and to save the positive ones, insofar as these are related by cause or consequence to EU processes. The inherent assumption is that it is possible to do this. However, *what, precisely, is a problem and what is a blessing, and what is a threat and what is an opportunity?* The amateur will find the question superfluous, because he or she believes the answer is self-evident, at least as far as it applies to him/her.

The professional knows that the answer can only come from the confrontation of a perceived fact (something that 'is or is not') with a chosen norm or value behind the norm (something that 'ought to be or not'). Logically, the two are independent of each other and are only connected by the formula of the *'if X and if Y, then Z'* approach: 'If this is the fact and if that is our norm, then we conclude that this is the challenge'. Every problem is hence, indeed, 'so-called'. Facts and norms are far from easy to identify objectively, as they are embedded in one's Pavlovian body full of strong beliefs, and are always contested in politics. The only certainty one has is that, in the last resort, a fact has an absolute character: it either exists or does not, it is present or absent. A norm or value, however, has ultimately a relative character, as it is one's subjective viewpoint or value judgement. To quote Shakespeare: 'There is nothing either good or bad, but thinking makes it so' (Hamlet, Act 2:2). Hence, in the last resort, every lobby group, including one's strongest enemy, is right in its choice of values and, if derived logically and consistently, its lobby targets. In all preceding resorts, however, many mistakes of identifying the real facts and best norms are possible and so is then the quality of their confrontation, resulting in the definition of a challenge. For example, many interest groups responded in a Pavlovian way to the 2008 'financial crisis' by only cutting costs, while others also saw opportunities and developed innovations [ComRes, 2009]. The work of defining a challenge is so strategic that every lobby group should keep it in its own hands. Asking befriended stakeholders and consultants for critical advice minimises Pavlovian mistakes.

The foregoing is summarised in Figure 5.1, presenting, in the upper part, the four situations that are logically possible. Two situations represent a problem or a threat: in one the perceived or expected fact does not accord with to the desire (cell B), and in the other that fact is feared (cell C). The two other situations amount to a blessing or an opportunity: in one the perceived or expected fact reflects the desire (cell A) and in the other that fact gives no grounds for fear (cell D). In half the situations of life, one has every reason to feel happy! Once the challenge has been defined, the solutions can be derived and even more happiness created. Because the number of solutions is always twice the number of problematic situations, as is clarified in the lower part of Figure 5.1, an intelligent problem-solver or lobbyist can only be an optimist and never complain about a situation, but develop one of the possible solutions. This is the field of the strategic management of challenges.

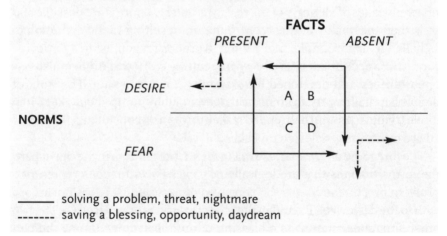

THE CHALLENGES OF PUBLIC AFFAIRS MANAGEMENT

I THE NATURE OF A CHALLENGE

		FACTS	
		PRESENT	ABSENT
	DESIRE	blessing opportunity daydream	problem threat nightmare
NORMS		A	B
	FEAR	C	D
		problem threat nightmare	problem opportunity daydream

II THE MANAGEMENT OF A CHALLENGE

———— solving a problem, threat, nightmare
------- saving a blessing, opportunity, daydream

Figure 5.1

To *solve a problem*, one might change either the fact or the norm. The first solution is targeted at changing the factual circumstances or developments. The way to do this is to turn cell B into A and/or cell C into D. This requires an enormous amount of work and a lot of physical energy over several years with, of course, an uncertain outcome. The second solution is to change one's chosen norm and to opt for another one. Then one turns cell C into A and/or B into D. This is a matter of thinking, which might be done quickly and has the greatest effectiveness. It only takes mental and not physical energy to reassess a fact feared yesterday as positive for tomorrow, or an unfulfilled desire as a blessing. Marcus Aurelius, the Roman emperor who observed the fall of his empire around 180 AD, achieved this change of mind in his 'Meditations' and did not term it a problem. Paradoxically, most organisations (and people) are, different from Aurelius, more doers than thinkers. They prefer years of hard work on changing facts rather than a short time on reconsidering norms. Some years later they often regret an EU law they lobbied for or praise one they opposed in the past. By neglecting half the number of possible solutions to a problem or a threat, they are not professionals.

Saving a blessing brings even more enduring happiness to the intelligent lobby group. In half the situations (cells A and D) it has every reason to feel happy now, although this is usually at risk in the future. After checking whether it still feels happy with such a situation and by preserving its facts, it can enjoy longer-lasting happiness. Paradoxically, most lobby groups hardly count their blessings and opportunities. Consequently, they forget to safeguard the benign facts and/or to validate their norms. By taking their current happiness for granted, they put it at stake. Only the most professional ones invest energy in saving a blessing or an opportunity. As they never complain about a problem but create a solution, they are never jubilant about a blessing but save it. They remember the fragility of earlier happiness. However, most organisations spend more energy on solving a negative challenge than on saving a positive one, let alone on safeguarding an old blessing. While trying to solve a problem, they may lose a blessing; and while trying to prevent a threat, they may miss an opportunity.

Strategic management is, indeed, a *difficult affair*. As the identification of real facts and best norms is always contested in reality, so is the choice of one or more solutions always at issue, first of all on the home front. Besides, many facts of life are not easily changeable or manipulable, at least not within the desired time period. For example, the variety of Europe with all its different interests will remain a fact of life for a long time. The change of norms has its limits as well. A company having its assets in a crisis sector like textile manufacturing or shipbuilding cannot easily decide to move to another sector, although the Finnish Nokia has managed to move from wood pulp to telecom. Every lobby group has to respect the dominant social norms as well, such as those on cartels, pollution and crime. If both the facts and the norms cannot be changed, as is possible in theory but seldom happens in practice, then there is no solution to the problem, and if there is really no solution, then neither is there a problem. The best attitude then is to be as relaxed as the sovereign Aurelius.

The approach to EU public affairs is, essentially, about achieving happiness at the EU level, even if it is only relative happiness in comparison to an opponent or competitor. In this case one has to move the opponent from his cells of happiness (A or D) to one of problems (B or C), by changing either the factual or normative conditions it holds. Whether hedonistic or warlike, this entire PA reasoning is generally applicable to any field of human concern [Rochefort and Cobb, 1994]. It is, however, most relevant for the EU playing-field with its permanently changing facts and, due to its variety of values and interests, its conflicting norms. The EU dynamics should invite every lobby group to review its current EU strategy and to invest energy regularly in critical *strategy development* [Hunger and Wheelen, 1998]. The amateurish group does this at random and incompletely. The professional group has within reach a PA unit for preparing it systematically and regularly. Its strategy development takes place as follows.

EU Strategy Development: Long-List, Shared-List and Short-List

Following Figure 1.2, strategy development takes three main steps. It starts with the creation of awareness about both oneself and the EU environment, which is done by monitoring and assessing the internal and external facts and values. To put it simply: the cells of the upper part of Figure 5.1 are filled with observed daydreams or nightmares, altogether constituting the *long-list* of challenges that are considered relevant in the period to come. Many come from the EU pipelines, and they easily amount to more than one hundred relevant challenges or dossiers, this being only six percent of all new EU laws on average per year. This long-listing requires much extroverted window-out lobbying for information or, better phrased, intelligence, as briefly noted at the end of chapter 1 and in Figure 1.2 (upper part). All this work may look tantalizing but has to be done as a means to select one's best possible PA agenda for the EU. The longer the long-list, the less chance of missing many challenges. The bulk of any long-list comes from the many sources of information mentioned in Figure 4.2, such as websites, Euro-

Feds and networks. The additional fine-tuning for one's own organisation can be done by the PA unit, with inspiration from staff and line at home. Critical aspects here are the creation of self-knowledge and the assessment of what should be desired or feared. Regarding the latter, every lobby group is fully free, due to the absence of an absolute yardstick for determining the norms, except for both the logical deduction from its ultimate value and the testing of the consistency with other norms. The difficulty of this is illustrated by many a strategy for tomorrow being based on the evaluation of today's situations with the help of yesterday's norms.

As a second step the *quick scan* (Figure 4.3) is made of the challenges of the long-list in order to get more nuanced insights. For every selected challenge or dossier the main stakeholders and their issues and preferences are roughly identified by a professional PA person or unit with the help of staff and line experts. The techniques of making the observations more reliable and complete, as outlined in the previous chapter, can be used here. They cover both the reasoned estimate and the repetitive observation, and they make use of, e.g., the corporate memory and the duplica method. The quick scan is not a goal in itself, but a necessary means to enable selectivity, as no lobby group can play single-handedly with a fair chance of success on more than a handful of EU chessboards simultaneously. Multinational companies like German Siemens, French Thomson, Swiss Novartis and British BAT perform such scans to obtain maximal selectivity. An NGO like Greenpeace, capable of spending most of its affluent resources just on lobbying, might play on a few more, but also has to be selective, as the total sum of desires and fears always outnumbers its resources. Many lobby groups find it difficult to be selective, as they consider the full long-list to be relevant and so it is, as relevance is always the sole criterion for long-listing. The most amateurish groups stick to their long-list, usually constructed at random, and will gather another long-list of disappointments.

The third step concerns exactly this selectivity that is conducted by breaking down the long-list into a *short-list* and a *shared-list*, the former being the list of dossiers to be lobbied primarily single-handedly, and the latter containing the dossiers to be lobbied through some collective platform. The semi-amateurish lobby group is aware of the need to downsize the long-list on the one hand to a short-list but on the other hesitant to entrust the remainder to a collective platform, and hence it sticks to a very long list with only grades of relevance. The *new trend* and now the mark of the professional group is to give priority to the shared-list, as a short-list dossier usually brings with it high costs (hardly burden-sharing) and low chances of success (little support from others), while a shared-list dossier gives a reversed balance. The professional thus prefers to get the shortest possible short-list and the longest possible shared-list. It prefers to drive its interests from a back-seat position. On the shared-list dossiers it prepays the price of compromising with other stakeholders, which in the EU must be paid sooner or later anyhow and tends to increase with time. By transporting these dossiers to a collective platform early on, being established or newly constructed, it chooses the high chance of many small wins on its shared-list, rather than the low chance of a single big win on its short-list. By using those platforms proactively, it soon expands the M of the magic lobby formula $E = MI^2$. Such a smart group practices *intelligent laziness*, i.e. it abstains from doing what others with more or less the same interest (identified by the quick scan) also want to do. It invests energy only in that early dossier transferral and in the remote control of what happens thereafter. Its short-list is the remainder of dossiers that cannot easily be shared with others and score high on relevance, such as in cases of infringement, unique interest or mere survival, and which have to be lobbied largely single-handedly. On second thought, however, such dossiers often appear to be appropriate or even profitable for sharing with others, because many others may be in a

DOWNSIZING THE LONG-LIST

- **MONITOR AND SCAN CURRENT DOSSIERS**
- **APPLY NEGATIVE SELECTION, GIVING SHARED-LIST**
- **REMAINDER, IF REALLY SHORT, IS SHORT-LIST**

IF THE DOSSIER IS ASSESSED AS:	*THEN IT IS BEST TO:*
1. 'NOT SO RELEVANT'	OUTSOURCE TO 'FRIENDS'
2. DAMAGING THE HOME FRONT	HANDS-OFF
3. POOR 'COST/BENEFIT' RATIO	LEAVE IT TO OTHERS
4. HARDLY URGENT NOW	OUTSOURCE IT TEMPORARILY
5. GOOD NON-PA ALTERNATIVE	CONSIDER IT
6. 'WINDS BEHIND'	TAKE FREE RIDE
7. HEADWIND-SITUATION	SEEK A COALITION
8. 'NO PINT TO CHOOSE'	LEAVE IT TO OTHERS

Figure 5.2

similar position or may be interested in sharing, just as the Philips company earns a fortune by sharing its unique patents. The difference between a dossier on its shared-list and one on its short-list is that the former requires little and the latter much energy. The shorter the short-list, the longer the shared-list can be and the less has to be, left to the winds.

The intelligent player breaks down the long-list into both a shared-list and a short-list in a paradoxical way. Unlike the more-or-less amateurish player, it does not select from the long-list the dossiers that are most qualified for the short-list, but those that are *not*. It applies not positive selection (everything remains important) but *negative selection*, by moving to the shared-list all challenges that can be solved or saved in other ways than solely by itself, or that otherwise might have to be left to the winds. The remainder automatically becomes the short-list, or may be left to the winds. The intelligent lobby group keeps this negative selection in its own hands, as cherry picking is a matter of personal taste. Standard criteria of negative selection include the following eight *(Figure 5.2)*.

(1) *Low relevance.* Not all challenges have equal relevance. If a challenge scores relatively low in terms of positive or negative impact on, for example, its profit or functioning in the future, it is better for the lobby group to give it lower priority, for example by leaving it to befriended stakeholders [Brown, 1979, 32]. This is clearly a matter of strategic thinking. For example, the 2006 proposals to complete the open market on postal services by 2009 (COM 2006/594) affects every post-sending organisation but is crucial for only a few, such as the state-run post monopolies, private couriers and mail-order firms.

(2) *Poor internal situation.* If the lobby group is internally seriously divided about a challenge, lacks sufficient knowledge, falls short of required resources or skills and/or expects a worsening reputation, it had better leave the challenge to the winds. Otherwise, it will become a loser in the best case and receive a boomerang in the worst case. Umbrella organisations like ETUC and BusinessEurope are frequently internally divided and wisely do little more than monitor such dossiers in dispute internally, maybe with some remote control.

(3) *Adverse cost-benefit expectation.* This is more than a summary variable of the aforementioned two: all sorts of side effects can be included. A great benefit from some action may be observed, but the costs of acquisition can make it unattractive. It is like the fine cherry at the very top of the tree, which would take too much energy or risk to pluck and is left to the birds. In a package deal, nobody can win it all, and everybody has to give in on some challenges, as otherwise one has to pay a higher bill.

(4) *Low urgency*. The lobby group can come to the conclusion that there remains plenty of time for action. The challenge remains in the future and immediate action is not necessary or is outsourced to a temporary consultant. The group consciously takes the risk that its competitors will act sooner, prearrange the arena by Triple P and make it difficult to intervene at a later moment. Green papers (suggesting a policy problem) from the Commission are frequently seen as not yet urging action, although they are early warnings of agenda setting.

(5) *Good alternatives to EU public affairs*. The mixed public-private multi-layers inside the EU may be considered alternatives to EU PA management. Many an EU challenge can be solved or saved through the domestic political system or private sector. Meat importers can shift the costs of veterinary inspection, obliged by EU legislation, to the consumers. The Philips company, feeling endangered by the lack of good EU copyright regulation, decided to sell its Phonogram music division in 1998. National ministries frequently shift the costs of adaptation to new EU laws to their decentralised governments rather than lobbying for better laws.

(6) *Free ride available*. Very often a free ride can be taken with another lobby group or coalition with the same preference but also a stronger interest in the outcome and a better capacity for action. SMEs, NGOs and regional governments frequently take a free ride or back-seat with bigger ones. This is particularly rational if the arena is friendly: most probably, the preference will prevail. In their fight for air-transport liberalisation, small air carriers like Virgin can, unlike in the early 1990s, take an almost free 'flight' with the Commission, British Airways, the US carriers and the consumer groups today.

(7) *Hardly any chance*. Conversely to the former case, the quick scan now reveals an extremely unfriendly arena. Due to a lack of support and unfriendly issues, the lobby group faces mainly cold and fierce headwinds. If it were to become active, it would hardly proceed. Therefore, it might rationally remain passive and save its energy for getting at least some loss-compensation. For example, the tobacco crofters in southern Europe, who have hardly a chance of collecting in the future such rich agricultural EU subsidies as in the past, can better lobby for loss-compensation. If there is really no solution at all, then there is no problem (being by definition manageable).

(8) *No pint to choose*. Even if the lobby group considers the challenge as relevant and feels it has a good chance of influencing the outcome, it may still believe that the created difference is at best hardly relevant. Comparing the situation before and after, it may feel it has been bitten by the dog instead of the cat (negative challenge) or pampered by the mistress rather

than the wife (positive challenge). In such cases it is more efficient to stick to the cat and to the wife. When the German government claimed to the Court that the Tobacco Ban Directive (EC 2001/37) was based on the wrong Treaty article, it won a ruling that the Treaty basis should be changed indeed, a change which did not make it happier at all. It could also have remained passive.

Setting the Targets and the Agendas

Downsizing the long-list into a shared-list and short-list can, as shown above, be organised as a *rational method* and even be computerised. By doing a quick scan, one can get a score based on the mentioned criteria for each challenge on the long-list, resulting in an informative matrix. If one considers the criteria to be of unequal importance, then one can add some weight to each of them at will. If, for example, a lobby group feels rich, it can freely delete the cost-benefit criterion, just as it can give this all the weight when feeling poor. If it wants to act anyway, for example for the purposes of publicity, then it can skip the free ride criterion. If it feels that the EU is endangering its survival, then it should give full weight only to the criterion of relevance. Under normal circumstances, however, it is better to consider not just one but many criteria. It may even be rational to give them all the same weight. The higher a challenge scores on the negative criteria, the less reason there is to lobby single-handedly on it and the more to put it on the shared-list. This selection of challenges should go on until preferably only a manageable, small number of them remains. It is not uncommon, however, that some not-so-rationally chosen challenge is added to the short-list, usually under pressure from the home front. In governmental lobby groups, there are always politicians at the top who want to include some item from their personal agenda, even if this is inefficient or ineffective at the EU level and only serves a small public at home, which has nothing to do with EU lobbying. Many a Council Presidency puts on its 'Agenda for Europe' some items for only domestic consumption, such as the French did in September 2008 by calling for more political control over the EMU.

On both lists of dossiers, *target-setting* first has to take place at home. In its ultimate search for the 'greatest happiness', the lobby group can start with a dream target for each dossier taking from its developed strategy, even if this is unrealistic, as this gives direction to the choices soon to be made. In the reality of the EU, it can only lobby for the 'greatest possible happiness', and so it has to define its next-best targets, which are acceptable to both itself and sufficient stakeholders and officials who want to have 'something in it for them'. In the early phase of window-in negotiations, it can best work with broad next-best targets that give room for trade-offs and fine-tuning during the process. Part of it should be target-setting for package-dealing by which it might compensate some possible loss. Finally, it must define targets at its bottom-line, which is equal to the current situation not becoming worse and perhaps being preserved or won through the Court. Below this line it should not negotiate, except for loss-compensation.

Sooner or later it has to *sharpen the targets* by making them as specific and precise as possible, so defining clearly its ambitions to get, for example, a particular provision in a Commission proposal, reference to a Treaty article, subsidy under an objective, position for playing Triple P, or another particular item considered desirable and realisable. Without sharp targets it can never really win (or lose) and only shop around for 'souvenirs from Brussels' furnishing memories instead of scores. With sharp targets it can also direct its intelligence lobby 'backwards' and play its support lobby 'forwards' more efficiently, so saving much energy. The quality of target-setting can be further enhanced by the tool of scenarios, which are prompted by the question, 'What might happen if x-y-z occurs and what is then the best course of action?', as outlined in chapter 4. By making a next-best scenario, a loss-compensation scenario and a bottom-line scenario for each dossier, the lobby group can anticipate possible situations better and move more efficiently and effectively during the process.

After the target-setting, the short-list and the shared-list dossiers can and should be managed as two different *agendas for action*. The short-list results in a short agenda of a few heavy matches, usually at high costs and with limited chance of great success. On it, the lobby group has to lobby for both information and support largely single-handedly, and to employ many of its resources and skills for preparatory work regarding both its home front and the arenas linked to its short-list, in addition to related activities such as actors to approach, factors to use and vectors to create, and not least the fine-tuned fieldwork (next chapter), all told a tremendous amount of work. The shared-list requires a similar amount of work that, however, now can be divided among the participants of the common platform or be pooled at its common PA desk. The many matches on the shared-list are easier to play as one is part of bigger teams (collective platforms) that provide cost-sharing and, of course at the price of early compromises, broader support giving good chances of small successes. On this shared-list agenda, every engaged lobby group still has, some work to do, however, particularly in the early phase of building both the common agenda and, if not yet existing, the common platform, and also in the end-phase of reaping its fruits. In between it can enjoy the efficiency of the shared-list by restricting itself to mainly activities of remote attention and control, such as the following.

- *Monitoring.* The challenges on the shared-list need a regular check of their progress, especially when changing facts or norms in either the arena or on the home front make a review necessary.
- *Correcting.* Some partners in a common platform may develop different interests as time goes on. That may happen under pressure from their home front, opponents, officials or outsiders. Corrective activities may then be necessary.
- *Repairing causes.* If a group regrets that a dossier had to be moved to the shared-list, for example due to the poor internal state (criterion 2), then one has to address this cause in the meantime.
- *Handling consequences.* For example, the case of low urgency (criterion 4) should be used for at least some preparatory groundwork and maybe for safeguarding a free ride (criterion 6), as otherwise a big problem may arise in future.
- *Exploiting nuisance value.* If the lobby group has put a dossier on the shared-list only for the purpose of nuisance value or loss-compensation, then it may have to become active at some point.
- *Testing consistency.* At various moments it is useful to check whether the various dossiers on the shared-list are still consistent with each other and not conflicting (unless so desired) or maybe overlapping.

So far, this *logic of strategy development,* resulting in two PA agendas, of course together forming one comprehensive agenda, may be seen as creating an unpleasant amount of studious work to be followed by even more. The lobby group with the ambition to win and not lose its interests cannot, however, escape it and will be rewarded afterwards. Only an amateurish group lobbies blindly, without any thoughtful strategy. Such a group usually lets the internal situation on the home front determine what should be realised externally. Long-listing, quick scans and shared-listing are empty catchwords in its view. Its PA agenda is a wishful daydream, so to say its 'greatest happiness' scenario, but only reflecting its demand side. When lobbying, it is at the mercy of the waves. In contrast, the professional or intelligent lobby group knows that the quality of all preparatory work is most crucial for the final outcome at the EU level. It defines consciously the best possible strategy, agendas and targets. It sees, once again, all these preparations for the fight not as a sacrosanct goal but only as a necessary means to success. If it would blindly believe in its preparatory work, it would not be a thoughtful player but rather a naïve bureaucrat. All preparations are useful only for some time to come, and to the best of available knowledge. The better their quality, the more they help to achieve the desired outcomes.

With What Result?

Take the following case. In the *1993 Banana Dossier,* the then Dutch Minister of Agriculture and former Minister of Development Aid Piet Bukman supported the Commission proposal (1992/359) to protect the 'ACP bananas' coming from poor countries in the first Council reading. In doing so, he created a qualified majority (very marginal) in favour of the proposal. In the second reading, however, he supported the opposite case of market liberalisation for the 'dollar bananas' (largely shipped through the Dutch harbour of Rotterdam) and became part of the overruled minority. Ultimately, he regretted his stupidity in not blocking the proposal at the first reading [Pedler, 1994]. The minister, being of two minds over what he wanted to support, clearly lacked a logically derived and consistent strategy. That may happen. An amateurish player wants to cover and forget such a mistake as soon as possible. An intelligent lobby group, in contrast, wants to learn from its mistakes in order to become smarter in future. Such a lesson is free as the price has already been paid by the loss.

The core question here is *how to assess the effectiveness* or success of particular lobby actions. The answer serves both the collection of hindsight wisdom that can enhance future success and the accountability or maybe prestige on the home front. Whatever the reason behind it, the answer is less simple than it may seem. Of course, the ultimate justification of a lobby action is that it did create the desired outcome, even if in daily practice the lobby group may already feel happy with less than this, such as with a good compromise from the EU, enduring respect from stakeholders and stable support from home, as stated at the start of chapter 3. The desired outcome remains, however, our reference point for the measurement of success. The professional group wants to see a causal relationship between its action and the EU outcome, the dependent variable. Its action is not necessarily a case of doing something. As with the indeterminate arena, it may be a case of not doing anything, and waiting and seeing instead. Whatever it decides, the group can be said to have influenced the EU if it has more or less caused an EU outcome as desired. However, causality is always difficult to determine. Following David Hume [1748], one can even prove that, for at least two reasons, causality in social life is impossible to prove perfectly. Firstly, during the time of the EU decision process, many more players may have tried and succeeded in influencing the outcome, which is normally a compromise. Due to this multicausality, a single impact is hardly possible to isolate. Secondly, the lobby group can never know what would have been the outcome if it had remained absent. The perfect control situation, necessary for the hard proof of causality, is not available in social life [Henning, 2004].

All this may be considered true and disappointing. The alternative, however, is not necessarily that one sees a decision process as a collection of incidents beyond any explanation. In terms not of strict causality but of *plausibility*, one can determine some dependency of the EU outcome on the action of the lobby group, by making use of four next-best methods of assessing an influence or an impact [Van Schendelen, 1998, 13-17]. In terms of validity, their rank-order is as follows.

(1) *Before-after.* Here one compares the initial targets of the lobby group and other stakeholders with the final EU outcomes and tries to explain the latter, as well and plausibly as possible, by using the former. Then one may see whether one or the other lobby group has plausibly acted as a factor or not.

(2) *Initial chances.* Now one re-assesses the initial position of the lobby group, as revealed by the arena analysis, and its inherent chances of success. A small impact in an unfriendly arena may have to be considered a greater achievement than a big one in a friendly arena.

(3) *Reputation.* Here the lobby group measures its reputation for influence among EU officials and stakeholders, for example by asking them as 'informed experts' to give their frank opinion about its performance in influencing the outcomes.

(4) *Backing at home.* This final one is a variant of the former. If the lobby group gets a stronger backing from its home front (such as facilities and mandate) after a lobby fight, even if this has not been won, then it has gained at least some success here.

These four next-best methods clearly have their weaknesses. They all fall short on strict causality and the last two also on high validity and reliability. Besides, only the first two are clearly linked to the EU arena and therefore appropriate for measuring the effectiveness of EU lobby actions, while the third is linked to the different arena of stakeholders and the fourth to that of the home front. However, if the best method is impossible, the *next-best methods* are the best possible. According to various surveys, even these are not applied very often. The large majority of 67 corporate PA officials takes 'cost-saving for the company' as the proxy measure of the first method, and 'recognition by high-level decision-makers' as the proxy measure of reputation [EurActiv, 2009-A]. A majority of 170 PA officials of EU federations relies on both the latter and 'feedback from (potential) members' as the proxy measure of backing at home [EurActiv, 2009-B] and that of 75 consultants relies on both 'clients satisfaction' as the proxy measure of backing and 'increase in turnover' as the proxy measure of comparing before and after [EurActiv, 2009-C].

For the sake of hindsight wisdom and improvement, the evaluation can and should be done much more ambitiously. This professional focus comes down to a systematic evaluation of the *quality of its preparations*, consisting of both its preparatory homework, the organisation of its home front and that of its fieldwork (chapter 6), altogether the variables most within its reach. It starts with the before-and-after comparison between targets and outcomes, preferably differentiated for the various decision phases ('where did it go wrong?'). To this it adds the hindsight study of initial chances. It wants to have any correlation between efforts and outcomes explained in plausible terms. The PA desk can prepare the evaluation and should be most interested in the unforced errors, which can never be blamed on others. For example, being misled by the smart Triple P game of a competitor is not necessarily an unforced error, but not having reckoned with this certainly is. From our previous and subsequent chapters it can distil a sort of critical questionnaire on crucial items of quality, such as regarding the window-out intelligence lobby, the downsizing to shared-list and short-list, the setting of targets, the supply side to others, the internal cohesion, the PA resources and skills, the briefing and debriefing on the home front, the performances on the playing-fields and much more. In short, it critically reviews its lobby process from start to finish and adds critical comparisons, such as between one phase and another, one arena and another, the recent past and the present, and itself and the main competitors. It can transform this hindsight into better self-knowledge, inspiration for improvement of its PA management, maybe even ideas for new R&D in PA, and cues for setting up training programmes for improving its weakest points.

The intelligent lobby group collects its hindsight wisdom not only from its PA desk but also from many people involved (board, staff and line) and even from outsiders. Then it can add the measurement of its reputation among stakeholders and officials and its backing on the home front. Useful *mirrors from outside* might be contacted EU officials, befriended stakeholders, indifferent ones, peer groups and colleagues in EU PU management. It is rare to canvass the opponent lobby groups, although such a sports-like review of the match may be extremely informative and even result in a friendly relationship. The various mirrors have, of course, their strengths and weaknesses and may yield different results. Frequently, a weakness is that, they tend to show satisfaction at home and admiration outsidedue to their social context, instead of accurate reflections on real performances. In order to avoid such measurement of only 'managed impressions', they should be constructed critically, maybe with the help of an outsider. All evaluation for the sake of learning can produce great competitive rewards in the future, as most competitors rarely evaluate their own performances and thus miss the opportunity to strengthen the plausible relationship between their actions and the outcomes.

Extra: The Multinational PA Model as Benchmark

No lobby group has its PA management in a perfectly organised state, but some are more perfect than others. In particular, some *multinational companies and NGOs* (MNCs and MNGOs), ranging from Unilever to Greenpeace, are the trendsetters in professional PA management, both internally and externally. They have to be. Internally, they have to cope with an exceptional diversity of cultures, role expectations and formal duties, this diversity being a potential richness for coping effectively with a diverse Europe, as said before. Externally, they are continuously challenged by planned EU decisions, such as regarding standardisation, open market, R&D subsidy, pollution, working conditions and external trade. Not coincidentally, the 1985 EU policy programme 'Open Market 1992' was drafted by the PA Department of Philips in 1982 and first discussed at the Round Table of Industrialists in 1984 [Verwey, 1994]. Most multinational lobby groups also possess adequate capacities to lobby, such as sufficient financial means, technical experts, cross-border networks and relevant positions, in which respects MNCs and MNGOs are not much different [Jordan and Maloney, 1996; Jordan, 1997]. Finally, many are perceived as having a good image that includes trust and importance and enables easy access to EU officials for exchanging information and support at even the working floor level.

Every lobby group might learn from these multinationals and their perceived best practices of managing PA on their home front [Sietses, 2000; Coen, 2007]. Even if the main lesson is *not* to follow their example, then such a decision is at least better reasoned. Of course, the multinationals are far from being all the same. Some are much more multinational than others, or are organised as country units rather than product or service units. More factors contribute to their variation, ranging from market position, economic sector and labour intensity to history, ownership, age, prestige and more. MNCs and MNGOs are frequently different by type of product or service (profit versus not-for-profit) and by internal authority pattern (top-down versus bottom-up). In spite of all this diversity, we observe among them a basically common pattern of PA organisation, which is pragmatically derived from the EU processes that have to be managed ('structure must follow processes'). The very nature of the EU means these processes are full of dynamic challenges, and cannot be managed by a standing bureaucracy, but only by a unit that is lean and mean, operates directly under the management at the top, and has close networks with the experts of both the specialised divisions and the country units. The three main parts of this basic structure, simplified and stylised in Figure 5.3, are as follows.

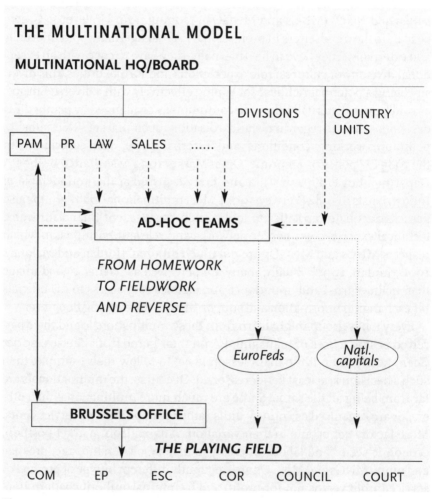

Figure 5.3

- *The Central Board* ('headquarters') is responsible for the general management of the whole organisation and has its own staff, such as on finance, law, sales, public relations (PR) and public affairs (PA). One member of the Board is directly responsible for the Central PA Desk and, for reasons explained in the next chapter, preferably for PR as well, and has a dual relationship with the PA officer. On the input side of the Board, where the corporate strategy is developed, the PA staff delivers crucial information about EU challenges and reasoned proposals to manage them, and on the output side of the Board, the PA staff receives the decisions made by way of a mandate that includes the strategic objectives for both the short-list and the shared-list, the room to manoeuvre, the allocated resources and the schedule for reporting. The *mandate*, given for a limited time period (frequently around one year), is mutually binding on PA strategy, sometimes on tactics but not on techniques, as the technical and partially the tactical sides belong to the PA profession. Under the mandate, the Board can forbid particular tactics, for example for reasons of reputation. The logic of binding the Board fully to the mandate is to insure that its members cannot cause blunders and boomerangs by lobbying at their initiative. They play a role only upon the request from PA.
- *The technical experts* of the specialised divisions and country units are part of the organisation's wider PA network. PA staff ensures that these experts get useful positions inside relevant collective platforms like EuroFeds, inside working-floor structures like committees and working groups of the EU, and in relevant countries and capitals. The technical experts operate there only under a mechanism of *briefing and debriefing* with the PA staff, based on shared interests and internal platform. The logic is that both the technical experts, with high expertise on the substance of a dossier but little on the playing-field and the game of playing, and the PA experts with the reverse qualities can only be successful at the EU level by briefing and debriefing each other closely. On short-list dossiers this mechanism is anchored in ad-hoc teams, led by PA and composed of technical experts and other staff, and on the shared-list it takes place online or otherwise.
- *The Central PA Desk* is lean and mean, as intelligent PA is most dependent on ounces of brains rather than pounds of body weight, and usually it has less than a handful of staff. Its real working force is its network with the technical experts, whose 'ears and eyes' help to gather useful information and whose 'hands and feet' help to build support, all embedded in briefing and debriefing. The Central PA Desk is focused not only on the EU but also on the global and domestic levels, because EU dossiers usually have

their origin or overflow there and thus may need multi-level lobbying. To support its daily fine-tuning of window-out and window-in lobbying, it usually has a small *local office* in Brussels and perhaps in some major capitals inside or outside the EU. The Central PA Desk co-ordinates all PA activities and reports directly to the Board member who is ultimately responsible for PA and gives the mandate. Within its mandate or otherwise assigned, the Central Desk has the following three core jobs to do.

Its first task is to get all the *preparatory homework* done. As summarised in Figure 1.2, this ranges from the window-out organisation of intelligence to the window-in organisation of sufficient support from outside. A proactive PA staff starts to think 'backwards' from the last step (support lobby) up to the first one (information lobby), which can it save much energy later on and improve effectiveness. Additionally, it is responsible for much more detailed work, as summarised in Figure 3.3 and outlined in our chapters. It must prepare for changes on the EU playing-field, new PA tactics and techniques, strategy review, scenario planning, set-up of corporate memory and the evaluation of past 'games, sets and matches'. Due to the overload of preparatory work, it has to play 'intelligent laziness', also internally, by entrusting parts of PA work to other staff people and technical experts, with internal co-operation as a by-product. In the mid-1990s, the PA Desk of the German company Siemens set a new trend ('Siemens method') by regularly asking its division and country managers to provide email feedback about the relevance of a long-list of EU challenges and actions needed on it. The mechanism of internal briefing and debriefing is, at the more detailed level, another form of intelligent laziness. The PA Desk clearly has a selfish interest in making the short-list the shortest possible and the shared-list long, as the latter brings in energy from external stakeholders gathered as a collective platform with a common interest.

The second task of the PA Desk is the internal *implementation* of the agendas. The standard approach is that for each short-list dossier an *ad-hoc team* is formed, led by a PA staff member as a kind of *chef de dossier*. The team consists of three sorts of relevant people. Firstly, members from other staff units, such as from Public Relations (to settle the issue of sound-in-public, to be discussed in the next chapter), EU Law (for legal aspects, including the bottom-line scenario), and Sales (as PA must contribute to the company's profits, a lesson learnt again by Shell during the Brent Spar affair). Secondly, technical experts from specialised divisions are included for tackling the technical side of an EU issue such as biotechnology, standardisation, the environment or engineering. Frequently, they hold a seat in an

EU expert group or EuroFed, through which they can contribute to window-out and window-in lobbying. Thirdly, people from relevant country units are invited to the team, as they may have different interests thatwould be better included than excluded, and supplementary capacities for lobbying, such as tapping information from their government, getting support in their country and contributing to the group's multinational orchestra. On shared-list dossiers similar sorts of people are engaged, but now more virtually than physically, for example by intranet, email, phone, fax and teleconferencing. The mechanism of briefing and debriefing keeps it all together.

The third task of the public affairs office is to realise the external window-out and window-in *fieldwork* regarding both EU officials and other stakeholders. For the short-list dossiers its main tool is the ad-hoc team, whose members operate as the multinational's orchestra that spearheads the communication with the primary stakeholders. Often these members already have a relationship with them, thanks to both their line position and their membership in a EuroFed or an EU expert group. For the shared-list dossiers, the main tool of the PA Desk is its external network, both in EuroFeds for turning the personal targets into collective ones; and on the EU work floors for monitoring and, if needed, fine-tuning the process. For getting all fieldwork done, the PA Desk uses both the mechanism of briefing and debriefing and, as its extension there, its Brussels office. This outpost is usually small-sized, consisting of one senior employee, one junior employee and a secretary, and has a location and budget that permit hospitality. It serves primarily as the 'ears and eyes' and, if necessary, the 'hands and feet' of the multinational on the Brussels playing-field. Going window-out, it monitors competitors and officials and forwards information to the Central Desk. Going window-in, it fine-tunes the lobbying by, for example, coaching the technical experts on the spot, talking with Commission officials, meeting competitors and engineering indirect links. It is, in short, the most direct tool of remote control the multinational has.

In the multinational PA approach to the EU, the *EuroFeds* and their variants clearly play an important role. In a relatively easy way the multinationals can get collective support for their interests here, so adding weight to the M of $E = MI^2$. Their shared-list dossiers are dragged to one or more of such platforms. They cannot easily transfer short-list dossiers to such a ready-made platform, and these they have to push and pull themselves until a tailor-made EuroFed comes within reach. Inevitably, the multinationals are greatly dependent for their success on the PA quality of their EuroFeds. The risks and costs of this they usually estimate as lower than those of a short-list dossier. If they are a direct member of a EuroFed, they can manage the risks by active role-playing inside, co-setting the common agenda, providing their technical experts, checking the effects of common actions, keeping their financial contribution at issue and, if needed, shopping around for an ad-hoc coalition. If not a direct member, they usually play similar games indirectly via one or more of their national associations that altogether form the EuroFed. Almost all EuroFeds consider EU lobbying as part of their *raison d'être* and invest both in their European image and in the PA quality of their EU affairs. Almost all have a small PA office (often the 'secretariat'), ad-hoc teams ('work groups') and standard procedures for arriving at a short-list with common targets [Greenwood, 2007]. Technical experts are usually recruited from among their members.

Many multinationals face two particular issues. One is the *issue of trust* between their Brussels office and the Central PA Desk. On the one hand, the Brussels office needs a clear mandate that gives room to manoeuvre as otherwise it cannot fine-tune their actions. On the other, the Central Desk wants to keep control over what is done or left undone. British, Dutch and Nordic multinationals usually give their Brussels office a free mandate for most window-out and window-in activities, which are scrutinised regularly for the results. Multinationals from the rest of Europe (and from the US as well) usually see their Brussels office as merely their local desk that needs strict instructions, more for going window-out than window-in, as they fear the local office becoming a player independent of the headquarters. The price they pay for this distrust in their Brussels office is frequently corporate passivity (or even absence) on the EU playing-field. Waiting for new instructions from Frankfurt, Paris or Madrid, the local officer sees them arriving after the game. Some multinationals have softened the issue of trust by compromising on distance: part of the week (usually Mondays and Fridays) the Brussels officer has to visit the Central Desk, which requires a lot of time and travelling. New communications technology might moderate the issue more.

The second special issue inside multinationals (and many other lobby groups) is the usefulness of hiring *PA consultancy firms*. A questionnaire among 140 Brussels-based PA officers, largely coming from big companies, reveals strong disagreement about the usefulness of PA consultants, with almost 35% in favour, 55% against and the rest not having an opinion [ComRes, 2008]. Due to a lack of in-depth research, one can only speculate about the reasons behind the negative appraisals. One is maybe the perception of poor quality of many consultants, among whom all varieties of quality can be found indeed. Many consultants advertise themselves as full-fledged PA experts, but in fact are either not experts at all or confined to only some PA niche, for example internet monitoring, image creation or contacting MEPs. Another reason may be the poor quality of the contract made with the consultant, for which the lobby group should blame itself. A quality consultant can, however, certainly create added value to a lot of preparatory homework, implementation and even fieldwork, particularly during rush-times [Spencer and McGrath, 2008, 73-77]. The person *cannot*, however, play at least three crucial PA roles. Firstly, the consultant can give advice or second opinion, but never bear responsibility for any important decision or choice. The person can, secondly, act in addition to the in-house PA Desk but, due to a lack of internal position, network and knowledge, never replace it credibly. Thirdly, the person can carry messages to and from stakeholders and officials, but never represent the organisation's interest in an authentic way, leave alone wheel and deal on its behalf [Warntjen and Wonka, 2004, 89].

The multinational model of PA management at the EU level is, in short, integrative by its inclusion of internal variety, studious by its preparatory homework, intelligent by its shared-listing, efficient by its flexible structures and potent by its early intake of support. Its organisation by way of a Central PA Desk with flexible ad-hoc teams and a Brussels outpost, all under supervision of a Board member, is like that of a flexible military intervention force. Thanks to its multinational background, an MNC and MNGO can, directly or indirectly, easily play prominent roles inside EuroFeds and thus promote their interests more efficiently and effectively. As noted, the model is a stylised summary of the basic pattern of PA management by many multinationals and, as such, allows that in reality many MNCs and MNGOs show their own variant of it, while some others hardly match it at all. In the EU, the multinationals have the reputation of leading the PA 'premier league', by scoring relatively well on issues, strengthening their position and enabling their people. They are, however, more admired in theory than really followed in practice. Most other EU lobby groups seem to find the application of the multinational model difficult.

Some Other Interest Groups Benchmarked

The multinational PA model at the EU level is only a generalised and stylised version of reality. Its basics have logical cohesion and might explain not only why so many multinational lobby groups have a reputation of influence and success in the EU, but also why non-multinationals seldom have this reputation. Maybe the latter fail to organise one or more basic elements of the multinational model well. In this section we shall use that model as a benchmark with a few other sorts of EU interest groups. Of course, the benchmark can only be tentative. Its objective is to make other lobby groups conscious about the basic elements that may be absent in their approach and should be installed.

Small-sized lobby groups in the fields of *SMEs, decentralised governments and NGOs* are most in contrast with multinationals. Small-sized firms, cities and citizen groups usually have a low sense of efficacy for EU action, few resources and skills, too parochial an image, weak common identity and a more domestic than European interest orientation. Their long-list is usually made introvertedly and their short-list is seldom really short. If they want to get something from the EU, they rely on their director or secretary and primarily go for help to their national ministry or domestic association. A small minority, largely consisting of decentralised governments, has a Brussels office. Frequently, the drive behind this is not PA, except for the case of EU subsidies, but getting visibility in the EU, thus public relations or PR. Their Brussels officer is often weakly embedded in the organisation at home and acts on the spot mainly according to circumstances. Only some medium-sized cities, NGOs and associations are active inside a EuroFed. Size seems to be an important factor indeed, as since the mid-1990s the larger regional governments and independent agencies have been jockeying for and attaining positions in the EU. They are sufficiently resourced, have their own Brussels offices, feel attracted to EU subsidies and hold positions in semi-formal and formal EU settings, ranging from expert groups to COR and, if coming from countries like Germany and Belgium, often even in the Council [Badiello, 1998]. Agencies, more than regional governments, also show a strong interest in EU legislation and often have access to comitology committees. By co-operating with other European regions or agencies as a EuroFed, network or ad-hoc group, they create a European face that gives mass and weight, in short more influence. A few examples are EIRA (steel regions), AEM (mountain areas), CTIP (fire & rescue) and EReg (vehicle and driver registration) [EPAD, annual]. However, many decentralised governments are still weakly organised at home. A major cause seems to be their government background. Agencies often fear supervision by the ministry, while regions fear that by both elected politicians and mass media at home. This fear hinders making a short-list with clear targets beforehand and critical evaluations afterwards. Therefore, the Flemish government innovatively created the independent agency VLEVA in 2005, composed of both public and private interest groups and acting as an open PA Desk for the promotion of Flemish interests at the EU level.

One might expect that *national ministries* have internalised most elements of the multinational model. Since the 1993 Treaty of Maastricht, and its broadening and deepening of EU policy domains, they all are dependent on EU outcomes now and might want to influence them, as their power to make binding decisions has become more limited at home and shifted to the EU level. At the Council level, they have their infrastructure of common facilities, meetings and work groups. The Commission invites them to take part in committees and agencies. Given such fine preconditions for EU lobbying, one might expect an internal approach to their EU affairs, akin to a multinational. Paradoxically, their real approach is frequently almost the opposite. Ministries usually operate as a standing bureaucracy and not as flexible response machinery, whose structures follow the EU processes. Internally, they are usually divided into directorates and units driven by domestic values and focused on domestic rather than EU affairs. Seldom do they have a specialised EU/PA Desk for preparing the homework, planning the fieldwork and, under a mechanism of briefing and debriefing with other staff and technical experts, for directing all activities. Their EU long-list, if one exist, is seldom reduced to both a shared-list and a short-list, and if they have a short-list, it is usually not short at all. Policy experts are involved in bits of EU fieldwork and, usually lacking PA expertise and being poorly resourced, they limit their EU activities to the reimbursed semi-formal layers of the Commission's committees and the Council's work groups, thereby neglecting both the informal build-up and the many stakeholders. Ministries rarely have a Brussels outpost or mistake as such their staff in the Permanent Representation that, however, is focused on the negotiations in the Council and pays little attention to both the pre-phase of secondary and the post-phase of delegated legislation. For the early europeanization of their interests, ministries usually do not have a EuroFed or they mistake as such, again, their Council setting. Of course, there are some exceptions to this general pattern. They can be found among small-sized Nordic ministries, among dossiers that are either highly politicised at home or fully fall under Council regime, among some cases of informal Councils and among a few ministries, such as Defence, Transport and Finance that, as mentioned in chapter 3, have some European ad-hoc network.

In theory, the *national governments*, defined as the domestic central government executives, also meet all conditions for edging out the multinationals on the PA management of EU affairs. Usually, they claim to have a strong interest in the EU outcomes, have many privileges as laid down in Treaty texts and possess plenty of resources such as manpower, financial means and technical expertise. At home they all have a procedure and structure for what is called national co-ordination. Reality is, however, much different from theory. Except for a few more 'statist' countries like France and the UK, the national government usually has not a Board or CEO at the topas multinationals have, but an inner arena of strongly competing ministries and parties. The internal tensions are fanned by the pluralism of the parliament, civil society and mass media, which are always divided about any EU challenge. Domestic interest groups who fear losing a domestic fight usually feel stimulated to lobby in Brussels against their government first. The procedure for national co-ordination usually covers only Commission proposals for secondary decision-making, thus bypassing all the rest before and after. Its outcome, prepared by a special office, is often equal to that of the internal rivalry, made coherent on paper and used for both determining the voting position in the Council and justifying this before the national parliament [Van Schendelen, 1993; Kassim and others, 2000 and 2001]. Only a few governments have a sort of Central PA Desk, like the SGAE in France and the EU Cabinet Office in the UK, but the French one lacks a serious mandate, and the UK one is focused on the short-list of the government party. Most governments usually behave reactively to proposals from the Commission and the Council chair and not proactively, let alone after carefully prepared PA homework on both a shared-list and short-list. However, when a new Treaty or their Council chairmanship is on the horizon or when a very special interest is at stake, most governments establish a high-level ad-hoc team for the listing of national priorities, usually without much window-out preparatory homework. They use their Brussels PR, mainly composed of policy experts from the ministries, primarily for preparing Council negotiations and hardly for proactive PA management regarding the other institutions and stakeholders around. Only informal meetings of the Councils and bi/multilateral ones of a few member states (like Benelux, 'Berlin-Paris') come close to an ad-hoc platform that might sometimes function as a EuroFed.

Continuing our 'intermezzo' in chapter 2, we can also benchmark the *European Commission*. The DGs of the Commission function on the one hand as open channels for the aggregation of public and private interests from the EU countries, but have on the other hand the selfish interest that these aggregated and competitive interests come to some targeted EU decision. The most manifest vehicles for this are the annual work programme and the specific proposals that have to pass the College. The Commission looks like a national government, as it is internally divided by DGs and layers and externally under pluralistic pressures from outside. But its responses to these challenges come close to those of the multinational model. The main layers of a DG are the policy units which, falling short of in-house technical expertise, in-source particularly from diverse interest groups. The 'chef de dossier' acts like a PA officer, who collects different internal experts and external partners on short-list dossiers. Some striking differences exist, too. The chef, firstly, usually wants to in-source diversity, thus not only potential partners but also opponents, and these external people are experts. They deliver varied expertise and support. In fact, the chef practices the shared-list method, while the PA officer also does a lot on a short-list. Secondly, the chef can play Triple P in-house, while the PA officer has to do so from outside. Thirdly, the chef gets the PA mandate usually from the head of unit, under remote control of higher levels. Fourthly, with so many chefs each managing a few dossiers, all the chefs taken together make the Commission look like a PA factory with numerous PA Desks and dossiers. This all makes the Commission a superb case of 'intelligent laziness'. By its early internalisation of external diversity in the EU, it can proactively play the 'backwards lobby'. For the few short-list dossiers not fit for the shared-list method, such as competition cases in the secondary process, it has to go window-out; in the latter case particularly towards the EP whose members, unlike the civil servants of the Council's governments, are absent in expert committees. Through its blue, green and white papers, the Commission efficiently monitors the EP's position in advance.

From this tentative benchmark one can draw the following observations and lessons.

– *PA Desk is crucial.* Interest groups without a qualified PA person or desk take a high risk by lacking the political expertise to monitor and manage the EU playing-field and the game of playing. Small-sized groups may consider its costs prohibitive, but not if they pool their limited resources on a common platform in, first of all, their domestic sector or region, from there connected to the EU. Other groups like national associations, ministries and governments cannot seriously consider the costs of qualified PA to be prohibitive, as the costs of non-PA are often exponentially higher.

– *EuroFeds are essential.* Any variant of a EuroFed gives indispensable leverage to the promotion of one's interest. Without it, one stands single-handed on the EU playing-field, has to bear the full costs of lobbying and misses a good chance of success. By becoming part of a EuroFed, any domestic lobby group gets a virtual multinational construction in its grasp, as the members of the different countries are, so to say, its country units that allow more multi-level lobbying (from local to global) and fine-tuned (diversity of tongues, cultures and countries). For almost every small group there exists a EuroFed that can be contacted via its domestic association or directly. Most ministries lack a European platform, so disadvantaging themselves; only a few have it under construction now.

- *Commission as example.* All EU lobby groups can learn from the intelligent way the Commission manages its PA. Even apart from the EU level and only for domestic purposes, they might profit from applying the 'internalised shared-list method' that the Commission practices by its insourcing of external stakeholders, as this brings in excellent information and commitment at a low price. At the EU level, the EuroFeds might follow this example of the Commission by in-sourcing more stakeholders from outside, for some special policy areas, into some of their work groups. Multinationals too might apply this method for their short-list dossiers by making their internal ad-hoc teams more open.

From the Home Front to the EU Fieldwork

Organising one's home front is clearly a difficult job. Indeed, it may take over half one's energy available for the EU RA management. It requires a lot of homework. Nobody can blindly produce cohesion, knowledge, resources, skills, image, strategy, targets, scenarios, evaluations and more. All these ingredients for cooking up success should be prepared carefully and thus selectively. This is purely a matter of *preparatory work.* The clearest example is the determination of the short-list, which requires negative selection from the long-list of challenges as identified by the strategic confrontation of perceived facts and chosen norms. Only after this can one know in which quantity and quality which ingredients are required. The lobby group neglecting all this homework will almost certainly be punished by extremely poor results from its EU actions.

The preparation on the home front is, of course, almost always *less than perfect.* If the costs of perfection exceed those of imperfection, this imperfection may be justified, as the best is the enemy of the better here. Merely the time pressure caused by EU deadlines frequently means the only real alternative to an imperfectly prepared action is no lobby action at all, which may be worse. If, however, a lobby group believes that its preparation is only better than that of its best competitor, then it should not feel justified in accepting its own imperfection, because it cannot count on always winning the 'tiebreaker' at the end. If the lobby group sees that some of its competitors are organising their home front better, then it has to improve its own preparation. This logic, true for every competition, is indeed the hard reality of the EU playing-field. More than ever, many interest groups want to create a desired outcome and invest in intelligent preparation for this at home.

The *multinational model* is, to be sure, not the last word on optimising one's home front. It looks well designed: integrative, professional and efficient, and it has earned a reputation of success. A few elements of it are widely followed now, particularly the establishment of a Brussels office. This, in consequence, is raising many questions of internal organisation, ranging from the making of the short-list and the contents of the mandate, to the involvement of staff and line people to be briefed and debriefed. The multinational model, looking so rational, is usually followed only piece by piece, starting with a Brussels officer and, years later, creating important changes deep inside the organisation at home. It remains, however, a question of research of whether the reputational claim, that this model of PA management at the EU level is significantly most successful, is really based on facts. Both the theoretical logic of the model and its reputation of success among practitioners favour the claim, but this is less than empirical evidence. The tentative benchmark suggests that even this model can be improved by incorporating some elements of the Commission's practices. Even if found necessary for success, the model can never be considered sufficient. It remains part of the preparation for the match and is not the match itself. The external fieldwork still has to come. This is a matter of fine-tuned lobbying and precise timing, the theme of the next chapter.

CHAPTER 6

MANAGING THE EU FIELDWORK

Lobbying: The Essential Link

In chapter 1, we referred to lobbying as an old effort to influence decision-makers by visiting some place (lobby, antechamber) near to them, or 'corridor behaviour', and we defined this behaviour technically as 'the build-up of unorthodox efforts to obtain information and support regarding a game of interest in order to get eventually a desired outcome from a power-holder'. We characterised in general terms the unorthodoxy of building such a position as indirect, informal, silent and charming behaviour. Modern insights from public affairs management tell us that even such a visit to a power-holder, called officials and stakeholders today, requires a lot of *study and prudence*, although the same basic insights can be taken from, for example, Sun Tzu and Machiavelli. In the preceding chapters we applied this insight to the study of the EU playing-field, the major actors, factors and vectors within reach there, the preparatory homework for approaching an EU arena and the management on the home front. The three main lessons from those chapters can be summarised as: countless variables determine success or failure; many of these variables are manageable to some degree; and this management requires permanent study and prudence. The third lesson is necessary but not sufficient for making the strategic, tactical and technical choices so as to become a professional rather than an amateur, intelligent rather than nonchalant and a winner rather than a loser.

In this chapter we focus particularly on the *technical choices* that have to be made concerning all activities on the playing-field, called corridor lobbying in the past and fieldwork now, in order to implement the strategic and tactical choices [McGrath, 2005-A]. Referring to Figure 1.2, this focus includes all field or corridor activities for both the upper arrow that stands for the window-out intelligence lobby and the lower arrow that represents the window-in support lobby. On the upper arrow the fieldwork contributes to the homework for organising the intelligence, and on the lower arrow the fieldwork is, reversely, directed by this organised intelligence for the creation of sufficient support. In combination with studious homework, the two forms of fieldwork give, so to speak, the E in the formula $E = MI^2$ its highest possible and ultimate value. Studious homework alone might sharpen the brains but remains useless in practice, and fieldwork alone is amateurish. In terms of workload, the former is even more important than the latter, as it is estimated that even the most qualified PA practitioners spent only 15% of their PA time on fieldwork [Spencer and McGrath, 2008, 18]. Although the focus on fieldwork is presented more at the end of the book here, in the daily life of lobbying it frequently comes much earlier. Among amateurs it is usually both the starting and the finishing point of their considerations, if they have any. The professional or intelligent lobbyists take the technical choices as part of one broader PA approach that includes strategy and tactics. Mentally they anticipate the technical choices proactively, in an early phase too, by thinking backwards and forwards in re-iteration (from step 5 to 1 in Figure 1.2 and vice versa).

The Surplus of Unorthodox Actions

On the EU playing-field every interest group has really *no shortage* of potential actions for the creation of a desired outcome. It can choose from an almost infinite menu of possibilities of going window-out and window-in. Firstly, it can use the orthodox ways and routes as mentioned in chapter 1, for which it does not have to lobby in the specific sense. Secondly, it can fall back on traditional techniques of influence, such as coercion, advocacy and argumentation, mentioned in chapter 1 as well. Thirdly, it can make use of the many unorthodox techniques that are discussed below. In fact, almost every variable is potentially instrumental. There are always manifold actors to approach, factors to be used and vectors to construct. The options 'exit, voice and loyalty' [Hirschman, 1970] or, in popular parlance, 'flee, fight, flirt', are only three of many. Every technique can be used in one or another direction, for example as stick or carrot, thus posing a perpetual dilemma. *Figure 6.1* presents a selection of frequently occurring dilemmas in EU fieldwork. The two first-mentioned categories directly apply to the actors, being the EU officials and the other stakeholders. The others refer to the factors and the vectors affecting them indirectly and they represent, as it were, dilemmas of meta-lobbying. The following exemplifies the dilemmas that every lobby group can face.

The officials. The lobby group can support or oppose the position officials prefer to adopt on an issue, thus making their life easier or more difficult. It can promote or damage their private careers, for example by good or bad

MAJOR DILEMMAS IN MANAGING THE FIELDWORK

REGARDING	DILEMMA
OFFICIALS	support or oppose / provide information or not / appease or disquiet
STAKEHOLDERS	mobilise or demobilise / reward or punish / divide or unite
RELATIONS	formalise or informalise / stabilise or destabilise / use old or make new ones
PROCEDURES	simplify or complicate / accept or litigate / interpret strictly or loosely
POSITIONS	recognise or challenge / take or leave / recruit by merits or spoils
ISSUES	politicise or depoliticise / broaden or narrow down / combine or split
FRAMES	keep frame or reframe / up-frame one's own or not / down-frame the opponent's one or not
DOSSIER LIFE	relieve or hinder / preserve or transform / push or delay time
ARENA	enter or leave / the one or the another coalition / restrict or expand
NEGOTIATION	use stick or carrot / overcharge or not / compromise or oppose
DECISION	accept or appeal / adapt to or escape / submit or undermine
LOBBYING	supplying or demanding / low- or high-key / direct or indirect / formal or informal

Figure 6.1

publicity. Some officials may be tolerant to practices of patronage and clientelism, and thus to receiving subtle favours like lunches and loyalties in return for compliance. All officials have an appetite for reliable real-life information, which the lobby group can satisfy or not. It can also appease or disquiet the concerns of the officials. Making a drama out of, for example, global competition or pollution is an evergreen technique of disquieting them, frequently resulting in the rapid creation of an EU agenda. Many more direct actions are possible with regard to the officials, such as changing their prestige, competencies, budget, workload, organisation or recruitment. Many officials frequently play these lobbying games against each other.

The stakeholders. One serious dilemma is whether or not to mobilise more of them. More friends give more support, but they take a larger share of the game as well. Another dilemma is either to reward the friends and those who surrender or to punish the opponents and the defectors. It is also possible to engender either division or unity among groups of stakeholders. Slumbering stakeholders might be kept sleeping or be awoken. Those wavering over an issue can be ignored, convinced or seduced. One can deal with irritating players by either excusing or accusing them in public, thus maybe bringing them either to obligation or to compromise. In 1998 the Dutch Minister of Finance Gerrit Zalm, defending his practices of fiscal aid to companies ('fiscal dumping'), forwarded to the Commission evidence that he had ordered from international accountancy firms whith which he showed even worse practices by other governments. This halted discussion on the issue for three years.

The relationships. The lobby group can make a relationship either more formal or informal, with semi-formal options in between. If it wants to have all three variants, then it has to cope with the dilemmas of their balancing and timing. It can also make a relationship more or less stable. Conflict can bring a better return than friendship [Coser, 1956], as in the CCMC/ACEA case of the car manufacturers (chapter 5). Another dilemma is whether to stick mainly to old relationships or replace them with new ones. Due to the continual circulation of EU officials and lobbyists, a lobby group often has no choice and has to invest in new relationships anyhow. After the 1999 reshuffle of the Prodi administration, many Commission people had to build-up new networks, and so did many lobby groups.

The procedures. These are part of the Triple P game. They can be made more simple or complex. Before the 2000 Commission's decision to allow Unilever to market its margarine Becel as 'healthy', the company lobbied for a simple procedure, and after that decision it preferred a complex one for keeping new competitors out. Every lobby group can either accept or challenge a procedure as well and, in the latter case, even go to the Court. The German government did this in 1998, when it questioned the Treaty basis of the Advertising Ban Directive. Another dilemma is about whether to lobby for a strict or loose interpretation of a procedure. Different language texts and daily practices ('precedents') allow room for new interpretations of procedures.

The positions. As part of Triple P, a lobby group can either recognise or challenge established bodies and positions, such as committees, agencies and officials. The proliferation of committees in the field of waste management, to as many as 25, has partially been caused by outside lobby groups complaining about the composition of existing committees. A lobby group can also decide to join or leave a body; the latter can indicate protest but also a desire for more freedom of action. The recruitment of people is full of dilemmas, for example in favour of or against one or another country, from one or more sectors, from inside or outside, and based on merit or on patronage (spoils). In 2000 the Commission decided, after many complaints about spoiled practices, to promote recruitment on merit.

The issues. One dilemma is whether to politicise or to depoliticise the facts, values and solutions that may be at issue. A standard technique of depoliticisation is to present an issue as 'technical', which many tend to take for 'less relevant'. For that purpose, an expert group on railway safety routinely placed a mathematical formula on the first page of its reports. Another dilemma is whether to broaden a single issue or to narrow it down. If some problem cannot be cut down to size, better for it to be enlarged. In the spring of 2000, Europabio pressed to extend the proposed liability for GMO to all sorts of nutritional products, so hoping to escape specific regulation and to broaden its coalition. A third dilemma is whether to combine various issues in a package, to keep them separate or to split them even more, which can also change the number and composition of stakeholders involved. The Commission and the Council frequently combine issues in order to satisfy many stakeholders a little bit.

The frames. Every interest contains one or more values, and because in pluralist societies every interest stands at issue, so each issue contains a clash of values. Different from a fight over facts, a clash over values is not solved by best evidence but by strongest support. As the real interest behind a value does not easily attract much support by its selfish nature, it should be framed or presented in a way that can mobilise much support [Daviter, 2007]. One dilemma is to reframe or not and, if so, in which direction. The allowance of novel foods on the market can be framed in terms of either health risks or liability, two sides of one coin. Another dilemma is to up-frame one's own interest or to down-frame that of the opponents. Figure 6.2 lists many EU examples of a selfish interest (first column) that has been upgraded by a more sociable and pleasant up-framing (second column) to attract wider support, just as the young lady Lorelei on her rock in the river tried to attract and catch many fishermen. Opponents shall try, of course, to prevent or block such an up-framing, to downgrade it to its selfish contents and/or to replace it by their own up-frame. Frequently, a lobby fight is between two or more competitive up-framed interests, for example liberty versus health on tobacco and smoking. An up-frame is most useful for an un-friendly arena and requires a lot of study of what important stakeholders, officials and the audiences want to hear. It took the European textile indus-try, looking to get rid of cheap imports, many years before it found the nicer frame of 'child labour'. Many NGOs are experts on this Lorelei technique and have hoisted such fine flags as 'public safety', 'sustainability' and 'hu-mane farming'. In 2005, trade unions of northern Europe campaigned against the Services Directive proposal (2004/001) that would allow cheap labour to go from central to northern Europe, down-framed this to 'social dumping' and up-framed their own position as 'for a social Europe'. 'Soli-darity' is frequently used as a Robin Hood up-frame to get EU budget funds transferred from the rich to the poor, from others to oneself. In 2010, popu-lar up-frames are 'climate change' and 'financial crisis'.

The life of a dossier. The lobby group can either help the passage of a dossier or make this difficult. The extreme example is the UK in the Council during the BSE affair (1996), when it simply blocked more than fifty dossiers (approved by rubberstamp afterwards). Another dilemma is whether to preserve or to transform the dossier contents. The latter, coming close to a reframing, is an indirect technique of time management that can solve or create a stalemate, and so push or delay the process. With the 1997 'Amsterdam' decision to reframe the matter of monetary stability as 'Stabil-ity *and Growth*', a stalemate was overcome. There are countless techniques for pushing or delaying the decision-making process. The most direct one is by moving a deadline forwards or backwards. Usually, it takes more ener-gy to push than to delay.

The arena. The lobby group can choose either to enter or to leave a spe-cific arena, with wait-and-see options in between. Inside the arena, it faces the dilemma of whether to join one or another coalition. Frequently, every coalition has its own mix of advantages and disadvantages, which can make a marginal difference and thus offers a real choice. A strong dilemma, dis-cussed in chapter 4, is whether to restrict or to expand the arena bound-aries. Such a change may result in a very different set of both issues and stakeholders. A lobby group can also choose to make one arena overlap or be separated from another one. If the lobby group takes multiple routes to the EU (Figure 3.2), it encounters the arena dilemma of whether to connect them in series or in parallel. Every lane, junction and roundabout on its way to the final EU arena amounts to a prelude arena.

The negotiation. A classical dilemma is to negotiate by stick or by carrot. Modern wisdom deems it best to show the carrot and to keep the stick cov-ered but in reach. Withholding the carrot is the first stick, and punishment

EU EXAMPLES OF UP-FRAMING

THE CORE INTEREST	THE UPGRADE
CAP (old)	Food supply
CAP (new)	Sustainability
Cheap textile import ban	Child labour
Tobacco smoking	Liberty
Tobacco ban	Public health
Tax-free shopping	Employment
Beer import limits	Environment
Charging private transport	Sustainable mobility
Shorter truck-trailer coupling	Public safety
Hands-free car-phone ban	Road safety
Fur industry (against)	Animal welfare
Laying hen (against)	Humane farming
Subsidies to Southern Europe	Social cohesion
ACP bananas (for)	Development aid
R&D subsidies	Global competition
Lower VAT (shoe repair, etc.)	Employment
Open labour market (against)	Social dumping
Open labour market (for)	Equality, Welfare
Chocolate definition up	Development aid
Subsidised food exports	Humanitarian aid
Subsidies to CEEC	Stability
Biotechnology (against)	Public health, Environment
Idem (for)	Development
Oil stocking	Security
SME support	Employment
Intervention in ECB (for)	Economic growth
Non-intervention in ECB	Monetary stability
Energy-saving products	Environment
Novel foods	Public health

Figure 6.2

by the real stick the ultimate one. In the game of giving and taking, another old dilemma is overcharging or underbidding or going straight to a fair deal. English negotiators have a reputation of disdaining those who cut straight to the chase. A related aspect is the dilemma whether to persist in one's position or to enter into a compromise. Governments in the Council, if this decides by unanimity, sometimes play the game of reluctance until 'five to midnight', as part of a loss-compensation game. In 2001, the Spanish government held up the Council decision regarding the timing of enlargement as a means of keeping the subsidies it gets from the Cohesion Fund. Another dilemma is whether to participate or, to block the process, to be absent. The latter choice is highly risky as the other participants can continue with an even easier formation of consensus.

The decision. Regarding the EU decision at issue, the lobby group can choose to accept the outcome or to appeal to for example the Court, as Germany did on the 1999 Tobacco Ban. A milder variant is to make use of the review clause that is part of many an EU law and to compile an agenda for retaliation. A dilemma at home is whether to adapt new EU legislation or to allow some escapes, as is often done for directives (needing domestic implementation) and by multi-layered countries such as Germany, Spain and Italy. Another dilemma is whether to submit to the decision or to undermine its implementation at the EU level (comitology) or at home. The costs and risks of appeal, escapes and undermining have become high, however, and indicate the rise of the EU as a system ruled by law.

Lobbying styles. Standard dilemmas in lobbying style are whether to behave in a supplying or demanding way, low-key or high-key, directly or indirectly, formally or informally, defensively or offensively, confrontationally or appeasingly, reactively or proactively and so on. The question of style is widely considered to be crucial. It is, in fact, the only one that is common to both the amateurish and the professional groups (Figure 3.3). But their answers differ, as we shall see at length below. The theoretical dilemma over lobbying as either legitimate or illegitimate behaviour is hardly one in practice. Every lobby group has every reason to fear the political isolation from behaviour considered illegitimate and causing scandals.

Coping with the Surplus

The most popular question posed by the dilemmas of EU fieldwork is, *'What is the best thing to do?'* Five types of answers can be heard in the world of EU lobbying.

(1) *Action reflex.* Amateurish groups tend to lobby by spontaneous reflex. Having an emotional feeling about an EU challenge, they go straight to EU high official of their own tongue and present their case there in a prolix, loud and selfish way. They are FiFo lobbyists: flying in, flying out. Or they make a stop in the national capital or association and try the same approach there. Driven by their emotions, they act almost Pavlovian, which is practically the same as at random. Unfamiliar with the labyrinth constructed on a

trampoline, as we characterised the EU playing-field before, they miss the many different backdoors and better moments. They consider the many dilemmas to be a problem rather than a blessing.

(2) *Rules of thumb.* Introductory manuals to EU lobbying [Venables, 2007; Guéguin, 2007; Randall, 1996; Anderson, 1992; Gardner, 1991] keep it simple as well. They describe the EU as a pyramid of dominant institutions and high officials connected by procedures, and with both the work floors and stakeholders at distance. They are formalistic and belong to the first wave of the study of EU PA management, focused on rulers. In addition, they give a number of rules of thumb, such as 'be to the point and on time', 'keep it low-key' and 'avoid over-lobbying'. Such general lobby caveats make some sense, of course, sometimes. At other moments, however, the opposites might be more effective, as we anticipated in chapter 4 ('best practices') and shall see below. The manuals hardly see the dilemmas and thus simplify the fieldwork.

(3) *Receivers.* According to the small amount of field research, many Commission officials [Burson, 2003 and 2005; Koeppl, 2001] as well as MEPs [Burson, 2001; Kohler-Koch, 1998; Katz and Wessels, 1999] want to be approached in a low-key, informative and friendly way at an early stage and not, as frequently happens, the opposite. Their consumer demands come close to the rules of thumb above. What is good for the receiver is, however, not necessarily good for the sender, as the former wants to be in the driver's seat and the latter to achieve a lobby target. Predictably, many MEPs say it is better to approach them than to try the Commission people. These findings coming from limited research do not distinguish between specific situations and neglect most dilemmas mentioned above.

(4) *Consultants.* Commercial consultants have been interviewed in connection with the aforementioned MEPs' pilot study [Kohler-Koch, 1998]. Overall they have strong but barely varying opinions about the best ways and moments for lobbying the Commission and the EP. Almost everything submitted to them in the interview they considered highly important. This has at least the suspicion of commercial self-interest. Of the highest importance they rank the informal contacts with the Commission officials during their preparation of a proposal, and with the EP's rapporteur during the writing of the report, all limited to only the secondary process. Other stakeholders and lobby styles remain unquestioned in this piece of research, let alone the many other dilemmas.

(5) *'It depends'.* The short answer of the thoughtful practitioners in EU lobbying to the question, 'What is the best thing to do?' is: it depends on the situation in the arena. In keeping with chapter 4 this is, of course, our posi-

tion, too. To make a lobby action more successful according to the yardsticks of effectiveness and efficiency, it must be fine-tuned to the specific situation. The amateurish lobby group usually feels unhappy with the surplus of options, as it has to choose without knowing how. The professional lobby group, by contrast, considers the surplus of dilemmas and variables of lobbying as a blessing rather than a problem. The higher their number, the more options it sees for solving or preserving a challenge. It can always find a friendly official, a supportive stakeholder, a pleasant up-frame, a promising deal, a better moment, an open route, in short, a chance to achieve the desired result. If it sees limited chances, the intelligent group usually knows how to enlarge them through the use of vectors. Thanks to this surplus of dilemmas and variables, which is larger than that of the game of chess, it can escape stalemates and overcome setbacks. Its lobbying is not random or based on rules of thumb, nor focused on pleasing the receivers or the consultants. It is based on a choice that is as rational as possible under consideration of its position in a particular situation.

The professional group has, of course, *no guarantee* of lobby success. As stated in chapter 4, a precise prediction of the effects of its actions is impossible for two reasons. Firstly, that relationship is full of multi-causality (same effect coming from different actions) and multi-finality (same action producing different effects), with many weak correlations. Secondly, the many volatile variables are beyond the reach of a complete and reliable calculation, as it already is with the simpler game of chess [Simon, 1979]. Therefore, also for its fieldwork, the intelligent group will not search for the maximal best choice, as this is a utopia in life and anyhow always comes too late, but for the optimal best choice derived from the menu of dilemmas. Full control over the chain-effects of its lobbying is also impossible, for essentially the same two reasons. The professional group thus takes the complexity and dynamics of any EU arena as facts of life that require permanent study and prudence. It may even feel confident enough to increase the complexity and dynamics, for example by creating new vectors and by crossing arena boundaries. It considers the absence of guaranteed success impossible to solve and thus not to be a problem.

This optimal choice is, again, an educated guess of the probable outcomes of suitable lobby actions, given the specific situation. Inevitably it is made under much uncertainty about the real outcomes. Therefore, *prudence* during the lobbying process is a permanent necessity, as it enables one to make all sorts of detailed corrections, similar to driving a car on a slippery road. It is based on solid knowledge about the playing-field and the variables, for example that it is easier to move from a soft approach (informal, silent, by carrot) to a hard opposite than the other way around. It is also anchored in the main chapters of qualified preparatory homework, such as the proactive window-out monitoring for the long-list, the assessment of an arena and the organisation of the home front. This knowledge helps to estimate the costs and benefits of whatever choice and its probable effects. An intelligent lobby group will even consider two other smart games of fieldwork. One is combining the two extreme options of a particular dilemma, for example the use of both stick and carrot. This requires precise engineering for different phases, stakeholders, issues or whatever variables present in the situation. Another game is faking the choice of an option by showing intentions of, for example, joining another coalition or 'going to the Court if this deal is all there is'. The two special games have, of course, their additional costs and benefits that require even more educated guesses and prudence.

Every lobby group is, of course, free to decide that choosing its actions by reflex, by rules of thumb, by serving the receivers or by following the consultants is no less rational than doing it by an educated guess. It then saves the costs of its own preparatory work. The chance of achieving the desired target is, however, low to zero in practice. The lobby group that acts by reflex becomes dependent on sheer good luck, on the crumbs from the table. If it acts by rules of thumb, it shall make many unforced errors. If it just serves the receivers or follows the consultants, it shall make them happier but probably not itself. Our approach remains *advisory* and not normative. There is no ultimate argument for why a lobby group should not be allowed to do all this instead of making a rational choice based on the best of its knowledge. However, if the lobby group seriously wants to solve or to preserve a challenge, then it should base its actions on such a rational choice, as this allows savings on the costs of inefficient or ineffective fieldwork. We shall now demonstrate this for the recurrent questions of the fieldwork, summarised earlier (Figure 3.3) as *'how to lobby, whom, on what, where and when?'*

Lobbying Whom?

At any particular moment, on any dossier, every lobby group can go to hundreds of stakeholders, including the officials having a stake in the dossier. However, no group can approach all of them in series, let alone parallel, and it should not want to do so, as maximal is the enemy of optimal. In its personalised lobbying it can better act *selectively*. The best cues come from the homework. Most helpful is the summary study of the arena (Figure 4.3). If the wind is blowing friendly, then the lobby group can confine its efforts to keeping the supporting stakeholders on board and to arranging a free ride. If, on the other hand, the wind is unfriendly, then it is better to approach a few opponents in order to divide them and also some waverers in order to get them on board. The best opponents to approach are those who have been assessed as primary (influential plus active) and as sharing the small-est number of preferences with other opponents. The most promising wa-verers are, by analogy, those having both primary status and high ambiva-lence. If, however, the winds are absent or circulating, thus making the arena indeterminate, then 'waiting and seeing' is more rational. In the meantime the lobby group should make scenarios for any wind which may arise, place Triple P pickets, intensify its monitoring and offer to a few pri-mary stakeholders a few arguments that match their interests and test their responses. The lobby group can read the names of these stakeholders from the vertical axis of its Figure 4.3.

It might do the same for *other dossiers* on its short-list and its shared-list. Usually it will discover that other stakeholders as well are involved in more than one dossier, have useful relationships with even more stakeholders and EU officials, and thus can be pulled or pushed indirectly. Among the many information sources (Figure 4.2) it can use its EuroFed(s) as easy shopping centre for names, contacts and more, in order to get its 'intelli-gent laziness' organised. Stakeholders that take friendly positions on dif-ferent dossiers deserve an intimate courtship. Those having mixed posi-tions may be made interested in some compromise. Strong opponents can be tackled, preferably indirectly upon their life-lines, for example those of support and budget. The lobby group can also work the other way around and identify those dossiers not on its own long-list but of great interest to primary stakeholders on their long-list. Dependent on their position on the latter, it can support or tackle them on their dossiers, thus repaying them almost free of costs.

In addition to these stakeholders, two *other groups of people* need attention here. Firstly, those on the home front. Well-done preparatory homework gives information about which people at home have the special expertise, status or relationship of interest to primary stakeholders. These people can be activated as liaisons in the external network. They only have to be briefed and debriefed. Some staff experts or line managers may already hold posi-tions in EuroFeds and EU committees that are useful for the current dossier. In the multinational model of managing EU public affairs, they of-ten become part of the ad-hoc team. If there are no such persons at home, the proactive lobby group still has some time to create them and to position them inside such EU platforms or nearby befriended stakeholders. Secondly, the people working inside the EU machinery need close attention. Acting under some functional and personal pressure, they need specific information and support at any given time, and all the more so if something is new to them. In any newly elected Parliament, usually the majority of newcomers is still inexperienced. Commission officials often circulate upward or to a different directorate. The sooner the lobby group can serve the newcomers with information and support, the more it can get an edge over its competitors. Related to this EU machinery are the many experts in committees and working groups. Those inside comitology deserve close attention.

The answer to the question *'lobbying whom?'* clearly depends on the specific situation. If the lobby group has knowledge of the situation as provided by careful study, it can benefit a lot from the checklist in Figure 6.1 by considering the use of additional dilemmas. Three examples follow. Firstly, if it has found a number of new stakeholders to be friendly often, it can promote a joint lobby for playing, for example, Triple P for safeguarding the common interests. Secondly, if it has identified some stakeholders as frequent opponents, it can pounce upon them in their own domain. For example, northern agricultural lobby groups, which now seldom interfere in EU olive committees, these being of high relevance to southern groups, might create an excellent trade-off by such an interference at low costs and risks on their own interests, like milk or R&D subsidies. Thirdly, if the lobby group has found that on a particular dossier only a few people of the relevant Commission DG are on its side, then it can delay the process expediently by lobbying them for a retardation of formal deadlines. To make all this personalised lobbying possible, the lobby group must keep its relevant EU directory updated and in close reach.

Lobbying on What?

No lobby group can tackle all the issues in all its dossiers at the same time. It has to be selective. For its specific *issue management*, the professional group relies heavily on its homework. The main source of inspiration is the summary assessment of any arena (Figure 4.3), which gives the clues to the best practices that have to be detailed. If, for example, the arena is essentially friendly, then the lobby group knows that it must keep the favourable issues high up and block opposing ones. From the cells of the arena description, it deduces which friendly issues deserve supportive evidence and which unfriendly ones the opposite sort. It can even personalise the mailing of messages, as it knows from the preparation which stakeholders are crucial on either its or the opposing side. If the arena is mainly unfriendly, then the lobby group can glean from its preparatory work which issues and whom it can best lobby for loss-compensation. This homework can also reveal which unfriendly issues are the most suitable to be up-framed into a more attractive Lorelei and on which issues it should lobby for changing the arena boundaries in order to get rid of opponents. If the arena, finally, is mainly indeterminate, then the lobby group can know from its homework on which issues and related to whom it has to intensify its monitoring, create a reframing or try a balloon.

If the lobby group has prepared itself well, it can even go beyond the issue boundary of an arena and use a different issue as the Achilles' heel of an opponent, which every player usually has (the columns at the right of Figure 4.3) and provide free sticks and carrots. One example of such *offensive lobbying* is the aforementioned option to interfere in EU committees on olives, on which one has no interest but some opponent much more so. In 2001, UK pharmaceutical companies, irritated about British Oxfam's issue-formation about their price-setting of AIDS drugs for South Africa, considered from their side fanning through local retailers the issue of Oxfam's local trade (as BINGO) that was, to the irritation of commercial retailers, largely free from local taxes. The enemy of one's enemy can be used indirectly as henchman. The pharmaceutical companies decided, however, to deal with the issue of AIDS prices directly, outside the EU, with the South African government. Making a virtue out of necessity, they offered cheap pricing in return for both approvals of new drugs and WTO agreements, and they beautified their public image somewhat. Again, excellent homework can pay its own way.

The lobby group can also practise *meta-lobbying* that deals with the actors, factors and vectors affecting an issue. The checklist of dilemmas can again be a source of inspiration. For example, the lobby group can decide to challenge the position of some opposing stakeholder, to move to another coalition or to lobby for a different procedure. Such behaviour may change the issues at stake. More specific is the meta-game of Triple P, intended to rearrange the playing-field and thus also to make the issues more friendly. The lobby group can get clues for this meta-lobbying on issues from its homework that also covers both the external arenas and general developments. For example, under secondary procedure, the conflict over the establishment of the European Food Safety Authority (EFSA) in 2000 was mainly about the layout of procedures and positions thereafter and hardly about the substantial issues of food safety. The latter usually cause more tension and friction and can best be settled afterwards, by authorised procedures and positions, which were proposed by DG SANCO at the suggestion of and with support from some lobbying ministries, producers and retailers in the food sector.

If the arena still remains unfriendly or indeterminate, the lobby group may have to return to its preparatory work regarding its home front. Maybe it has engaged in a *mission impossible*. Disappointing field experiences are useful input for studious review. They help in checking the reliability and completeness of the previous homework. The lobby group may have to come to the conclusion that it has to redefine the challenges, if necessary based on a reassessment of facts and norms, and maybe its break-down between shared-list and short-list as well. In the most extreme case, it may have to conclude that its chances of winning something are close to zero or only exist at a disadvantageous cost-benefit ratio. Then it had better remove the dossier from its short-list, put it on its shared-list or even leave it to the winds, as Unilever did in 2000 with its GMO challenge, after which it decided to spend the saved lobby energy on the more promising dossier of the one-stop EFSA.

How to Style One's Lobbying?

The question of 'how to lobby' is the oldest one on the subject, going back to the days when lobbying was confined to political corridors and antechambers. It is also the only question that is posed by both amateurish and professional lobby groups. No group lobbying for a desired outcome can escape it, because the answer ultimately shapes and styles its behaviour. Specific dilemmas in answering are whether it is better to behave in a supplying or demanding way, formally or informally, and directly or indirectly. Very topical is the dilemma of whether it should act silently or noisily. Of course, it can always behave at random, follow some rules of thumb, simply please officials or act on consultants' advice. All this would make most preparation indeed superfluous. The following shows that, if one wants to win on targets, one should solve those dilemmas rationally, based on homework.

Supplying or Demanding
Every lobby group has to develop both a supply and a demand side. Without the first, it cannot attract interest from other stakeholders, and without the second it cannot get its own interest included in the outcome. As far as some rule of thumb makes sense, the lobby group should be more conscious about its supply than its demand side, as it usually has, by almost nat-

ural instinct, the latter so much in the forefront of its mind that it must try hard not to forget its supply side. Besides, when entering an arena, it has to obtain and maintain a position, which is better achieved through charming and offering than demanding behaviour. Therefore, the professional group invests in its *image of charm*. It likes to be seen as interesting, pleasant, friendly and ultimately trustworthy. It plays courtesy and diplomacy, as an EU arena is as risky on fortune and fate as the Ruler's court or the stage of international politics. It distributes such symbols of charm as small talk, nice dinner or casual drink, and it hopes to be rewarded with an informal relationship that can tell more about the demand side of the other. Behind its face of charm and its hands full of carrots, it hides its selfish interests and its sticks in the event of an emergency. As tone makes the melody, it up-frames even its objections as a friendly 'of course yes, but'. Window-out, it shows interest in the well-being of others, so trying to get information about particularly their problems and agendas, as this gives the best input for developing a supply side that can solve their problems without hurting its own interests. On substance most stakeholders and EU officials usually desire expertise and support to satisfy their needs. The lobbying art is to discover their appetite precisely. What they say they need, if reliable, provides clues about their strengths and weaknesses. EU officials from their side have on offer their capacity to push or block a desired outcome. All this seemingly charming behaviour lays the ground for the crucial window-in practices, which must result in achieving the deals as desired.

The rational lobby group, in short, tries to satisfy its demand side by pushing forward its supply side. A good deal finally links up one's own demand and supply sides with those of the crucial stakeholders and officials. This friendly looking style of lobbying comes close to *political marketing*, albeit usually not for mass markets but for niche markets like EU arenas [O'Shaughnessy, 1990; Andrews, 1996; Harris and others, 2000; Dermody and Wring, 2001; Baines and Egan, 2004]. Here too, desired outcomes such as sales and profit can no longer, as frequently in the past, just be imposed, tied-in, advertised or talked-up. Even for the current mass markets, they now have to be prepared by careful research into what consumers may want and what may satisfy them. An EU arena too is usually a niche market, with a lot of open competition among multiple stakeholders and with rounds of wheeling and dealing, eventually resulting in a sufficient consensus. As an aside here: organisations that have excellent PA expertise probably also excel in their commercial market or policy domain (and vice versa), as they behave in a substantially extroverted manner. Many marketing techniques can help to improve a supply side, ranging from branding and merchandising to export licensing and 'after sales'. Their parallels in the EU arena are reputation building, displaying attractive items, appointing an intermediary, and servicing friends after a deal. On the latter, lessons can be taken from former MEPs who frequently complain that, from the date of their departure onward, they are forgotten by many previously most friendly lobbyists. By telling this to their successors, they silently punish these lobbyists for being so amateurish.

The preparatory work provides the best possible indicators for the *design* of the supply side. The lobby group can, contrary to a popular rule of thumb, sometimes even demand more than it supplies. For example, in an overwhelmingly friendly arena (a buyers' market) it can take a free ride and get more of its demands fulfilled without having to supply much. By carefully studying the situation, it can work out on which issues it can take a free ride and from whom. In a most unfriendly situation it might decide rationally, contrary to a rule of thumb again, to overcharge its demand side for the purpose of creating nuisance value, getting more loss-compensation or delaying the process. It has to fine-tune, such aggressive lobbying, of course, to the proper issues and stakeholders, which perspective it can obtain from having done good homework. In a mainly indeterminate situation it has the least reason to push its demand side above its supply side, because it still has to build up its position. An intelligent group fine-tunes its style with a wider view to both its other current interests and the near future, as it is always concerned about possible boomerangs. If it over-demands according to crucial stakeholders or officials, it may get the bad image of a greedy player and be punished for it. If it oversupplies, it might be seen as a softie and be treated accordingly. It is all a matter of studious and prudent lobbying.

Formal or Informal

Many lobby groups are inclined to take the skeleton of the decision process as a real process and thus to behave formally. Focusing on the desired end-result of the lobby process, they look for the signature of some high official or authority, such as the chairman of a EuroFed, a Commissioner or the Council, and approach them formally by way of an official letter sent by their chairman. Many EuroFeds and national ministries hold the *formal belief* that for a desired outcome, formal support from the beginning to the end of the process is both needed and even sufficient. They are amateurish, as neither is true. Many decision-making processes start at some lower level or even outside the boundaries, and proceed upwards through higher officials that put comments in the margins and usually sign. If their desired outcome is for no decision to be taken at all, then no approval is needed either. If the desired approval has been granted, the required measures can still fail to be taken or implemented. A formal decision can produce the decided outcome with time, but this is never certain. The EU open market for labour and capital was decided by 1987 SEA but is still slowly developing two decades later. Those having opposed that decision have lost the treaty game but not (yet) their real interest.

In at least the following *four situations*, the formal style of lobbying is not very appropriate.

– *Wanting no decision*. The lobby group may want no decision at all to be taken. This is a matter of blocking and delaying the build-up of issues, agendas and decisions (Figure 4.1), which usually can best be achieved by informal and semi-formal techniques.

– *Window-out*. If the lobby group has to go window-out, it usually gathers crucial information better through an informal chat or a semi-formal meeting than by a formal demand.

– *Work floors*. Those having to approve the desired decision are seldom the same as those who composed it. The work floor is usually much more relevant than the boardroom. The mid-level experts, clerks and other apparatchiks can often best be approached in non-formal ways, as they are human beings usually with some discretionary powers.

– *Window-in start*. If the lobby group wants to make a window-in deal with a supportive, opposing or wavering stakeholder or official, it can best start informally.

The latter applies particularly to the situation in which formal approval is really needed. This can best be built up step by step, from informal to semi-formal and finally formal. It works by *creating trust*. It is, as said before, just like engaging a partner in life, a process that is best started informally, then leads up to some semi-formal formula of 'living apart together' and finally may result in a formal marriage, which sequence hardly works the other way around. Informally, one gets the best information and networks. Efficient tools for this first step are the quiet restaurant, pleasant outing and social networking in leisure time, and all framed by an attitude of pleasant respect. In this way the informal relationship can come to incorporate common interests ('something in it for both of us') that engender trust in its most solid basis, as loyalty to the other has become self-interest. The arising informal understanding continues, secondly, semi-formally, for example by ad-hoc group, expert committee or working group. So far the prudent lobby group keeps its position paper in its head or luggage and never puts it on the table, as otherwise it cannot negotiate ('give and take') well and may lose face. An example is Commission officials who in the past often put their proposals on the table early and now increasingly issue tentative papers (blue, green, white) for evoking comments, so hiding their hand. The third step is to get the semi-formal position formally approved, which after so many rounds of ever better trust, understanding and negotiation is usually a matter of formality. In private affairs, the informal build-up can take years, the semi-formal engagement half that time, and the final day of marriage usually only one day.

From its preparatory homework, the lobby group can read which stakeholders it should approach informally and on which issues. To this it adds useful information about their personal *idiosyncratic preferences*, such as walking in a park, having a drink or visiting the theatre. The office of the German region of Bavaria once had on hand a private plane to take people to, for example, a Munich football match. One person likes to talk about family or career, another about politics or philosophy. One takes familiarity as a sign of friendship, another takes it as impoliteness or even as contempt. One loves a phone call, another sees it as disruptive. High officials tend to open only hand-written envelopes and leave pre-printed ones to their secretary. Some people even dislike being approached informally at all and allow this behaviour only after a formal beginning. The professional lobbyist takes all these idiosyncrasies very seriously, as they are crucial when trying to cross a physical or a mental threshold. Among lobbyists such personalised information is frequently exchanged. Some consultants have it for sale.

Direct or Indirect
Direct ways of lobbying are those that go straight from the lobby group to the targeted audience, a person, committee, platform or wider public. Indirect ways are those by which the lobby group makes use of a U-turn as its medium for sending its message. The menu of both direct and indirect ways to lobby is richly varied, as is shown in Figure 6.3 that presents a selection drawn from aforementioned case and field studies and is subdivided consecutively for intimate, formal and noisy variants.

The *direct ways* show great variety. Some are highly informal and personal, such as the face-to-face and ear-to-ear ('lobby by body') personal visit, phone call and invitation to the opera. Others are more formal and functional, such as going to a meeting or a hearing, presenting a position paper and sending an official letter or delegation to a stakeholder or official. Some direct ways are low-key or silent, for example the informal face-to-face meetings behind closed doors. Others are high-key or loud, as they make

EXAMPLES OF DIRECT AND INDIRECT EU LOBBYING

DIRECT WAYS

Personal visit, letter, phone, email
Social invitation
Committee membership
Hearing participation
Presentation of position
Formal visit, contact, delegation
Formal request, petition
Folder or brochure
Mass media participation
Political advertisement
Press conference
Manifestation, demonstration
Love-site, thanksgiving, applause
Hate-site, boycott, blockade, strike
Litigation, Court procedure

INDIRECT WAYS

(Sub)national association
(Sub)national government
(Cross-)sectoral (Euro)Fed
Foreign (non-EU) network
Ad-hoc coalition
Affiliated interest groups
Science: scientists, studies, seminars
Working visits, trips, tours
Well-known personalities
Mid-level civil servants
Caretakers and friends inside
Brokers and consultants
Cyberlobbying
Political parties
Mass media mobilisation, polls
Under-cover action

Figure 6.3

use of public platforms, such as an advertisement, press conference or public demonstration. Some direct approaches are friendly, such as the invitation for pleasure trips, the launch of a brochure or the public thanksgiving to a group of MEPs. The lobby group for Animal Welfare did the latter shortly after the EP's 'improvement' of the directive on Animal Testing in April 2001. Others are more confrontational, for example the hate-site, boycott and litigation. A direct way frequently has, by choice or effect, a mixture of characteristics. The choice for a press conference is almost automatically one for a formal, loud and possibly confrontational way. New rules of public registration in force, particularly in the EP and Commission (chapter 7), require that formal visits and presentations there almost always become public.

The *indirect ways* also have many variants, ranging from informal to formal, low-key to high-key and appeasing to confrontational. Established U-turns are those via a domestic umbrella organisation, EuroFed and foreign (non-EU) platforms like the WTO. Underused as a U-turn but potentially highly effective is the OECD in Paris, which is a high-expert producer of definitions, standards and methods consumed by the Commission as input for its policy framing [Dostal, 2004]. Ad-hoc coalitions are frequently set-up for the purpose of broader-based and fine-tuned communication. Scientific studies, scholars and 'wise men', if under control but seeming independent, give an aura of authority to the sender and the message, which is highly effective if the receivers are both willing and uninformed. Seminars under the flag of a Commission DG or EP committee have a similar presence. The same applies to the use of popular personalities such as, for example, the Spice Girls, who demonstrated at the EP in 1998 against the draft Copyright Directive, to the displeasure of music producers. People inside the system, like mid-level civil servants and friends, are excellent for plugging a message. Political parties can be used for the politicisation of an issue. Many lobby groups use mass media for disseminating information off the record and for promoting an EU issue or agenda. Many lobby groups (wealthier), such as ministries, MNCs and MNGOs, order public opinion polls, as these have the image of being 'the voice of the people', and they publish the results if supportive and not if disappointing to their interest. A lobby group can create a new U-turn by, for example, parachuting a friend into a useful position (part of its Triple P) and other undercover practices.

Highly ingenious is the interconnection, in series or in parallel, of various U-turns. In this way the lobby group can arrange a *polyphonic orchestra*, sending the same message through various sound boxes to the targeted audience that thus becomes more easily convinced. A trend-setting example was given by EACEM, the association of consumer electronics companies like Philips and Thomson, when lobbying for their high-definition TV (HDTV) in 1986 [Verwey, 1994; Cawson, 1997]. Through their different units in the member countries they, now experts in political sound as well, approached many national ministries, trade associations and other stakeholders in a parallel setting, and they subsequently connected in series the key people inside these organisations to the relevant people in EuroFeds, the Commission, EP and the Council, particularly at the work floor levels there. In 1995, DG Environment, in cooperation with both national ministries and NGOs in its field, launched a similar campaign in favour of sustainability. Politicians can easily be used for such an interconnection, as they belong to party-political families that connect the local, regional and national level to the EP, the COR and the Council officially and often to other EU institutions unofficially.

The surplus of so many different ways of lobbying is a richness that makes a reasoned choice possible and necessary, as every way has its own costs and benefits and also its own probable effects. *Efficiency and effectiveness* are thus useful general criteria for choosing. There is no rationality in applying rules of thumb and the like. In their daily lobbying, many lobby groups still show a bias in favour of direct ways. The reasons for this can be manifold, for example lack of capacity (such as expertise, relationships and maybe resources) to manage indirect ways, or lack of time due to their late arrival in a process. Indirect ways require, indeed, investments made in the past and early preparations of games to come. An ad-hoc group of stakeholders or a prestigious group of scientists easily requires half a year of formation and two years before becoming effective. Some other disadvantages or costs of a U-turn can be the return to be paid, disclosure of the sender, distorted transmission and lack of visibility on the home front. Finding the best balance of costs and benefits of going either directly or indirectly is clearly a matter of studious consideration and contributes to the prudence of the choice. Often the costs of indirect ways are outbalanced by greater benefits, such as the following four.

- *Cue-givers helpful.* When lobbying for information or support from a new or not well-known stakeholder or official, one can receive more from them by going first to intermediaries, who always exist and may provide cues and manuals for the best way to approach them.
- *Hands free.* By going through another group, one can gain invisibility or anonymity and thus free hands for the moment. For example, when launching a balloon in an indeterminate arena, one can try best from another platform than one's own.
- *Generalised interest.* By sending a message through a different channel, targeted receivers may take it as more convincing and perhaps as representing a more general interest, which is one of the main functions of a BONGO or GONGO.
- *Less backlash.* If opposition arises, this does not immediately strike back at the real sender but only on the U-turn.

The intelligent lobby group selects from the full menu of options the ways that score best on efficiency and effectiveness, given the specific *arena situation* in which it finds itself. If it still has much to choose, it usually prefers indirect rather than direct ways, not only because the former provide lower visibility but also because, as a matter of prudence, it is easier to go from indirect to direct than the reverse. For the same reason of prudence it prefers to go an informal rather than formal route, let alone loudly announcing its every move. Sometimes, however, even the professional group has not much choice, as the best possible solution depends on the specific arena situation. If it finds itself in a friendly arena, it can, for example, make some direct informal visits to the friends it has identified, and after having secured their support, together they can engineer some U-turns for producing messages that keep the wind blowing favourably. In a chilly arena it can best make use of, for example, scientific reports for reframing and mass media for up-framing the unpleasant issues. In an indeterminate arena, as is usually the case in an early phase of a dossier, it may be better to invest in building up a collective platform or getting prestigious scientists on its side in order to impress wavering stakeholders and officials. Good preparatory study gives information about the most efficient and effective ways to influence crucial stakeholders and officials, to tap or inspire their networks, to encircle them with polyphonic sound and/or to deliver support in ways they like. The fieldwork can then be engineered backwards from the targeted receiver(s) to the lobby group. This requires a lot of fine-tuning as otherwise the end result may become a costly mess.

The Fine-Tuning of 'Sound'

A challenging part of the big question of 'how to lobby?' regards the use of silence or noise in public, in short the *sound button*. As a variable on a continuum the button can go up or down. Many lobby groups produce a lot of public noise on the EU playing-field. When feeling weak, they want to attract attention and if strong, to show their greatness. When they see something they desire or fear, they easily voice their pleasure or anger. Arrogant or pompous actions are soon widely known, and formal visits and letters are usually registered and thus easily noticed by the numerous stakeholders and many hundreds of EU journalists making Brussels a transparent village. National ministries and business associations cannot easily avoid publicity as they are often called to their parliament or their members in order to account in public for their plans, actions and results. Some NGOs have to communicate with thousands of members and cannot keep the information flow confidential to a committee inside or by intranet. In short, many groups more readily produce noise than silence. Noise around a lobby group is, however, not necessarily the outcome of its incapacity to avoid it and can also be the product of others, such as befriended stakeholders unable to avoid it or opponents who provoke it, or even engineered by the lobby group itself. An example of the latter, standing in between the two extremes of the continuum, is the limited soundtrack to a select audience, for example to selected members of a EuroFed, EP committee or Commission units. Clearly engineered for the purpose of creating the broadest possible publicity are the hate site, press conference or advertisement. This 'outside lobbying' by way of an issue-specific publicity campaign stems particularly from grassroot NGOs and newly arriving US lobby groups, such as in the past Philip Morris, Monsanto and the AmCham.

The amount of *outside lobbying* in the EU is remarkably low in comparison to the US [Thomas, 2004; Mc Grath, 2005-A]. The explanation can hardly be a difference of pluralism, at least not among lobby groups from civil society. However, in the EU more than in the US, most existing groups are connected to several layers of government (local, regional, national and EU), so having their feet already inside the mixed public-private systems (chapter 1) and less reason to lobby outside. Two factors can explain the high volume of outside lobbying in the US. Firstly, it is particularly directed at the elected politicians in the legislature (like Congress) and administration ('spoils' recruitment), who have vulnerable grassroots and (also financial) lifelines in their constituency. They can rather easily be influenced by lobbying their voters directly. Secondly, the litigation procedure that takes place in public is a conventional direct way of lobbying in the US. These two factors are weak in the EU, where only the British have a constituency system, and litigation at the Court proceeds without mass media. In the past many US lobby groups arrived in Brussels poorly prepared for the very different EU arena. Being more silent now, they have apparently learnt their lesson.

In EU public affairs management, the window-out information lobby runs most smoothly by listening and watching, as information enters through the ears and eyes and never through the mouth. Therefore, the variable of public noise or sound is usually considered risky. As easy as it is to create noise, it is as difficult to keep its effects under control and to restore silence if needed. Noise is, technically, an almost one-directional variable of manipulation. Once the *ghost of noise* is out of the bottle, it is very difficult to stuff it back in. In the window-in support lobby, the main effect of public sound is the mobilisation of more stakeholders and thus the widening of arena boundaries. Absent stakeholders may be encouraged to enter the arena, thus bringing in their own interests and issues. They may even take the opportunity to build up nuisance value if only for the possibility of exchanging this for another value. The new stakeholders delay the decision-making process, as they need time to find their position and to become party to the deal. Silence, in contrast to noise, has the opposite effect. It keeps the arena boundaries narrow, and if a compromise can be found, it usually speeds up the decision-making process. No lobby group can, however, easily control the chain-effects from public sound, and therefore the prudent group tends to dislike it.

This one-directional character of the sound variable explains why professional lobby groups usually believe that silence is safer than sound. Their management of sound is, in fact, *silence management*. Particularly at the start of processes, they usually prefer the silent approaches of intimate meetings, networks or circuits held in conference rooms of offices, hotels and restaurants. As long as it proves useful, they want to remain silent about their underlying position, targets, interests and values. Making the latter public would not only damage their effectiveness, but also be useless because most other stakeholders, holding different interests and values, cannot ultimately be converted as, from their perspective, they are fully right as well. Constructing a common interest out of various interests is the best result one can attain, and this form of engineering is better achieved under silence than noise. If necessary, more silence can be created by applying special factors and vectors, such as making a dossier more complex or technical, by bringing it under comitology or by inserting one's own people into the apparatus. The more a dossier is seen as 'low politics', the easier it is to negotiate on it silently and conveniently.

This issue of the sound button also explains why, in the multinational model of EU public affairs management, a member of the Central Board is often responsible for the use of it, which is frequently at issue between the *units of PR and PA*. The PR office may have a vested interest in continuously making a lot of impressive sound, which yet remains sound, whereas the PA office may have strong reasons to be firmly against this and to prefer silence. The decision to turn the sound button up or down is then left to the Central Board member. This person has to solve the dilemma of whether sound or silence is in the interests of the organisation. The choice for sound may damage its interests at the EU political level but promote them on the home front, on the market or elsewhere, and silence may have opposite effects. Sometimes the risks of the one or the other choice are kept limited by some internal compromise, for example on the timing or on the contents of the sound, but even so the risk of undesired chain-effects lies in wait.

Avoiding the ghost of sound might seem to be a rational rule of thumb, but this is not true for various arena situations. One regards the arena being assessed as *unfriendly* at some stage of the dossier's life. If a lobby group wants to push a proposal but fears that this will not pass any of the six thresholds of the decision-making process (Figure 4.1), then it may feel it is doomed. It may have the same feeling about the reverse situation, when it fears that an undesired proposal cannot be blocked and will inexorably cross the next threshold. In such situations it can rationally cause some noise, preferably indirectly. If the frequently aggressive sound produced by some NGOs at the EU level is rational indeed, then it indicates that they have a lot of problems with crossing thresholds; if not, they take high risks and probably make mistakes in lobbying. By making noise, the lobby group that feels itself to be in a chilly arena automatically widens the arena boundaries, thus bringing in new stakeholders and issues that almost certainly delay the process (Figure 4.4). In this rational case there is, however, no guarantee of a stay of execution. The crowds may love to see a loser put to death, as with the *tricoteuses* when Marie Antoinette was executed on the Place de la Concorde in 1793. By making identifiable noise, such as crying jeremiads, the lobby group might even destroy its chance of getting some loss-compensation. If it feels close to imminent demise and wants to escape by noise, then it should, firstly, up-frame its message and, secondly, use only indirect media that fully hide the sender's identity.

Also when the arena is largely *friendly*, it may sometimes be better for the lobby group to apply some noise rather than full silence. The friendly issues have to be kept buoyant. Orchestrating supportive sound indirectly and with up-framed contents can do this excellently, for example by releasing new scientific evidence that the desired outcome will produce extremely positive effects for a high social value that benefits many. This may drive out counter-issues. In the meantime the promising dossier can be pushed by calling for an early deadline, as was done by the 1985 Round Table of Industrialists for the creation of the Open Market by 1990 (that became 1992). In the *indeterminate* arena, making a little bit of noise can also be rational by trying a balloon or calling for support, as the Commission does with its early statements and calls. Indifferent and wavering stakeholders here have to be put at ease and won over. If they are dispersed over many countries and sectors, the lobby group may have no alternative to public sound, in which case it may start a public campaign for reframing the crucial issues. In accordance with its interest in this wait-and-see position, it can lobby in public, particularly for more research and learning practices like OCM.

In the section on 'supplying or demanding' above, we referred already to some useful insights from political marketing for the niche markets of EU arenas. To this we can add at least four *general uses of sound*, which are not related to a specific arena and can be handled jointly by the units of PR and PA [Johnson, 2008].

- *Trustworthiness*. Every lobby group is heavily dependent for its licence to lobby, on this part of its general reputation, as ultimately given or withheld by mass media and the public. Similar to 'corporate imaging' in marketing practice, the lobby group can contribute to the public perception of its trustworthiness by disseminating evidence of its honest and sincere behaviour. It should not this type of broadcasting itself but leave it, indirectly and unidentifiably, to others it can mobilise.
- *Public thanksgivings*. EU officials and particularly MEPs and ministers are usually sensitive to lyric applause in the mass media. A lobby group should preferably apply this negotiating chip only after having achieved the desired outcome and only in general terms unrelated to its specific interests, like the Eurogroup for Animal Welfare did in 2001. This is like 'after sales' in marketing and incorrectly often forgotten in EU lobbying.
- *Early up-framing*. A lobby group might want to give a most early up-frame, to its constantly arising new challenges and subsequent interests in order to stop them being passed or blocked in the beginnings of EU agenda-building. When turning up the sound button for influencing public opinion, it should use language credibly linked to popular concerns, such as 'safety', 'sustainability', 'welfare' or 'security' in the recent past. This is no different from 'product positioning' in marketing.
- *Sound for silence*. In order to distract or divert the attention of competitors away from its real interests, the lobby group may rationally make noise about something else, for example on its plans for the distant future or foreign areas, just as in marketing it may help to launch publicly different vistas in order to hide what is in the current pipelines. There is always some room for theatrics. However, the lobby group must remain credible and thus be a professional player that is not unmasked as an amateurish comedian.

In the case of sound, it is often the *tone that makes the melody*. In the intimate meetings with stakeholders and officials, the prudent lobby group knows how to strike a melodious note. It wants to be seen as charming, to show a sense of humour and to avoid any direct arguing over who is right or wrong, as this would easily result in a zero-sum game [Warleigh and Fairbrass, 2002; McGrath, 2007]. When some argumentation is asked for, it says not what it wants to say, but what the other wants to hear or accepts. Its language is not intellectual speak but salesman's talk, adapted to a market where both sides want to become happier (variable-sum game). When it finds that this soft approach is not working well, it may decide to make its tone gradually more hostile. Due to the almost one-directional nature of tone, it knows that going from hostile to friendly requires an excuse first, which can only work sometimes and requires an honest performance. This is no different for public sound. The Lorelei-technique of up-framing one's selfish interest (Figure 6.2) is the salesman's pitch to lure followers. Between the making of sound in private circles and the public domain there is, however, one remarkable difference. The disarming *power of humour* is almost unused in EU public spaces. The messages sent to the mass media and mass publics are usually very serious, without irony or smiles. At most they are accompanied by some light entertainment, such as the Spice Girls at the 1998 EP. Using the weapon of humour may be easier in intimate than in public settings, but at the domestic level it is often applied in public settings, too. As humour is culture-bound, the most probable explanation for the near absence of humour at the EU level is that, so far, there is no European sense of humour, which is another indicator that Europe is not (yet) a community of common cultures.

The fine-tuning of the sound button is thus fully dependent on professional crafts and maybe arts. The lobby group that makes spontaneous noise is like the brainless bird that twitters a lot when seeing bread in the garden, thus attracting many competitive birds plus the cat. Given the one-directional nature of noise, the prudent lobby group prefers to apply silence management as the starting-point of its fieldwork, while it is free from a mindless phobia about the ghost of noise, because then it would neglect the many rational exceptions. From that starting-point on, it wants to identify the rational exceptions and not make unforced errors. This is a matter of preparatory homework and prudence. Without this, there can be no fine-tuning of sound or silence.

Lobbying Where?

'Brussels' is only the *pars pro toto* name for the EU machinery, as it is the physical location of most institutions and offices. The relevant place of lobby action can, however, be anywhere. Of course it can be in the EU buildings of Brussels, but also in the nearby restaurants or in the offices of lobby groups. It can also be the places where EU institutions and agencies meet or are located, such as the EP's sessions in Strasbourg (where MEPs usually have more time available), the Court in Luxembourg, the ECB in Frankfurt, the EFSA in Parma and EUROPOL in The Hague. The place to meet can also be a hotel along the road to Paris, the country holding the Council chair, the office of a WTO panel or anywhere else where stakeholders or officials get together [Greenwood, 2007, 13]. The old *lobia* or antechamber is now often a quiet seating area close to a conference room in an office, hotel or restaurant. Most stakeholders and officials work and live elsewhere. MEPs travel a lot and have a home in their own country. Council ministers meet only incidentally in Brussels, and their civil servants live mostly at home. The same goes for the experts of Commission committees, Council working groups and EuroFeds. In short, 'Brussels' stands for a hub system with Brussels at the centre of a wide network full of routes and places [De Groof, 2008]. Most people can be met at many different locations and often in their home country. Only the staff of the Commission, Parliament and Council (including Coreper) lives predominantly in Brussels or nearby. The Commission officials, in their role of lobbyists, hold the easiest position as most EU stakeholders come to them spontaneously or by invitation, for example through their experts, lobbyists or letters. All other lobby groups have to travel to a location. They cannot be everywhere at the same time and thus have to be selective once again.

The matter of *locating the meeting* may seem trivial, but without a meeting place it is hard to lobby, and without a satisfactory place it is difficult to be successful. Therefore, the professional lobby group takes this seriously and selects its areas of operation rationally. First of all, if based in Brussels, it considers carefully the location of its office there. It can learn from the Dutch PR, which has maintained an office for almost twenty years far away from the main EU buildings around Place Schuman, on the road home, a detour most others are unwilling to make, thus necessitating its staff to travel to other people's offices (unwise for negotiations), a restaurant (difficult due to lack of budget) or their rooms in the Council building Justus Lipsius (where all the others can guess what is going on). Secondly, the prudent lobby group wants to know where it might meet other stakeholders and officials. The preparatory work on the former question 'to whom?' can provide the information, as most of them have regular locations and routine behaviour. The lobby group only has to know their behavioural map, in fact their agenda. As many stakeholders prefer to keep low profiles, it must build up relationships of trust with them first, which require background information about their life. Professional groups collect this as part of the vertical axis of arena study (Figure 4.3) and keep it up to date in their EU directory. A few consultancies sell personalised information.

The choice of location can be optimised. For the physical *window-out* monitoring of stakeholders, Brussels is a fairly good place that attracts numerous lobby offices. Many lobby groups have their office or representation here. Many more travel to and from Brussels and can be watched or met here. Many other stakeholders identified as primary on a dossier are located elsewhere, however. Visiting them there can be a costly affair. Remote contacts such as by post or email are efficient but only effective after personal trust has been established. Multinational groups might be contacted at some country office and national ministries through their attachés at the embassy. Every group, wealthy or poor, can ask consultants or befriended people elsewhere to assist in monitoring stakeholders located in their vicinity. Such indirect use of local representatives is often both efficient in its cost savings and most effective, as these local people usually have a superior capacity to monitor, as they speak the local tongue, have contacts and do not look foreign. The identification of both primary and befriended stakeholders elsewhere is clearly a matter of good preparation.

For its *window-in* meetings with crucial stakeholders, the professional group should dovetail the behavioural maps (agendas and schedules) of both the other groups with its own. Brussels may seem an efficient location for negotiations, but it frequently has the disadvantages of, for example, being full of social control, not being neutral terrain and not being relaxed at all. Regardless, many crucial stakeholders live outside rather than inside the city, in which case even Lisbon or Budapest may be a better place for this meeting. At the most detailed level this optimising is all a matter of route planning and navigation (Figure 3.2), with stops included along the way. Similarly, the lobby group can arrange multilateral meetings with primary stakeholders on its side, which sooner or later have to take place to aggregate common interests to a strong and potentially winning (pushing or blocking) coalition. It is all a matter of dovetailing. With some stakeholders the lobby group may already have regular contacts, for example through a EuroFed or expert committee. Then it can use the day before or after the regular meeting for holding the extra one. If the regular one concerns an expert committee, the Commission shall reimburse most variable costs of the extra one. Some members of expert committees even lobby for more regular meetings in order to get more extra ones scheduled.

A topical question is whether a physical place can be replaced by a virtual one, in short by *tele-lobbying or cyber-lobbying*. The answer is varied. For the window-out information lobby, new tools such as websites, news alerts and search machines are certainly helpful. Since passing its 2006 e-Participation Initiative, the Commission holds even more public consultations online. As holds for any source or tool, the quality of information (reliability, validity and completeness) can never be taken for granted and has to be improved by traditional means. Chat-sites, discussion-sites, webinars, hate-sites and more variants that raise or discuss some value produce a rapid and cheap splitting of that value into different issues and frames. Sharing information with trusted others in, for example, the home organisation or an EuroFed, is facilitated by tools like email, intranet, web-conferencing and web 2.0, but their security (hacking) and privacy are new problems of quality here. For the window-in and thus confidential support lobby, new tools such as intranet and tele-conferencing are hardly useful, as they fall short of security, privacy and particularly the necessary ambiance of trust. If the lobbying for support is directed at a wider audience or even a mass public, for example in order to construct an issue or agenda or to escape an unfriendly arena, many new tools can be used for such cyber-activism [Illia, 2003], from weblogs and rogue-sites to buzzing (the old Tupperware-method of 'mouth to mouth') and RSS-feeds (packages of messages), except when the sender has to remain unknown. In spite of all the theoretical possibilities of cyber-lobbying, most Brussels PA practitioners are, according to surveys [ComRes, 2008; EurActiv, 2009-A/B/C], not big users of it, except for the information lobby online and the information sharing by email. Many, fearing uncontrollable effects, even distrust it and still prefer traditional tools of communication. In early 2008 the European Banking Federation (EBF) emailed to the EP its critical position on the proposal for Consumers Credit, which Word-document included two earlier draft versions, generating embarrassment. Our conclusion is that cyber-lobbying has provided only limited benefits so far. The acquisition of relevant information and support is, maybe paradoxically in the age of internet politics [Chadwick and Howard, 2008], still largely a matter of personal trust and contact and thus of meeting places. Nonchalance on this matter causes boomerang effects, the price of imprudence.

Lobbying When?

'Lobbying when?' is the last of our leading questions relating to the fieldwork. The rule of thumb in simple manuals urges the lobby group to be early in the process, because then it can prearrange the playing-field and take the lead. An early player, however, is also visible at an early stage, spends a lot of scarce energy and can be bypassed by the competitors joining the match later. As in cycling, usually only amateurs and helpers rush ahead of the pack at the start. For professionals the proper timing is always a difficult balance between being not too early and not too late. Precise timing is almost an art. It also requires from the lobby group a time culture, in particular an excellent memory (past time), a long-term perspective (future time) and a lot of patient tenacity (between times). Although the EU pace of decision-making has gone faster [Jordan and others, 1999] and is often faster than in most national capitals, it still takes on average about twenty months for a secondary proposal to be adopted by the EP and Council [DN: IP/01/323.2001], which does not include the time the Commission needs for drafting, estimated to be on average at least the same. For the domestic implementation of directives, the national governments take on average slightly more time than the EP and Council together. All these averages have, of course, a wide range of values around them. The leading question for lobbying is: *when precisely is the best moment?* The answer depends, of course, on the situation, which is dynamic due to the dossier life cycle (Figure 4.1). So far this cycle has been presented as a stylised model with six phases and thresholds, developing from social problem formation to inspection.

This stylised and analytical cycle falls short of reality, however, as it has the following subtleties that, if neglected, easily cause mistakes in determining timing.

- *Feeding forward and back.* The move from the one to another phase is frequently not at all clear-cut. One phase usually feeds both forward and backward into another phase. There is, for example, the EU saying that 'those who define the problem take half the decision'. Even the die of inspection is usually cast long before its phase starts.
- *An open cycle.* In reality the cycle can have no fixed sequence of phases and be open to a start anywhere. For example, an expert group can initiate a dossier and then search for a social problem to be attached. A new dossier can be the spin-off from another agenda, a package deal or a finding from an inspection. An EU official may adopt a social problem as discretionary for direct policy implementation.
- *No outcome.* An outcome may never occur in reality. At any time, the officials can decide to terminate a dossier. Many a dossier even fades away without such a decision and dies as, for example, a non-problem or non-output that is often caused by stakeholders opposing the dossier outright.
- *The attention curve.* Public attention is not always at its highest during the formal decision-making phase and lowest during the phases before and after. Most parts of Treaty texts, Council decisions and delegated decisions hardly attract high public attention during their formal phase, and neither before nor after. By contrast, public attention can be high for a green paper defining a problem, a white paper suggesting solutions or an

inspection report criticising a policy.
- *Mobile players*. Stakeholders are not locked in to positions in the early phases of problem formation and officials not in some phase thereafter, as some suggest [Schaeffer, 1996]. In every phase an official can move to the role of a stakeholder and so can a non-official. Often, EP inter-groups and EuroFeds create agendas, experts from civil society make decisions, companies act as inspectors of competition practices, and the Commission directs the delegated legislation almost from start to finish.
- *Micro cycle*. Even a single player such as an EP rapporteur can go through the full cycle, from redefining the social and political problem to getting a formal decision from the plenary, to scrutinising the outcomes.

The best moment for lobbying is clearly not easy to determine. True, it depends on the arena situation, but for almost every dossier this is a dynamic affair, with stakeholders and issues changing during its life cycle that is full of subtleties. The formal procedure may give some handhold or cue for scheduling one's lobbying, but almost only the co-decision procedure gives some standardised deadlines; in almost all other cases the deadlines, if any, are variable and subject to lobbying. For the rest there are only high or low probabilities based on experience and intelligence. The only rational rule of thumb on timing here regards the following two activities, to be started at the earliest moment and continued thereafter.
- *Preparatory homework*. This enables reasoned answers to the questions 'who acts why, for what, to whom, on what, how, where and with what result?', leaving open only the question of 'when'. The more alert and proactive the preparatory work, the more time there is for an anticipatory action that can change the factor of time from an independent into a dependent variable, and the passive concept of time into the active one of timing. For example, a prudent government going to chair the Council should start its homework preparations at least twenty months before, being the average time of the secondary process, plus preferably another twenty months for monitoring the Commission's draft phase, altogether taking up three to four years. Such anticipated timing is no different for a company, NGO, ministry or region that really wants to score success.
- *Anticipatory action*. The preparatory homework may reveal that some anticipatory action is necessary or helpful and hence should be considered for an early moment of whatever phase. For example, an NGO having to abandon an EU challenge only due to its internal weaknesses should swiftly address them. A Commission official observing that a playing-field is unfriendly should quickly start a Triple P game. A ministry ob-

serving that it lacks sufficient network support must start further networking soon. A company discovering that its interests are controversial should anticipate this by soon considering an up-frame and launching a campaign.

In contrast to these two early activities, the window-in activity of negotiations can usually best be done much later on. In many a case, the lobby group makes the best bargains not early on but much later. The timing for this *deadline lobbying* is found through its preparatory work. In an unfriendly arena and with a lot of nuisance value it can usually claim the best loss-compensation just before the last minute. Important but wavering stakeholders can be approached early an but create the greatest impact if brought on board at a late stage. In a friendly arena, the lobby group should act reserved, wait it out and not show impatience. In an indeterminate arena, the wait-and-see strategies require the lobby group to remain slow to enter into negotiations. Otherwise it will trade off some interests that it may have to re-trade later, when the arena turns friendly or unfriendly. If it learns from the homework that the best deal can be made at the last moment, for example in the meeting of the Council ministers, then it should not act earlier. The early preparation and some anticipatory action will suffice here. This was done by the national air carriers in the 1992 Air Transport Slot Case [Van den Polder, 1994] and the French agricultural lobby in the 1998 Transgenic Maize Case [Bradley, 1998], mentioned earlier.

While the preparatory work and the anticipatory actions can best be done at an early stage and the negotiations at a much later stage, the *other fieldwork* activities of EU public affairs management cannot be allocated any single best time. They should remain adapted to the current situation and thus be reactive. Resetting the strategy, updating the short-list, extending the network or playing Triple P can all have many good or bad moments for action but, dependent on the situation, some moments are better than others. For example, a EuroFed in a friendly arena wanting to speed up the process should not necessarily arrange an early appointment with, for example, the EP rapporteur. In order not to alarm the opponents early, its absence, late arrival or U-turn might speed up the process the most. This is clearly a matter of detailed homework and no different from the delaying and the wait-and-see strategies in the unfriendly and the indeterminate arenas, respectively. The good moment for action here depends on the details. For example, the lobby group that wants to reframe its issue can hardly do so in the Commission's draft phase if the Commissioner has a personal commitment to the policy line. It might consider the expert meeting stage, but may know from experience that experienced experts there tend to be cynical about reframing, as they are experts on this too. In this case the lobby group can better wait for the decision phases of the EP and Council, if they are involved, and for now do only the preparatory homework and take some anticipatory actions.

The dilemma of time and timing is not separate from the many *other dilemmas* of the fieldwork mentioned before, such as those regarding lobbying styles. In the early phases of the dossier life and at the early stages of its involvement, the lobby group can usually best behave in a supplying mindset, informally, indirectly and low-key. This helps it become accepted as an interesting stakeholder, to build-up relationships, to keep its hands free and to avoid early opposition. The early homework and the anticipatory actions should reflect those styles, too, as the lobby group will gather better information and greater opportunities at lower cost. During the negotiations at the later stages, it may have to become more demanding in order to get the desired outcome and to act formally if it wants to get a real decision, which is not necessary if it only wants to block or delay. The use of direct and noisy ways remains subject to the many considerations mentioned above. The timing of actions that do not have an easily identifiable best moment can best remain linked to the other dilemmas, as every specific situation requires a comprehensive approach. The amateur lobby group neglecting this runs the high risk of managing its EU public affairs in the wrong ways at the wrong moments.

Extra: The Ideal Profile of the EU Public Affairs Expert

Improving the chance of getting a desired outcome from the EU is clearly a matter of fine-tuned and well-timed fieldwork and so a matter of special knowledge or expertise. This raises the question about the *ideal profile* of the expert in EU public affairs, working for whatever lobby group or as a self-employed consultant. The work to be done can be distilled from Figures 1.2 and 3.3. The person must, ideally, be a threefold master: a Socrates in posing the fundamental questions for every case of lobbying, a Max Weber in developing rational answers by preparatory work, and a Niccoló Machiavelli in synthesising ambition, study and prudence. The expert performs all homework and fieldwork systematically and on time. Superficial work completed on time is as useless as perfect work done after the deadline.

The skills needed for the *preparatory homework* are the following ones, the first three being scientific skills and the last three applied ones.
– *Research-minded*. The public affairs expert is research-minded, with

strong descriptive and analytical capacities, and with a hungry appetite for valid and reliable observations or, as they may be called, facts.

- *Value relativism.* The expert possesses a strong sense of relativism for values when assessing the facts, because no fact is good or bad by itself but only in confrontation with some independently selected value. Every value or position may be sensible, even that of the opponent. A phlegmatic expert can even turn a threat into an opportunity and keep a nongonised attitude to challenges.
- *Critical.* All this is done with a critical or discriminating mind. The expert is conscious about, *inter alia*, the limits of his/her knowledge, the alternatives to every option, and the difference between shadow and substance.
- *Familiar with EU.* The expert is familiar with the developing EU system and the major actors, factors and vectors at play. He/she knows the relevant people, places and ways to enter the system. Thanks to this, the expert can compose menus for action on the playing-field.
- *Rooted in home front.* While keeping one eye on the EU, the PA expert stays firmly within his/her own organisation, which is the source of every interest. This implies at least an overall knowledge of what happens there: the internal dynamics, the main processes, and its position in society.
- *Pragmatic.* The expert has a sense of pragmatic efficiency, as constraints of time, resources, knowledge, support and much more always exist. Maximising the striving for perfection may bring an academic award, but will nullify one's position on the EU playing-field. The expert optimises the search for the best possible lobby.

For the *fieldwork* on a dossier, two skills are most essential. First of all, the PA expert must have the capacity to connect it in a two-pronged approach with the preparatory work. From the one side, the expert is able to take field experiences as an inspiring source of inductive creativity for a different approach to the homework. Even seemingly trivial information may indicate an important change of issues or stakeholders that requires additional arena analysis. On the other side, the expert is able to apply the homework by methodical deduction to the playing-field. For example, building a broader coalition, upgrading an issue, supplying support or delaying a process is all driven by preparatory homework. Such two-pronged connection between homework and fieldwork gives the best possible solution to all dilemmas of lobbying. The second specific skill falls in the area of classical diplomacy [De Callières, 1716]. The direct fieldwork in particular is highly personalised behaviour. In direct contacts with stakeholders, the expert looks like a diplomat, communicative, reasonable and pleasant according to the various standards of the others. The person masters the leading languages, including body language and the informal codes. During negotiations the expert is seen as reliable, generous and flexible, and has a lot of patience and tenacity for coping with long and difficult matches. A basic sense of humour and optimism is important, not only for the positive image but also for one's own mental survival. Due to the paradoxical necessity of remaining both non-agonised and yet looking human under all circumstances, the expert can play some theatre: smiling in stormy weather and grumbling when the sun comes out. As a diplomat, the person remains charming and respectful to the others who have different preferences, simply because the others are warriors with nuisance value, despite how irritating their preferences may be. The expert behaves like a sportsman who is eager to score but in a courteous way, because there is always another match coming. All these qualities the expert performs in an unspectacular and quiet way, with a seeming concern only for the common interest.

In addition to these specific skills, the PA expert possesses two *general attitudes*. Firstly, the person has a broad curiosity regarding any development related to the EU playing-field. This curiosity is not limited to the EU machinery with its countless variables such as procedures, personnel, issues and stakeholders. It extends to seemingly marginal developments such as the new political culture in Italy, the devolution of the French state or the rapid industrialisation of Turkey. With some time lag all these developments may affect the EU playing-field in the near future. Curiosity functions as the engine for updating one's understanding of the varieties and especially the irritating differences in Europe. It helps to get an anticipatory grip on the EU method of living together peacefully. Secondly, the expert has a strong commitment to his/her interest group and acts as a warrior on behalf of it. The PA expert wants to win, or at least not to lose. This dedication gives him/her a licence to operate as the representative lobbyist. It also feeds back to the interest group, in the form of a flow of useful information and creative thinking. The expert is capable of, for example, defining a challenge, recommending how to save a blessing or solve a problem and eventually turning a threat into an opportunity.

If advertised, this ideal profile of the expert on EU PA management will certainly attract a number of applicants. Many of them hold the self-confident belief that they are naturally gifted and have the right talents for the job. They say they have the professional management of EU public affairs at their fingertips. Almost certainly only a very few applicants will, however, come close to the profile. Even among the many PA practitioners working in Brussels, only a very small minority is widely considered to be professional and all-around players. The majority is often nonchalant on studious homework and prudent fieldwork and/or plays only limited roles such as desk researcher, representative or platform manager. Expertise is always a scarcity, as expertise is a match of talents and skills for one or more specific roles. The talents may be those for assessing facts and values, going through labyrinths constructed on trampolines, fine-tuning fieldwork and behaving like a diplomat. To some degree they can be developed and brought out through training. But there are always people who hardly benefit from whatever training, making clear the difference between talent and training. Training without much talent can make a person a good player, but not a Kasparov. Talent without skills shows high potential but is still far from playing at the top. Talent plus skills creates art.

The development of skills is easier than that of talents. So far, most people working in the field of EU PA management have not received any special training for it. They have developed their abilities largely through an *éducation non-permanente*. Only the happy few have received from their predecessor some teaching 'from father to son', including the inheritance of mistakes. Seniors rarely train juniors up to an advanced level. In most lobby groups the learning takes place just by doing, with much trial and error. Most persons in EU public affairs are self-made people. Coming from a different job, frequently in line management, they are dropped without any parachute into the work of EU PA management. Most lobbyists from government organisations (central and decentralised) have this type of curriculum vitae and tend to confuse their policy expertise with PA expertise. Those from MNCs and MNGOs often have received some minor training from a 'godfather' or a centre outside, the latter being offered by a few institutes and consultancies.

The public affairs official is, of course, not necessarily a person but can be a *small team* as well. This formula can be found among multinational organisations like Siemens or Greenpeace. This team is usually supported by other staff such as experts in European law, by line people for technical expertise, by colleagues from units in other countries and, if necessary, by specialised consultants. In a team, all the work of PA might be divided according to the talents and skills of the members, but even this is more theory than practice. Most small teams are formed by incidental chance rather than conscious design. By the latter method, one can organise a team like a small chamber orchestra with professionals in limited roles and the whole team acting both professionally and as all-rounders. Then, one might even gain advantage from the scarce academic research on the profile of 'best lobbyist'. The findings suggest that officials who are lobbied regard the full-timers, women and government officials as the most influential lobbyists [Nownes, 1999]. Full-timers are seen as more experienced and expert, women as more patient and able to compromise, and government people as more concerned about the general interest. These different virtues are provided more easily by a well-organised small team than by a single person.

There is, in short, much *room for improvement*. The easiest thing to organise and to improve is internal training. Any Board should allow its PA people to spend about ten percent of working time on maintaining and improving their PA expertise by study, reading and training. A senior should invest in a junior, even if the latter might overtake him/her or depart to join a competitor. Regular sessions with staff and line personnel involved in EU affairs can create a common concern for shortcomings at the home front and so a common agenda for improvements. The evaluation of any game played is, as said before, a great but highly underused source of learning and training. PA people invited from the outside, even if they lack great experience, may add value to internal training as they can stimulate learning by comparison. Recognised experts from outside can be asked to give peer review. Another way of learning is by going out and meeting PA colleagues from different lobby groups informally, as happens in the Netherlands (the King William Circles), France (AFCL), UK (ECPA), Austria (ALPAC) and Germany (DIPA), to mention a few examples. The British monthly PA News is a network of subscribers exchanging information. In many countries a few institutes and colleges offer short EU training sessions with a chapter on PA, as do some institutes and consultancies in Brussels. Most recommendations are, however, still a daydream of almost all practitioners.

There is *no university programme* in this field available in Europe. A few Master's programmes exist, such as at the Political Studies (Sciences Po) in Paris, the British University of Ulster and Brunel University and the Brussels settlements of Kent University and United Business Institutes UBS. In fact, in Europe the field of PA is still adolescent and falling short of mature professionalization as indicated by, for example, a competitive supply of university programmes, academic research, published findings and more [McGrath, 2005-B; Fleisher, 2007]. If a full curriculum were to be created, it should be interdisciplinary. The major courses recommended here are the following five: science and methodology for understanding value-relativism and research, political science for learning the flesh-and-blood of the EU system, EU law for knowing the EU skeleton, psychology for comprehending the human side of public affairs, and economics for grasping phenomena like interests, scarcity and efficiency. Minor courses should be given on European cultural variety, European history and geography, negotiations in complex situations, comparative country studies and special EU policy areas. Some European languages would have to be studied as options. Other electives are information retrieval techniques, communication and maybe, as useful for the understanding of political engineering, chemistry (how to control an effect), construction (how to construct a linkage and U-turn) and mechanical engineering (how to make it work). Finally, the students would have to complete, both individually and in groups, some exercises, case studies, case-related homework and essays and to participate for some time in a PA department of an EU-oriented lobby group. Such a university programme would, of course, not be a panacea. It would merely help to develop the talents people may have and to replace costly trials and errors at the start of a PA job through preliminary training.

From Potentials to Limits of EU Public Affairs Management

At the end of the third chapter, we explained our choice to start the presentation of EU PA management with the homework for both the external arena and the home front and of ending with the fieldwork. This design is justified from an *educational* point of view. The homework should be the basis of the fieldwork. To avoid an egocentric or introverted approach towards the EU playing-field, it is better to start with the external arena rather than with the home front. The alternative design, starting with the fieldwork, would only produce questions and no guiding answers. But, as emphasised before, the various activities of the preparatory work and the fieldwork, all distinguished analytically, are closely interwoven in practice. In daily life, all the questions and activities found in Figure 3.3 lie, simultaneously on the table of every lobby group, whether it is conscious of this or not.

The paradox is that the more one keeps the various questions and activities separated analytically, the more one can safely interweave them for the production of a desired EU outcome. The greatest skill is in *interconnecting* all questions and activities systematically, thereby acquiring new insights for both the fieldwork and the homework regarding both oneself and the arena. To do this perfectly is, of course, only a dream. Even in the easier game of chess, such a multi-variable decision game cannot be solved perfectly, but one can strive for it. The more experience with homework and fieldwork one gets, the easier one makes the connections between the two, and the more one grows in expertise. The reward will be a better choice of the next activity for the fieldwork and homework, which can bring the lobby group closer to the desired EU outcome. In every case of strong competition, it is the margin that makes the difference.

By this interconnection one gets both *homework-based fieldwork* and *fieldwork-based homework*, which is the perfect match. The preparatory work, then, is as much a source of inspiration for playing the game as playing the game is for preparatory work. Through this process, one also creates a real *R&D* of EU PA management, resulting in even more options, tools, menus and dilemmas and, in addition, more manageable factors and constructible vectors. The surplus of potential actions becomes even larger and is, theoretically, unlimited. For the professional this is not an embarrassing problem, but a pleasant opportunity that provides more ways through the EU labyrinth. What is unlimited in theory can, however, have many limits in practice. That is the theme of the next chapter. To jump to a paradoxical conclusion: the professional, already taking greater advantage from the surplus of potential actions than the amateur does, suffers less than the amateur does from the limits in practice.

CHAPTER 7

THE LIMITS OF EU PUBLIC AFFAIRS MANAGEMENT

From Tantalus to SCARE

Our preceding chapters on the management of EU public affairs are full of buoyant spirits. The attractive flowers and trees of the EU playing-field seem to be within the reach of every lobby group. Cultivating them is, however, not easy as this requires much homework and fieldwork, to be carried out carefully and energetically. Many lobby groups hold the optimistic belief that, after their digging, fructifying and pruning, sooner or later a lot of flowers and fruits can be brought home as trophies. Many see room for planting even better varieties. *Tantalus*, in Greek mythology the hero unable to pick the grapes in Hades, would have loved to go to Brussels. In PA management, however, the sky is not the limit, but the players, the playing-field, the issues, the game, the audiences and all other features of a situation are. Most of them are variables that can indeed be manipulated or managed to engineer a desired outcome, but only to some degree. The limit that is both most crucial and in reach, or manageable, is intelligence, being the summary variable of all preparatory homework regarding the three arenas of home front, stakeholders and officials and giving clues for the best possible support lobby to assure success. This summary variable is dependent on many factors that can pose limits to success and hence deserve closer attention here.

The various limits can be classified under different headings. One distinction is between limits that are endogenously linked to a lobby group and those that exogenously come from outside. Another one differentiates between structural limits caused by patterned behaviour and cultural ones set by the individual and the collective minds. More concrete is the typology that is based on communication categories or *SCARE*. The limits in this case come from the Sender or lobby group, the Channels that transmit messages, the Arena where all information is exchanged, the Receivers such as

EU officials and stakeholders, and the Environment conditioning the other four categories. In this approach, all limits of PA in the EU are viewed from the perspective of the lobby group sending a message. This message can have substantial form and contents but also be a non-message; for example, silence or absence meant to convey a position.

We shall now examine this SCARE typology and identify a few typical limits for each category. Their identification mirrors that of potential actions, shown in the preceding chapters, in two respects. Firstly, like potential actions, limits cannot be listed exhaustively. Theoretically, their numbers are infinite. We confine our description to some major ones existing in the daily life of PA management in the EU, as published by practitioners in interviews or by scholars in case studies mentioned earlier. Secondly, for the management of these limits, we shall discriminate again between amateurish and professional lobby groups. The catchword for the amateur is *nonchalance* and for the professional it is *prudence*. More than the amateur, the professional is scared of making unforced errors and thus of becoming one of his own strong opponents. As a prudent player, the professional remains conscious of the many possible limits, tries to escape or to remove them in advance, and respects the unmanageable ones.

The assessment of a limit is once again a matter of expertise on realising the formula $E = MI^2$ and basically not different from that of a *challenge*, discussed in chapter 5. Every lobby group must, firstly, establish whether or not a limit exists in a specific situation. The same channel, arena and receiver may set limits on one stakeholder, but give free passage to another, as limits are relative and not absolute. The group has, secondly, to determine whether a limit is a problem or a blessing. If an existing limit is helpful for the group's targets, it is a blessing that should be preserved by efforts to keep it. If it is harmful, then it is a problem that can be solved either by removing the limit and its consequences, or by reconsidering its harm. By analogy, the absence of a limit, if found to be a challenge, can be managed as either a blessing to be preserved or a problem to be solved. The professional group does this sort of homework not only for its own organisation, but also for primary officials and stakeholders. They all have their own variable collection of limits.

The Sender's Mental Limits

PA management is a highly human activity. The person or team in charge must continually search for the next best move. Brains, enriched by talents and skills, are crucial. Inevitably, all sorts of *human shortcomings* can play a disturbing role. For example, due to some personal drama even one's private life can become an obstacle and undermine one's PA performance. Someone's character may be so full of arrogance and vanity that it turns him into his own worst enemy on the playing-field. One may be mentally obsessed with one's own interest, an opponent, an issue or something else that is part of the playing process. These examples at the individual level can easily be transferred to the organisational level. Here we focus on mental limits caused by human shortcomings and discuss three cases: emotions, dogmas and myths.

Emotions

The list of potential emotions is infinite. A lobby group can become *imbalanced* by, for example, the threat or the opportunity attached to a challenge. While carrying out his cost-cutting operation Centurion in 1992, Philips CEO Jan Timmer emotionally blamed the Commission for its delaying of his great HDTV mission. He only succeeded in attracting more opposition. A lobby group can also exhibit voracity, as a result of which it cannot reduce the long-list to a manageable shared-list and shortest possible short-list. Another frequent emotion is that of political (in)efficacy, the belief that it is one's fate to be the winner or loser. Many emotions crop up during the game, for example resulting from the perceived unfair behaviour of another stakeholder. Many a lobby group often feels disturbed and acts agonised thereafter. In the Biotechnology Dossier, opponents of GMO introduced the norm of 'zero risk' and publicly blamed the proponents for putting mankind at maximum risk. Part of the food industry behaved, indeed, as if it were emotionally imprisoned by this black-and-white debate. A lobby group can also have the emotional belief that some important stakeholders, such as Commission officials or MEPs, are autistic, biased, unreliable or in some way vicious. For their part, many EU officials display emotions of distrust regarding what lobby groups really want. An emotional sender easily resorts to voicing annoyance, even if this hurts its interests, thus throwing the tomahawk instead of unaffectedly offering the peace pipe. A frequent emotion arises from uncertainties. The inevitable lack of useful information can be upsetting, especially when both the stakes and the time pressures are high.

Emotions are a strong variable in the double sense that they can both strongly affect lobby behaviour and exhibit strong variation. Regarding the latter, there even exist specific *nation-wide* emotions, such as the British allergy to EU federalism (the 'F-word'), the French aversion to takeovers by foreign companies, and the Polish distrust of EU food law that limits their exports. Emotions can be bound to the *type of organisation,* too. SMEs frequently hold the emotion of inefficacy, while many a multinational regularly expects that it will be one of the winners. Issue-driven NGOs usually have an emotion anchored in their central policy value, such as 'green environment' or 'safe and healthy labour'. National ministries may attach emotional value to a specific EU dossier, especially if this has priority at home, for example in their parliament or mass media. Such a priority is seldom based on sound preparatory work and can soon create the problem of having to save face. The same can happen to a national government chairing the Council and being urged by its parliament to bring better order to the EU. In 1991 the Dutch government launched an overambitious campaign for European Political Union (EPU). In a few weeks it experienced its 'Black Monday' and became so bewildered that in 1997 it publicly gave up any ambition for its new chairmanship.

Such emotions are part of human life or nature, like earthquakes. *Professional* groups, however, know that, to some degree, earthquakes can be foreseen and some most devastating effects can be controlled. This awareness is the precondition of prudence and a matter of good preparation. It is not that professional players have, necessarily, fewer emotions than amateurs have, but they filter the emotive stimuli better and react in a more reserved way than amateurs do. They are disciplined about heeding their homework and remaining concentrated on their targets. They take the emotions of other players as useful indicators, of their feelings of weakness (unless those are smart comedians), and any unfairness from them they return as free boomerang or leave until later. In the multinational model the professionals are able to remain cool by such measures as the critical ad-hoc team, the regular update of the short-list and the construction of scenarios. Even so, they remain susceptible to emotional behaviour, but less so than amateurs. This difference can be crucial for the desired outcome.

Dogmas
Dogmas are strong beliefs in being right, and they tend to be immune to critical debate. Policy experts frequently believe that their policy analysis is the best one, and during meetings with colleagues from other groups and countries, they can easily start dogmatic clashes. Party-politicians frequently claim their ideology to be the best and preach that salvation lies in following their message. Issue-driven NGOs tend to have great difficulty with any compromising on their core value. Many lobby groups are inclined to stick to a strategy once it is set and, seeing a problem, prefer to deal with the unpleasant facts rather than their fixed norms (Figure 5.1), thus losing half the

number of solutions. In monitoring a dossier arena (Figure 4.3), they may have strong beliefs about who are primary stakeholders and what are the issues at stake, thus neglecting empirical reality. A peculiar dogma is that of national coordination. Its source is usually the national parliament or even the constitution that demands the central government act as one body that voices one message, thus denying all domestic pluralism. At the EU level, a dogmatic group can easily irritate others. Dogmas deny the realities of pluralism and value relativism [Galston, 1999]. They heat up emotions and hinder negotiations.

There seems to be some *national variation* in dogmas. Lobby groups from the Protestant areas of Europe frequently have the reputation of selling their dogmas as expertise. The French are frequently dogmatic on central planning, the Dutch on accommodative compromising, the British on rule of law and the Romanians on flexible implementation. Some variation by *organisational type* seems to exist as well. Governments, usually lacking a PA unit and using their policy experts as their agents, frequently take dogmatic positions, particularly if their elected body instructs them to do so. The same pattern can be found in private organisations if policy experts set the tone. Many NGOs take their mission as dogma and easily launch a 'fanfare doctrinaire à Bruxelles', as portrayed by James Ensor. Many companies do so when their core product or service and ultimately their licence to operate are at stake.

Amateurish groups adopt dogmas more easily than *professionals* do, as the latter are more critical about their own strategic norms and values. Therefore, in the multinational model the PA experts must counterbalance the policy experts at home. Proactively, they include the dogmas of other stakeholders in their plan of action. Professionals are more inclined than amateurs to stay away from public platforms like press conferences and mass media that function as consuming markets for dogmas. They act publicly only in the specific situations mentioned in the previous chapter, for example in the voicing of an upgraded dogma that mobilizes more support. They know that the decision-making process consists of negotiations, which can best take place in inner rooms, far away from public platforms. Even a professional, however, is seldom free from dogmas and may hold a sacrosanct value. The amateur is only less free, and this difference is important for the outcome.

Myths

A myth is a cherished preconceived image of reality. It is taken as true, but in fact it is merely fiction formed by, for example, tradition, prescripts, folklore, propaganda or tabloids. Figure 7.1 exemplifies this through ten popular myths about the EU, all taken from the headlines of mass media and with their meaning put in italics below. Most have a large following, even when they partially contradict each other, such as the claims that the EU is both corporatist and dominated by governments. The ten myths are as follows. 'Brussels' is said to be a big bureaucracy, but in real terms of budget or number of civil servants, it is miniscule. The EU is seen as centralist, but a large part of its decision-making process takes place on work floors and lower levels and is in reality firmly in the hands of public and private interest groups. The skeleton of formal powers is mistaken for the flesh-and-blood of influence. Interest groups of organised management and labour, interwoven with EU officials, make the EU look like a corporatist system, but in reality they rarely amount to a closed policy cartel in any way. The EU is seen as elitist, but usually it is an open decision-making system or, as it is sometimes called, a polyarchy [Dahl, 1971] of many competitive groups, which is almost the opposite of an elitist system. National governments are seen as

TEN POPULAR EU MYTHS

1. 'BRUSSELS': A BIG BUREAUCRACY
   The number of EU civil servants is extraordinary high.
2. CENTRALIST UNION
   'Brussels' governs top-down.
3. FORMAL POWERS = REAL INFLUENCE
   Those who have the formal powers are the influential ones.
4. CORPORATIST UNION
   The employers, trade unions and officials together run the EU.
5. ELITIST UNION
   Those running the EU form a closed group.
6. DOMINANT GOVERNMENTS
   The national governments have the final say.
7. DEMOCRATIC DEFICIT
   The people and the Parliament are politically marginal.
8. AXIS PARIS-BERLIN
   France and Germany together run the EU.
9. 'NOT SO RELEVANT FOR US'
   The EU is much ado about nothing.
10. 'TOWARDS ONE HOTCHPOTCH UNION'
    All varieties are cooked down to one bland average.

Figure 7.1

dominant, as prescribed by the Treaty of Rome, but in reality they are each only one player among many and, acting as the Council, they approve only about 15 percent of total EU legislation per year. With regard to the EP, it is claimed that the EU has a democratic deficit, but in many respects and compared with many national systems, it has more of a democratic surplus. The allegedly strong 'Paris-Berlin axis' is in reality a red-hot junction between two rivalling capitals amidst 25 other ones at present. In particular, small-sized interest groups frequently attach little relevance to the EU, but in fact they only feel small in a large relevant system. A hotchpotch Union has often been predicted, but goes counter to growing regional and cultural differentiation. In fact, all ten popular myths are incorrect 'strong stories' indeed.

Every person or group holds some myths and is thus misled by preconceived images of reality, but some are more under the influence of myths than others. There seems to be some *national* variation. Most myths are widely followed in the United Kingdom. The democratic deficit myth is popular in Scandinavia. The myth of formal powers is cherished in more formalistic countries like France, Poland and Spain. The myth of little relevance is, except for subsidies, widely held in Greece, Romania and Italy, where legislation is often considered as a recommendation rather than binding. Some myths are typical for a *type of organisation*. National governments frequently hold the myth of their own importance, except when they are defeated on important dossiers. Ministries of Home Affairs and Justice, being latecomers at the EU level, tend to believe that their influence equals their formal powers. Newly arriving member states and NGOs often believe that 'Brussels' is a big bureaucracy, full of centralism and elitism. Among many SMEs the myth of little relevance is popular and used as an excuse for passivity.

Amateurish groups hold many myths. They follow the popular stereotypes, gossip and newspapers. For example, they go to Brussels even when they should really be somewhere else, or they put trust in the Council when the Commission makes the real decisions. *Professionals* may have their myths as well, but usually in lower quantity and with less certainty. When faced with challenges from the EU, they act by conscious reflection rather than myth-bound reflex. The discipline of preparatory work gives them the best possible protection against an enduring EU mythology. For example, their dossier-bound inventory of stakeholders is an open-minded exercise regarding whatever layer, axis or platform of the EU. In the multinational model, the professionals have such additional safeguards as the critical examination of the homework by the Board member, ad-hoc team or peer review. A general risk to all is the generalisation of a single experience, which gives a post-conceived image of reality with again mythical contents. The dynamics and complexities of reality keep nobody fully free from belief in myths. Some may be only slightly freer and less bound than others, and this difference can tip the balance towards winning or losing.

The Sender's Organisational Limits

Not only its mental situation, but also its state of internal organisation can set serious limits for a lobby group's EU PA management. Staff and line people may cross each other on the EU playing-field, where the public relations (PR) staff can thwart the PA unit on the use of sound, and the legal staff can do so on litigation. In a voluntary association such as a EuroFed, some members can weaken the common position. In a multinational group the various country units may choose their own way to lobby Brussels. Many a lobby group lades important resources, such as good reputation, strong leadership and sound strategy. NGOs constructed by government (GONGO) or business (BONGO) can be unmasked as fake ones and lose credibility, and those seen as not representative may suffer a similar fate [Warleigh, 2003]. In short, all organisational variables can limit the effectiveness and the efficiency of EU public affairs management. Here we shall focus on three typical cases: dissent, scarcity and lack of leadership.

Dissent

The lack of sufficient cohesion is one of the most common and most serious causes of poor performance in PA. Every lobby group has a certain amount of internal pluralism, indicated by different values, role expectations and duties. To some extent this is a blessing, as it promotes internal creativity and external adaptability. But this richness has its optimum form as internal dialectics can hurt external performance. If a lobby group sends different messages to the same audience within a short time, then it may soon lose credibility as a stakeholder, and if it does so as part of a comedian diversion, it may lose reliability. Every lobby group has some record of serious dissent observed by other stakeholders, who can exploit it to their advantage. In its lobbying on the 2001 Tobacco Ban Directive (EC 2001/ 37), the market leader Philip Morris profited from the weak cohesion of its main competitor British American Tobacco (BAT). If a group has grassroots layers, as applies to voluntary associations, the display of dissent on major issues is a normal part of its internal life and easily noticed externally. The same holds true for vertically segmented dissent, such as between divisions or country units of an MNC, the ministries or agencies of a national government and the DGs or agencies of the Commission. Settling an internal cleavage costs a lot of time, compromise and management. Then the lobby group might even best abstain from playing and leave its interest to the winds.

Dissent may be a regular feature of every lobby group, but it is highly variable in frequency, intensity, form, contents, methods of solution and other aspects. There seem to be some patterns to the variations. One is *national*. In Denmark and the Netherlands, many interest groups have grassroots layers taking up much internal debate and other costs. In France and Germany, internal dissent is often embedded in procedures and formalities, and solved by decree from the top to the rank and file being trained in paying lip service. In Italy internal dissent tends to follow lines of clientelistic factions, with patrons seeking accommodation. *Organisational* variation is another pattern. Government organisations show much dissent due to pressures from mass media and politicians. Their opponents can easily exploit their internal cleavages. Inside NGOs, the voluntary members frequently voice their different positions on an issue publicly. Confederations like ETUC and BusinessEurope are frequently paralysed by internal dissent, more so than rather homogeneous EuroFeds like CIAA (food industry), EMF (metalworkers) or Europabio (biotech firms). Multinational groups often show strong dissent between both their divisions and country units and SMEs have this frequently inside their domestic associations.

The most striking variation exists between the amateur and the *professional* lobby group. Through its preparatory work, the latter has an early-warning system for any internal dissent arising on an issue, thus enabling it to anticipate it by, for example, discussion, compromise or internal deal. If it fails to bridge the gap, it can rationally decide to remove the issue or full dossier from its agenda and to remain passive, thus avoiding any further waste of energy. By its preparatory homework it can also profit from the observed dissent inside any other stakeholder group. A relevant friend may thus be helped, a wavering group won or an enemy split. Such a result, of course, has a good chance of success but is not guaranteed. The amateur group, however, does not even get the chance as, due to its neglect of the homework, it lacks the early warning system and can only muddle through.

Scarcity
Important resources such as expertise, networks, positions and financial means are always scarcities, either by quantity or by quality. Even more so

are the skills of acquiring expertise, networking, positioning and financing. Knowledge about the EU generally or about the arena specifically has limited reliability and completeness. A lobby group may have the finest reputation, but this is always less than sacrosanct. Time is almost always scarce. At the operational level of EU public affairs, qualified people are an utmost scarcity, and it takes a long time to get talented people well trained. Once they are qualified, they may switch to another position or organisation, taking with them their qualifications. Often the successor has to start almost from scratch. Every asset, in short, is hard to obtain and can soon be lost. Scarcity is a fact of life, making the economy or efficiency of PA management a must.

There are hardly indications of *national* variation in scarcity, but the resource of networks and the skill of networking come close to having such a variety. Interest groups from northern countries are often more rigid and those from new member states undecided about networking than those from southern areas. Hence they have a lower quantity and quality of informal networks. In the case of the northern countries, this poor networking is probably caused by their culture (Protestant), and in that of the new member states, by their unfamiliarity with the EU. The rest of the scarcities do not seem to be distributed differently among the member countries. The variation in scarcity by *organisational* type looks more striking. The most notorious example of resource scarcity is the Commission with its extremely small staff and budget compared to other bureaucracies. Governments may frequently look capable and skilful, but usually fall short of PA resources and skills as they mainly rely on technical experts without PA back-office support. Many established NGOs have skilfully built up resources like nuisance value, popular image and, if they are not dogmatic, interesting supply sides. New NGOs often compensate for their lack of resources with great ambition, studiousness or creativity. MNCs regularly suffer from their reorganisations that hurt or halt their PA work in the EU, as shown in the crisis year 2008 [ComRes, 2009]. SMEs often have weak resources and skills, but have received from the Commission more preferential treatment since the mid-2000s.

There exists a clear difference between amateurs and *professionals*. The latter manage their scarcities more prudently and are more selective in, for example, adopting a dossier for their short-list, developing a network, mapping a promising route or negotiating over a target. Their selectivity comes from their homework. Through this economic behaviour they can save on their scarce resources and skills or exploit them more successfully. By identifying their allies at an early point, they can arrange cost-sharing of the monitoring, networking and other fieldwork for the EU lobby. Amateurs, in contrast, behave more wastefully and are exhausted sooner. This difference can be dramatic for the desired outcome.

Lack of Leadership

Management deficits can take many forms. No management is ever fully free from emotions, dogmas and myths. It can, for example, be emotional about a competitive stakeholder, dogmatic about its strategy once set and mythical about its position on the EU playing-field. It is also never free from dissent and scarcity on the inside. All this is normal, but the special duty of management is to control and to relieve all these mental and organisational limits. Here management meets its own limits: its decision on strategy is frequently not based on regular and open-minded assessment of preferred norms and observed facts, but on indolent compromise between, for example, the old and desired strategy, one or another emotion or two rival board members. Frequently, it starts its consensus management not by stimulating the rich internal dialectics, but instead by leaping to formally imposed consensus. Even if it starts in the right way, it may fail to transform the dialectics into better synthesis. Many managers have a poor span of control, thus leaving the various units to drift, including that in PA with as a result, for example, an uncontrolled short-list, wasteful fight with PR over sound, and imbalance between targets and means.

Management deficits have their variations and even *nation-specific* ones. In countries where some emotions, dogmas and myths persist, the managers usually have great difficulty in overcoming them. In rather hierarchical countries such as Germany, France and Greece, lobby groups often fail to create consensus dialectically. In the Netherlands, managers are, for the opposite reason, often indolently compromising on setting strategy. In Protestant countries, managers frequently neglect the utility of undignified wining and dining for networking. In most new member states, coming from a centralist past, there is no strong tradition of building broad consensus. More specific are some *organisational* variations. The management of government organisations often fails to develop a realistic next-best scenario and to keep its staff and line cohesive. Smaller-sized regional and local governments show much variation, but some, like the German region of Bavaria and the Spanish one of Catalonia, have a reputation of strong leadership over their PA in the EU. EuroFeds and other NGOs are frequently characterised by the weak position of their management. The chairman and board are usually selected, replaced and pressurised by the grassroots. In MNCs and MNGOs with vertical segmentation (divisions, country units), the management often has only limited control over PA operations. The management of SMEs has to meet, in addition to its internal limits, the external ones of European associations, necessary for remote control.

Amateurishly organised lobby groups have clearly more management deficits than *professional* ones. They are more affected by mental limits and by internal dissent and scarcities. Their managers are more doers than thinkers and more led by reflex than by reflection. They are, in short, highly dependent on good luck and thus often suffer bad luck. The management of professional groups, in contrast, oversees its EU public affairs more or less as sketched in the multinational model (chapter 5). It has its mental and organisational limits better under control, thanks to its early warning system obtained through homework and enabling it to anticipate limits. It usually has less numerous management deficits, but it still encounters limits to its ability to manage EU public affairs successfully. However, these are less the result of its own deficits and more of external circumstances, as discussed below.

The Limits of Channel Management

A channel is a transmission system for sending messages. There are many different types of channels. Figure 7.2 presents a selection of the analytical variety. Through the various possible combinations, the number of channels can be infinite. A channel can be one-way, either sending or receiving a message, or two-way (or more), for interactive communication. There may be just one channel or a multiple channel system, forming a network. A channel can be connected either to a receiver or to another channel, or it can have a dead end. If there are more channels, they can be connected parallel or in series. Channels may go directly or indirectly to some place, similar to the direct and indirect ways of lobbying a stakeholder (chapter 6). A channel can be open or closed. In the former case, it is free like a public road, and in the latter case it requires a fee to be paid, a ticket to be obtained or a password to be given, as for a toll road, a party or an intranet. The channel can also be general for any member of the public or specific only to a particular group. Some channels are natural like a river, while others are constructed or engineered like pipelines or canals. A channel can be either permanent or temporary, being there irrespective of its use or only for as long as it is used, like a moving vehicle. Some channels are old, established and tested, while others are newly developed and experimental.

Channel thinking is highly inspired by the three metaphors of water, sound and electricity. Through cybernetics and systems analysis it has made its imprint on political science [Deutsch, 1963; Easton, 1965]. In applied political science, with PA management in the EU as the selected chapter, the key question for every sender is *how to get a message, in the desired form and with the desired contents, delivered only to the desired place and at the right time?* Much can go wrong with this objective. During the channel process, the form can be affected and the contents changed. The message may be delivered to the wrong place and at the wrong time. These four problems of form, content, place and time can occur in combination, resulting in 24 different problem cases. The message can even be lost, disappear and not be delivered at all. If the transmission is good, it may have been delivered not exclusively but widespread, resulting in rumours going around and politicising the interest.

All these problems may not be due either to the sender or to the receiver but be channel-related. Many causes are possible. It may be that the chosen channel is not correctly connected to the desired place, has limited capacity that delays delivery, contains a filter that affects the contents of the message, or produces its own noise and echo that make the message widespread. All these and more channel properties are, of course, variables. To some degree they can be manipulated or managed by both the sending lobby group and

VARIETY OF CHANNELS FOR PUBLIC AFFAIRS MANAGEMENT

ONE WAY OR TWO/MORE WAYS

SINGLE OR MULTIPLE (NETWORK)

CONNECTED OR DEAD END

PARALLEL OR IN SERIES

DIRECT OR INDIRECT

OPEN OR CLOSED

GENERAL OR SPECIFIC

NATURAL OR ARTIFICIAL

PERMANENT OR REVOLVING

ESTABLISHED OR NEWLY DEVELOPED

Figure 7.2

every stakeholder. The former wants to get the message delivered as desired, while the latter may wish to distort, change, delay, misplace, obstruct or politicise the transmission. Both have many options, but any option has its limits as well. Next we shall discuss three typical cases of channel limits: power, quality and configuration.

Power

Some channels are more powerful than others, just as there are turbulent rivers and calm waters. National ministries and EuroFeds, if used as channels of information and influence, tend to be powerful with regard to, for example, the Commission officials. Ministries have some nuisance value at the Council level, for example by linking different dossiers in a complex way. EuroFeds are seen as authoritative as long as they aggregate the interests of sectoral groups from different countries, thus saving the Commission officials a lot of hard work. But the same national ministries may be a dried-up channel with regard to MEPs or stakeholders from different countries, while EuroFeds have little authority over each other. For communication with the members of an expert committee or a working group, scientific reports are usually more powerful vehicles than mass media, but for communication with the mass public, their status is almost the reverse. For making a political claim public, a press conference in central Brussels is a useful channel, but for the pursuit of inside negotiations it can reverse the current to adverse.

The power of a channel depends to some degree on the *relationship* between the sending and the receiving side. It is strongest if there is a balance of interests between the two sides, by which the message can indeed be delivered to the right place, at the right time and with the planned form and contents. The two sides have to be connected, of course. This can happen in many different ways, as shown in Figure 7.2. Some ways are certainly more powerful than others, but they are less so by necessity than by specific circumstances related particularly to the arena and the life of the dossier. If there are many opposing stakeholders, it may be better to use, for example, channels in parallel rather than in series, thus decreasing the chance of failing transmission. In case of such opposition, it may be even better, to combine parallel and indirect channels, thus concealing one's identity as the sender. Opponents may try to reverse the current, for example by the issuance of a counter-message through the same channel, thus causing severe confusion. Or they may try to change the EU playing-field, for example by playing Triple P and installing veto points [Cowles and others, 2001], making the sender's desired place and time out of reach.

The possibility to manipulate the power of a channel is limited because, to some other degree, the power belongs to the channel and not to its users. For example, a general channel like the mass media is extremely difficult to keep under control. Even a specific and closed channel like intranet is not easy to keep fully closed in practice. The limited management of *power limits* requires good preparatory work. This helps to identify which channels are the most powerful and how their power can remain under some control and perhaps be made immune to opposing actions. For obvious reasons, outlined in the previous chapters, even this homework has its limits. However, any difference in study and prudence can make a lot of difference to the desired outcome. The amateur group neglecting its homework uses the power of a channel like a novice sailor. Wanting to transmit its message to 'Brussels', it goes, for example, directly to the mass media or to the national government, with the risk of becoming overpowered. As a trained sailor, the professional group prudently tries to avoid that outcome. It fears falling at the mercy of the waves and usually prefers a channel with power and safety in balance. However, the professional has no guarantee, but only a better chance of not being sunk.

Quality
Some channels keep a message intact during transmission, while others do so much less. In the ideal case both the form and the contents remain unchanged, and the message is delivered only at the planned place and time. Frequently, however, the transmission has poor quality. Several variants of *disturbed transmission* can be distinguished. One is that the channel adds signals that affect the form and/or the contents of the message. Mass media produce a lot of channel noise. A message can be distorted or changed when going via central government, due to bureaucratic conflicts or, euphemistically called, national co-ordination. A second variant is that parts of the form and/or the contents are lost during transmission. A channel usually contains some filters, locks and lock-keepers. For example, in an EP session, the rules of order, the timetable and the clerks can be selective in recording messages. A third variant regards the delivery by place and time. The message may end up at a different address by going through a side-channel. Many a company or NGO trying to send some idea through its EuroFed to the Commission sees it falling off the table, not reaching the targeted official or being consumed by someone else. In a fourth variant the transmission is kept intact, but not exclusive. The channel may have a memory system, which can be tapped by others. A formal letter to or from the Commission may arrive perfectly at its destination, but due to its regis-

tration it might be noticed, identified and read by other stakeholders and journalists.

Channels have a large amount of *quality variation*. The informal face-to-face contact in, for example, a quiet restaurant is the channel with frequently the highest potential for quality. The time and place are fixed, the form is determined, and the contents are directly transmitted from mouth to ears. But the meeting can be leaked to or be noticed by others, such as the secretary, the chauffeur, an opponent or a journalist passing by chance. Even some traces of the meeting, such as the invoice or a scribble, can be found by others. All other channels contain even greater risks of distorted transmission. In contrast to the informal meeting, a press conference is like shouting out the message. Journalists attending the conference can interpret the message however they want. The off-the-record tip to a journalist is just stored in his/her memory and may be ferreted out by others. Every channel has its limits as it gives chances of faulty rather than intact transmission.

No lobby group on the EU playing-field can operate without channels, however. Everyone is dependent on others and has to communicate. To some degree an interest group can manage *the quality limits* and make them slightly wider or narrower. The sender can take measures to check the quality of transmission during the process and afterwards, but doing this in advance is more difficult. It is much easier for an opponent to disturb a transmission than for the sender to prevent this, as it is easier to spread rather than stop rumours. Amateur groups suffer more from the channel limits than professionals. The latter have a better knowledge of the usual quality of a channel than the former. For many situations they know that they should prudently choose a less risky channel, take some measures of quality control and maybe widen a few limits. When playing the role of opponent, they know how to narrow the limits of a channel used by the enemy that sends a message. They are aware that even such an act of channel management must be considered prudently, because it may boomerang back.

Configuration

Seldom does a channel connect only two or more places. Usually, it is part of a configuration of many transmission elements created by nature or mankind. The main ones are *capacities, flows, regulators, collectors and sites*, as in the following examples. The Commission's free capacity (what is left after current workload) to channel new political demands is very limited due to its small staff. The volume or contents of new messages easily overload it. Traffic jams at the Commission and/or overflows to other channels are the usual consequences. The EP is renowned for its multiple and parallel flows to and from institutions, countries and interest groups. Some flows it accelerates through an inter-group like that on animal welfare, others it delays, as happened to the GMO dossier in the late 1990s, and yet others it converts into a circular flow like that on workers' codetermination in the 1990s. The multiple and parallel flows can easily collide inside the EP, which my then adopt contradictory resolutions that, if noticed, shock MEPs and mass media. Every channel has regulators that propel, slow down or redirect flows. Some are inherent to the flow, such as the French Council initiative on the 'financial crisis' in autumn 2008 that at first propelled the flow forwards, then was slowed down by traffic-jammed counter-proposals and finally was redirected by multiple circular discussions. Others are constructed, such as the secretariat of a EuroFed and the white-books of the Commission. Channel collectors are, among many others, the *chef de dossier* of the Commission, the rapporteur of the EP and the PA official of a lobby group. Virtual collectors are the memory storage, the bureaucratic pipeline and the policy dossier. The sites of a channel refer to the areas around it, such as expert groups around the Commission. They connect with other channels, provide room for overflows and feedback loops and receive all sorts of more or less fertile residues.

All such elements, together forming the channel configuration, may be considered *limitations or facilities*. On the one hand, they put limits on perfect transmission, as much can go wrong due to the channel system. A local government, a Commission unit or a multinational NGO, wanting to send a message to an EU stakeholder, may end up in a traffic jam, circular flow, dried-up channel, pipeline or overflow. On the other hand, all these elements are three-fold facilities as well. Firstly, they enable one to monitor the channel process, because every element is a potential indicator that, after homework, can contribute to better fieldwork. Secondly, all limitations also exist for the opposing stakeholders. One has seldom any reason to fear that their messages will go through whatever channel smoothly and perfectly. By monitoring the configuration, one can observe their bad or good transmission and respond accordingly. Thirdly, as partially manipulable variables, the elements provide some room for configuration management and engineering. An example is the Triple P game, which looks to create a configuration by the early instalment of lock-keeping persons, positions and procedures.

The configuration elements place limits on every sender, but fewer on professional lobby groups than amateurish ones. Professionals have better *management skills*. By monitoring a configuration carefully and watching the streaming closely, they can take advantage by getting wider limits for themselves and narrower ones for their opponents, or the reverse. Even a small change, for example regarding a deadline or destination, can strongly improve the outcome they want. Professionals can never fully get rid of all channel-related limits and their consequences, as many of these fall outside their control.

The Limits of Arena Management

The four main components of every arena, discussed in chapter 4, are issues, stakeholders, dossier life and arena boundaries. Each of them can pose limits on every lobby group every time a new conflict arises. As contested facts, values or solutions, the issues are claimed by many stakeholders. The stakeholders want to become part of the winning coalition and not the losing one. The life of a dossier is always unpredictable, and consequently it falls largely outside the control of a single group but not necessarily of a collective platform. The boundaries of an arena are normally open, thus allowing entry and exit of issues and stakeholders. Each lobby group, being always only one among many, has every reason to feel overwhelmed more by the limits than by the opportunities of an EU arena. From the many arena limits, and continuing their discussion in chapters 1 and 2, we select the following three: pluralism, complexity and dynamics.

Pluralism
Europe is full of irritating differences regarding perceived facts, preferred values and cherished solutions. Many lobby groups believe, like common people, that both differences and irritations come from outside. Any irritating difference or issue is, however, embedded in public and private interest groups and fought among and usually inside them. It can be found among EU institutions, domestic governments, NGOs and companies. Their competitions come close to a *civil war*, no matter how civilised. Each lobby group can have only a marginal grip on its development and outcomes. It may try, of course, to push or to block the passage of an issue or a dossier. Many competing stakeholders will try as well, with the result that the dossier's life frequently ends up like a truck with many drivers behind the wheel, steering in different directions. It is also an open truck, easily permitting passengers to jump on or off. Its trailer-load of stakeholders and issues is seldom fixed. In this pluralistic setting many stakeholders are eager to develop their own networks, coalitions and cartels, in order to get a better grip on the arena and its outcomes. Even the most corporatist arena allows the insiders only

limited control, as there are always some challengers inside and even more outside.

The pluralistic character of the EU poses significant limits to every lobby group [Hoffman, 1963]. An arena is seldom inviting: only the stakes may attract, as the grapes did Tantalus. The lobby group nonchalantly entering an arena runs all the risks of becoming isolated or even victimised, so it must behave prudently. Any issue can be a threat or opportunity, every stakeholder can be a friend or enemy, every dossier can come to a good or bad end, and any boundary can become wider or narrower. The professional player, behaving prudently, tries to figure out all these possibilities beforehand. Indicators for drawing conclusions can be obtained from the preparatory homework. This may also reveal which other stakeholders are acting prudently and therefore have to be taken seriously. The professional group can discover finally that, *thanks to* the pluralistic nature of the EU, there are always some beneficial issues and some friendly stakeholders, both inside and outside the EU institutions. It only has to discover them by doing its homework, whereafter it can more or less manage them by fieldwork. In this way, it can even contribute to an increase or a decrease in the arena's pluralism, for example by launching a new issue or by compromising on an old one. But it can never dictate the desired outcome, and neither can any competing stakeholder. This is the essence of pluralism. The professional understands this better than the amateur, and through his prudence stands a better chance of a desired outcome.

Complexity
Every arena is like a labyrinth, and even a seemingly small issue is complex. The contested facts, values and solutions are related to different interest positions, each being right in their own way. Even such a black-and-white dossier as the Tobacco Ban Directive 2001 is as complex as an ancient Greek drama, with all parties fighting for noble but irreconcilable values: the one for liberty and pleasure and the other for safety and health. Most stakeholders have complex structures as well. For example, the Commission is full of both horizontal and vertical segmentation, not to mention its assistant bureaucracy of a few thousand expert committees. Almost always an interest group has a formal skeleton that is different from its real flesh-and-blood. This is also true for the relationships among interest groups. They range from rather formalised EuroFeds to informal ad-hoc networks, and frequently they cut across both institutional and territorial borders. This makes it difficult to identify their membership and has resulted in such a vague and modish concept as *governance* [Kohler-Koch, 2003; De Schutter

and others, 2001; COM Governance, 2001]. The dossier's life is no less complex. It can suffer a premature death and always has its mini-loops during institutional phases. There is no fixed relationship between an institutional phase and a decision phase, as every EU official and other stakeholder can take part in every phase. Comitology even looks like 'a dark glass' [Bradley, 1992]. Combining dossiers by package dealing is a very complex practice. Last but not least, the arena boundaries are seldom fixed, rigid and concrete and usually variable, open and abstract, in short, complex. They almost always cut across those of other arenas, thus facilitating even more combining of issues and dossiers.

The amateurish interest group can easily lose its way in the labyrinth-like arena and plead for reduced complexity. The professional player, however, understands both the limits and the opportunities caused by complexity. Assuming that every labyrinth has a structured pattern, however irregular this may be, it tries to discover it. *Thanks to* the complexity, it at least enjoys the extra room for playing created by those who lost their way. It discovers that there is always more than one front door, back door, hopper window, passage, connection, by-pass, exit or escape. The expert can even try to increase the complexity for others and especially for the opponents, for example by engineering a fake entry or another dead end. The professional group remains conscious about the limits of all advantages from complexity and prudent about their use. It may lose its way as well or fall into its own trap. Complexity sets its limits on all, but on some more than to others. This margin can be crucial.

Dynamics
To some extent an arena is dynamic like a trampoline. Newly chosen values, perceived facts or preferred solutions may cause issues to rapidly change. A main actor in this is the Commission. Repeatedly, it launches new decisional values, research reports and policy proposals, such as those on financial stability in 2009, or it reframes old ones, such as moves from production-oriented to sustainable agriculture. Lobby groups have changing agendas, too, in the best case due to the reconstructions of their long-list, shared-list and short-list. Their organisations change permanently under countless pressures from both outside and inside, ranging from reorganisation, growth and decline to reputation and turnover of personnel, which altogether change their capacities and performance. NGOs may beget a GONGO or a BINGO. All stakeholders can break off an engagement with others and enter a different one. The life of a dossier is full of dynamics. Many stakeholders try to push or to block its development, and all of them do this

in different directions. Through negotiations, they can bring a dossier to life or death and, by reframing, even to reincarnation. Many a dossier spills over into different policy areas. The arena boundaries are flexible, too. Old issues can fade away, and new ones arise, as happened with the Biotech dossier in the late 1990s, when its core issue changed from product improvement to human safety, also changing its composition of stakeholders.

In every arena the lobby group has reason to fear the trampoline, as it can easily fall down and/or off. Expertise is, of course, rewarding here, too. *Thanks to* the dynamics, the professional group, recognising some patterns of change, can survive longer and sometimes even make a leap forwards. It has a comparative advantage over the amateurs, who often ask for a more static arena. It might try to make the arena even more dynamic, for example by pressuring for earlier deadlines or provoking new issues and stakeholders to enter the arena. The professional group that creates scenarios is prepared for change and can thus anticipate events. Even in bad times it knows that a better moment will always arrive. By its managing of time, it hopes to promote the desired outcome. Notwithstanding all these potential rewards, even the most professional group is limited by the arena dynamics. It has to respect the natural forces of any boisterous and wild arena, but through prudence it will cope better with it than the amateurs.

The Limits on the Receivers' Side

Not only stakeholders, including EU officials, are receivers, but also outside groups and mass media. The outsiders, not being on the 'mailing list' of the sender, may have got the message by accident, echo or leaking channel. They may become stakeholders and can limit the effectiveness of a message. If a message has been sent, channelled and gone through the arena perfectly, it may have been poorly received by the targeted receiver, due to for example its internal affairs, confusion or indifference. Or it has been received well but interpreted wrongly, in which case it acquires a different urgency, procedure or meaning. Even if received and interpreted correctly, it can still fail on the receiver's side that overreacts, does not react at all or does the opposite of what is desired. All this can happen not only with a message that has form and content, but also with a non-message, such as non-verbal action or silence of a sender. To put all this in terms of communication theory: the message may have been incorrectly registered (*syntactic* filter), understood (*semantic* one) or taken into account (*pragmatic* one) [Cherry, 1966]. The threefold distinction runs parallel to that between the input, throughput and output side of any body. From the many receiver-related limits, we select three for elaboration here: inattention (syntactical), satiation (semantic) and neutralisation (pragmatic), which all set limits on the lobby group that sends a message.

Inattention

Just as a sender can have his mental and organisational limits, a receiver can have emotions, dogmas and myths that can lead to selective perception of a message, by which some signals are neglected and others over-registered. A receiver suffering from internal dissent, scarcity or lack of leadership can be equally inaccurate in his reception of a message. The *syntactical* case of inattention may have many causes. For example, an EP rapporteur with a bias in favour of a particular outcome is easily blind to the counter-message provided by an opponent sender. A national ministry, believing it is perfectly right on its policy position, will for a long time remain deaf to any warning report from the playing-field. A national parliament, believing the myth that it is always the Council that decides, shall neglect what happens before and after the Council phase. Small-sized lobby groups can be inattentive due to their limited resources and their belief in the myth that the EU is not so relevant. Many groups have the experience that both their strong opponents and close allies hardly take in their messages, as the former may not be at all receptive, and the latter may feel glutted. Much inattention is caused by poor internal organisation, leading to an introverted focus on internal dissent or pending reorganisation. The PA function may be scattered over various units and people, not be linked to the Board or simply be unmanned due to vacancies or staff holidays.

Every receiver can have such a syntactical filter of inattention on its *input side*. Amateurishly organised receivers tend to be more inattentive than professional ones. Their antennae are poorly attuned to the stakeholders that are potentially relevant to them. Often they lack qualified people for monitoring, or they are hardly aware of their mental and organisational limits, which make them deaf or blind to a message. By poor intake they limit the effectiveness of the sending lobby group and probably that of their own response. The way the Commission usually organises its input side, namely by launching public calls for interests and keeping open its doors for many experts, makes it a most professional receiver of messages at its input side. In contrast, some parts of DG SANCO and DG ENVI lose professionalism when allowing in only 'entitled groups'. Amateurs irritated by an inattentive receiver may be inclined to either send a stronger message or renounce the receiver altogether. Through preparatory work, the professional senders, in contrast, try to anticipate the attention limits of targeted receivers or to take advantage of this. They might even send fake messages indirectly, in order to test a receiver's attention. When noting the receiver's inattention, they try to repeat the message prudently, for example indirectly and quietly. But even the best professional cannot prevent or remove all causes and cases of inattention among all targeted receivers. Nobody can be seen or heard by those who remain blind and deaf.

Satiation
One variant of the *semantic* filtering of an incoming message is that the receiver may soon have had enough of it. Most information has a rapidly decreasing marginal utility or, to put it differently, an explosive marginal irritation value. This curve-shaped indifference exists in politics as well as economics. Receiving a message twice, in the same form and with the same contents, is in the best case taken as an indicator of disorganisation on the part of the sender and in the worst case as an insult to the receiver. MEPs frequently complain about repetitious lobbyists, as the latter often do about the former. Most receivers feel bored with senders who believe that only they are perfectly right on an issue and who send their argumentation again and again. The reiteration of identifiably the same findings of research is often counterproductive by its provocation of counter-research. The nicest Lorelei labels used for up-framing a core issue (Figure 6.2) tend to become obsolete after a few years. All over-lobbying easily activates the filter of satiation at the receiver's end. In such cases, the receiver may soon lose any interest in both the message and the sender and even become irritated. Satiation, in short, always lies in wait.

The semantic filter of satiation can always become active during the *throughput* of a message. Amateurishly organised receivers are most vulnerable to this. They either believe they have received a message already or do not read it closely but only cursorily, so missing details. Feeling satiated, they can easily feel fed up and irritated, which weakens their attention capacity even more. Professional receivers, however, take even the reiteration of a message as information and like to know whether it is caused by, for example, nervousness or disorder of the sender or something else, like a channel's echo. Then they can benefit from their findings and, for example, soothe the sender or exploit his disorder. In reaction to the satiation of targeted receivers, the senders can be very greathy. Amateurish senders may react in more irritating ways, such as by repeating the message louder or blaming the receiver. Professionals, in contrast, prefer to send an important message through a 'polyphonic orchestra' of befriended stakeholders or newly created platforms, such as a BONGO, federation or ad-hoc coalition (chapter 6). In their R&D on PA, they search for new vehicles. The reiteration, then, comes to the receiver as being fresh. Professional senders gain free advantage from the irritation of the receivers caused by amateurish opponents. They have no reason to whine or whimper. To exacerbate the receiver's satiation with those messages from amateurs, they might even joke with their opponents as parrots. However, even they cannot fully manage the risk of falling victim to the satiation of a targeted receiver. All receivers have their moments of satiation and indigestion.

Neutralisation

No sender is the sole one with a message sent to a targeted receiver. On every dossier, the latter receives different messages from mutually opposing senders. The receiver has, in theory, many *pragmatic* options for response, ranging from doing nothing to meeting the request or doing the opposite of what is suggested. In reality, the receiver has less freedom of choice, due to for example its own interests, current commitments or power positions. But this freedom can be restored by the *paradox of cross-pressures*: the higher the number of contradictory messages, the lower the impact each one tends to have and the more freedom of choice. The many different lobby efforts to influence a single stakeholder should, in mathematical terms, not be added together or multiplied, but divided by each other as they create room to manoeuvre. The limit of neutralisation, which is found everywhere, is a corollary of the paradox of cross-pressures. The Commission's *chefs de dossier* and the EP's rapporteurs, being approached by many different stakeholders, usually enjoy this paradox. Stakeholders also receive messages from numerous others inviting them to take their side. If one offers support to a targeted receiver, another stakeholder may overbid. If one presents some evidence, another may show it to be false and refute it. Research is always vulnerable to neutralisation, as delivery of counter-evidence may take only three months. If a message gets public attention, then it may become neutralised in mass debate. The lobby to limit the import of cheap textiles from third-world countries by the up-frame of 'child labour' soon became neutralised by mass media reporting that those children had an even worse fate, as they went to work in crime or prostitution instead of factories, let alone schools.

To some degree, every receiver has such a pragmatic filter of neutralisation at the *output side*. Professional receivers will feel happy with it, as cross-pressures give room for choice. Under the flag of 'democratic consultation', many EU officials are eager to stimulate more stakeholders to send their views, as this not only saves them much monitoring work but also gives them, thanks to incompatible replies, more freedom of choice. Amateurish receivers, however, tend to feel unhappy with cross-messages, as they find it difficult to exploit choice and room. Neutralisation may bring freedom or embarrassment to the receiver but also to the sender. Amateurish senders, dreaming of being the only one, usually regret the neutralisation limit, except when their opponent is incidentally neutralised. Their message being refuted within three months makes them upset and maybe aggressive, causing new mistakes to be made. Professional senders, however, consider the neutralisation limit as normal for any pluralistic system. As part of their arena study, they explore the probable cross-pressures in advance. Their homework helps them to immunise their own messages against cross-messages and to produce their own cross-messages against opponents in good time. To achieve better bargaining positions, they may simulate or stimulate new messages that cross the counter ones. On the GMO dossier, the counter-messages from lobby groups like Europabio finally gave the Commission the legitimate option of not closely following Greenpeace's line. But no sending lobby group can always or fully control the neutralisation limit, as this belongs to the receiver.

The Limiting Environment

Seldom is a PA communication system a closed one that only contains senders, channels, arenas and targeted receivers. Usually, it has *openings and gaps* both to and from the outside. A sender may fail to keep his message in a closed circuit, for example when it, feeling weak, looks for outside support or when a journalist smells smoke. Channels can produce all sorts of echoes and noise that attract attention from outsiders. Stakeholders and issues can catch the eye of the outside when crossing arena boundaries. Receivers can be accountable to an open forum, as happens to Commissioners in the EP and to Council members in their home parliament. There is also the case of reverse openness, from the outside to the inside. Outside interest groups, hearing about a dossier, may want to interfere in order to influence or to cash in on nuisance value. Lobby groups that are not well established, such as some SME alliances, citizens' groups and those from new member-states, frequently do so at a late stage. Journalists from the mass media or professional press love to enter an arena and nose around, to please their public. Domestic politicians, being sensitive to such reports, often urge their government to interfere. Such outsiders bring in their own norms, values and interests that can come to life inside the arena. They may, for example, push or block new agendas, decision practices or policy lines. In fact, they indicate the widening of europeanization. We now present the following three examples of the limits-setting environment: reputation, prescripts and outside groups.

Reputation

The reputation of a person or a group is never stable property, but a *temporary assessment* by others according to their current norms and morals. Especially mass media and the public play major roles in making or breaking a reputation, and different from stakeholders and officials (chapter 5), they take this reputation as trustworthiness alone and not, sympathising with David rather than Goliath, also as indicative of importance. Many lobby groups have learnt to care about their reputation, as this can give or withhold a licence to operate in the EU, as stakeholders and officials are shy to contact a scandalised player such as the controversial tobacco producer Philip Morris. Every interest group can more easily break than make its reputation, as the latter is largely dependent on the values and views held by outsiders. A helpful aspect is the aura of 'general interest' that common people attribute most to government organisations, secondly to NGOs and least to companies [Eurobarometer, 2000, 98]. This aura may, in objective terms, be incorrect as retailers might contribute more than NGOs and governments do to a general interest like a wide supply of healthy food, but the subjective view matters here. Therefore many companies set up a BONGO and many NGOs a GINGO, too improve their image. A good reputation is helpful but never sufficient for getting a license to operate, however. A lobby group that does not respect, for example, procedures, deadlines or demand sides is easily vilified and neglected, as happened to Unilever in 2007 when it had missed deadlines of the regulation on health claims (COM 2003/165). The fastest way to get a bad reputation is to lobby in ways that might be viewed as sneaky or tricky. Since 2005, NGOs like Spinwatch and Friends of the Earth have organised online their 'Annual Worst EU Lobbying Award', won in 2007 by German car producers. To neutralise this, a few established PA groups inaugurated their 'EPAD Awards in PA Excellence' in 2008. NGOs can be scandalised, too, as happened to Corporate Europe Observatory CEO for its 'one-man-band show' without citizens. Reputations are now the targets of PA and lobbying and thus contested.

Amateurish lobby groups tend to be nonchalant about reputation limits. When they have a good reputation, they see it as fixed asset, and when they have a bad one, they hope that nobody cares. When wanting to pick a pretty flower along a ridge, they take high risks with their reputation as they may topple into the gorge of fallen names. This fate befell Greenpeace after it had provided false information on the Brent Spar oil platform in the mid-1990s, and to Alter-EU after its biased study in 2008 that blamed the Commission for being 'biased for businesses' in its expert committees. *Professional* groups know that competitors, stakeholders and journalists can watch them. They are prudent and allow any flower on the ridge to stay. They respect the various values and morals, maybe not with conviction but at least out of fear of being caught and scandalised if they would offend them. Their *Praxismoral*, as it is called in Germany, is based on preparatory work and up-framed as Corporate Social Responsibility [Baines and Harris, 2006]. They know that lobbying styles allowed in one country, sector or arena can cause scandal in another. They manage their reputation, for example by up-framing their contested interests, outsourcing risky behaviour to others or creating an image of openness. If they suffer the fate of scandal, they soon play an act of integrity presented in a creative form that attracts friendly attention, as Shell did after Brent Spar in its 1999 Listening and Responding campaign, aimed at better dialogue with stakeholders. Prudent groups try to build up a higher standard or premier league of players, by organizing circles of selected members. However, even with the most prudent anticipation and management, no lobby group can fully control its reputation, as this is ultimately set by others.

Codes of Conduct

In 1991, the Dutch socialist MEP Alman Metten privately published *The Ghost of Brussels*, in which he reported that during three months he had received almost 150 letters from lobby groups, 90 percent from trade and industry alone. He concluded that lobbying is neither transparent nor balanced and proposed both a register of lobbyists and a code of conduct. His action resulted in much mass-media attention, the first EP hearing on lobbying in 1992 [Doc En/CM/118767] and the first EP rules on a register and code of conduct for lobbyists in 1997. The Commission followed the EP by issuing codes of conduct for their personnel and registration forms for outsiders. In 2005 Siim Kallas, the Estonian Commissioner on Administration and Anti-Fraud, launched his *European Transparency Initiative* ETI, aimed at tighter registration and conduct rules for lobbyists, and he invited the EP and Council to join. In 2008 the College adopted this ETI, the EP made an even tighter version (rapporteur: Alexander Stubb from Finland), and the Council abstained. Common elements of the two texts are the exclusion of lobbying by government officials (local, regional and national) and the inclusion of financial disclosure. The main differences are twofold (Figure 7.3). Firstly, the Commission's register is voluntary and limited to

CODES OF CONDUCT (fragments)

EUROPEAN COMMISSION (from COM 2008/323)

'Interest representation' activities for which registration is expected are defined as 'activities carried out with the objective of influencing the policy formulation and decision-making processes of the European institutions'. Excluded from this definition are activities of legal procedure (fair trial)... under the social dialogue (unions and employers)... and responding to Commission's requests...

Only entities engaged in interest representation activities (...) and not individual persons are expected to register (...), with the exception of local, regional, national and international public authorities.

Interest representatives shall always:

1. identify themselves by name and by the entity(ies) they work for or represent;
2. not misrepresent themselves as to the effect of registration to mislead third parties and/or EU staff;
3. declare the interests, and where applicable the clients or the members, which they represent;
4. ensure that, to the best of their knowledge, information which they provide is unbiased, complete, up-to-date and not misleading;
5. not obtain or try to obtain information, or any decision, dishonestly;
6. not induce EU staff to contravene rules and standards of behaviour applicable to them; and
7. if employing former EU staff, respect their obligation to abide by the rules and confidentiality requirements which apply to them.

EUROPEAN PARLIAMENT (from A6-0105/2008)

Agrees with the Commission's definition (cf above) and 'emphasizes that all players, including both public and private interest representatives, outside the EU institutions falling within that definition and regularly influencing the institutions, should be considered lobbyists and treated in the same way: professional lobbyists, companies' in-house lobbyists, NGOs, think-tanks, trade associations, trade unions and employers' organisations, profit-making and not-profit-making organisations and lawyers'. Excluded are 'regions and municipalities of the Member States, as well as political parties at national and European level and those bodies which have legal status under the Treaties'.

Code of conduct (Rules of Procedure, 16th ed. 2008, Annex IX, art. 3):

1. In the context of their relations with Parliament, the persons whose names appear in the register provided for in Rule 9(4) shall;
   a. comply with the provisions of Rule 9 and this Annex;
   b. state the interest or interests they represent in contacts with Members of Parliament, their staff or officials of Parliament;
   c. refrain from any action designed to obtain information dishonestly;
   d. not claim any formal relationship with Parliament in any dealings with third parties;
   e. not circulate for a profit to third parties copies of documents obtained from Parliament;
   f. comply strictly with the provisions of Annex I, Article 2, second paragraph (i.e. financial interests);
   g. satisfy themselves that any assistance provided in accordance with the provisions of Annex I, Article 2 is declared in the appropriate register;
   h. comply, when recruiting former officials of the institutions, with the provisions of the Staff Regulations;
   i. observe any rules laid down by Parliament on the rights and responsibilities of former Members;
   j. in order to avoid possible conflicts of interest, obtain the prior consent of the Member or Members concerned as regards any contractual relationship with or employment of a Member's assistant, and subsequently satisfy themselves that this is declared in the register provided for in Rule 9(2).
2. Any breach of this Code of Conduct may lead to the withdrawal of the pass issued to the persons concerned and, if appropriate, their firms.

Figure 7.3

entities ('not persons'), while the EP's is required for anybody wanting to get a pass. Secondly, the EP text explicitly states that also lobbyists from NGOs, trade unions and the like must fall under its code, and, moreover, it calls for one inter-institutional register ('one-stop shop'). In the summer of 2009, the Commission and EP reached an agreement to set up a common register and code that would also fully include think-tanks. The Council, the oyster of Brussels, remains at a distance.

The current texts can be seen as semi-formal prescripts in response to both social demands and their own desires to get rid of irritating ways of lobbying [Burson Marsteller, 2001 and 2003], but certainly not of lobbying as such, which they praise explicitly as a positive contribution to EU decision-making. The texts are not much different from regulations on lobbying and lobbyists that exist elsewhere [Bertók, 2008; Spencer and McGrath, 2008, 13-72; McGrath, 2008]. In addition, most EU institutions have their internal regulations regarding (former) officials [Demmke and others, 2007]. The new codes and forms make both the sending and the receiving sides of lobbying more transparent, thus stimulating social control, the 'mother of all control'. In mid-2009, the Commission's register held about 1700 entities, with two refused (one being CEFIC, the big umbrella of chemical industry) for lack of financial disclosure. Most registered entities here are consultancies, followed by companies and EuroFeds and last by NGOs and think-tanks. The EP's register also lists about 1700 entities and 4300 persons, most with a permanent pass. Many groups of lobbyists, such as EPACA and SEAP, make their own code of conduct as a tool to create a better image.

Amateurish lobby groups may believe that everything not forbidden or prescribed is permitted or left open and may conclude that the prescripts are mildly and loosely formulated, thus leaving much lobby freedom. Acting nonchalantly, they may easily become scandalised and even lose their license to be in arenas. *Professional* groups interpret the prescripts strictly, monitor their application closely and respect them prudently. Considering them as both a blessing in disguise and a comparative advantage, they support them, and some even ask for more [ComRes, 2008]. By observing the prescripts correctly, they gain respected and seemingly legal status and can keep amateurish groups at a distance. Of course, they try to influence the prescripts, which are always open to reformulation. Regularly, they renew their own informal codes and offer these to the institutions. This sort of lobbying is no different from influencing whatever new regulation and is closely watched by critical NGOs on transparency. The prescripts have become a new category of limits. They exist for all lobby groups, but the professionals apply them internally better than the amateurs. This margin of prudence can also make a crucial difference for the desired outcome.

Outside Groups

There are always newly arising interest groups that sooner or later enter the playing-field. In the early 1980s only a very few MNCs, regional and city governments, and NGOs had their facilities in Brussels. At best, they had indirect representation through domestic umbrellas that had their Eu-roFeds. Interest groups from outside the EU area were almost completely absent, without direct or indirect representation, and many mass media had only a part-time reporter in Brussels, to cover Belgium, NATO and the EU altogether. A few decades later, numerous interest groups from governments and civil society have both a network of indirect linkages and a direct presence, either part-time or permanently. Hundreds of non-EU interest groups now have their facilities in Brussels, and many mass media have set up permanent desks for the EU alone. New outside groups can be expected in the future. Additional interest groups from SMEs, local governments, domestic agencies and social groupings like the elderly and even immigrants entered in the mid-2000s, usually through a EuroFed. Any EU enlargement brings in new interest groups dealing with different issues of, for example, religion, literacy, trade, income and tradition. Sooner or later their values and interests will come to play a stronger role inside the system and change current balances. Newcomers may pose new lobby limits for the insiders. At very least, they want to be taken into account.

Amateurish groups inside the system, seeing EU decision-making as a zero-sum game and thus fearing to lose what another group receives, consider newcomers to be intruders. Before the fifth enlargement in 2004, many Spanish interest groups were worried about losing their EU subsidies to applicant states, and many member states feared having to give in on voting points, EP seats and other privileges. *Professional* groups inside the EU are more prudent. Considering decision games to be variable-sum, they take their old subsidies and privileges as bargaining chips for other desired outcomes. New interest groups, such as immigrant shopkeepers, retired people or applicant states are assessed as potentially useful stakeholders and included in their preparatory work and anticipatory lobbying. In the late 1990s, Dutch lobby groups on road transport, including the ministry, politically supported the Hungarian trucking sector, then their main competitor outside the EU, so anticipating its EU membership. Professionals also try to benefit from new issues promoted by new groups, for example by using the issues of growth and welfare in Central Europe as leverage for blocking, pushing or changing current EU policy lines. If in an unfriendly EU arena, they like to embrace newcomers that can manipulate the arena elegantly in their favour. Being more proactive than the amateurs, they can harvest opportunities brought in by outside groups and perhaps turn imported problems into virtues.

Extra: The Limited National Government

To every interest group one can apply the typology of SCARE and thus to the national government too. Defined narrowly, this is a country's central government as composed of cabinet, parliament and ministries, in short the national capital. The broad definition also includes forms of decentralised government such as municipal and regional governments (territorial) and more-or-less independent agencies (functional). By written or unwritten constitution, the exercise of power is divided among several institutions, which makes national government in Europe almost synonymous with *limited government* [Friedrich, 1974]. Here we shall follow the narrow definition and focus on limits of the national capital in its relationships with the EU. For each capital the assessment varies, of course, with time, place and other circumstances, as it does for every interest group. Some general observations can be made, however. When sending messages to the EU, many a capital and particularly its parliament hold the dogma of national co-ordination and the myth of Council decision-making. Its external effectiveness is usually limited by conglomerate structure, multi-layered operations and much pluralism internally. In communicating with the EU, it often uses open and noisy channels that start in parliament and mass media at home and are out of control thereafter. Its own complex and dynamic pluralism at home is usually no secret to foreign capitals (embassies) and EU institutions. Inside the Council, it finds its messages often falling on satiated soil, and it is seldom warmly welcomed by the Commission and EP. It has to cope with countless domestic interest groups, including decentralised governments that all easily challenge and by-pass it by going to the Commission and EP directly. It faces three disadvantageous limits that are typical for any capital: transparency, pressures from elected politicians and the dogma of general interest.

National capitals score high on *transparency*. Their formalised procedures often have a public character. Only in its domestic domain of delegated legislation can it usually keep its decision-making behind closed doors. In many countries, citizens and journalists can, however, urge the government to make internal documents public. Much information has to be presented to the national parliament, either according to the constitution or at the MPs' request. Due to divisions within and among both ministries and political parties, many facts, values and solutions relating to past, current or planned decisions and policies are leaked out and openly disputed. Journalists can relatively easily gather news from inside their capital, particularly if the parliament is involved. Due to openness willy-nilly, governments have an awkward position as both sender and receiver of lobby messages, by which confidential information easily becomes public.

In comparison, private groups such as companies and NGOs have an easier position on transparency. Many strategic and operational decisions do not have to be made public. Outsiders are seldom legally entitled to demand inside information. Shareholders and other stakeholders normally receive only summary information through yearly reports and official statements. Some information may leak out or be obtained by journalists, but its volume is usually modest compared to that from the capital. The *tragedy* of government transparency is that it gives the national capital, compared to private groups, a disadvantage in the EU. Intelligent interest groups can rather easily gain information about its internal divisions and positions and thus anticipate and exploit them. MNCs and MNGOs can do this for many capitals efficiently through their country units. From their side, the private groups, being rather well-informed about their capital, are hesitant to provide crucial information to it, as this functions as an almost open and often noisy channel to the wider public and thus to their own competitors in the EU as well. If they provide such information at all, they want to receive in exchange some substantial support in the EU or at home. In the EU, however, the capital being positioned as one out of many in the Council ('the last phase of about 15 percent of legislation') cannot deliver much in return there. This is one of the reasons why it is increasingly by-passed.

The *pressures from elected politicians* are a second comparative disadvantage. In most countries the members of parliament (MPs) tend to have unstable positions and short horizons, thus discouraging the government to take the longer view. Due to their high turnover, most new MPs hardly have basic EU knowledge, memory or experience. They are basically uninformed about the flesh-and-blood of the EU machinery and almost fully ignorant about its delegated legislation and how this streams into their country, largely by-passing their parliament. Their party-political competition easily causes politicization of domestic issues for the EU. In some northern and eastern countries, they can formally instruct their government and impose on it any domestic dogma, ranging from policy preference to high EU position. They like to hang on to the myth of an EU led by national governments based on parliamentary sovereignty. Often they deny the pluralist nature of the EU and take an uncompromising position. All this applies more to countries in the north and east than in the south. In the latter, the government frequently behaves in a more authoritarian way, and the parliament is less critical of EU integration [Raunio and Wiberg, 2000]. But the northern example is spreading out over the EU [Auel and Benz, 2005; O'Brennan and Raunio, 2007]. In for example the French *Assemblée Nationale* and the Spanish *Congreso*, more MPs than ever now push demands for the EU to their government, require information about Council sessions and politicise home issues for bringing about EU action. Except those from Spain and Malta, all parliaments now have a small desk, located in the EP, for informing it early on of pertinent developments.

In comparison, private groups rarely have an openly elected and representative body that discusses in public and instructs or questions the Board on its lobbying in the EU. A few NGOs have a council that is said to represent the many members, but it is usually composed by selection and not accountable to the public. In companies, the workers and shareholders tend to regard the management of EU affairs as an executive task. Their workers' council meets in closed session and is usually only interested in labour issues. Managers are free to meet their stakeholders behind closed doors. The *tragedy* of parliamentary democracy at home is that it can bind the capital rigidly before, during and after its negotiations in the Council and on the EU playing-field at large, thus limiting its much-needed room to manoeuvre there. Any new election can change these limits any time, thus making the government's position inside the EU unstable. Parliamentary procedures and practices take much time and energy from the government. Parliamentary democracy sets, in short, limits to both the effectiveness and the efficiency of the capital as an EU interest group.

The dogma of *general interest* creates a third comparative disadvantage for the national capital. In a pluralistic society, no interest is, shared by all. Yet, the government is expected to consider all sorts of interests at home and not only those of, for example, some MNCs or SMEs, working or retired people and one sector or another. Also, it is held responsible for collective goods, these being consumer goods to be delivered free or at subsidised price, such as infrastructure, public health and public transport. The capital cannot, however, be everybody's friend. It always has to make choices regarding, as called, its general or national interest, so making it less general or not so national. The choice is made informally by negotiations behind the scenes and, regarding the Council, formally by national co-ordination procedure (chapter 5), which tries to get different ministerial positions more coherent on paper. Involved in both cases are usually only some ministers, sometimes the national parliament and leading MPs, and domestic interest groups hardly or not at all. The outcome is always that many interests at home are not included, although they may be formally or *pro forma* by procedure. The by-passed interest groups often voice their protest at home, freeze their loyalty to the government or take the exit route to Brussels. Due to the dogma of general interest, the capital has to manage the gap between trustful expectations at its input side and distrustful disappointments at its output side, which is a Tantalus job.

In comparison, private groups can cope with their different internal interests much easier. Their specific interests are usually flexible. The Board can even close or sell a division, as Philips did with its Polygram division in 1998, but a government cannot easily or fully close its department for elderly people or sell it to the private sector. The *tragedy* of the general interest orientation is that the capital always has an overload of different specific interests of its own. When choosing, it always has to follow a complex procedure or to make a complex compromise. It cannot easily define a short-list and, if it presents one as such, it is really long and controversial. For every dossier on its list, it almost never defines clear targets. It usually has too many priorities, adopted under domestic pressure. Its problem is, in short, that its real home front is the whole of the country, which is always most pluralistic. Any attempt to define the general interest is, in fact, a mission impossible.

The three disadvantages or tragedies of the national government have a strong common denominator. In all EU countries, the capital is largely *driven by domestic politics*. The elections are still largely dominated by domestic issues and parties [Pennings, 2006; Poguntke and others, 2006]. The MPs feel accountable to domestic citizens. The cabinet and the ministers are accountable to this parliament and need stable majority support from it. Also at the lower levels of ministries, the political winds from the inland are often blowing stronger than from the EU. Contained in introverted structures and processes at home, the cabinet and ministries should none the less be extroverted when performing in the EU, where increasingly crucial policy decisions are being made. They can only feel torn by the very different demands from their two playing-fields. Their disadvantages at the EU level, caused by domestic politics, are particularly voiced by the MPs. This body is still the most national and at the farthest distance from EU. Although all parliaments have an EU committee and a few (Nordic and some Eastern ones) even a scrutiny committee that can instruct the cabinet on its Council position, their impact on the EU remains very limited [Auel,

2007]. Besides, these scrutiny committees scrutinise only a small sample of proposals for secondary legislation, a few percent of the total. Most MPs hardly have expertise and networks in the EU and rely for information largely on ministries, mass media and, sometimes, befriended interest groups. If they come to a majority position in front of the cabinet at all, the latter can easily pay lip service and report later on that the mission was over-ruled in the EU.

For the following five reasons, the three tragedies do not make the capital a tragic hero, as exists in ancient Greek drama.

(1) *Comparative advantages.* Compared to particularly decentralised governments, NGOs and SMEs at home, the capital has some outstanding resources, such as budget, manpower and formal powers. It can easily shift costs, re-order its many troops and influence domestic stakeholders, also by traditional techniques such as coercion by law and encapsulation by subsidy. Regional governments and big cities suffer from the three tragedies too, but have an easier escape to the EU. Domestic agencies can have the better of two worlds, as they are free from the three tragedies and often possess formal powers and many resources. Private groups have more limited resources, but particularly multinational groups compensate for this disadvantage by intelligent PA in the EU.

(2) *Tricks and games.* The cabinet and ministries can control the parliamentary factor of the three tragedies to some degree, in order to lose less in the EU. It can keep its real EU short-list secret partially or temporarily, just enough for confidential talks there. By delegation, decentralisation and privatisation, it can move dossiers from parliament to the administration, agencies or civil society, so weakening pressures from MPs. It can overload the parliament with documents, so making it confused and compliant. The definition of general interest it might leave to open procedure with 'calls for interests', like the Commission, thereby gaining paradoxical room to choose at will.

(3) *Virtues out of necessities.* Cabinets and ministries can also enjoy advantages from the tragedies. Their visible divisions show to all stakeholders outside that they have friends (and enemies) inside and thus easily attract allies free of cost. In unfriendly EU arenas, they usually need secrecy and silence less than publicity and noise, which are plentiful. Usually, the cabinet has fixed control over the majority of MPs and can order sufficient support. It can use the notion of general interest elegantly for up-framing its choice for whatever domestic interest. All cabinets do so sometimes. If they cannot get rid of the disadvantages, they have to use them. The Danish government, often eager to proclaim its own virtues, used domestic noise after the

Danish negative referendum on the 1992 Maastricht Treaty to get concessions; and by drafting its instructions from the Folketing, it uses them as pressure on the Council.

(4) *Change in the air.* Every capital is always subject to change due to domestic and foreign factors. One factor is failures and losses in the EU that stimulate a capital to adapt its internal structures and procedures better to EU processes, a lesson often learnt by private groups and agencies at home. To its PR, which feels the rift between domestic politics and EU reality the most intensely, many capitals allow increasingly discretionary room for finding negotiable positions there. They try to reduce domestic problems with consequences of EU legislation, often caused by weak management in the draft phase, by ordering better briefing and debriefing of their experts there. Some ministries promote direct coalitions with ministries abroad, informal Council meetings or even a sort of EuroFed. Parliaments now try to substantiate the subsidiarity procedure under the Lisbon Treaty. Some parties inside already behave like shopping members of a trade association that join the majority position if comfortable and go outside if not. For example, many single-issue parties (human rights, environment) work in alliance with Amnesty and Greenpeace in the EU. In 2006, the Flemish parliament, wanting to by-pass its federal parliament (that includes Walloons), discussed this party-political shopping and the set-up of a PA desk to serve its parties.

(5) *Professionalization.* Tragedies are manageable. Transparency may be a fact of government life, but a display of division and turmoil is not. MPs are the voice of parliamentary democracy, but this is not necessarily synonymous with amateurish performance. Really general interests may not exist, but they can be defined and explained by procedure, just as a company's board defines its strategy and defends it to shareholders. All capitals can learn from the Commission that must cope with the consequences of its much higher transparency on secondary legislation, pressurising MEPs and challenges from countless lobby groups that want their interests included in proposals. The Commission exploits its comparative advantages, plays smart tricks and games, makes virtues out of necessity, uses change in the air and, above all, usually behaves professionally by studying and managing the arenas of the EP and Council in advance and by in-sourcing interest groups from outside, so gaining room to manoeuvre. Most capitals are laggards in such professional PA on their home front.

The question remains whether capitals can realise *basic preconditions* for success. They often lack PA expertise for the EU properly positioned in their structures and procedures. Introverted in their observation of domestic politics, they operate in the EU without sufficient proactive homework and attuned fieldwork far before and beyond any meeting in the Council, so neglecting the Commission and EP and particularly the relevant stakeholders. Their office of national co-ordination is more for soothing their parliament than for preparing EU matches. Most ministries rely for EU work floors on their policy experts, as if these experts on substance can replace PA experts on influence management. Many ministries in Europe hardly brief their policy experts before a Brussels meeting and debrief them afterwards [Schneider and Baltz, 2005], thus hardly make use of them. Their few talented and skilled people in the PA management of EU affairs are usually self-taught, insufficiently resourced and without a rewarding career perspective. A short-list and shared-list with clear targets is seldom made, let alone a thorough analysis of selected arenas. The tragedies of transparency, pressurising MPs and dogmatic general interest lack professional counterbalance.

However, even if the capital were to better exploit its comparative advantages, play tricks and games, make virtues out of necessity, use changing winds and get more professionalised, it would never be able to overcome all general limits of EU/ PA management. No player can. To some degree and in an ever-changing mixture, the limits, summarised under the label of SCARE, will remain real to any capital, too. It will, for example, always be troubled by some myths and internal dissent, remain dependent on channels that distort and are beyond its control, be surprised by the dynamics and complexity of EU arenas, encounter inattentive receivers and run up against reputations and outside groups. But all such limits are variables and, as such, partially manageable. There is no necessary reason why the national government must be so much like Tantalus.

The Limits of PA Management in EU: Problem or Blessing?

All of the limits discussed above may seem self-evident. Yet they are largely neglected both in the literature and by the buoyant zealots of PA management. They are, however, much discussed by PA professionals working in the EU. As a reminder, these people are not necessarily those with full-time or commercial PA jobs, but those who carefully prepare and prudently do the fieldwork, whatever their job position is. These professionals regard the *understanding* of the limits as the most useful knowledge for various reasons. They want to respect the limits that fall outside their control, as otherwise they would not only be inefficient and ineffective but also damage their reputation. They also like to be aware of the limits that apply to their rivals in order to profit not only from this knowledge but also from maybe their rivals' nonchalance. Already knowing that the many possibilities of EU/PA management have their limits, they understand that these limits can also provide opportunities, at least for gaining an edge over nonchalant players. So they can avoid unforced errors, enjoy virtues out of necessities and improve their room for manoeuvring prudently. All the various limits clearly have not an absolute but a relative status. The same limit can exist for the one lobby group, but be absent for another. The one group may consider the presence or absence of the same limit a problem and another to be a blessing. This assessment should, of course, not be based on instinctive reflex but on careful reflection upon the specific situation. Therefore, the professional group tries to identify both its comparative advantages and disadvantages. The former it wants to save as blessings and the latter to solve as problems. It may even try to engineer more disadvantageous limits for rivals. In the preceding chapters we have viewed such practices, possibilities and limits of PA and lobby management in the EU primarily from the perspective of a lobby group. In the next and final chapter, we shall review them from the broader outside perspective of democracy and examine the question of whether this PA and lobby management and particularly its professional variant is good or bad for *EU democracy*.

CHAPTER 8

LOBBYING AND EU DEMOCRACY

Democracy as a Criterion

Lobbying on the EU playing-field is frequently and publicly *criticised* for its previously noted damaging effects on the democratic functioning of the EU. In particular, mass media in countries recently discovering the phenomenon of EU lobbying launch strong criticisms and fears, as has happened in Britain during the 1980s, Scandinavia in the 1990s, Germany in the early 2000s and the southern and eastern countries currently. This can be considered as a positive development because, so far, such an outburst of normative concerns has appeared to be only the first phase of empirical attention, followed by a much wider acceptance and even application of more prudent EU lobbying.

At the aforementioned 1992 EP hearings on lobbying, which gave birth to the debating forum at the EU level, lobbying received three *major criticisms*. Firstly, it was said that the most dominant interest groups such as, allegedly, industrial MNCs lobby the most. The inference here was that they create an imbalance in decision-making, to the disadvantage of weaker interest groups such as workers, consumers and small enterprises. Secondly, much lobbying was said to take place behind closed doors, which by inference creates a lack of transparency that frustrates competitors, mass media and officials. Thirdly, much lobbying was accused of abuses and immoral practices, such as document robbery, blackmail and bribery. The inference here was that this should be forbidden.

Whether these accusations and inferences were valid or not, they brought the public debate on lobbying within the frame of democracy. The critics of lobbying believed that the allegedly opaque and immoral lobbying was putting EU democracy in danger. This frame of democracy is, of course, only one public *choice* out of many alternatives, as the phenomenon of lobbying could have been (and, in future, may be) debated within different frames as well. Three examples are the following. One alternative frame is the value of integration that questions whether the various stakeholders, lobbying for their issues and coming from different countries, sectors, regions and other constituencies, contribute to a more stable EU decision-making system or not. A second alternative frame can be that of efficient EU decision-making: does lobbying make it easier for EU officials to come to a decision or not? A third possible frame addresses the welfare of citizens: does lobbying contribute positively or negatively to socio-economic welfare or not at all?

Given the current dominance of the democracy frame, we shall focus here on the *impacts* of EU lobbying on EU democracy. In academic language, democracy is the dependent variable and lobbying the independent one. An effect of lobbying may be positive, negative or indifferent for the state of EU democracy. The positive and negative effects are the most relevant for the debate, and form our focus here. In order to assess these effects, we shall have to define what is meant in Europe by the word 'democracy'. But before we can do this, we must put aside the following four different but closely related and equally interesting questions.

Firstly, we shall bypass the old and still relevant question on the *applicability* of nationally formulated notions of democracy to the EU system fully or, such as for the EP, partially [Weiler, 1995; Goodhart, 2007; Hix and others, 2007] and simply pursue the current public debate in which they are applied. Secondly, we shall not enter into a discussion about the question of what the *best concept* of democracy is. As we shall see below, there is no generally accepted criterion to help determine this. Hence we shall, thirdly, also not raise the question of whether the EU is *democratic at all* [Andersen and Eliassen, 1996]. To this question as many answers are possible as different notions exist. For example, the observation that 'the EU has a democratic deficit' [Lord, 1998] is contradicted by both that of having a 'democratic surplus' [Meunier-Aitsahalia and Ross, 1993] and by the observation that in Europe the 'real problem of democracy' lies at the national rather than the EU level [Zweifel, 2002; Schmidt, 2006]. Finally, we leave the *inverse* relationship between democracy (as the independent variable) and interest group behaviour (as the dependent one). An open society, active citizenship and limited government are, indeed, excellent democratic preconditions for the flowering of lobby groups [Popper, 1945]. Our single question remains: do lobby groups have specific impacts on EU democracy?

Notions of Democracy

In Europe (and elsewhere) not just one notion of democracy exists, but *many notions* are popular to some degree. Many are also disputed at home and even more at the aggregate EU level Pollack, 2000-B], where their variety, developed over the years, becomes visible [Pinder, 1999]. For example, in countries with a presidential-like system, like France or Britain, there is frequently more emphasis on the notions of accountability and rule of law, and less on those of pluralistic competition and consensual decision-making, than in countries with a parliamentary system such as Italy or Sweden. In countries with strong and volatile political parties, like Spain and Hungary, the notions of parliamentary government and discursiveness tend to be popular, while those of corporatism and responsiveness are more prevalent in countries with well-developed interest groups, like Austria or the Netherlands. In contrast to weakly organised interest groups of SMEs and NGOs, the established social groups including the educated and the wealthy tend to attach more importance to the notions of direct channels and limited government and less to those of competitive elections and common identity.

More fundamental than this socio-political variety in notions of democracy is the main conclusion from the science of knowledge that, ultimately, every value has not an absolute but a *relative* status [Brecht, 1959]. A scientifically sound criterion to determine the single best notion of democracy is simply beyond reach. This idea of relativity opens the door to manifold competitive and newly arising notions of democracy. They all may make sense. 'Democracy', in fact, is an open container full of different notions, negatively conjoined by their common contrast to the (equally broad) notions of tyranny, despotism and the like [Dahl, 1989; Held, 1996]. The notions of democracy differ largely on what they stand for positively and are variously presented as core ideas, preconditions, elements, indicators, factors or outcomes of it. Some notions are value-related, such as 'freedom', 'tolerance' and 'legitimacy', while others are process-related, such as 'elections', 'majority rule' and 'responsiveness'. Confusingly enough, the notions of democracy sometimes differ only seemingly, as different words can be used for the same fundamental idea. For example, 'liberty', 'freedom' and 'autonomy' are frequently used as synonyms for the personal capacity to act as one wants. The reverse can happen as well, when the same word is used for different ideas, sometimes even by the same author. For example, the term 'democracy' is on one occasion seen as containing such elements as legitimate authority and identity, and on another as one element of the wider notion of legitimate authority [Lord, 1998; Beetham and Lord, 1998]. An established taxonomy of notions of democracy is clearly absent.

For our purpose it is not necessary to decide upon the best definition of the concept of democracy with regard to the EU. For the construction of our dependent variable it is sufficient to assemble the most popular notions of democracy as they feature in the public debate about the EU. They are listed in Figure 8.1, subdivided into four categories, respectively related to the input side of EU, its throughput of decision-making, its output side and its feedback-loop in civil society [Easton, 1965]. We shall briefly explain them first.

Input Notions
The general idea of the input concept of democracy is that the decision-making system must offer *openness* to all sorts of people and groups wanting to get a desired outcome. The openness is not discriminating or selective, but gives an equal and fair chance to every desire regarding the outcome of a decision. A desire may involve anything: one or another decision or no decision at all regarding binding laws, policies, allocations, implementations, recruitment, sanctions or any other outcome. Openness, equality and permeability do not necessarily have to be real for every desire at any moment, but, after some time, every type of demand, information or support should find its way into the system. The permeation of competitive civil pluralism into and inside the political system needs, vehicles of course. At least three of them have become specific notions of democracy on the input side. One is the notion of regular competitive elections, based on equal-

POPULAR NOTIONS OF DEMOCRACY

INPUT NOTIONS
- OPENNESS, PERMEABILITY
- PLURALISTIC COMPETITION
- COMPETITIVE ELECTIONS
- DIRECT CHANNELS
- REPRESENTATIVE CHANNELS

OUTPUT NOTIONS
- LEGITIMACY
- LIMITED GOVERNMENT
- RULE OF LAW
- ACCOUNTABILITY
- RESPONSIVENESS

THROUGHPUT NOTIONS
- REPRESENTATION
- MAJORITARIAN DECISIONS
- CONSENSUAL DECISIONS
- POLYARCHY, OPPOSITION
- LEGITIMATE AUTHORITY
- DISCURSIVENESS
- TRANSPARENCY

FEEDBACK NOTIONS
- CITIZENSHIP
- TOLERANCE
- IDENTITY
- FREEDOMS AND RIGHTS
- LINKAGES TO INPUT

Figure 8.1

ity and fairness, for the purpose of distributing formal positions of power. A second is that direct channels must exist for the transportation of desires. They may range from a national referendum and personal visit to an orderly petition and street protest. Finally, indirect channels that represent civil desires must exist by way of political parties, interest groups, mass media, bureaucracies or any other platform with an intermediary capacity.

All the general and specific input notions have some varying degree of *popularity* in European countries, which is another way of saying that they are contested. People and groups appear to differ in their preference for one or another input notion and for one or another vehicle, as the following examples may show. The openness of the French government to the employers' organisations rather than to the trade unions is at issue there. Everywhere the electoral system is regularly under debate, for example concerning its capacity to create either equal effects of votes (proportionality system) or stable government (district system). Direct channels are popular in countries like Denmark, Greece and Poland, in regions like Flanders and Bavaria, and in concentrated sectors like consumer electronics and the environmental movement. Examples of strongly supported indirect channels are political parties in Italy, mass media in Britain, bureaucracies in the Netherlands, central governments in Scandinavia and Baltic States, churches in Austria and trade unions in Germany.

These different input notions have, to some extent, all been put into practice *at the EU level*, frequently clash there and cause some europeanization of them at home. The EU shows substantial and remarkable openness to old and new desires coming from the countries, regions and sectors and permeating into the EU system, where they all stand at issue and finally may contribute to for example the expansion and reform of policy fields like environment and agriculture. Some established groups may take a lead, but the current overtaking by SMEs, NGOs and regions indicates a remarkable degree of equality for those entering the system after some time. The accessibility of the main institutions is, according to a sample of lobbyists, another affair, as the EP is found to be most accessible, followed by the Commission and the Council the least [ComRes, 2008]. The pluralistic competition inside member countries has a possibility imperfect but real continuation at the EU level, as indicated by their lobby groups. There are elections, although only directly for the EP seats and held on a national basis. Direct channels are available, ranging from national referendums to corridor lobbying and street protest in Brussels. All major indirect channels are used by political parties, interest groups, civil servants and journalists from the member countries. In some cases these channels may be considered to be still weak and under development. For example, most political parties are only weakly organised on a transnational basis, and many journalists function more as sports reporters on the output side by commenting upon scandals and scores than as providers of informationon the input side. In any event, the input notions of democracy have a firm position in the EU.

Throughput Notions

The general idea here is that the government must be *representative* of what the people desire. This idea of representation is another container-like notion resuscitated in the 1960s. A group of officials may be said to be representative if, for example, it mirrors the social features of the people (such as age, sex and ethnicity), their opinions, their interests and/or their votes [Birch, 1971]. All that may apply to an elected body ('electoral representation'), but also to a nominated committee, a corporatist platform or a bureaucracy ('functional representation') [Krislov, 1974]. The representatives are assumed to act on behalf of the larger population, instead of whom they govern. In their 'acting for the people' [Pitkin, 1967 and 1969], they may behave as either a delegate or a trustee [Pennock and Chapman, 1968], although the one role does not necessarily preclude the other. Regarding elected politicians there exist the two formalistic notions that, so to say by definition, the elected people are representative due to the ballot box and their institution due to the constitution. Some notions of representation even jump ahead to the output and feedback side of government and emphasise both the responsive allocation of desired outcomes [Eulau and Prewitt, 1973] and the promotion of civil society [Pateman, 1970]. Two groups of throughput notions of democracy may be seen as more specific. The first is focused on *methods* of government. One variant is the notion of majority rule, usually with an amendment for a qualified majority if there is an inequality of either size or passion [Dahl, 1989]. Another variant replaces this amendment by the notion of consensual or even consociational government, by which different preferences are continually accommodated by new compromises [Lijphart, 1977; Taylor, 1996]. Between them is the variant emphasising the notion of polyarchy, which stands for a system that is permanently open, highly competitive, full of opposition and without any group being always in either a majority or minority position [Dahl, 1971]. The second group stresses specific *values* of government process, such as legitimate authority [Friedrich, 1963], discursive considerations [Dryzek and Niemeyer, 2008] or transparency [Deckmyn and Thomson, 1998; Bunyan, 1999], to mention only the most popular values.

All these throughput notions of democracy have differing levels of *popularity* in European countries [Schmidt, 2006], as the following few examples show. In Britain and the Central European countries that in the early 1990s acquired party-political competition, there is a threefold strong belief in elected representation based on party-political delegation, in majority decision-making, and in the value of transparency. Most popular in the Germanic countries are the notions of functional representation by experts acting on behalf of their segment of society, consensual decision-making and the value of discursiveness. In France, the preference for functional representation is largely limited to both administrative experts and experts from the employers' side, while the value of transparency is supported after rather than during the decision-making process. In Italy, there exists broad support for electoral representation on a party-political trustee basis, for consensual government and for polyarchy and opposition. In the EU area, one single dominant set of throughput notions is absent. The various notions compete with one another [Pollak, 2007].

To some degree all throughput notions undergo europeanization and have, as an outcome of compromises, been put into practice to some degree at the *EU level*. All institutions have a demographic composition that reflects somehow the different nationalities involved. At the administrative level, this is informally arranged ('fourchette') and at the political one it is formalised through seats, voting points and positions. Through their respective institutions, the political groups (EP), interest groups (ESC), regions (COR) and member states (Council) import into the system a wide variety of opinions and interests. By the way of expert groups, comitology and agencies there is much functional representation, which is closely linked to the Commission that acts as a bureaucracy, representing particularly sectoral and regional constituencies. Electoral representation is directly rooted in the EP and indirectly in both the COR (politicians from decentralised councils) and the Council (governments based on national elections). The specific notions of throughput democracy also have some EU design. All main *methods* of government have been put into practice. Variants of majority decision-making are present in the Commission's College, the Parliament and the Council. In all institutions the informal routine is consensually directed at reaching broad compromises. Polyarchy and opposition are vested in both formal power distributions and informal conflicts. Indicators of the latter are revolving disagreements about nominations, policy objectives, regime values and constitutional change, including notions of democracy. The *values* of legitimate authority, discursiveness and transparency are hardly at issue as such, but intensely upon their application. Examples are the often contested authority of the Commission, discursiveness of the Parliament and transparency of the Council. These issues cause both public debate and new proposals, so indicating that the values are taken as serious notions of democratic government.

Output Notions

The general idea of output notions is that the government's products should be *legitimate* or be widely considered as acceptable. There are various potential sources of legitimacy. One is satisfaction with the government's outputs that meet social needs like health, employment, education and housing. The throughput process can be a source of legitimacy if widely regarded fair and just. Then even a disappointing output is accepted as 'all part of the game', and a compromise among different groups as 'the best possible result' that comes the closest possible to 'general interest'. Another source of legitimacy is the personal authority or charisma of responsible people. Margaret Thatcher, Felipe González and Helmut Kohl (former 'heads of state' of Britain, Spain and Germany, respectively) have had their moments of speaking *ex cathedra* and getting what they wanted. Legitimacy can also be provided by prestigious vehicles such as tradition and science. If an outcome links up nicely with a famous past or is based on scientific evidence, it may be more easily accepted. More specific output notions of democracy are the following, two of which come close to being *methods*. One is limited government, which from the perspective of effective government is frequently considered a vice (chapter 7), but from that of democracy a virtue. This notion has at least three dimensions: checks and balances among institutions, decentralisation and restrained interventions in the private spheres, and sectors. The last two dimensions are also covered by the notion of subsidiarity. The other method regards rule of law: outputs of government should ultimately be based on formally binding decisions, produced through prescribed procedures, approved by a formally representative platform and open to judicial appeal. Specific output *values* exist as well. One is that the officials who produce outputs should be accountable for what they do or do not do [Lord, 1998] and particularly that nominated officials be accountable to the elected ones and the latter to the electors. Another popular value is that the outputs should be responsive to the desires imported into the system at an earlier stage [Eulau and Prewitt, 1973]. This responsiveness may be that the government generally performs what it has promised before, but also be specific for regions, sectors or groups [Eckstein, 1971].

The output notions of democracy gather variable levels of *popularity* at the country level, and thus adverse reactions as well. The outputs of government are often widely considered legitimate, as is indicated by relatively high levels of civil obedience and low levels of civil protest in most countries. If protests occur, they are mainly limited to the special issues of regional separatism (such as in the Basque region, Corsica or Northern Ireland), sectoral decline (farming, trucking or mining, for example) and failing government performances (such as in CEEC states like Hungary and Romania). All countries have some form of limited government in one or more of its three dimensions (checks and balances, decentralisation, private freedoms). Most notable among these are Germany, which scores high on all three, and the formerly communist countries of Central Europe, which are rapidly creating more limited government. France is seemingly at the opposite end of the spectrum, but behind the formal show of central state dominance exist such realities as conflicts between Matignon and Elysée, public decentralisation and sectoral privatisation. The notion of rule of law is hard and most popular in Britain, while in the continental countries it often includes soft law (semi-formal agreements) as the outcome of consensual decision-making and resulting in what is called rule of consent. In all countries, the value of accountability is in some way contained in formal arrangements between representative councils and electors, and in basic freedoms of mass media. For its responsiveness, every government is widely evaluated by public opinion and through the ballot box. In countries like Italy, Belgium and Bulgaria, clientelism that pampers selected socio-political groupings is part of this.

The different notions and practices of output democracy increasingly undergo europeanization and vie with each other at the *EU level*. To some degree, they all exist in some form. Legitimacy is rooted in popular policy values ranging from open markets to healthy food, in decision-making procedures that are generally accepted as basically fair, and in special vehicles such as charismatic leadership (like that of Walter Hallstein or Jacques Delors), tradition (from the old Idea of Europe to the practices of representation) and science (as by expert groups) [Schmitt and Thomassen, 1999]. People in southern countries attach even more legitimacy to EU institutions than to their national ones [Norris, 1999]. Protest behaviour is limited to incidental interest groups demanding less or more from EU policies, and to increasingly domestic political parties that feel caught between domestic politics and EU decision-making. The notion of limited government is practiced by institutional checks and balances and, with regard to both the domestic levels and the private spheres, by growing respect for subsidiarity. The main form of EU government is rule by law, including soft variants such as OCM. Discretionary decisions regarding subsidies and procurements must have a legal basis. Binding laws are formally devised according to procedures based either on treaties (secondary law) or on secondary laws (delegated law), and unlike in some member states, they are open to appeal at the Court. The enforcement of law, vulnerable by its dependency on national co-operation, is yet remarkably effective, although more for civil societies than for central governments. Evidence of accountability is found in three developing formal practices: EU officials are becoming gradually more accountable to the EP, Council ministers to their home parliament and both EP and ministers to their ballot boxes. Besides, there is ever more accountability to interest groups and mass media. Responsiveness to demands can be seen in both general policies and specific support to selected regions and sectors.

Feedback Notions

The general idea here is *citizenship*. The people are not just subjects of government, but are seen as citizens with the personal capacity to internalise the values of government selectively (civic spirit) and to behave accordingly (civic behaviour). This applies not only to individuals but also to groups and organisations called corporate citizens, and which include NGOs and companies. As government should be open and permeable to citizens' demands, so the citizens should be open to demands from government. Their internalisation may be selective but, if rejecting some values of government, citizens ultimately have to account for this in front of a court. With their civic spirit, they take into consideration both the desired and the perceived functioning of government. Through their civic behaviour they express their own views, which may range from full support to intense protest. A democracy cannot exist without such a civil society [Fine and Rai, 1997; Fullinwider, 1999]. There are more specific feedback notions, two of which concern *values*. Firstly, citizens need to be tolerant of each other and allow peaceful resolution of any irritating difference [King, 1976]. Secondly, to avoid a breakdown of society, citizens must have a stable sense of some common identity that is based on, for example, social indicators (such as sex, income or ethnicity), belief systems (religion or ideology), regions ('we, the Flemish'), sectors (like agriculture, industry or education), recent drama (formerly communist CEECs) and/or national past and pride ('La France'). The more the various identities cross-cut each other, the more social cohesion they produce. Two other specific notions involve *methods*. Firstly, citizens must possess substantial freedoms and rights [Friedrich, 1963]. This notion implies that citizens are entitled to have, negatively, a private domain outside ('free from') government and, positively, opportunities to participate in ('free for') government if they wish. Secondly, the cultures and structures of civil society should be linked to the input side of government. The feedback channels must be part of civil society and consist particularly of political parties, interest groups and mass media [Luttbeg, 1968]. Without them, the government cannot be considered capable of reflecting the general notions of openness, representation and legitimacy and be called democratic.

All feedback notions of democracy have some degree of *popularity* at the country level and thus are to some degree contested. In behavioural terms, however, in every country only a minority of individual or corporate citizens displays high levels of civic spirit and behaviour [Van Deth and Scarbrough, 1998], while the mass of citizens tends to follow that minority as a way of citizenship. Tolerance ranks high as a social value, as indicated by widespread public disapproval of open discrimination against, for example, immigrants, women or the elderly. New or deviant values and activities are frequently accepted as part of the pluralism of society, as long as they do not break current laws or irritate others. All sorts of group identities exist in the European countries. However, those based on belief systems seem to be weakening in most countries (except in Scandinavia), like those based on nationalism (except in CEECs). Regionalism as a common identity is still going strong in countries like Spain, Germany and Belgium and taking off in Poland, Romania and Hungary. Basic freedoms and rights have been institutionalised everywhere. Freedom from government has been promoted under the frames of privacy and privatisation, which have diffused from the north to the south of Europe. However, a backlash against privacy occurred after 'September 11, 2001', and against privatisation in the aftermath of the 2008 financial crisis. Feedback linkages to government are widely supported. In northern countries, they shift from political parties to interest groups and mass media [Klingemann and Fuchs, 1995].

As part of their europeanization the various feedback notions and practices compete at the *EU level*. No different from the domestic levels, individual citizenship is clearly the weakest realised notion here, and difficult to realise in a Union of about 500 million people. There is, however, much corporate and represented citizenship that more or less represents individuals, as indicated by both countless lobby groups acting on behalf of individuals (workers, clients, members) and, to a lesser degree, political groups that represent citizens in the EP. There is a moderate level of individual tolerance for people from other EU countries, as is shown by sympathy scores that tend to be the highest for one's own countrymen (except in Italy, Sweden and Belgium) and higher for northern than southern people (chapter 1). Corporate tolerance is indicated by most organisations' willingness to settle their disputes and irritations by peaceful and compromising decision-making. Most people feel some degree of EU identity, which is largely grounded on a sense of utility [Van Kersbergen, 2000] and weaker than their district, regional and country identity [Eurobarometer 51, 1999, 8; Scheuer, 2005]. Among corporate citizens the sectoral identity is the strongest. Under the Lisbon Treaty the notion of freedoms and rights gets its first constitution-like status, including a Europe-wide referendum. The main linkage system between civil society and the EU is through interest groups. Mass media and political parties still maintain a largely national focus. Their feedback to the EU goes mainly through the indirect channels of domestic officials.

The Impacts of EU Public Affairs Management on EU Democracy

All the above-mentioned notions of democracy clearly play some role in both the member countries and at the EU level, but they are all *disputed* as well. Some people attach high value to, for example, direct channels rather than to representative ones, while others take the opposite view. Still others differentiate further and want the direct channels to be open only to individuals, and the representative ones only to political parties. Their preferences may conflict with those of others that put their trust in interest groups as agents of democracy. Some consider political parties and interest groups as two contradictory channels, while others see them as complementary. This sort of critical debate exists for all other notions, too. No notion gathers absolute or unconditional support from all people. Because in a pluralistic society each notion competes with other notions and results always in some compromise, its realisation is never perfect. At the more abstract level this is even true for the whole 'container' of democracy that has to compete with such other high values as welfare, stability or effectiveness. Therefore, the maximisation of a high value would be the enemy of its optimisation and certainly cause trouble in society. The notions of democracy need equal optimisation rather than maximisation. For example, perfect transparency, rule of law or tolerance would seriously injure other notions of democracy and even other high values, such as better integration and greater welfare.

As stated earlier, it is not our objective to assess here the state of EU democracy. For our case, it is sufficient to observe that all notions have achieved some form of realisation at the EU level. The state of EU democracy is clearly an *amalgam* of them, each having its support basis somewhere and sometimes. As examples of europeanization, these practices of EU democracy can be seen as compromises between often irritatingly different notions of democracy that exist in the EU countries, regions and sectors. Their contested character there is continued at the EU level, acquiring more intensity and greater heterogeneity. Our objective is to explore the *dependency* of EU democracy, with its variety of notions, on the behaviour of lobby groups, an approach which others have followed recently [Karr, 2006; Greer and others, 2008]. Can outcomes of EU democracy be explained by this behaviour? Or: do lobby groups have a positive or negative impact on them, or none at all?

Input Impacts
In a comparative perspective, the EU clearly is a highly open and competitive system. Three indicators, *inter alia*, are the constant influx of new issues resulting in new agendas, the regular permeation of new regime and policy values, and the massive in-sourcing of experts from interest groups. The strong competition between issues, values and experts reflects the pluralism of the countries. Lobby groups play a significant *positive* role in keeping the system open and competitive. Evidence of this comes not only from their role in decision processes, as documented by the case studies referred to before, but also of the imaginary control situation in which lobby groups are absent. If this were the case, the EU would be a system only of COM officials, members of EP, ESC and COR, Council ministers and Court personnel, with only two types of linkages with the member countries; one being the direct election of the EP and the other the indirect linkages between the Council, ESC and COR on the one hand, and the national capitals and societies on the other. This virtual system would certainly be much more closed for many issues, values and people from private and even public interest groups, and altogether be much less open and competitive than it is in reality now.

On the *vehicles* of input democracy, lobby groups have different positive impacts. There is hardly any evidence that they play a strong role in the direct elections for the EP, although some try to influence party manifestos, lists of candidates and public debates at the domestic level, as happens in Britain. Lobby groups dig their own channels, either indirectly through EuroFeds or directly by sending their experts to the EU and opening a Brussels office. The Commission and EP aggregate channelled issues, values and people, functioning as a kind of representative bureaucracy and parliament. Most domestic political parties hardly have well-established direct links with the EU's input side. Their indirect links go largely through their

EP's sister party, sometimes via befriended interest groups, as the green parties and green movement exemplify, and incidentally through party-political friends in the Council and COR [Lindberg and others, 2008]. With a very few exceptions mass media are almost never directly present on the EU input side.

Lobby groups may be called *helpful but not sufficient* for EU input democracy. In terms of equality of entry, some types of lobby groups can have better chances of permeation than others [Coen, 2007, Greer and others, 2008] and certainly, have, according to some NGOs such as Alter-EU, Spinwatch and Friends of the Earth in 2008, groups which lobby against lobbying. Established groups like national ministries and multinationals (MNCs and MNGOs) can have a permanent ticket to enter their policy domain, but never have passe-partout entitling them to enter any room. Professional groups find the system particularly open and permeable, because they carry out a lot of preparatory work before lobbying. They are simply smarter than the amateurs and can arrive early on in the right place. The electoral vehicle is potentially most open to NGO-like lobby groups that suggest representing more general interest. The direct channels are mainly used by better-resourced groups that can afford the costs, such as multinational groups, EuroFeds and national ministries. The representative channels are the least discriminating, as they are open to every group that meets the minimum conditions of organisation. Of course, there are always some insufficiently organised outside groups, such as retired people and immigrant entrepreneurs, which we shall discuss in the section on feedback impacts.

Lobby groups can also have at least two forms of *negative* impacts on EU input democracy. The first comes from short-sighted lobby groups that try to make the access to the EU less open to competitors. This is the paradox of openness that can lead to closure. Along the access routes to the EU, such groups form a coalition for getting priority treatment at the entrance. Once inside, they erect thresholds that keep their rivals at a distance behind them and try to transform their coalition into a policy cartel that preferably includes EU officials. The proposed Aarhus Convention Regulation (COM 2003/622), precooked by the green movement's European Environmental Bureau (EBB) and limiting participation on green issues to 'entitled groupings' belonging to its family, is one example of such a negative impact on input democracy. The second source of negative impacts belongs to all lobby groups together. Because so many groups seek to enter and to permeate EU operations, they can overload the system through either the volume or the contents of their demands. This is the paradox of openness creating its own blockage. Some issues, values and groups are then held up, stockpiled, refused or otherwise not provided entrance. Each of these negative impacts may result in an imbalance of lobby groups on the input side.

The possibilities of entry inequality and negative impacts are at least partially addressed by three system-linked *correction mechanisms*. Firstly, many doors are opened from the inside. In their appetite for new information, support and demands, the EU officials invite even incipient, amateurish and penniless interest groups having an interest in the EU. Incumbent groups that want to turn a headwind inside the arena often widen the arena boundaries and open the doors. Entry thresholds are, in short, often only temporary. Secondly, lobby groups that stand outside and want a position inside often get doors opened from the outside and make the EU even more competitive. Usually, they receive a provisional ticket, start their professionalization and find ways to be present or represented. Thirdly, the overload problem is tackled from the inside by new collectors of inputs, such as new expert committees and online consultations. A lobby impact on the EU input side should, however, not be equated with a final impact, as more corrections may come from what follows during throughput, output and feedback.

Throughput Impacts

In many respects the EU decision-making system is fairly representative for the member countries, although this is not necessarily the performance of lobby groups alone. Commission civil servants and MEPs can also act as agents of representation, for example by soliciting opinions, anticipating interests, recruiting people or distributing positions. The presence of lobby groups is, however, frequently a *positive* factor of better EU representation. With these groups nearby, the officials can anticipate demands better. Each day they receive fresh information and indications of support from all sorts of lobby groups. The experts representing lobby groups make the work floors of the EU demographically more representative of the various sectors, regions and countries. From their side, the lobby groups that provide information, even if it is selective, stimulate the representative and discursive discussion inside the institutions [Neyer, 2000], and by indicating support they promote a decision-making process that is more representative of the various interests.

The *methods* of decision-making are also at least partially made more democratic by the presence of lobby groups. This positive dependency is, once again, selective. Lobby groups prefer the majority-vote method only if this is most likely to give them the result they desire. Being aware that the official bodies formally control this method, they tend to prefer consensual decision-making more than majority vote and see such consensus, once achieved, usually adopted by the official bodies. In fact, they prefer the big chance of winning part of the game by consensus to the small chance of taking the full game by majority vote. For the same reason, they are quick to register their opposition to what they dislike. By adopting a nuisance position, they may get a better negotiating stance and larger piece of the pie. If the arena is highly competitive and turning toward a stalemate, they usually push officials to cook up a representative compromise. The more the lobby groups compete, the more they willy-nilly contribute to the polyarchic method of decision-making.

Many lobby groups enhance the democratic *values* involved in the throughput process as well. The individual group primarily demands, of course, not so much more legitimate authority, discursiveness or transparency as to win and not to lose its interest. Knowing, however, that this interest is frequently indeterminate for some time, it often has a next-best preference for those three values. It considers them safeguards against conspiring practices by rivals. Those fearing to lose a match usually demand that the legitimate authority makes the decision in a discursive and transparent way. Many improved democratic practices result from such demands, as exemplified by the Commission's authority relying on expert committees, the EP's sympathy with popular views and the Council's (slowly) improving transparency. The support from many lobby groups for the three values is at least partially based on their self-interest, which is usually the most solid basis of support. The main boost in favour of more open access to EU documents and against the opposing Council members since 2001 comes from NGOs like Statewatch and Transparency International, and some Nordic governments like Sweden's, that in 2009 prioritised this dossier for its Council chair later that year.

All the activities of lobby groups during the decision-making process and particularly their supply of experts, information and interests are *helpful but insufficient* for making decision processes fully representative. The aggregate supply can be unbalanced, when representing only some kinds of interests, and officials can be self-obsessed or deaf for whatever reason. From this supply they frequently gain much room for choice and manoeuvre thanks to the paradox of the neutralisation effect (chapter 7), that the stronger the competition among lobby groups is, the more they occupy the position of trustee with free mandate to devise a compromise acceptable to most stakeholders. Many officials have indeed a vested interest in strong lobby competition, which on the one hand provides more free experts, information and support, and on the other more freedom to decide. But this freedom might be that of a cook having to make dinner with ingredients provided by the diners. The more varied the ingredients provided, the more the kitchen is representative of what nature provides. The countless lobby groups are very helpful in this regard.

The lobby groups can, however, also have *negative* impacts on the throughput process. Given their primary drive to win and not to lose, interest groups value democracy rarely as a goal and only as a means to be used flexibly. Professional groups, unlike amateurs, want to respect the forms, methods and values of democratic decision-making, but on this they are optimisers and not maximisers. When feeling they are on the winning side, they often dislike any proposal that would make the process even more representative than it, from their point of view, already is. They may even fear the three methods, because the majority-vote holds the risk of becoming identified as minority, the consensual one of having to make wider concessions and the polyarchic one of attracting new challengers. They may have little interest in furthering the values of authoritative, discursive and transparent decision-making. The professional group in a marginal position or losing mood is usually no different in its instrumental approach to democracy, but only in its final preferences. In this situation it is usually inclined to pledge for more representative, consensual and polyarchic decision-making and for stricter application of the three values. It may remain silent only on the majority-vote method, as this might reveal that it belongs to a defeated minority.

The possible negative impacts are subject to at least three system-bound *correction mechanisms*. Firstly, no arena has fully closed boundaries. There are always groups watching, which are a source of social control and may decide to become active. When joining an arena, they can make it more representative by both their quantity and variety, and challenge the current forms, methods and values of decision-making. Mass media happily report on what they see as undemocratic practices. Secondly, from inside the EU officials often have a vested interest in making the process more democratic, because this will bring them, ultimately, more firmly into the driver's seat. Lobby groups inside an arena in a losing mood can have the same preference for more democracy, as this is a means that can hinder the near-winners. Thirdly, the output side that requires legitimacy may already cast its shadow. There are more quality tests of democracy to come.

Output Impacts

In all member countries an absolute or relative majority of people supports their EU membership, being the summary indicator of its legitimacy or acceptance, and in almost all countries similar majorities consider this membership to be largely beneficial [Eurobarometer, 70, 2008; Scheuer, 2005]. The specific output notions that promote EU legitimacy, such as the methods of limited government and rule of law and the values of accountability and responsiveness, are also widely accepted. These *positive* scores of democracy on the output side are not necessarily the products of interest groups that lobby. Many national politicians, members of EP, COR and ESC, Commission officials and Court judges also contribute to the legitimacy of the EU and to the formation of its specific methods and values. Often, however, they do so under pressure from lobby groups that consider EU legitimacy and its methods and values maybe not so much as an ultimate goal but as a useful means to promote their specific interests. Even policy values that now attract much sympathy and thus acceptance have usually once been promoted by lobby groups with roots in society. Examples are the popular values of open markets, healthy food, sustainability and social cohesion. Lobby groups frequently push for new regime practices that may make even undesired outcomes acceptable as being 'all part of the game'. Examples are the practices of better regulation, open consultations and expert meetings on the EU work floors. Some groups add their own charisma, as the European Round Table did, adopt traditions like functional representation and act with a show of science and expertise. Output legitimacy can also be promoted by lobby groups from the private or public sector.

This positive contribution is no different for the identified *methods and values* of output democracy. Many interest groups have lobbied actively to put limits on the EU's government by campaigning for more openness, representation and legitimacy. Citizens' groups have pressed for the EP to become a more checking and balancing power. Many lobby groups are in favour of rule of law, as they find any alternative being worse or because they come from countries with a legalistic tradition. The British BONGO 'Bruges Group', founded in 2008, strongly campaigns against any EU law that adds costs onto UK firms, so making rule of law subordinate to its commercial interests. Groups that suffer losses during EU decision-making and go the Court paradoxically strengthen the rule of law. British groups successfully pressed for more accountability in the EU. The general and specific responsiveness of EU policy outputs can only be well explained if lobby groups are also taken as a factor in this.

The existence of lobby groups is *helpful but insufficient* for the creation of EU output democracy. The officials that approve and sign the decisions may remain deaf or blind to lobbying efforts from outside and may give priority to their own values and interests, as happens in every system. As players, too, they can patronise selected lobby groups by applying discriminating procedures to others, as happened on the Aarhus Convention (COM 2003/622). They may undermine limited government by making deals and coalitions across institutional, territorial and sectoral boundaries. Officials outside the Court can weaken the supremacy of law by their discretionary capacity to interpret EU laws at their desire and to fall back on supplementary law. They can use procedures of accountability for highlighting their own performances, to get sunshine publicity. In 2008 the British NGO 'Open Europe' blamed the Commission for its expensive campaigns full of 'biased propaganda'. All this can happen in any system and thus in the EU as well.

Lobby groups can, of course, also have *negative* impacts on the EU's legitimacy. The rationale behind it is, again, their prime aim of coming close as possible to the desired outcome for a dossier. Professional groups may be able to see opportunities for managing or manipulating methods and values that produce more or less EU legitimacy, but as prudent players they feel restrained in using them. Amateurish groups frequently take higher risks on this by not respecting notions like limited government or accountability. For example, on the 2008 European Transparency Initiative (ETI) many NGOs were reluctant to account for their funding. The output side can, indeed, reflect shortcomings of legitimacy caused by lobby behaviour.

Three system-linked *correction mechanisms*, however, prevent such potentially negative impacts from easily becoming reality. Firstly, even if inside the system some legal and social controls on the officials are not working well, many others remain operative thanks to the system's redundancy. A rapporteur, being one soul with a lobby group, has to get his report accepted by shadow rapporteurs, groups and plenary. Commission officials are subject to control from competitive offices, higher officials and other institutions. A dramatic example is the 1999 demise of the Santer Commission. Secondly, even more controls come from the numerous and varied lobby groups that spend much energy on closely watching each other. The more professional, established or resourced groups are becoming less certain about their comparative advantages, since more groups are acquiring such qualities. Groups that feel themselves on the losing side may launch critical campaigns and blame the officials for a lack of legitimacy or accountability. The mass media need only a wisp of smoke in order to report a fire that may burn the officials. Thirdly, the feedback mechanism can cast its long shadow. If an output is widely considered as falling short of democracy, it may evoke serious feedback reactions. The lobby group aware of the risk of scandals disciplines its behaviour beforehand. That is prudence.

Feedback Impacts

The basic unit of citizenship is the mass of individual citizens. In the large-scale EU they are highly dependent on intermediate organisations that range from NGOs and companies to government offices, parties and mass media. Whether these organisations are really intermediate or, as they are also called, corporate citizens, depends on their representativeness for their members, clients or, in short, their following among the citizens. The feedback loop from citizens to, in our case here, the EU is in its turn fed by the flow of information about what happens in the EU. The topics can be anything and range from draft-legislation and institutional changes to specific issues and scandals. The sources of information can range from official EU statements and domestic comments to local media and gossip. Even if incomplete, distorted or misperceived, this flow of information can stimulate citizens willy-nilly to develop EU citizenship. There are always some (organisations of) citizens that react to what happens at the EU level (or not). This is where citizenship comes in as a *positive* feedback loop of democracy. Citizens can react by either only their civic spirit or by their civic behaviour, too. In the former case they develop new beliefs, values or judgements regarding the EU or confirm their old ones; and in the latter case, they even react by activities that support or oppose what happens. Usually, this feedback loop runs through the indirect channels of intermediate organisations that adopt some interests of their following at home and act for it at the EU level. Much EU lobbying has indeed this history of a multi-layered feedback loop, which starts at the mass level of consumers, farmers or workers and takes shape through organisations that act as corporate citizens.

The loop can also positively affect specific *values and methods* of feedback democracy. Examples are the following. The extension of the internal market as pushed by MNCs and consumer groups has reinforced the value of tolerance for people, products and ownership from foreign countries. Intolerance meets more retaliation now than in the past, thanks to some NGOs at the EU level. Regional groups have promoted new forms and procedures for the value of identity, such as regional cohesion and subsidiarity. Private groups lobby for even more freedoms and rights, since they enjoyed the taste of market liberalisation and free movement in the EU. Many interest groups have stimulated the Commission, being prone to follow out of its own interest, to establish better linkage systems by inviting interest groups to provide information and to sit in expert groups. In most countries, domestic political parties and mass media are, however, still more a dead-end route, giving only selective and frequently biased information to their public rather than being a fixed part of the feedback loop [Binnema, 2009; De Vreese, 2007].

The lobby groups are *helpful but insufficient* for the promotion of feedback democracy in the EU. Citizenship has many more determinants, such as (lack of) welfare, education, free time and social interest [Milbrath and Goel, 1977]. Their unequal distribution may explain why there is so much variation of EU citizenship between corporate and individual citizens and also within each category. Thanks to the EU, the values of tolerance and identity have acquired new meanings and forms, but their status in society is also dependent on much more than the EU and its lobby groups alone. For example, respect for pluralism is also determined by the social situation at street level, and frequently the place of tension is there. The formation of new identities, such as the regional ones, is often primarily caused by local factors such as language or religion, and only catalysed via the EU. Lobbying for the proclamation of freedoms and rights through the Official Journal is not sufficient, because such values must be embedded in wider social demands and adequate infrastructures as well. EU stakeholders pushing for more and better feedback linkages can fail in their efforts, as the weak feedback linkages by most political parties and mass media show.

Lobby groups can also have *negative* impacts on the state of EU democracy. If people would come to believe that the EU is only a sort of republican court with lobbying groups and factions patronising them, they may get the feeling of not being clients at all, lose civic spirit or behaviour and become indifferent or passive. The lobbying in favour of tolerance and identity can cause the opposite to occur, in the form of rising social conflicts and cultural confusion. For a job vacancy, house purchase or parking space, people may dislike competition from equally entitled foreigners. Counter-lobbies in the EU may challenge domestic freedoms and rights, such as regarding the Dutch coffee shops selling soft drugs, the Austrian 2000 cabinet formation bringing right-wing party leader Haider to power, the Spanish sports of bull-fighting, the British working hours and the CEEC's appetite for formally unhealthy but good-tasting meat and wine. Organisations pretending to be corporate citizens but in that fact hardly act on behalf of their following set EU feedback democracy at risk [Warleigh, 2001].

These potential or real negative impacts remain limited, so far, by the workings of at least five *correction mechanisms*. Firstly, the EU officials, getting feedback on negative lobby impacts, frequently interfere and take some measures to deal with them. Commission officials like to get on board outside groups, MEPs include weak special interests within their intergroups, and Council ministers, being under pressure from their parliament and public opinion, lobby for keeping such domestic folklore as coffee shops and working hours. Many EU lobby groups, secondly, search for new support groups and potential clients. In the field of DG R&D policies, big companies had to make new alliances with SMEs, universities and NGOs. At the domestic level, thirdly, new protest groups may arise. In many countries now the great example of this is the national parliament, feeling itself marginalised on EU affairs. In such cases, the parliament feeds back its feelings of concern either indirectly through its government or directly, as Nordic parliaments do. Fourthly, formerly outside groups learn to organise better for EU action. The previously weak groups of consumers and workers have become respected EU lobby groups now. Groups of patients or retired people are growing in importance, and immigrant groups may follow. Finally, there is social control. If a lobby group is widely seen as misbehaving according to some notion of democracy, it easily acquires a bad reputation and an isolated position among its citizens, members or stakeholders. The fear of this boomerang is a self-correcting mechanism.

Improving EU Democracy by EU Lobbying

The relationship between lobby groups as for two reasons independent variable and EU democracy as the dependent one is more complex than could be described above. Firstly, there is the *multifinality* of lobby groups. They create more impacts than solely that upon democracy, as is shown by the following examples. By their cross-border group formations, they strengthen the integration of Europe. Their direct settlements, of irritating differences outside the EU, contribute to EU stability and their creation of standards to promoting EU economic growth and welfare. By providing information and manpower to the Commission, they promote its effectiveness and efficiency. They also have impacts upon the formation of special EU policies, such as those on the environment, agriculture or R&D, which subsequently may have positive or negative effects on EU democracy, for example by changing the openness or legitimacy of a policy domain. The lobby groups are, of course, usually driven not by the intention to create such impacts, but by their selfish ambition to win and not to lose. Selfishness thus has many side effects, including highly appreciated ones [Mandeville, 1705].

Secondly, there is the *multicausality* of EU democracy. Many more independent variables than lobby groups alone can have impacts upon it. Among them are the following three. Firstly, EU officials can and do contribute to EU democracy, as shown by the contributions of the Commission to better stakeholders' participation and public accountability, of the Parliament to discursiveness and transparency, and those of the Council, by its new treaty formation, to more limited government and EP empowerment. A second cause is mass media that barely contributes to EU democracy, or negatively rather than positively. Most media are poor observers of the EU. They hardly report about anything more than official statements, scandals and results of games surrounding decision-making, as if they are covering Eurosports instead. With such news, citizens can hardly come to reasoned judgements useful for their citizenship. Cyber-democracy might become a third cause of EU democracy in the near future [Dai and Norton, 2007; Wilhelm, 2000], but basic assumptions about cyber-communication between citizens and officials in the EU are still doubtful [Hindman, 2008].

Under consideration here, however, is not how EU democracy can or should be explained or strengthened. Given all the contested notions of democracy at the EU level, the dependent variable is still developing and not yet sufficiently stable. Not denying the importance of many other actors and factors that contribute directly or indirectly to EU democracy, we remain focused on the lobby groups as one of its important factors. Inevitably, the lobby groups contribute to a europeanization of notions of democracy. In many cases they determine practices of democracy, at least partially. Some impacts fit nicely with current notions of democracy, and can thus be considered positive. Others are potentially or truly at odds with them, but can be subject to system-bound correction mechanisms. Our leading question now is how EU democracy can *benefit more* from lobby groups, even if such a benefit is only an unintended side effect of lobbying. This big question can be downsized as follows. Can the positive impacts be strengthened and increased? Can the negative ones be reduced or blocked? Can the correction mechanisms be promoted and reinforced?

Strengthening the Positive Impacts
Referring to Figure 8.1, we conclude that lobby groups have some positive impacts on all elements of democracy, with two exceptions. One is the input method of competitive elections, and the other the throughput method of decision-making by majority vote. Most lobby groups keep their hands off these two. To the other notions they contribute, willy-nilly, positively, although with a strong *variation in behaviour*. Of course, only the active groups can contribute positively. The passive ones are irrelevant on the positive side. In the previous chapters, the established and professional groups emerged as the most important among the active groups. The established

ones, usually not falling short of resources, have not only the capacity and the drive but frequently also the invitations from officials to participate. They produce the high quantity of lobby impacts on EU democracy, both positively and negatively. Professional groups, of course being not identical to established ones, produce the best-quality impacts on democracy. Thanks to their preparatory work, they prudently manage the many limits of behaviour by, for example, supplying useful information and support to officials, promoting legitimate consensus and behaving as corporate citizens.

The positive impacts can, in consequence, be strengthened by the *triple approach* of activation, establishment and professionalization. The more the interest groups in the EU area are activated, well-established and professionalized, the more they can produce beneficial impacts on democracy. Only a few active, established and either amateurish or professional lobby groups may be a big danger to democracy, but a surplus of purely professional groups is a blessing. They can keep the system open and competitive, make the process more representative and discursive, bring the officials into the driver's seat of polyarchy and create a more developed citizenship and feedback linkage, to mention only some effects. Time is already on the side of the triple approach [Meny and others, 1996]. Increasing numbers of interest groups are becoming more active in PA management for the EU, are building up more established positions and are gaining professionalism. They do so under pressures from the perceived relevance of the EU and stronger competition from numerous other stakeholders. They are also encouraged to do so by Commission officials and MEPs that have a vested interest in active, established and professional lobbying of interest groups.

Reducing the Negative Impacts
The main negative impacts of lobbying on EU democracy, mentioned above, can be summarised as follows. Lobby groups that enter and permeate the system may set up thresholds for others, form cartels and overload it at its input side. In the throughput phase the insiders may hinder others from representing their interests, act as a closed shop, pay lip service to polyarchy and legitimate authority, and minimise discursiveness and transparency. On the output side, they may injure legitimacy, including key elements like limited government, rule of law, accountability and responsiveness. At home they may dispirit citizens, disregard the values of civil tolerance and common identity, and discredit the freedoms and the linkages of competitors. Such risks of lobbying are worries primarily among

citizens and journalists. Whether they really occur much depends on the *type of behaviour* of lobby groups. Paradoxically, also the passive interest groups contribute to them, precisely because they are passive and leave more room for action to the active ones, thus weakening the competition. In a basically open system like the EU, a threshold or closed shop, erected by the active few, can only endure if the many remain passive. Among the active groups, the many semi-established ones create the great quantity of negative impacts. Falling short of, for example, a strong organisation, an established position and a regular ticket to manoeuvre about, they are more concerned about their short-term impacts on officials and stakeholders than about anything else. In contrast, the non-established groups that play only occasionally hardly have any impact at all, while the best-established groups have most to lose in becoming the talk of the town. The qualitatively worst negative impacts, however, come from the semi-professionals with limited skills in political engineering, such as monitoring and issue reframing, or applying them nonchalantly. They try to pick flowers on the ridge by, for example, acting arrogantly, erecting thresholds to others, obstructing transparency or limiting the freedoms of others. In contrast, the real amateurs lack the skills to damage much more than their own interests, while the full professionals respect the limits of PA management in the EU prudently, as they fear the risk of boomerangs from scandals caused by allegedly undemocratic behaviour.

The negative impacts can best be reduced by the same aforementioned *triple approach*. Firstly, the more the many domestic interest groups are activated to play a role as EU lobby group, the less they provide free room to the active few. The best activation usually comes from the rank and file of interest groups and ultimately from individual citizens. After better training, even mass media and political parties, now barely part of the EU feedback loop, might contribute to that activation by making citizens more aware and concerned about their interests in the EU. Secondly, the better established the lobby groups become, the more they shall lose by creating negative impacts on democracy. Their greatest risk is of becoming scandalised and isolated and thus losing their ticket to operate. Often they feel encouraged to become professionals, which is the third key to the reduction of negative impacts. The more the lobby groups behave fully professionally, with both technical skills and a sense of prudence, the less they cause serious damage to democracy. Time, again, is already on the side of the triple approach. Public interest groups are activated by their citizens and private ones by their members or workers. Rank and file people push their board towards being better established on the EU playing-field. Well-established groups learn from each other how to avoid the pitfalls of nonchalant lobbying. On the receiving end of EU lobbying, the officials and other stakeholders, fearing any fall-out from scandals, demand more prudent behaviour.

Reinforcing the Correction Mechanisms
Of course, there will always remain some negative impacts from lobbying on EU democracy. Nobody can prevent a lobby group, wilfully or accidentally, installing an undemocratic practice or distorting an existing democratic one. Only a tyrannical system, totally unconcerned about democracy, can outlaw lobby groups, but such a system is, paradoxically, always run by a single lobby group, for example by the military, clergy or single party. In a democracy, lobby groups are an essential part of the open society [Popper, 1945]. Their positive impacts on democracy can be taken for granted and enjoyed as free benefits. Their negative impacts can be reduced by reinforcing the system-bound correction mechanisms. These mechanisms are summarised in Figure 8.2. We concluded already that the system-bound correction mechanisms are most dependent on both the quantity and quality of the active lobby groups. The higher the number of active groups, the more of them will enter EU arenas, become established, increase the competition, bring officials into the driver's seat and search for new support from outside, thus stimulating new entrants. The higher the number of better-established groups, the more of them will create the aforementioned effects continually as they care about their acquired positions and start to professionalise. The better the quality of lobby groups, the more they behave adequately, proactively and prudently, driven as they are by the double desire to win a current game and to keep their licence to play further. Of course, any increase in active, established and professional lobby groups may attract more lazy, wandering and amateurish groups as well, but as long as they behave as followers and not as leaders, they hardly endanger democracy. Many newcomers take, indeed, the more active, established and professional lobby groups as an example to follow.

Any effort to strengthen the correction mechanisms should, therefore, be focused on increasing both the quantity and the quality of the active lobby groups. The first is a matter of *stimulating participation* of all sorts of interest groups at the EU level. There is, however, hardly any need for a kind of official EU stimulation policy for this. Many interest groups already have strong desires to participate, as caused by perceived threats and opportunities. Many also feel sufficiently compelled by their competitors in the market or policy sector. The invitations from inside the EU are at most only a temporary problem, as many officials and groups inside want to get new

SELF-CORRECTING EU LOBBY DEMOCRACY

INPUT SIDE
- SCRAMBLING GROUPS OUTSIDE
- OPENINGS FROM THE INSIDE
- PROVISION OF POSITIONS

THROUGHPUT
- OFFICIALS' SELF-INTEREST
- WATCHING GROUPS
- OUTPUT ANTICIPATION

OUTPUT SIDE
- INTERNAL CONTROLS
- EXTERNAL CONTROLS
- FEEDBACK ANTICIPATION

FEEDBACK
- OFFICIAL INTERFERENCES
- LOOKING FOR SUPPORT
- PROTEST GROUPS
- NEW GROUPS
- REPUTATION

Figure 8.2

groups on board. Most obstacles to participation relate to insufficient capacity at home, as manifested by internal dissent, lack of knowledge, poor mix of resources and skills and/or a bad image. Their improvement is up to the interest group, maybe with some help from stakeholders. The second focus regards *quality improvement*. This too is strongly dependent on the quantity of lobby groups. The higher the number of active and established groups, the stronger will be both their competition that stimulates homework and the social control that stimulates prudence. The two factors together stimulate their professionalization, being ultimately in their own hands and hardly needing specific EU policy either.

To keep the system open and competitive, some watchdogs are needed. DG Competition sets the example to follow here. It rarely develops specific competition rules for different trades, but relies on general rules to keep all markets open and competitive, and it intervenes when receiving information from companies or consumers that feel hurt by market failures. A similar approach is appropriate for the political market of EU decisions. *Open entry* and *fair competition* are the two preconditions for strengthening the inbuilt correction mechanisms that subsequently promote EU democracy. To a great extent, the current state of competitive lobby groups already fulfils these two preconditions. A single or a few groups may try to close off the entrance, but the effort usually fails soon afterward, thanks to both pressures from outside and corrections from inside. A single or a few groups may also try to play tricks, but a boomerang endangering their licence to operate will usually hit them. Watchdogs are helpful in strengthening the two preconditions and, as in the case of competition policy, the best possible watchdogs are critical stakeholders and the mass media. If some closed shop or unfair practice is observed or reported, then some EU officials and stakeholders may always open doors or interfere. This can work even better once EU mass media, now still underdeveloped but facilitated by the 2008 ETI, become more serious watchdogs. Although the notions of openness and fairness still differ by arena, sector and country, they are under europeanization. Many more lobby groups, therefore, erect safety margins now. Wanting to avoid the risk of being misunderstood and thus scandalised, they become more prudent.

The idea of a basically self-regulating lobby democracy is far from new. It was well-developed by the US founding fathers in their *Federalist Papers* [1788], a misleading title to cover more centralist rule, and ever since the source of confusion about the F-word in the EU. In Paper 10, James Madison developed the following logic. A lobby group, called a faction, he considered to be a normal phenomenon of free human life. If such a selfish group is seen as devilish, then there are two possible solutions. One is to remove the causes. This can only be done either by tyrannical rule or by an equalisation of interests, which are respectively undesirable and impossible. The other solution is to reduce the negative effects of lobby groups. This can best be done by keeping the system as open and competitive as possible, which requires attracting into the system the maximum number and the highest variety of factions. In this situation they will all compete with each other. Quoting Madison: 'Extend the sphere and you take in a greater variety of parties and interests; you make it less probable that a majority of the whole will have a common motive to invade the rights of other citizens; or if such a common motive exists, it will be more difficult for all who feel it to discover their own strength and to act in union with each other.' In short: one or a few devils can best be exorcised by letting in as many different devils as possible. Then they will not become saints, of course, but human beings controlled by other human beings. This ingenious vector rather than factor approach is the solution Madison recommends. In addition, he pleads for a limited government, with many formal checks and balances, in order to prevent the state becoming a devil.

Extra: Improving EU Democracy by the Study of EU PAM

Our proposition here is that the study of PAM at the EU level can greatly contribute to EU democracy, as measured by the various notions of democracy. The better *developed* this study is and the more *widespread* its knowledge and application are, the smaller the chance of closed shops and unfair practices in real EU life. Those two conditions are inseparable. A well-developed science can be used for better or worse. Those who master it exclusively have the choice of both and can use their knowledge for either strengthening or weakening practices of democracy. But once knowledge is widely spread among many, it loses its potential to overpower others. Then, the many others can counterbalance any single master, and all together they, willy-nilly, respect each other and abstain from abuses of power. The widely diffused knowledge must, however, have a sufficiently sound scientific basis as well. If people take their beliefs or myths as knowledge or neglect chain reactions, they may cause a lot of damage as well, maybe not by criminal intent but by stupid mistakes, which is even worse according to the French politician Charles de Talleyrand-Périgord (1754-1838). In short, the *combined* development and diffusion of sound empirical knowledge about intelligent lobbying regarding the EU playing-field may enhance EU democracy.

In chapter 2, we described the state of knowledge about the EU as once widely considered unsatisfactory. Different grand theories and big concepts, mainly derived from international law and international relations, were applied to the EU. If normative rather than empirical, they hardly have explanatory power, let alone predictive value. Three new trends followed. The first is *empirical* research by more direct field observations. It shifts the intellectual interest away from the EU's skeleton to its flesh-and-blood by raising questions such as the following. What are the real facts, as found by controllable research and not refuted by evidence? What are explanatory causes or factors and their probable consequences? Which vectors might produce similar consequences? The second trend is *inductive* reasoning, thanks to field research. Which interpretation of the findings and their relationships makes sense? Is there a driving force behind it, for example the influence of lobby groups? How can this new conjecture be further tested? The final component is *mid-level theorising*. If some interpretation is repeatedly considered reliable and valid, how can it be systemised into coherent theory? The old pretension, to tell the grand story, is clearly replaced by the modest ambition to make mid-level statements. These must be reliable and valid at least for the crucial variables of some part of the EU, for example a policy sector, a type of arena or an influence approach.

Mainly younger and often American scholars have given rise to the new trends, but they were not alone. The growing family of PA practitioners who, due to their profession, want to know *how the EU really works* criticised the old body of pretentious knowledge silently, by preferring to rely on their own trials and errors and, in some advanced cases, on their own training and R&D on PAM in the EU. They discovered, for example, the work floors of the EU, mid-level Commission's officials and delegated legislation and developed their own methods of homework, Triple P, fine-tuned lobbying and more. Many of their experiences are still not discerned as potentially relevant and valid by many academics, except a few like this author. Few scholars and practitioners dare to walk over the fragile bridge between *academia* and *societas* and have organised joint meetings, activities and outlets, mentioned at the end of chapter 1. Between the two a perfect match is possible. The practitioners have real-life information based on experiences and want to get more useful knowledge, while the scholars want to gather empirical information and to deliver valid and reliable knowledge. Together they have a common interest in improving the knowledge basis of EU PAM and in supporting the new trends.

If kept exclusive, the better knowledge and insights might be used against EU democracy as well, of course. But they already tend to be rapidly disseminated among many people, particularly through four *channels of diffusion*, as indicated in chapters 1 and 6. Firstly, the growing results from research on EU PAM get wide circulation through more new books and journals, like the *Journal of Public Affairs*. Secondly, some consultants working for different lobby groups and thus gathering different experiences disseminate these insights among their clients. A few also participate in the aforementioned networks with academics for stimulating or tapping their brains. Thirdly, on a more or less commercial basis private institutions and postgraduate schools are increasingly offering open courses on EU PAM. The lecturers usually come from the same mixed networks of experienced practitioners and researching academics. Finally, there are the few university programmes with a research-based major or minor course on EU lobby behaviour. Their students get a basic taste of PA and maybe an appetite for more. However, a full programme on EU PAM still does not exist. In overview, the knowledge and insights are charting improvement and wider diffusion. Everybody can acquire them.

By contents, the channels now disseminate three *types of knowledge*. First-ly, they provide the results of research. As in a restaurant, the consumers are less interested in the cooking than in the meal. They want to know the facts of, for example, the EU work floors and the networking of various officials. Secondly, useful tools are taught. The consumers of lobby knowledge are most interested in checklists regarding, for example, the making of a long-list and its downsizing to shared-list and short-list, the assessment of the specific situation that tells 'what is best to do', the fine-tuning of lobbying or the better organisation of EU PAM on the home front. Much less interest is shown in the methodology of constructing such checklists. Thirdly, the con-tents are highly prescriptive for what is better to do or not to do. The fre-quently silent criteria are effectiveness and efficiency, as lobby groups want to know how to score better and more easily. The prescriptions are usually placed in a longer-term perspective, with attention given to chain reactions and thus with an emphasis on prudence. The contents are most focused on useful knowledge and, as such, satisfy the practitioners often more than the scholars. This threefold diffusion of practice-based knowledge and insight indicates a popularisation and democratisation of EU PAM.

There remains plenty of room for even more improvement, and two pri-orities can be suggested. First of all, the *diffusion* needs more ramified chan-nels and balanced contents. To the current channels are mainly connected private organisations with an EU-wide position, such as MNCs, MNGOs and EuroFeds. Interest groups of central, regional and local governments and small-sized private businesses and NGOs should get connected, too. Most interest groups in southern and eastern countries still lag behind in the awareness and practice of EU PAM, not to mention its body of knowl-edge. Electronic means (e-learning) and visiting scholars (travelling facul-ty) are now underused for their diffusion potential. The contents of pro-duced knowledge, besides, deserve better balance between the demand sides of practitioners and researchers. If the former would gain interest in more than only simplified results, checklists and prescriptions, and be-come eager to understand the methodology behind, they could inspire the researchers better and be rewarded with even more useful knowledge.

Secondly, the channels of diffusion should be fed with more ambitious *research agendas* [Andersen and Eliassen, 1995], such as the following three that, for the sake of this chapter, are all related to EU democracy. The first should regard the limits of EU PAM. The current knowledge on these lim-its comes more from logical thinking based on observations and experi-ences than from systematic empirical research. In particular, the limits set by the arena, receivers and environment are most relevant for the state of

EU democracy. The negative effects coming from the possible practices of closed shops and unfair competition are just one example. If the results of research refute such practices, they are useful for unmasking popular beliefs and myths. If not, they will certainly alert mass media acting as watchdogs for EU democracy and hence strengthen correction mechanisms. Once publicised, tricks simply become less effective. The second agenda should be on the question of why some sorts of interest groups, such as immigrant shopkeepers and national ministries, often fall short of activism, establishment or professionalism, three features of lobbying that have the strongest impacts on EU democracy. The results of research can help the currently passive or nonchalant interest groups to strengthen their lobby capacities, to engineer an efficient establishment and to improve their performance. As a third agenda we plea for researching the europeanization of the various notions of democracy, an agenda of classical political science which might help all stakeholders to adapt their behaviour better to the arising common norms of EU democracy.

The two general priorities of better diffusion and more research are justified here for their contributions to the broad value of EU democracy, but can be based on other values, too. As said before, EU lobbying can also contribute to values like European integration, efficient EU decision-making and/or socio-economic welfare, which can all benefit from the science of PA management in the EU. It is, however, not necessary to have any other justification for whatever study than simply 'wanting to know' or 'art for art's sake'. Yet, we advocate these two priorities of research as being especially beneficial to EU democracy.

Final Reflection before the Action

The EU is a most ambitious experiment in living together peacefully in Europe, partially or fully replacing the old practices of accommodation by resignation, leniency, war, imitation and ad-hoc negotiation. The machinery of common EU decision-making has acquired the reputation of *highest relevance*, thanks to the priority of EU law over domestic law in particular. Increasingly, all sorts of interest groups coming from the pluralistic member countries try to intervene in the workings of the machinery, which provides much openness and permeability. Frequently, lobby groups get a more or less desired outcome, being the pushed-for decision or the prevention of a feared decision. The EU officials and politicians inside the machinery widely welcome the arrival of new issues and stakeholders that give more relevant contents to their machinery. Like the lobby groups, they also make use of the vectors of europeanization, so integrating the domestic and the European level and also the public and the private sectors more than before. The EU has become a major forum for political action.

The new influence technique of *public affairs management,* and especially its professional application, is better adapted to the realities of the EU than the traditional techniques are. It is essentially based on respect for the many (frequently irritating) different values and stakeholders in any arena. However, the respect is not for the value or the stakeholder as such, but for their power of retaliation. This can best be compared with the respect that fighting soldiers, wanting to survive a risky battle, have for their armed enemies. This respect is indicated by their careful preparation for the battle and by their prudent behaviour during it. The EU lobby groups that take their PA seriously likewise want to survive. When going window-out, they are well-prepared and act prudently. They search for better ways within the labyrinth and better moments on the trampoline of EU decision-making. Unlike real soldiers and the era of Machiavelli, they cannot hope to kill off their opponents forever. They have to lobby for peace, by negotiating a deal and finding a compromise, by going window-in with crucial stakeholders and by settling issues. This is a second indicator of respect.

This approach to any EU arena, euphemistically called a playing-field, requires a lot of *reflection* for action. There are so many challenges, options, menus and dilemmas that, in comparison, the game of chess may look easy. On the home front, the lobby group has to consider the real nature of challenges and the presence of such preconditions as sufficient cohesion and a good image. The mere downsizing of the long-list of EU daydreams and nightmares to, preferably, a shared-list with realisable targets requires intense study of the playing-field. For every specific arena, one has to observe and consider the issues at stake, the stakeholders involved, the time dimensions and the arena boundaries, and also to reflect on their best management. The fieldwork is full of dilemmas, such as regarding styles of behaviour, using voice and timing activities. The numbers of potential actors to approach, factors to use and vectors to create are always too high for managing them all and thus require selectivity. The lobby process is full of limits requiring attention too. Lobby groups must be aware of all these factors while deciding intelligently.

Intelligent reflection upon action enhances the chance of success, but is *neither necessary nor sufficient* for at least some chance. A lobby group can also act by reflex or haphazardly. Then it may even, with some luck, achieve a desired outcome incidentally. However, the chances of this happening are slight and usually absent in practice. If one wants to win, or at least not lose, either one's game, one's respect from others and/or one's backing at home, one is advised to act by reflection. The more thoroughly this is done, the better the chance of success, although there are never guarantees. Reflection is always more or less imperfect, due to, for example, incomplete information, lack of time or unreliable support. Even with thorough reflection, the lobby group may be the victim of bad luck caused by an unforeseeable event, like the 1998-99 fall of the Commission Santer, the sudden rise of the 2001 issue of 'terrorism' or that of the 2008 financial crisis, to mention these high-profile cases. As bad luck can always occur, the best responses to it are scenario planning and prudency.

Reflection is not the goal, but a most *useful means* to increase the chance of more successful EU lobby activities in a specific arena. This does not imply that specific activities always have to follow. After reflection a lobby group may come to the conclusion that it can better remain passive, for instance because it considers the cost-benefit ratio of any further action to be unattractive. Then it is at least mentally active by its awareness of the current situation and its preparation for change to come. If it decides to play an active role, it has to be prepared thoroughly, which ranges from effectively organising the home front to carefully analysing the arena. Its purpose is to find and establish optimal positions regarding issues, stakeholders, moments and boundaries considered relevant. During the preparatory work, the balance of activities will gradually shift from window-out to window-in behaviour. Then the lobby group has to negotiate on issues with both stakeholders and officials, in order to become part of the winning coalition.

If the lobby group wants to find the approaches that will score the highest on efficiency (cost-benefit ratio) and effectiveness (desired outcome), it must make a substantial investment in *collecting sound information* about both its own position and the EU arena and, for gaining intelligence, reflect upon this. This investment is an ongoing activity. It must start before the action and continue both during it and afterwards. Only then the lobby group can gather information needed for making sound decisions with regard to its participation in the arena, its responses during the interactive lobbying and its primary lessons for future games. The 'best practices' are never permanently fixed but dependent on both the specific situation and new insights and thus always in development. Many lessons can also be taken from different groups lobbying on the same dossier, people working on the receiver's side or in the transmission channels, observing journalists, colleagues in PAM and academics researching lobby group behaviour. In PA, the real professionals are insatiable in their demand for enhanced knowledge and learning.

They are also *prudent* for two reasons. Firstly, every arena contains certain risks. A lobby group may become part of either the winning or the losing coalition. During the arena process it may lose old friends, get a hostile setting, be caught in issue reframing, be taken as a scapegoat, become divided on the home front or be subjected to any other experience suitable for a nightmare. It may ultimately have to live with a most undesired outcome from the EU for many years. Therefore, like soldiers wanting to survive in a risky field, professional lobby groups want to behave prudently by conscious preparation and cautious action. The second reason for prudency is that every lobby group wants to keep safe its license to operate in future arenas considered relevant. By acting prudently in every arena, the lobby group may sometimes lose part of its interest at stake, but retain its respect from others and its backing at home. If it would become the subject of controversy or scandal due to its nonchalance, it may be out of any other arena at the same time or in the near future, thus almost certainly lose more interests.

One general conclusion from all this is that *professional* lobby groups are both the most successful in influencing the EU and inadvertently greatly contribute to EU democracy, as they respect others, behave prudently and strengthen the system-bound correction mechanisms. The semi-professional or more nonchalant groups not only make more mistakes to their own disadvantage, but also care less about for example reaching a compromise, criticism from public opinion or interest groups which have long been outsiders. As semi-professionals they can learn from professionals or by trial-and-error and in due time contribute a bit to democracy. The many interest groups that remain passive for whatever reason and complain about EU outcomes and processes have the worst influence on EU democracy.

The second general conclusion is that the flowering of the *study of PAM*, being highly dependent on open and competitive democracy, also contributes significantly to this. Its results help many more groups to lobby the EU in an active, established and professional manner and diminish the possibility that only a few groups will win games, sets and matches. In conclusion, EU democracy is dependent on many groups and ultimately on many people knowing how to participate in the EU machinery of common decision-making, including how to lobby professionally. Nature has assured that most people possess more or less the same amount of brains or mental capacity, being the most important tool for acquiring the expertise in our formula $E = MI^2$ that promotes effective lobbying. They are, of course, free to leave that capacity underused or unused. Such people should

not complain about undesired EU outcomes, but address their own ignorance and nonchalance. The prevention of more such complaints has been
the educational objective of this book.

REFERENCES

Abbreviated reference to journals

APSR American Political Science Review
CEP   Comparative European Politics
CMLR Common Market Law Review
EJM   European Journal of Marketing
EJPR   European Journal of Political Research
ELJ   European Law Review
EUI   European University Institute
EUP   European Union Politics (paper series)
JCMS Journal of Common Market Studies
JEPP Journal of European Public Policy
JLS   Journal of Legislative Studies
JPA   Journal of Public Affairs
LSQ   Legislative Studies Quarterly
WEP   West European Politics

Alesina, A. and others (2002), *What does the EU do?*, Firenze: EUI (paper RSC 61).

Alkhafaji, A. (1989), *A Stakeholder Approach to Corporate Governance*. Westport: Quorum.

Almond, G. and G. Powell (1966), *Comparative Politics*. Boston: Little Brown.

Andenas, M. and A. Türk, editors (2000), *Delegated Legislation and the Role of Committees in the EC*. London: Kluwer.

Andersen, C. (1992), *Influencing the EC*. London: Kogan Page.

Andersen, S. and K. Eliassen (1995), 'EU Lobbying: The New Research Agenda', in: *EJPR*, Volume 27, 4, 427-441.

Andersen, S. and K. Eliassen, editors (1996), *The EU: How democratic is it?* London: Sage.

Andrews, L. (1996) 'The relationship of political marketing to political lobbying', in: *EJM*, Volume 30, 10, 68-91.

Antalovsky, E. and others, editors (2005), *Cities in Europe, Europe in the Cities*. Vienna: Europaforum.

Archer, C. (2004), *Norway Outside the EU*. London: Routledge.

Arnull, A. (2006), *The EU and its Court of Justice*. Oxford: Oxford University Press.

Auel, K and A. Benz, editors (2005), 'The Europeanization of Parliamentary Democracy', in special issue *JLS*, Volume 11, 3-4, 303-421.

Auel, K. (2007), 'Democratic Accountability and National Parliaments' Scrutiny in EU Affairs', *ELJ*, Volume 13, 4, 487-504.

Bache, I. and A. Jordan, editors (2006), *The Europeanization of British Politics*. Basingstoke: Palgrave.

Bache, I. (2008), *Europeanization and Multilevel Governance*. Lanham: Rowman and Littlefield.

Badiello, L. (1998), 'Regional Offices in Brussels', in Claeys and others (1998), 328-344.

Bainbridge, T. (2002), *Penguin Companion to the EU*. London: Penguin, 3rd edition.

Baines, P. and Egan J. (2004), 'Political Marketing', in special issue *JPA*, Volume 4, 3, 218-299.

Baines, P. and Ph. Harris, editors (2006), 'Corporate Social Responsibility', in special issue *JPA*, Volume 6, 3-4, 171-307.

Bauer, R. and I. De Sola Pool (1960), *American Businessmen and International Trade*. Glencoe: Free Press.

Bauer, R. and others (1963), *American Business and Public Policy*. New York: Atheston.

Bauer, M. (2008), 'Reforming the European Commission', in special issue *JEPP*, Volume 15, 5, 625-780.

Baumgartner, F. (2007), 'EU Lobbying: A View from US', in *JEPP*, Volume 14, 3, 482-288.

Beach, D. and C. Mazzucelli (2007), *Leadership in the Big Bangs of European Integration*. Basingstoke: Palgrave.

Beach, D. and T. Christiansen, editors (2007), 'Political Agency in the Constitutional Politics of EU', in special issue *JEPP*, Volume 14, 8, 1163-1332.

Beetham, D. and Lord, C. (1998), *Legitimacy and the EU*. London: Longman.

Bellier, I. (1997), 'The Commission as an Actor: An anthropologist's view', in Wallace and Young (1997), 91-115.

Beloe, S. and others (2003), *The 21st Century NGO*. London: Sustainability.com.

Bergström, C. (2005), *Comitology*. Oxford: Oxford University Press.

Berkhout, J. and D. Lowery (2008), 'Counting Organised Interests in EU: A comparison of data sources', in *JEPP*, Volume 15, 4, 489-513.

Bertók, J. (2008), *Lobbyists, Governments and Public Trust*. Paris: OECD.

Bertrand, G. and others (1999), *Scenarios Europe 2010*. Brussels: European Commission (working paper Forward Studies Unit).

Beyers, J. and B. Kerremans (2007), 'Critical Resource Dependencies and the Europeanization of Domestic Interest Groups', in Coen (2007), 128-149.

Bindi, M. (1998), 'The Committee of the Regions', in Van Schendelen (1998), 225-249.

Binnema, H. (2009), *How parties change*, Amsterdam: Free University (Ph.D. thesis).

Birch, A. (1971), *Representation*. London: Pall Mall.

Bisson, T., editor, (1973), *Medieval Representative Institutions*. Hinsdale: Dryden.

Borragán, N. (2003), 'The EU organisation of Central and Eastern European Business Interests', in Greenwood, 2003, 213-225.

Borrás, S., editor (2004), 'The open Method of Co-ordination and EU Governance', special issue *JEPP*, Volume 11, 2, 181-337.

Boucher, S. (2004), *Europe and its Think-tanks*. Paris: Notre Europe.

Bouwen, P. (2007), 'Competing for Consultation: The Commission and Parliament', in *WEP*, Volume 30, 2, 265-284.

Bradley, K. (1992), 'Comitology and the Law: Through a Glass, Darkly', in *CMLR*, Volume 29, 4, 693-721.

Bradley, K. (1998), 'The GMO Committee on Transgenic Maize', in Van Schendelen (1998), 207-222.

Brandsma, G. (2010), *Backstage Europe: Comitology, accountability and democracy*, Utrecht University (Ph.D. thesis).

Braun, D. and F. Gilardi, editors (2005), *Delegation in Contemporary Democracies*. London: Routledge.

Brecht, A. (1959), *Political Theory*. Princeton: Princeton University Press.

Broscheid, A. and D. Coen (2007), 'Lobbying activity and fora creation', in *JEPP*, Volume 14, 3, 346-385.

Brown, J. (1979), *The Business of Issues*. New York: Conference Board.

Buchholz, R. (1990), *Essentials of Public Policy for Management*. Englewood Cliffs: Prentice Hall, 2nd edition.

Bugdahn, S. (2008), 'Travelling to Brussels via Aarhus', in *JEPP*, Volume 15, 4, 588-606.

Bull, M. and M. Rhodes (2007), 'Italy: A contested polity', in special issue *WEP*, Volume 30, 4.

Bulmer, S. and C. Lequesne, editors, (2005), *The Member States of the EU*. Oxford: Oxford University Press.

Bunyan, T. (1999), *Secrecy and Openness in the EU*. London: Kogan Page.

Burns, C. (2004), 'Codecision and the European Communities', in *JEPP*, Volume 11, 1, 1-18.

Burson Marsteller (2001), *A Guide to Effective Lobbying of the European Parliament*. Brussels: BKSH.

Burson Marsteller (2003), *A Guide to Effective Lobbying of the European Commission*. Brussels: BKSH.

Burson Marsteller (2005), *The Definitive Guide to Lobbying the European Institutions*. Brussels: BKSH.

Calori, R. and P. Lawrence, editors (1991), *The Business of Europe*. London: Sage.

Caporaso, J. (1974), *Structure and Function of European Integration*. Pacific Palisades: Goodyear.

Carrol, A. (1989), *Business and Society: Ethics and Stakeholders Management*. Cincinnati: South Western.

Cawson, A. (1995), 'Public Policies and Private Interests: The role of business interests in determining Europe's future television system', in Greenwood (1995), 49-61.

Cawson, A. (1997), 'Big Firms as Political Actors', in: Wallace and Young (1997), 185-205.

Chadwick, A. and P. Howard, editors (2008), *Handbook of Internet Politics*. London: Routledge.

Cherry, C. (1966), *On Human Communication*. Cambridge: MIT Press.

Christiansen, T. and others, editors (1999), 'The Social Construction of Europe', in special issue *JEPP*, Volume 6, 3, 527-719.

Christiansen, T. and S. Piattoni, editors (2003), *Informal Governance in the EU*. Cheltenham: Elgar.

Christiansen, T. and T. Larsson., editors (2007), *The Role of Committees in the EU Policy Process*. Cheltenham: Elgar.

Christiansen, T. and S. Vanhoonacker (2008), 'The Council Secretariat', in *WEP*, Volume 31, 4, 731-770.

Chryssochaou, D. (2001), *Theorizing European Integration*. London: Sage.

Church, C. editor (2006), *Switzerland and the EU*. London: Routledge.

Cichowski, R. (2007), *The European Court and Civil Society*. Oxford: Oxford University Press.

Circa (2008), *Political and Economic Dictionary of Central and South-Eastern Europe*. London: Routledge.

Claeys, P. and others, editors (1998), *Lobbying, Pluralism and European Integration*. Brussels: EIP.

Closa C. and P. Heywood (2004), *Spain and the EU*. Basingstoke: Palgrave.

Coakley, J. and M. Gallagher (2004), *Politics of Ireland*. London: Routledge.

Coen, D. (1998), *The Large Firm as a Political Actor in the EU*. London: Routledge.

Coen, D., editor (2007), *EU Lobbying: Empirical and Theoretical Studies*. London: Routledge (also special issue *JEPP*, 2007, Volume 14, 3, 333-488).

COM (European Commission)...
- *Eurobarometer: Public Opinion in the EU*, bi-annual.
- *Europe in Figures*, periodical.
- *General Report*, annual.
- (2001), *European Governance*, Brussels (white paper).

ComRes (annual survey), *The State of PA*. London: www.comres.eu.com.

Coplin, W. and M. O'Leary (1976), *Everyman's Prince*. North Scituate: Duxbury (2nd ed.).

Coplin, W. and M. O'Leary (1983), *Political Analysis through the Prince System*. New York: PSA.

Corbett, R., P. Jacobs and M. Shackleton, (2007), *The European Parliament*. London: Harper, 7th edition.

Coser, L. (1956), *The Functions of Social Conflict*. London: Routledge.

Cotta, M. and L. Verzichelli (2007), *Political Institutions in Italy*. Oxford: Oxford University Press.

Culpepper, P. and others, editors (2006), *Changing France*. Basingstoke: Palgrave.

Daemen, H. and M. Van Schendelen (1998), 'The Advisory Committee on Safety, Hygiene and Health Protection at Work', in Van Schendelen (1998), 129-147.

Dahl, R. (1971), *Polyarchy*. New Haven: Yale University Press.

Dahl, R. (1989), *Democracy and its Critics*. New Haven: Yale University Press.

Dahl, R. (1991), *Modern Political Analysis*. Englewood Cliffs: Prentice Hall (5th ed.).

Dai, X. and P. Norton, editors (2007), 'The Internet and Parliamentary Democracy in Europe', special issue *JLS*, Volume 13, 3.

Daviter, F. (2007), 'Policy Framing in EU', in *JEPP*, Volume 14, 4, 654-666.

Dean, J. and R. Schwindt (1981) *Business, Government and Society: Reading Lists and Course Outlines*. Durham: Eno River Press.

De Callières, M. (1716), *On the Manner of Negotiating with Princes*. (edition University Press of America, Washington, 1963).

Deckmyn, V. and I. Thomson, editors (1998), *Openness and Transparency in the EU*. Maastricht: EIPA.

De Groof, R., editor (2008), *Brussels and Europe*. Brussels: ASP.

Delhey, J. (2007), 'Analysis of Trust between EU Nationalities', in *JCMS*, Volume 45, 2, 253-279.

Demmke, C. and others (2007), *Regulating Conflict of Interest for Holders of Public Office in EU*. Brussels: Commission (BEPA).

Dermody, J. and D. Wring, editors (2001), 'Political Marketing', special issue *JPA*, Volume 1, 3, 198-280.

De Schutter, O. and others (2001), *Governance in the EU*. European Commission, Brussels.

Deutsch, K. (1963), *The Nerves of Government*. New York: Free Press.

De Vreeze, C. (2007), *The role of media and news in embedding Europe*. The Hague: WRR.

Dinan, D., editor, (2000), *Encyclopedia of the European Union*. London: Macmillan.

Dinan, D. (2006), *Ever Closer Union*. Basingstoke: Palgrave.

Dostal, J. (2004), 'Campaigning of Expertise: the OECD' in *JEPP*, Volume 13, 3, 440-460.

Drake, H., editor (2005), *French relations with EU*. London: Routledge.

Dryzek, J. and S. Niemeyer (2008), 'Discursive Representation', in *APSR*, Volume 102, 4, 481-494.

Duina, F. and P. Kurzer (2004), 'Smoke in Your Eyes', in *JEPP*, Volume 11, 1, 57-77.

Dyson, K (2003), 'The Europeanisation of German Governance', in Padgett and others (2003), 161-183.

Easton, D. (1965), *A Systems Analysis of Political Life*. New York: Wiley.

EC Committee (1994), *Issue Management Summary*. Brussels: American Chamber.

Eckstein, H. (1971), *The Evaluation of Political Performance*. London: Sage.

Eilstrup-Sangiovanni, M., editor (2006), *Debates on European Integration*. Basingstoke: Palgrave.

Eising, R. (2004), 'Multinational Governance and Business Interests in EU', in *Governance*, Volume 17, 2, 211-245.

Eising, R. (2007), 'Access of business interests to EU institutions', in *JEPP*, Volume 14, 3, 384-403.

Elgie, R. (2003), *Political Institutions in Contemporary France*. Oxford: Oxford University Press.

Elgström, O. and Smith, M., editors (2000), 'Negotation and Policy-making in the EU', special issue *JEPP*, Volume 7, 5, 673-834.

Elgström, O., editor (2003), *EU Council Presidency*. London: Routledge.

Emerson, M. and others (1988), *The Economics of 1992*. Oxford: Oxford University Press.

EP/ European Parliament (2003), *Lobbying in the EU*. Brussels: AFCO 104.

EPAD (annually), *European Public Affairs Directory*. London: Dods.

Epstein, R. and U. Sedelmeier, editors (2008), 'Postcommunist Europe after Enlargement', special issue *JEPP*, Volume 15, 6.

Eulau, H. and K. Prewitt (1973), *Labyrinths of Democracy*. Indianapolis: Bobbs-Merrill.

EurActiv (2009-A), *Corporate Survey 2009*. Brussels: EurActiv.

– (2009-B), *Federations Survey 2009*. Brussels: EurActiv.

– (2009-C), *Consultancies Survey 2009*. Brussels: EurActiv.

– (2009-D), *PA Memberships*. Brussels: Euractiv.

– (2009-E), *What do EU actors think of ETI?* Brussels: Euractiv.

Eurobarometer: see COM.

Featherstone K and C. Radaelli, editors (2003), *Politics of Europeanisation*. Oxford: Oxford University Press.

Fine, R. and S. Rai, editors (1997), *Civil Society: Democratic Perspectives*. London: Frank Cass.

Fleischer, C. (2007), 'Developing the PA Knowledge Body', in *JPA*, Volume 7, 3, 281-290.

Fligstein, N. and J. McNichol (1998), 'The Institutional Terrain of the EU', in Sandholtz and Sweet (1998), 59-91.

Fligstein, N and A. Sweet (2001), 'Institutionalizing the Treaty of Rome', in Sweet and others (2001), 29-55.

Flora, P. (1988), *Growth to Limits: Unity and Diversity*. New York: Walter De Gruyter.

Flora, P. and others (2005), *European Regions*. Basingstoke: Palgrave.

Fombrun, C. and C. Van Riel (2007), *Implementing Practices for Effective Reputation Management*. London: Routledge.

Fouilleux, E. and others (2007), 'Council Working Groups', in Christiansen and Larsson (2007), 96-119.

Franchino F. and C. Radaelli, editors (2004), 'Europeanisation and the Italian Political System', special issue of *JEPP*, Volume 11, 6, 941-1111.

Franchino, F. (2007), *The Powers of the Union*. Cambridge: COP.

Frederick, W. and others (1996), *Businessmen and Society*. New York: Mc-Graw (6th edition).

Freeman, R. (1984), *Strategic Management: A Stakeholder Approach*. Boston: Pitman.

Friedrich, C. (1963), *Man and his Government*. New York: McGraw-Hill.

Friedrich, C. (1974), *Limited Government*. Englewood Cliffs: Prentice Hall.

Fullinwider, R. (1999), *Civil Society*. Lanham: Roman and Littlefield.

Galston, W. (1999), 'Value Pluralism and Liberal Political Theory', in *APSR*, Volume 93, 4, 769-778.

Gardner, J. (1991), *Effective Lobbying in the EC*. Boston: Kluwer.

Geddes, A. (2004), *The EU and British Politics*. London: Palgrave.

George, S. (2000), *An Awkward Partner: Britain in the EC*. Oxford: Oxford University Press.

George, S. and I. Bache (2001), *Politics in the EU*. Oxford: Oxford University Press.

Geuijen, K. and others (2008), *The New Eurocrats*. Amsterdam: Amsterdam University Press.

Giddings, P. and G. Drewry (2004), *Britain and the EU*. London: Palgrave.

Gigerenzer, G. and others (1989), *The Empire of Change*. Cambridge: Cambridge University Press.

Goodhart, M. (2007), 'EU as Challenge for Democracy', *Perspectives on Politics*, Volume 5, 3, 567-584.

Gorges, M. (1996), *Euro-corporatism?* Lanham: University Press of America.

Gornitzka, A. and U. Sverdrup (2008), 'Who consults? Expert Groups in EU', in *WEP*, Volume 31, 4, 725-750.

Gottweis, H. (1999), 'Regulating genetic engineering in the EU', in Kohler-Koch and Eising (1999), 61-82.

Grabbe, H. (2005), *The EU's Transformative Power*. Basingstoke: Palgrave.

Grant, W. (1989), *Pressure Groups, Politics and Democracy in Britain*. London: Philip Allan.

Grant, W. (2003), 'Trust: a sceptical view', in Greenwood 2003, 197-204.

Graziano, P. and M. Vink, editors (2007), *Europeanization: New Research Agendas*. Basingstoke: Palgrave.

Green, S. and others (2007), *The Politics of the New Germany*. London: Routledge.

Greene, R. (1998), *The 48 Laws of Power*. London: Profile Books.

Greene, R. (2003), *The Art of Seduction*. London: Profile Books.

Greenwood, J. and others, editors (1992), *Organised Interests and the EC*. London: Sage.

Greenwood, J., editor (1995), *European Casebook on Business Alliances*. Englewood Cliffs: Prentice Hall.

Greenwood, J. and M. Aspinwall, editors (1998), *Collective Action in the EU*. London: Routledge.

Greenwood, J., editor (2003), *Change in EU Business Associations*. Basingstoke: Palgrave.

Greenwood, J. (2007), *Interest Representation in the EU*. Basingstoke: Palgrave (2nd edition).

Greer, S. and others (2008), 'Mobilizing Bias in Europe', in *EUP*, Volume 9, 403-433.

Griffin, J. (2005), 'The Empirical Study of Public Affairs', in Harris and Fleisher (2005), 458-480.

Griffith, S., editor (1963), *Sun Tze: The Art of War*. Oxford: Oxford University Press.

Grossman, E., editor (2007), 'France and the EU', special issue *JEPP*, Volume 14, 7, 983-1150.

Guéguen, D. (2007), *European Lobbying*. Brussels: Europolitics.

Guyomarch, A. and others (1998), *France in the EU*. London: Macmillan.

Haas, E. (1958), *The Uniting of Europe*. Stanford: Stanford University Press.

Häge, F. (2007), 'Who decides in the Council of EU?' in *JCMS*, Volume 46, 3, 533-558.

Häge, F. (2008), *Decision-making in the EU Council: The role of committees*. Leiden University (Ph.D. thesis).

Hagemann, S. and J. Declerck (2007), *Old Rules, New Game: Council Decision-making after 2004 Enlargement*. Brussels: CEPS.

Halman, L. and others, editors (2005), *Atlas of European Values*. Leiden: Brill.

Hanf, K. and B. Soetendorp, editors (1998), *Adapting to European Integration*. London: Longman.

Harris, P. and others, editors (2000), *Machiavelli, Marketing and Management*. London: Routledge.

Harris, P. and C. Fleisher, editors (2005), *Handbook of Public Affairs*. London: Sage.

Haverland, M. and M. Romeijn (2007), 'The EU Transposition Deficit', in *Public Administration*, Volume 85, 3, 757-778.

Hayes-Renshaw, T. and H. Wallace (2006), *The Council of Ministers*. London: Macmillan (2nd edition).

Hayward, J. and A. Menon, editors (2003), *Governing Europe*. Oxford: Oxford University Press.

Heath, R. (1997), *Strategic Issues Management*. London: Sage.

Heisenberg, D. (2005), 'Consensus in the European Council', in *EJPR*, Volume 44, 65-90.

Heisenberg, D. (2008), 'How should we best study the Council of Ministers?', in Naurin and Wallace (2008), 261-276.

Held, D. (1996), *Models of Democracy*. Oxford: Polity Press.

Henning, C. (2004), 'Modelling the Political Influence of Interest Groups', in Warntjen and Wonka (2004), 94-112.

Heslop, L., editor (2005), 'GMO Food Concerns', special issue *JPA*, Volume 5, 3-4, 193-345.

Hindman, M. (2008), *The Myth of Digital Democracy*. Princeton: Princeton University Press.

Hirschman, A. (1970), *Exit, Voice and Loyalty*. Cambridge: Harvard University Press.

Hix, S. (1999), *The Political System of the EU*. London: Macmillan.

Hix, S. and others, editors (2003), 'Fifty Years of Research on the EP', special issue *JCMS*, Volume 41, 2, 191-353.

Hix, S. (2005), *Political System of EU*. Basingstoke: Palgrave.

Hix, S. and others (2007), *Democratic Politics in the EP*. Cambridge: Cambridge University Press.

Hix, S. and A. Noury (2009), 'Voting Patterns in the Sixth EP', in *LSQ*, Volume 34, 2, 159-174.

Hoffman, S. (1963), 'Discord in Community', in: Wilcox and Haviland (1963), 3-31.

Hojnack, M. and D. Kimball (1998), 'Organized Interests and the Decision of Whom to Lobby in Congress', in: *APSR*, Volume 92, 4, 775-790.

Hooghe, L. and G. Marks (2008), 'European Union', in *WEP*, Volume 31, 1, 108-129.

Howell, K. (2000), *Discovering the Limits of European Integration: Applying grounded theory*. Huntington: Nova.

Hudock, A. (1999), *NGOs and Civil Society*. Oxford: Polity Press.

Hume, D. (1748), *An Enquiry Concerning Human Understanding*. London: Cadell.

Hunger, J. and T. Wheelen (1998), *Strategic Management*. Reading: Addison Wesley (6th edition).

Hurwitz, L., editor, (1980), *Contemporary Perspectives on European Integration*. London: Aldwyck.

Huxham, C., editor, (1996), *Creating Collaborative Advantage*. London: Sage.

Illia, L. (2003), 'Passage to cyberactivism', in *JPA*, Volume 3, 4, 326-337.

Jans, J. and others (2007), *Europeanization of Public Law*. Groningen: Kluwer.

John, S. (2002), *The Persuaders: When lobbyists matter*. Basingstoke: Palgrave.

Johnson, D. (2008), *Handbook of Political Management*. London: Routledge.

Jordan, A. (1997), *The Protest Business*. Manchester: Manchester University Press.

Jordan, A. and W. Maloney (1996), 'How Bumblebees Fly: Accounting for Public Interest Participation', in: *Political Studies*, Volume 44, 4, 668-685.

Jordan, A. and others (1999), 'Innovative and Responsive? A longitudinal analysis of the speed of EU environmental policymaking 1967-1997', in: *JEPP*, Volume 6, 3, 376-398.

Jørgensen, K. (1997), 'Studying European Integration in the 1990s', in: *JEPP*, Volume 4, 3, 486-492.

Judge, D. (2005), *Political Institutions of the UK*. Oxford: Oxford University Press.

Judge, D. and D. Earnshaw (2008), *The European Parliament*. Basingstoke: Palgrave.

Karr, K. (2006), *Democracy and Lobbying in EU*. Frankfurt: Campus.

Kassim, H. and others, editors (2000), *The National Co-ordination of EU Policy* (Volume I). Oxford: Oxford University Press.

Kassim, H. and others, editors (2001), *The National Co-ordination of EU Policy* (Volume II). Oxford: Oxford University Press.

Kassim, H. (2003), 'The European Administration: Between Europeanization and Domestication', in Hayward and Menon (2003), 139-161.

Katz, R. and B. Wessels, editors (1999), *The EP, the National Parliaments and European Integration*. Oxford: Oxford University Press.

Keading, M. (2006), 'Rapporteurship Assignment in the EP', in *JLS*, Volume 11, 1, 82-104.

Keessen, A. (2009), *European Administrative Decision*. Groningen: Europa Law.

Keohane, R. and S. Hoffmann, editors (1991), *The New European Community: Decision-making and Institutional Change*. Boulder: Westview Press.

Key, V. (1964), *Politics, Parties and Pressure Groups*. New York: Crowell.

King, P. (1976), *Toleration*. London: Allan and Unwin.

Kingdon, J. (1984), *Agendas, Alternatives and Public Policies*. Boston: Little Brown.

Klingemann, H. and D. Fuchs, editors (1995), *Citizens and the State*. Oxford: Oxford University Press.

Knapp, A. and V. Wright (2006), *The Government and Politics of France*. London: Routledge (5th edition).

Knoke, D., editor (1996), *Comparing Policy Networks*. Cambridge: Cambridge University Press.

Kobrin, S. (1982), *Managing Political Risk Assessment*. Berkeley: California.

Koeppl, P. (2001), 'The acceptance, relevance and dominance of lobbying the EU Commission', in: *JPA*, Volume 1, 1, 69-80.

Kohler-Koch, B. (1998), 'Organised Interests in the EU and the EP', in Claeys and others (1998), 126-158.

Kohler-Koch, B. and R. Eising, editors (1999), *The Transformation of Governance in the EU*. London: Routledge.

Kohler-Koch, B., editor (2003), *Linking EU and National Governance*. Oxford: Oxford University Press.

König, T. and others (2006), 'Quantifying European Legislative Research', in *EUP*, Volume 7, 4, 553-574.

König, T. (2008), 'Analysing the Process of EU Decision-making', in *EUP*, Volume 9, 1, 145-165.

Krasner, S. (1999), *Sovereignty: Organized Hypocrisy*. Princeton: Princeton University Press.

Krislov, S. (1974), *Representative Bureaucracy*. Englewood Cliffs: Prentice Hall.

Krouwel, A. (2003), 'Measuring Presidentialism and Parliamentarism', in: *Acta Politica*, Volume 38, 4, 333-364.

Kurpas, S. and others (2008), *The European Commission after Enlargement*. Brussels: CEPS.

LaGro, E. and K. Joergensen, editors (2007), *Turkey and EU*. Basingstoke: Palgrave.

Lahusen, C. (2004), 'Social Movement Organisation at the EU', in *Mobilisation*, Volume 9, 1, 55-71.

Larsson, T. (2003), *Precooking in the EU*. Stockholm: ESO.

Larsson, T. and J. Murk (2007), 'The Commission's relations with expert groups', in Christiansen and Larsson (2007), 64-95.

Laurencell, S. (1979), *Lobbying and Interest Groups: A Selected Annotated Bibliography*. Washington DC: Congressional Research Service.

Legendre, A. (1993), 'The State's Power under Pressure', in Van Schendelen (1993), 51-66.

Leonard, M. (1999), *Networks Europe*. London: Foreign Policy Centre.

Lewis, J. (2000), 'The methods of community in EU decision-making and administrative rivalry', in: *JEPP*, Volume 7, 2, 261-289.

Lijphart, A. (1997), *Democracy in Plural Societies*, New Haven: Yale University Press.

Lindberg, L. (1963), *The Political Dynamics of European Economic Integration*, Stanford CA: Stanford University Press.

Lindberg, L. (1970), 'Political Integration as a Multidimensional Phenomenon', in *International Organization*, Volume 24, 4, 649-731.

Lindberg, B. and others, editors (2008), 'The Role of Political Parties', in special issue *JEPP*, Volume 15, 8, 1107-1265.

Lindblom, C. and Cohen, D. (1979), *Usable Knowledge*. New Haven: Yale University Press.

Linsenmann, I. and others (2007), *Economic Government of EU*. Basingstoke: Palgrave.

Lintner, P. and B. Vaccari (2007), 'Comitology and EP's Scrutiny', in Christiansen and Larsson (2007), 201-226.

Loewenstein, K. (1973), *The Governance of Rome*. The Hague: Nijhoff.

Lord, C. (1998), *Democracy in the EU*. Sheffield: Sheffield Academic Press.

Loughlin, J., editor, (2001), *Subnational Democracy in the EU*. Oxford: Oxford University Press.

Luitwieler, S. (2009), *The Black Box of Nice Treaty Negotiations*. Rotterdam: Erasmus University (Ph.D. thesis).

Luttbeg, N., editor, (1968), *Public Opinion and Public Policy*. Homewood: Dorsey.

Machiavelli, N. (1513), *The Prince*. Edited by A. Gilbert (1964), New York: Hendricks House.

Magone, J. (2008), *Contemporary Spanish Politics*. London: Routledge.

Maloney, W. and G. Jordan (1997), 'The Rise of Protest Business in Britain', in Van Deth (1997), 107-124.

Mandeville, B. (1705), *The Fable of the Bees: Private Vices, Public Benefits*. London: Garman (1934).

Marks, G. and others, editors (1996), *Governance in the EU*. London: Sage.

Marks, G. and others (2002), 'What do subnational offices think they are doing in Brussels?', in *Regional and Federal Studies*, Volume 12, 3, 1-23.

Marshall, A. (2005), 'Europeanization at the Urban Level', in *JEPP*, Volume 12, 4, 668-686.

Matthews, D. and J. Stimson (1975), *Yeas and Nays: Normal decision-making in the US House of Representatives*. New York: Wiley.

Mattila, M. and J. Lane (2001), 'Why unanimity in Council?', in *EUP*, Volume 2, 1, 31-52.

Maull, H., editor (2006), *Germany's Uncertain Power*. Basingstoke: Palgrave.

Mayes, D., editor (1992), *The European Challenge: Industry's response to 1992*. London: Harvester Wheatsheaf.

Mazey, S. and J. Richardson, editors (1993), *Lobbying in the EC*. Oxford: Oxford University Press.

McCormick, J. (1999), *Understanding the EU*. London: Macmillan.

McDonagh, B. (1998), *The Paradox of Europe: An account of the negotiation of the Treaty of Amsterdam*. Dublin: Europe House.

McElroy, G. (2006), 'Committee Representation in the EP', in *EUP*, Volume 7, 1, 5-29.

McGowan, L. and D. Phinnemore, editors (2006), *Dictionary of the EU*. London: Routledge (3rd edition).

McGrath, C. (2005-A), *Lobbying in Washington, London and Brussels*. Ceredigion: Edward Mellen.

McGrath, C. (2005-B), 'Towards a lobbying profession', in *JPA*, Volume 5, 2, 124-135.

McGrath, C. (2007), 'Persuasive communication', in *JPA*, Volume 7, 3, 269-281.

McGrath, C. (2008), 'Development and Regulation of Lobbying in New EU Member-states', in *JPA*, Volume 8, 1-2, 15-32.

McLaren, L. (2006), *Identity, Interests and Attitudes to European Integration*. Basingstoke: Palgrave.

McLaughlin, A. (1994), 'ACEA and the EU-Japan Car Dispute', in Pedler and Van Schendelen (1994), 149-166.

Meerts, P. and F. Cede, editors (2004), *Negotiating European Union*. Basingstoke: Palgrave.

Meny, Y. and others, editors (1996), *Adjusting to Europe*. London: Routledge.

Meunier-Aitsahalia, S. and G. Ross (1993), 'Democratic Deficit or Democratic Surplus', in: *French Politics and Society*, Volume 11, 4, 57-69.

Michalowitz, I. (2007), 'What determines influence?', in *JEPP*, Volume 14, 1, 132-151.

Milbrath, L. (1963), *The Washington Lobbyists*. Chicago: Rand MacNally.

Milbrath, L. and M. Goel (1977), *Political Participation*. Chicago: Rand MacNally.

Mitchell, R. and others (1997), 'Toward a theory of stakeholder identification and salience', in: *Academy of Management Review*, Volume 22, 4, 853-896.

Moravcsik, A. (2000), 'Integration Theory', in Dinan (2000), 278-291.

Morgenthau, H. and K. Thompson (1985), *Politics among Nations*. New York: Knopf, 6th edition.

Naurin, D. and H. Wallace, editors (2008), *Unveiling the Council of EU*. Basingstoke: Palgrave.

Neunreither, K. and A. Wiener, editors (2000), *European Integration after Amsterdam*. Oxford: Oxford University Press.

Neyer, J. (2000), 'Justifying Comitology: The Promise of Deliberation', in Neunreither and Wiener (2000), 112-128.

Neyer, J. (2004), 'Explaining the unexpected in EU decision-making', in *JEPP*, Volume 11, 1, 19-38.

Nicolaides, P. and A. Suren (2007), 'Rule of Law in EU: What numbers say', in *Eipascope*, 1, 33-39.

Niemann, A. (2006), *Explaining Decisions in EU*. Cambridge: Cambridge University Press.

Norris, P. (1999), 'The Political Regime', in Schmitt and Thomassen (1999), 74-89.

Nowak, T. (2007), *The Influence of the ECJ on the EU's Legislative Process*. Groningen: University (Ph.D. thesis).

Nownes, A.J. (1999), 'Solicited Advice and Lobbyist Power: Evidence from three American States', in *LSQ*, 24, 113-123.

Nugent, N. (2003), *Government and Politics of the EU*. Basingstoke: Palgrave (5th edition).

Nugent, N. (2006), *Government and Politics of the EU*. Basingstoke: Palgrave (6th edition).

Nugent, N. (2001), *The European Commission*. Basingstoke: Palgrave.

Nutt, P. (1999), 'Surprising but true: Half the decisions in organisations fail', in *Academy of Management Executive*, Volume 13, 4, 75-90.

O'Brennan, J. and T. Raunio, editors (2007), *National Parliaments in the Enlarged EU*. London: Routledge.

O'Shaughnessy, N. (1990), *The Phenomenon of Political Marketing*. London: Macmillan.

Padgett, S. and others, editors (2003), *Developments in German Politics*. Basingstoke: Palgrave.

Page, E. (1997), *People Who Run Europe*. Oxford: Clarendon.

Papadimitriou, D. and D. Phinnemore (2008), *Romania and EU*. London: Routledge.

PARG (1981), *Public Affairs Offices and Their Functions*. Boston: University.

Pari, I. (2003), 'Members from the South in EU Associations', in Greenwood (2003), 207-212.

Pateman, C. (1970), *Participation and Democratic Theory*. Cambridge: Cambridge University Press.

Patterson, L. (2000), 'Biotechnology Policy', in Wallace and Wallace (2000), 317-344.

Pedler, R. and M. Van Schendelen, editors (1994), *Lobbying the EU*. Aldershot: Dartmouth.

Pedler, R. (1994), 'The Fruit Companies and the Banana Trade Regime', in Pedler and Van Schendelen (1994), 67-92.

Pedler, R. and G. Schaefer, editors (1996), *Shaping European Law and Policy: The Role of Committees and Comitology in the Political Process*. Maastricht: EIPA.

Pedler, R. (2002), *European Union Lobbying*. Basingstoke: Palgrave.

Pennings, P. (2006), 'Empirical Analysis of the Europeanization of National Party Manifestos 1960- 2003', in *EUP*, Volume 7, 2, 257-270.

Pennock, J. and J. Chapman, editors (1968), *Representation*. New York: Atherton.

Peters, B. and V. Wright (2001), 'National co-ordination of European policy-making: Negotiating the quagmire', in Richardson (2001), 155-178.

Peterson, J. (2001), 'The Choice for EU Theorists', in: *EJPR*, Volume 39, 3, 289-318.

Pierre, J. and Peters, B. (2000), *Governance, Politics and the State*. London: Macmillan.

Pijnenburg, A. (1998), 'EU lobbying by ad-hoc coalition', in *JEPP*, Volume 5, 2, 303-321.

Pinder, J., editor, (1999), *Foundations of Democracy in the EU*. London: Macmillan.

Pitkin, H. (1967), *The Concept of Representation*. Berkeley: California University Press.

Pitkin, H., editor (1969), *Representation*. New York: Atherton.

Poguntke, T. and others, editors (2006), *Europeanization of National Political Parties*. London: Routledge.

Pollack, M., editor (2000), 'Democracy and Constitutionalism in the EU', in *ECSA Review*, Volume 13, 2, 2-7.

Pollack, M. (2005), 'Theorizing EU Policy-making', in Wallace and others (2005), 13-48.

Pollak, J. (2007), 'Contested meanings or representation', in *CEP*, Volume 5, 87-103.

Popper, K. (1945), *The Open Society and its Enemies*. London: Routledge and Kegan Paul.

Priestly, J. (2008), *Six Battles that Shaped Europe's Parliament*. London: Harper.

Raffone, P., editor (2006), *Italian Lobbies in Brussels*. Brussels: CIPI.

Randall, H. (1996), *A Business Guide to Lobbying in the EU*. London: Cartermill.

Rasmussen, A. (2008), 'The EU Conciliation Committee', in *EUP*, Volume 9, 1, 87-113.

Raunio, T. and T. Tiilikainen (2003), *Finland in the EU*. London: Frank Cass.

Raunio, T. and M. Wiberg (2000), 'Does Support lead to Ignorance?', in *Acta Politica*, Volume 35, 2, 146-168.

Reese, Th. (1996), *Inside the Vatican*. Cambridge: Harvard University Press.

Richardson, J., editor (2001), *European Union: Power and policy-making*. London: Routledge.

Richardson, J., editor (2006), *European Union: Power and policy-making*. London: Routledge.

Ringland, G. (1998), *Scenario Planning*. New York: Wiley.

Rochefort, D. and R. Cobb, editors (1994), *The Politics of Problem Definition*. Kansas: Kansas University Press.

Rometsch, D. and W. Wessels, editors (1996), *The EU and Member States*. Manchester: Manchester University Press.

Rosamond, B. (2000), *Theories of European Integration*. London: Macmillan.

Rosenthal, G. (1975), *The Men Behind the Decisions*. Lexington: Lexington Books.

Sandholtz, W. and A. Sweet, editors, (1998), *European Integration and Supranational Governance*. Oxford: Oxford University Press.

Savage, G. and others (1991), 'Strategies for assessing and managing organizational stakeholders', in *Academy of Management Executive*, Volume 5, 2, 61-75.

Schaefer, G. (1996), 'Committees in the EC Process', in Pedler and Schaefer (1996), 3-24.

Schaefer, G. and others (2000), 'The Experience of Member State Officials in EU Committees', in *Eipascope*, 2000, 3, 29-35.

Scheuer, A. (2005), *How Europeans See Europe*. Amsterdam: Amsterdam University Press (Ph.D. thesis).

Schimmelfennig, F. and U. Sedelmeier, editors (2005), *The Europeaniza-tion of Central and Eastern Europe*. Ithaca: Cornell University Press.

Schlozman, K. and J. Tierney (1986), *Organised Interests and American Democracy*. New York: Harper and Row.

Schmidt, V. (2006), *Democracy in Europe*. Oxford: Oxford University Press.

Schmitt, H. and J. Thomassen, editors (1999), *Political Representation and Legitimacy in the EU*. Oxford: Oxford University Press.

Schmitter, Ph. (1996), 'Imagining the Future of the Euro-Polity with the Help of New Concepts', in: Marks and others (1996), 121-150.

Schmitter, Ph. and W. Streeck (1999), *The Organization of Business Interests*. Köln: Max Planck Institute (mimeo).

Schneider, G. and S. Baltz (2005), 'Domesticated Bureaucrats', in *Acta Po-litica*, Volume 40, 1, 1-27.

Schneider, J. (2007), *Lobbying and Interest Representation*. Brno: Masaryk University Press.

Sciarini, P. and others (2004), 'How Europe hits home: Swiss evidence', in: *JEPP*, Volume 11, 3, 353-375.

Scott, A. and M. Hunt (1965), *Congress and Lobbies*. Chapel Hill: North Car-olina University Press.

Sepos, A. (2008), *Europeanization of Cyprus*. Basingstoke: Palgrave.

Shaw, J. (1995), *EU Legal Studies in Crises?* Firenze: EUI (RSC 95/23).

Sietses, H. (2000), *The Fragmented Interest Representation of Big Dutch Business in the EU*. Rotterdam: University (mimeo Faculty of Manage-ment).

Simon, H. (1979), *Models of Thought*. New Haven: Yale University Press.

Smismans, S. (2004), *Functional Participation in Social Regulation*. Oxford: Oxford University Press.

Smith, A. (1776), *The Wealth of Nations*. New York: Modern Library edition (1937).

Spence, D., editor (2006), *The European Commission*. London: Harper (3rd edition).

Spencer, T. and C. McGrath, editors (2008), *The Future of Public Trust*. Lon-don: Dods.

Spinelli, A. (1965), *The Eurocrats*. Baltimore: Hopkins University Press.

Stacey, J. and B. Rittberger (2003), 'Dynamics of formal and informal EU change', in *JEPP*, Volume 10, 6, 858-883.

Steunenberg, B. and J. Thomassen, editors (2002), *The European Parlia-ment*. Oxford: Rowman and Littleffield.

Stout, H. (2005), *The EU Papacy*. Maastricht: Metajuridica.

Sun Tze: see Griffiths (1963).

Suvarierol, S. (2007), *Beyond the Myth of Nationality*. Delft: Eburon (Ph.D. thesis).

Sweet, A. and others, editors (2001), *The Institutionalization of Europe*. Oxford: Oxford University Press.

Swenden, W. and others, editors (2006), 'The Politics of Belgium', in special issue *WEP*, Volume 29, 5.

Tallberg, J. (2007), *Bargaining Power in the European Council*. Stockholm: Sieps.

Tanasescu, I. (2009), *The European Commission and Interest Groups*. Brussels: VUB.

Taylor, P. (1996), *The European Union in the 1990s*. Oxford: Oxford University Press.

Telò, M., editor (2001), *European Union and New Regionalism*. Aldershot: Ashgate.

Thomas, C., editor (2004), *Research Guide to US and International Interest Groups*. Westport: Praeger.

Thompson (1967), *Organizations in Action*. New York: McGraw Hill.

Timmins, G. and others (2007), *Politics of the New Germany*. London: Routledge.

Töller, A. and H. Hofmann (2000), 'Democracy and the Reform of Comitology', in Andenas and Türk (2000), 25-50.

Tombari, H. (1984), *Business and Society*. New York: Dryden.

Trondal, J. (2004), 'Resocializing Civil Servants: The Transformative Powers of EU Institutions', in *Acta Politica*, Volume 39, 1, 4-30.

Trondal, J. (2008), 'Balancing roles of representation in the Commission', in *Acta Politica*, Volume 43, 4, 429-452.

Tsebelis, G. and S. Proksch (2007), 'The Art of Political Manipulation in the Convention', in *JCMS*, Volume 45, 1, 157-186.

Urban, S. and S. Vendemini (1992), *European Strategic Alliances*. Oxford: Blackwell.

US/ Congress (1977), *Senators: Offices, Ethics and Pressures*. Washington: GPO.

US/ GAO (1999), *Federal Lobbying: Differences in Lobbying Definitions and their Impact*. Washington: General Accounting Office.

Van den Polder, R. (1994), 'Lobbying for the European Airline Industry', in Pedler and Van Schendelen (1994), 103-119.

Van der Heijden, K. (1996), *Scenarios*. New York: Wiley.

Van der Heijden, H. (2006), 'Multi-level environmentalism and the EU', in *International Journal of Urban and Regional Research,* Volume 30, 1, 23-37.

Van der Voort, W. (1997), *In search of a role: The ESC in EU Decision-making.* Utrecht University (Ph.D. thesis).

Van Deth, J. and E. Scarbrough, editors (1995), *The Impact of Values.* Oxford: Oxford University Press.

Van Kersbergen, K. (2000), 'Political allegiance and European integration', in *EJPR,* Volume 37, 1, 1-17.

Van Kippersluis, R. (1998), 'The Waste Management Committee', in Van Schendelen (1998), 47-67.

Van Rens, P. (1994), 'Dutch Trade Union Federation and the EU Works Council', in Pedler and Van Schendelen (1994), 283-300.

Van Schendelen, M. (1984), 'The European Parliament: Political influence in more than legal powers', in *Journal of European Integration,* Volume 8, 1, 59-76.

Van Schendelen, M. and R. Jackson, editors (1987), *The Politicisation of Business in Western Europe.* London: Croom Helm/ Routledge.

Van Schendelen, M. (1990), 'Business and Government Relations in Europe', in *European Affairs,* Volume 4, 2, 81-87.

Van Schendelen, M., editor (1993), *National Public and Private EC Lobbying.* Aldershot: Dartmouth.

Van Schendelen, M. (1996), 'The Council decides: does the Council decide?', in *JCMS,* Volume 34, 4, 531-548 and Volume 35, 1, 171.

Van Schendelen, R., editor (1998), *EU Committees as Influential Policy-makers.* Aldershot: Ashgate.

Van Schendelen, R. (2002), 'At issue with EU', in *Dutch Crossing,* Volume 26, 1, 27-42.

Van Schendelen, R. and R. Scully, editors (2003), *The Unseen Hand: Unelected EU Legislators.* London: Frank Cass.

Van Schendelen, R. (2003), 'Insourced Experts', in Van Schendelen and Scully (2003), 27-39.

Van Schendelen, R. (2008), 'Brussels as the Place for Lobbying the EU', in De Groof (2008), 197-214.

Van Thiel, S. (2000), *Quangocratization: Trends, Causes and Consequences.* Utrecht: ICS (Ph.D. thesis).

Venables, T. (2007), *Tips for the Would-be European Lobbyist.* Brussels: ECAS.

Verwey, W. (1994), 'HDTV and Philips', in Pedler and Van Schendelen (1994), 23-40.

Vos, E. (1999), *Institutional Frameworks of Community Health and Safety Regulation: Committees, Agencies and Private Bodies*. Oxford: Hart.

Waddell, H. (1952), *The Wandering Scholars*. London: Constable.

Wallace, W., editor (1990), *The Dynamics of European Integration*. London: Pinter.

Wallace, H. and A. Young, editors (1997), *Participation and Policy-making in the European Union*. Oxford: Clarendon.

Wallace, H. (1997), 'Introduction', in Wallace and Young (1997), 1-16.

Wallace, H. and others, editors (2000), *Policymaking in the EU*. Oxford: Oxford University Press (4th edition).

Wallace, H. and others, editors (2005), *Policymaking in the EU*, Oxford: Oxford University Press (5th edition).

Wallace, H. (2007), *Adapting to Enlargement: Institutional practices since 2004*. Brussels: Tepsa.

Warleigh, A. (2001), 'Europeanising civil society', in *JCMS*, Volume 29, 619-639.

Warleigh, A. (2003), 'Informal Governance: Improving EU Democracy', in Christiansen and Piattoni (2003), 22-35.

Warleigh, A. and J. Fairbrass, editors (2002), *Influence and Interests in the EU*. London: Taylor and Francis.

Warntjen, A, and A. Wonka, editors (2004), *Governance in Europe*. Baden-Baden: Nomos.

Warntjen, A. (2007), 'Steering the Union: The impact of the EU Presidency on legislative activity', in *JCMS*, Volume 45, 5, 1135-1157.

Weiler, J. (1995), *European Democracy and its Critique*. Firenze: EUI (RSC 95/11).

Werts, J. (2008), *The European Council*. London: Harper.

Wessels, B. (1999), 'European Parliament and Interest Groups', in Katz and Wessels (1999), 105-128.

Wessels, W. and others, editors (2003), *Fifteen into One: The EU and its Member States*. Manchester: Manchester University Press.

Westlake, M. and D. Galloway (2004), *The Council of the EU*. London: Harper.

Wiener, A. and T. Diez, editors (2009), *European Integration Theory*. Oxford: Oxford University Press.

Wilhelm, A. (2000), *Democracy in the Digital Age*, London: Routledge.

Williamson, D. (2006), 'The conciliation procedure', in *JLS*, Volume 12, 1, 1-7.

Winand, P. (1998), 'The US Mission to the EU in Brussels', in Claeys and others (1998), 373-405.

Wright, J. (2004), *The Jesuits*. London: Harper Collins.

Zweifel, Th. (2002), 'Who is without sin cast the first stone: The EU's democratic deficit in comparison', in *JEPP*, Volume 9, 5, 812-840.

INDEX

References to key passages